Little by little, I've grown used to my failing eyesight except for one thing: It's annoying to have to put glasses on before I go out. I don't wear any accessories — not even a wristwatch (the reason being that I'd lose it so quickly, heh!) So I'm sure it's only a matter of time before I lose my glasses too. I'm prepared for the worst, but so far so good. Still, I wonder if there's any way to cure aging eyes. Maybe after the serialization ends and I can take it easy, they'll get better. It's a faint hope. (My current weight...69 kg!! Yeah-yaw!!)

—Mitsutoshi Shimabukuro, 2016

Mitsutoshi Shimabukuro made his debut in **Weekly Shonen Jump** in 1996. He is best known for **Seikimatsu Leader Den Takeshi!**, for which he won the 46th Shogakukan Manga Award for children's manga in 2001. His current series, **Toriko**, began serialization in Japan in 2008.

TORIKO

TORIKO VOL. 41
SHONEN JUMP Manga Edition

STORY AND ART BY **MITSUTOSHI SHIMABUKURO**

Translation/Christine Dashiell
Weekly Shonen Jump Lettering/ Erika Terriquez
Graphic Novel Touch-Up Art & Lettering/ Paolo Gattone and Chiara Antonelli
Design/Veronica Casson
Editor/Marlene First

Published by VIZ Media, LLC
P.O. Box 77010
San Francisco, CA 94107

10 9 8 7 6 5 4 3 2 1
First printing, February 2018

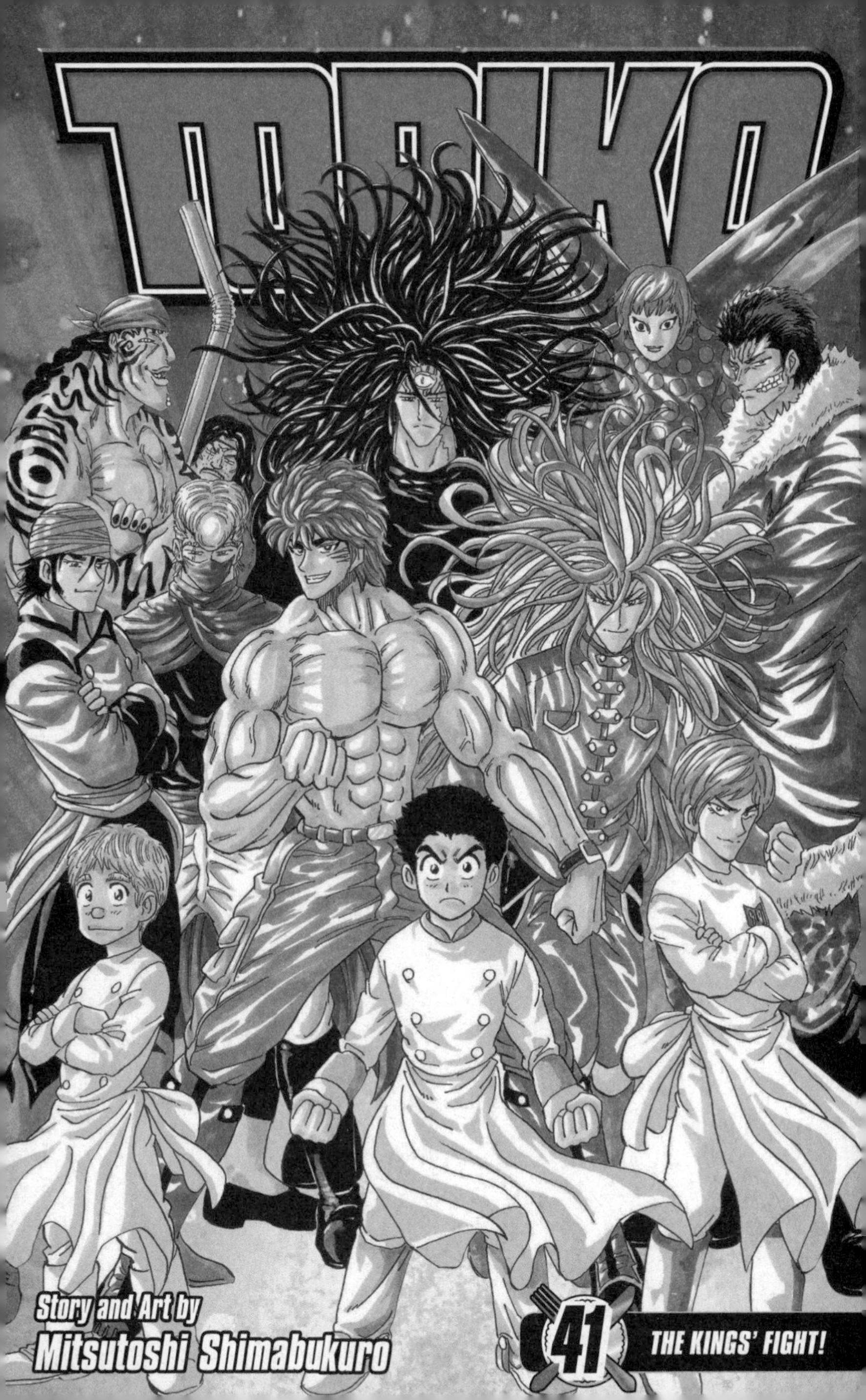
TORIKO
Story and Art by
Mitsutoshi Shimabukuro
41
THE KINGS' FIGHT!

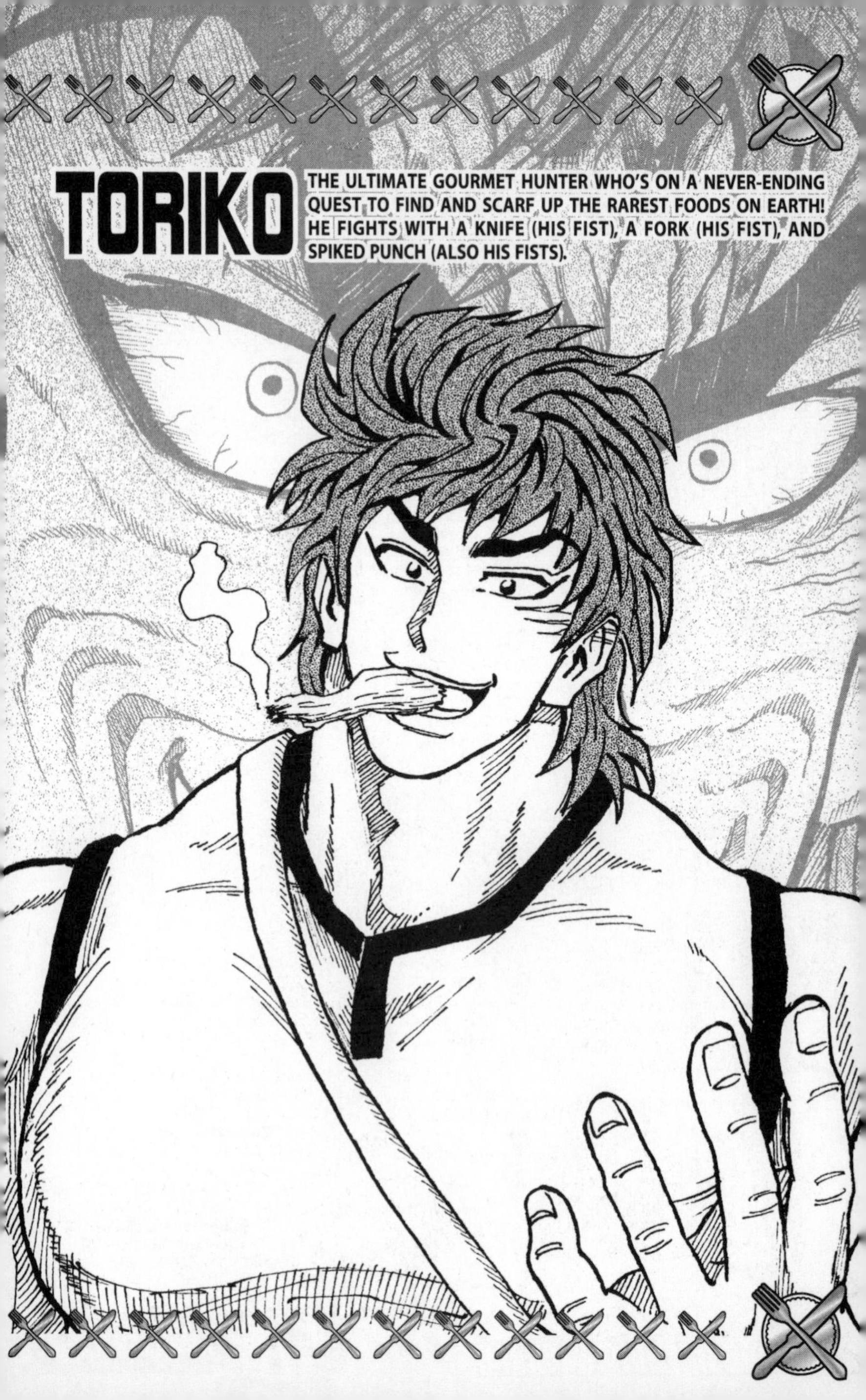
TORIKO
THE ULTIMATE GOURMET HUNTER WHO'S ON A NEVER-ENDING QUEST TO FIND AND SCARF UP THE RAREST FOODS ON EARTH! HE FIGHTS WITH A KNIFE (HIS FIST), A FORK (HIS FIST), AND SPIKED PUNCH (ALSO HIS FISTS).

WHAT'S FOR DINNER

THE WORLD IS IN THE AGE OF GOURMET! THE GOURMET HUNTER, TORIKO, AND A CHEF WHO POSSESSES THE UNIQUE ASSET OF "FOOD LUCK," KOMATSU, HAVE A FATEFUL MEETING AND EMBARK ON NUMEROUS ADVENTURES TOGETHER. MEANWHILE, THE IGO AND THE EVIL ORGANIZATION GOURMET CORP. START AN ALL-OUT WAR. THE WAR DESTROYS MOST OF THE INGREDIENTS ON EARTH AND THE HUMAN WORLD ENTERS A FOOD SHORTAGE CRISIS! GOURMET CORP. TAKES THE BRUNT OF THE DAMAGE, THOUGH, THANKS TO A NEW EVIL POWER KNOWN AS NEO LED BY THE INFAMOUS CHEF JOIE!

IN ORDER TO SAVE HUMANITY, TORIKO AND KOMATSU, ALONG WITH THE OTHER FOUR KINGS, COCO, SUNNY AND ZEBRA, EMBARK ON AN ADVENTURE TO THE GOURMET WORLD TO GO AFTER ACACIA'S FULL-COURSE MEAL!

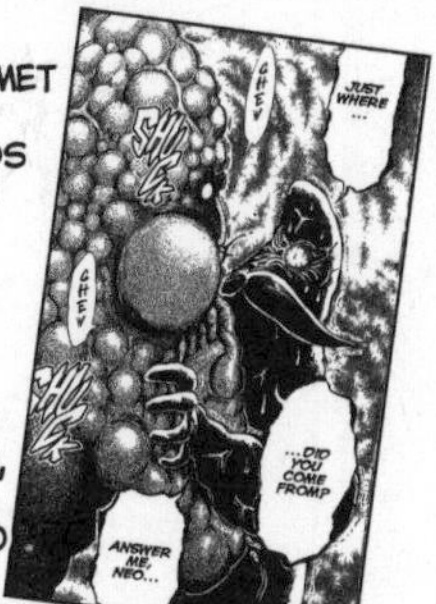
JUST WHERE...
...DID YOU COME FROM?
ANSWER ME, NEO...

MEANWHILE, THE GOURMET ARISTOCRATS, THE BLUE NITRO, HAVE BEEN SPENDING THOUSANDS OF YEARS WORKING TO PREPARE ACACIA'S FULL-COURSE MEAL ON THEIR OWN. THEIR GOAL IS TO FULLY RESURRECT ACACIA'S GOURMET CELL DEMON, NEO, AND SEAL HIM AWAY. BUT RIGHT AS THEY ARE ABOUT TO SUCCESSFULLY RESURRECT HIM, PIECES OF NEO ESCAPE THE BLUE NITRO'S BASE AND HEAD TO EACH AREA. TO MAKE MATTERS WORSE, ACACIA HIMSELF DISAPPEARS TOO!!

TO PREVENT NEO FROM DESTROYING THE WORLD AND STOP HIS RESURRECTION, TORIKO AND THE GANG SPLIT UP TO CAPTURE THE REMAINING INGREDIENTS IN THE FULL COURSE. AFTER GATHERING THE COURSES, TORIKO AND HIS FRIENDS CONSUME THEM TO REVEAL THEIR GOURMET CELL DEMONS AND POWER UP BEFORE THE FINAL BATTLE.

MEANWHILE, ON THE CUSP OF ACACIA'S RESURRECTION, NEO CHANGES FORM AT DIZZYING SPEEDS AS HE SETS ABOUT CONSUMING DON SLIME AND TURNING JIRO TO DUST. JOIE, WHO FOLLOWS IN ACACIA'S FOOTSTEPS, THEN PREPARES AND SEALS AWAY MIDORA TOO.

THE GOURMET ECLIPSE CLOSES IN AND GOD SUDDENLY APPEARS! DESPITE ITS GENTLE APPEARANCE, IT DEMONSTRATES FEARSOME PREDATORY POWERS BY DEVOURING THE MOON. KOMATSU LETS HIS GUARD DOWN FOR A SECOND AND GETS SWALLOWED WHOLE TOO! TORIKO AND THE OTHERS ARE RESOLVED TO CHALLENGE THE KING OF INGREDIENTS!!

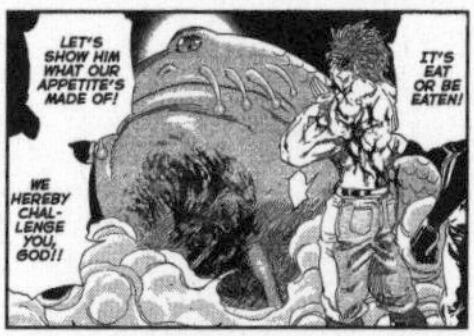
IT'S EAT OR BE EATEN!
LET'S SHOW HIM WHAT OUR APPETITE'S MADE OF!
WE HEREBY CHAL-LENGE YOU, GOD!!

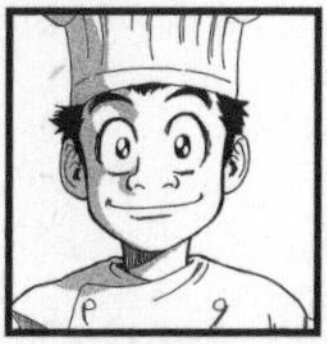

● **KOMATSU**
TALENTED IGO HOTEL CHEF AND TORIKO'S #1 FAN. HE POSSESSES FOOD LUCK.

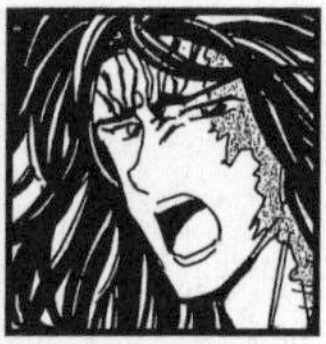

● **STARJUN**
A VICE-CHEF FROM GOURMET CORP. MIDORA ORDERED HIM TO HELP TORIKO AND THE GANG DESPITE BEING A FORMER ENEMY.

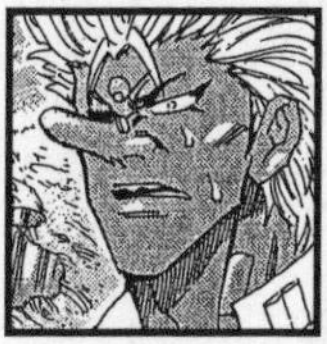

● **BRUNCH**
A CHEF FROM HEX FOOD WORLD WHO LOOKS LIKE A LONG-NOSED GOBLIN. HE'S BEEN WORKING HARD AS AN INTERMEDIARY WITH GOURMET CORP.

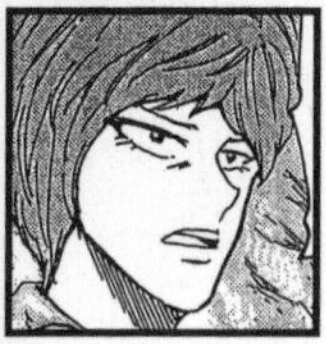

● **OTAKE**
KOMATSU'S FRIEND. AFTER BEING PICKED AS THE 99TH TOP-RANKED CHEF IN THE WORLD, HE WAS KIDNAPPED BY GOURMET CORP.

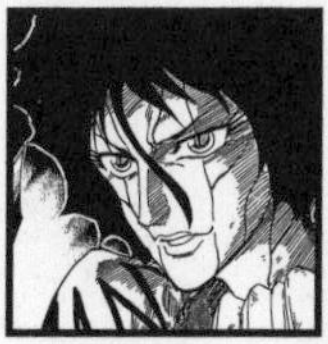

● **JOIE**
A SHADY CHEF WHO DEFECTED FROM GOURMET CORP. TO JOIN NEO. POSSESSES FROESE'S REVIVED BODY.

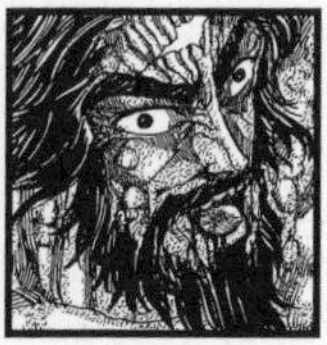

● **ACACIA**
A LEGENDARY GOURMET HUNTER KNOWN BY MANY AS THE GOURMET GOD. HE PLANS TO REVIVE HIS GOURMET CELL DEMON, NEO.

Contents

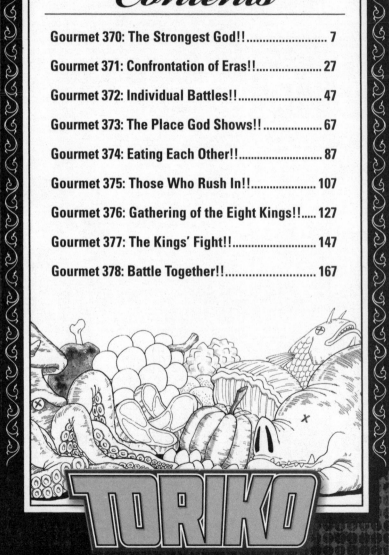

TORIKO

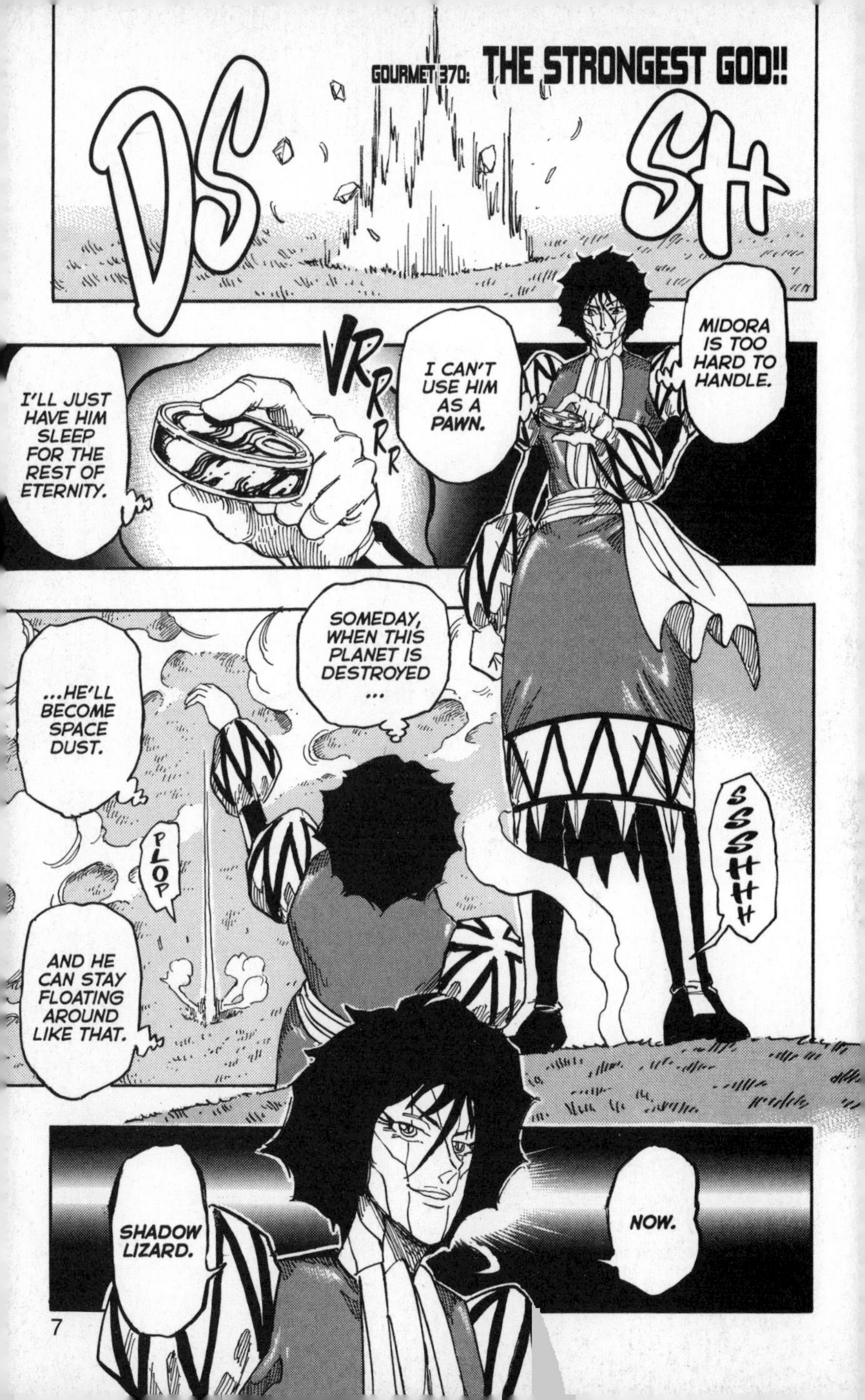
GOURMET 370: THE STRONGEST GOD!!
SH
DS
MIDORA IS TOO HARD TO HANDLE.
I CAN'T USE HIM AS A PAWN.
VRRRR
I'LL JUST HAVE HIM SLEEP FOR THE REST OF ETERNITY.
SSSHHH
SOMEDAY, WHEN THIS PLANET IS DESTROYED...
...HE'LL BECOME SPACE DUST.
PLOP
AND HE CAN STAY FLOATING AROUND LIKE THAT.
NOW.
SHADOW LIZARD.

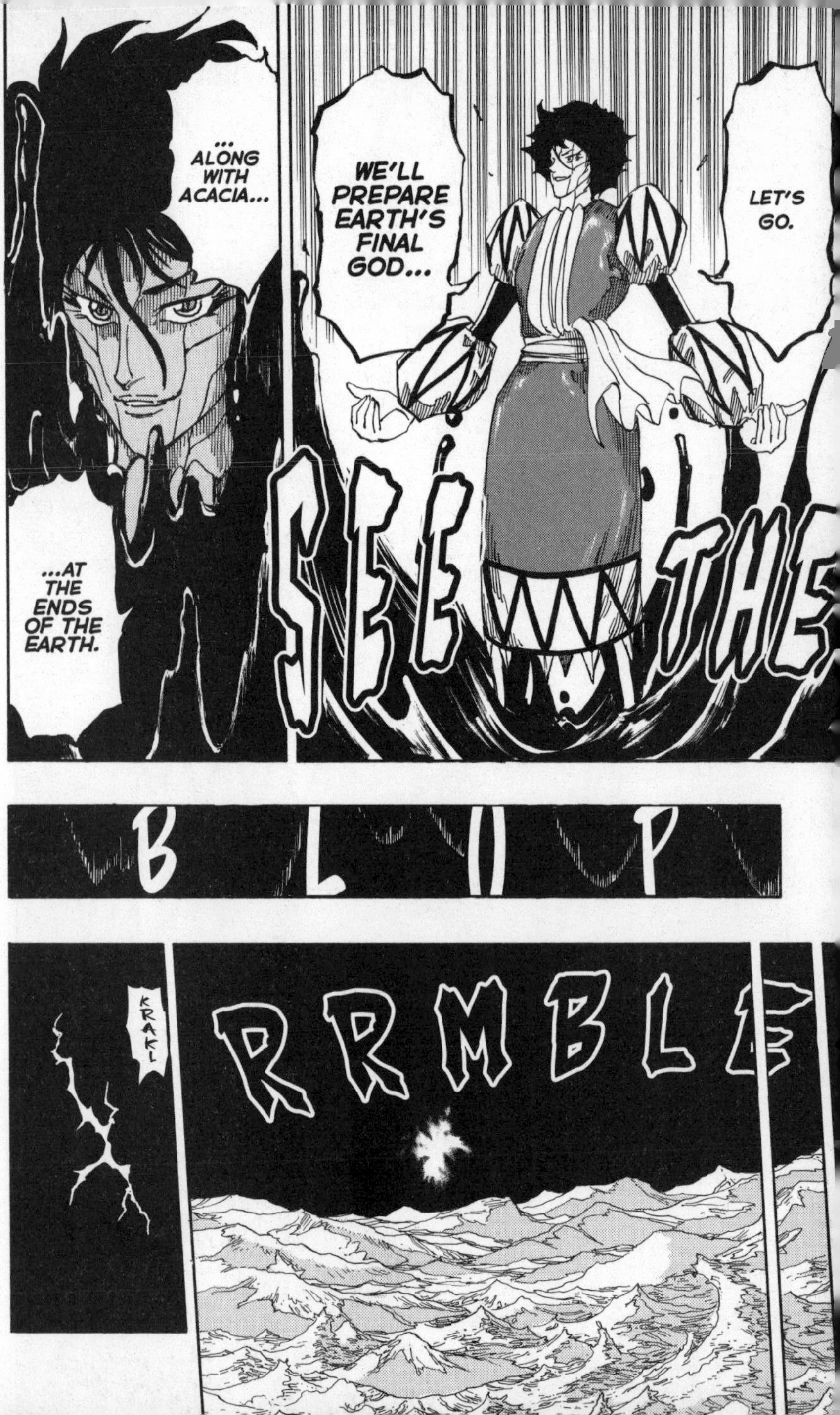
LET'S GO.
WE'LL PREPARE EARTH'S FINAL GOD...
SEETHE
... ALONG WITH ACACIA...
...AT THE ENDS OF THE EARTH.
BLIP
RRMBLE
KRAKL

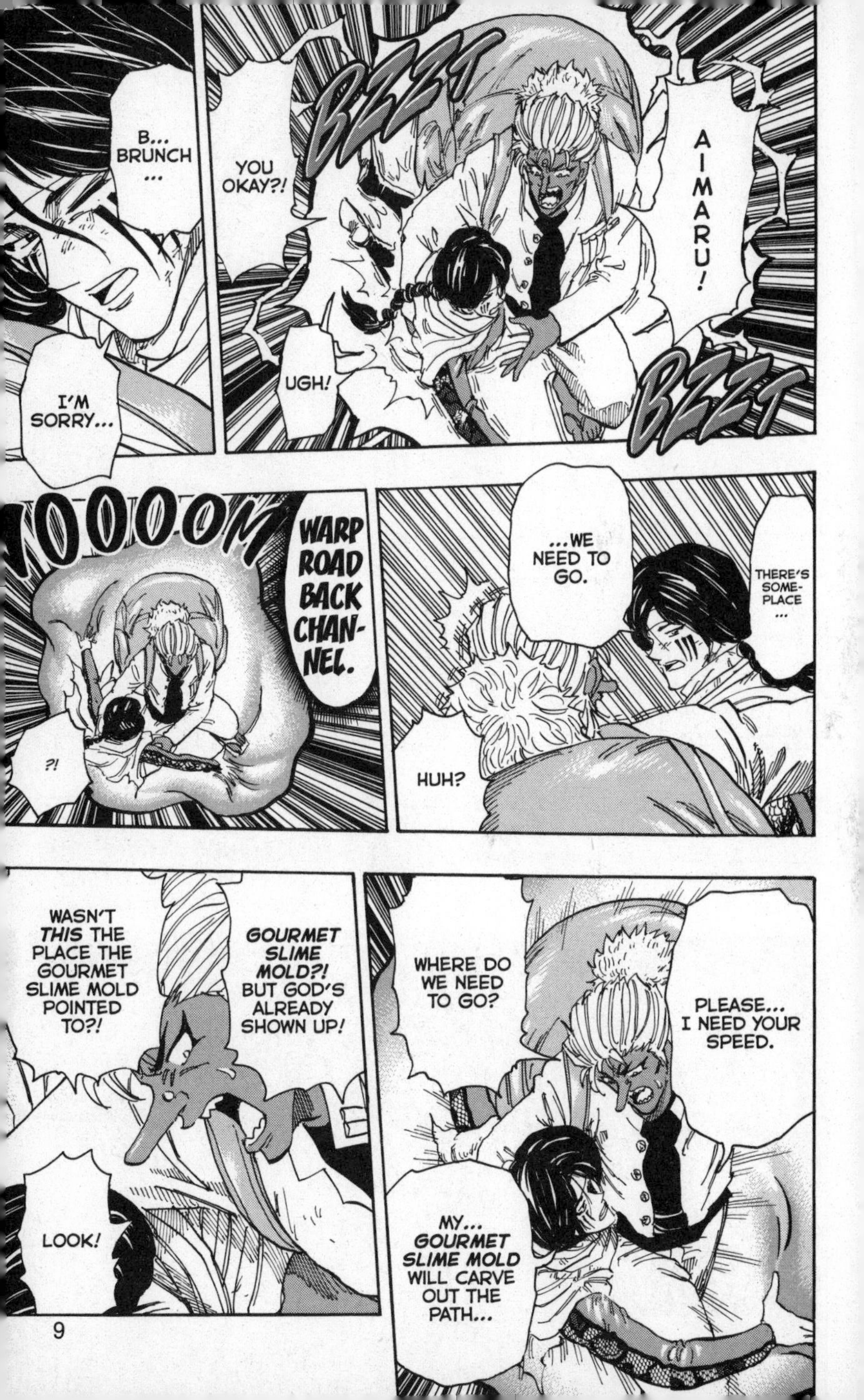
A I M A R U !
BZZT
YOU OKAY?!
BZZT
UGH!
B... BRUNCH ...
I'M SORRY...
THERE'S SOME-PLACE ...
...WE NEED TO GO.
HUH?
WARP ROAD BACK CHAN-NEL.
OOOOOM
?!
PLEASE... I NEED YOUR SPEED.
WHERE DO WE NEED TO GO?
MY... *GOURMET SLIME MOLD* WILL CARVE OUT THE PATH...
GOURMET SLIME MOLD?! BUT GOD'S ALREADY SHOWN UP!
WASN'T *THIS* THE PLACE THE GOURMET SLIME MOLD POINTED TO?!
LOOK!

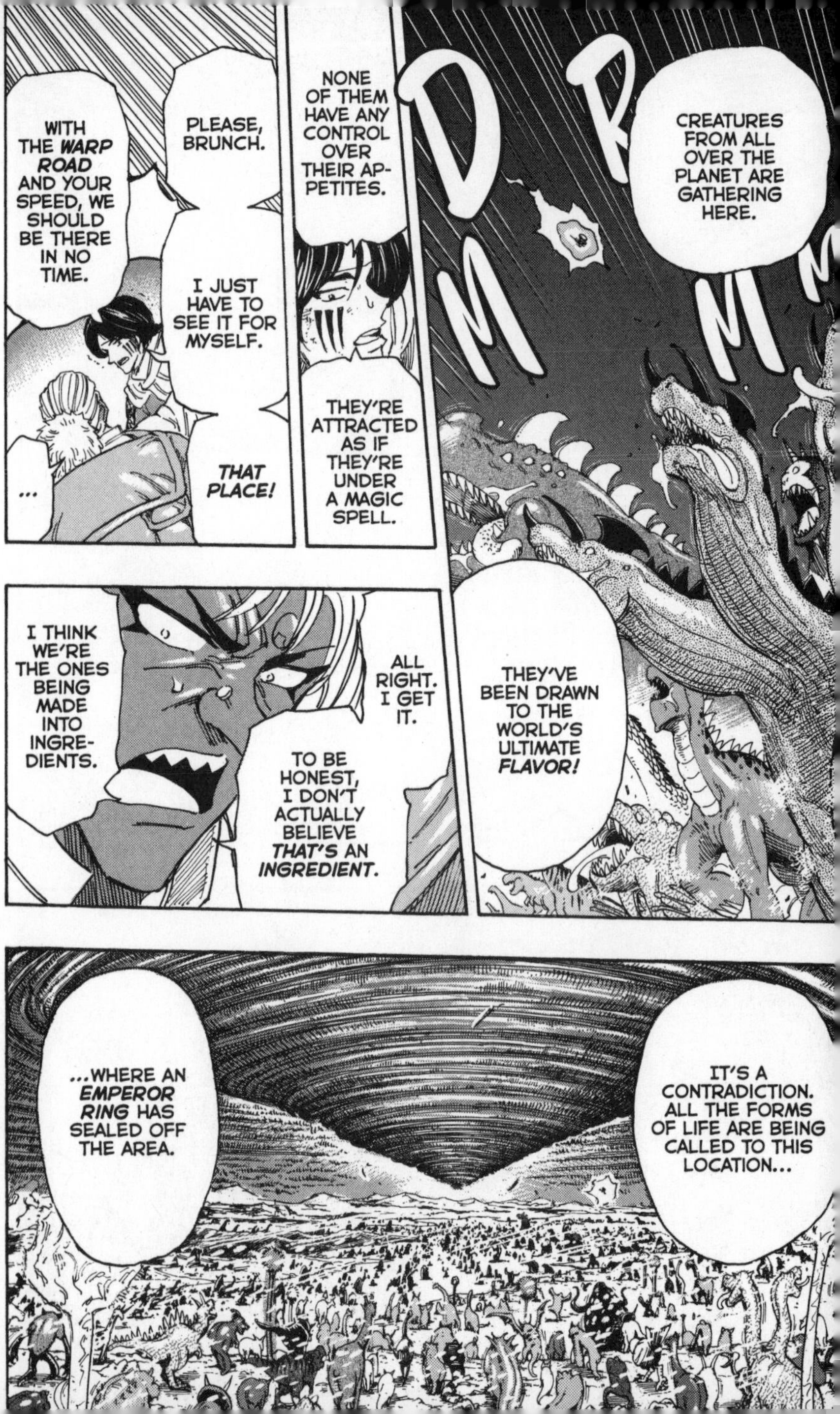
DRMMM
CREATURES FROM ALL OVER THE PLANET ARE GATHERING HERE.
THEY'VE BEEN DRAWN TO THE WORLD'S ULTIMATE *FLAVOR!*
NONE OF THEM HAVE ANY CONTROL OVER THEIR AP-PETITES.
THEY'RE ATTRACTED AS IF THEY'RE UNDER A MAGIC SPELL.
PLEASE, BRUNCH.
I JUST HAVE TO SEE IT FOR MYSELF.
THAT PLACE!
WITH THE *WARP ROAD* AND YOUR SPEED, WE SHOULD BE THERE IN NO TIME.
...
ALL RIGHT. I GET IT.
TO BE HONEST, I DON'T ACTUALLY BELIEVE *THAT'S* AN *INGREDIENT*.
I THINK WE'RE THE ONES BEING MADE INTO INGRE-DIENTS.
IT'S A CONTRADICTION. ALL THE FORMS OF LIFE ARE BEING CALLED TO THIS LOCATION...
...WHERE AN *EMPEROR RING* HAS SEALED OFF THE AREA.

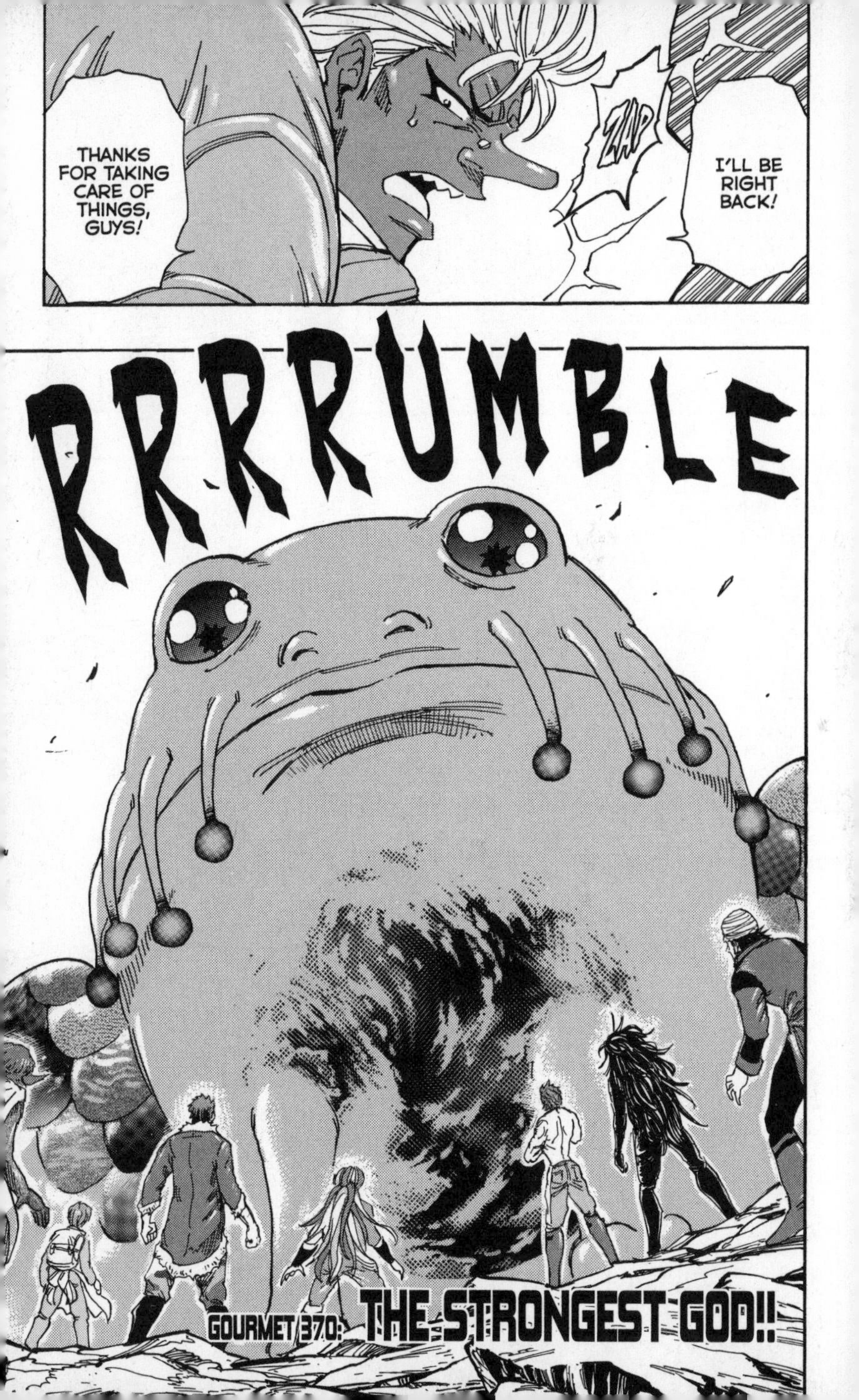
I'LL BE RIGHT BACK!
ZAP
THANKS FOR TAKING CARE OF THINGS, GUYS!
RRRRUMBLE
GOURMET 370: THE STRONGEST GOD!!

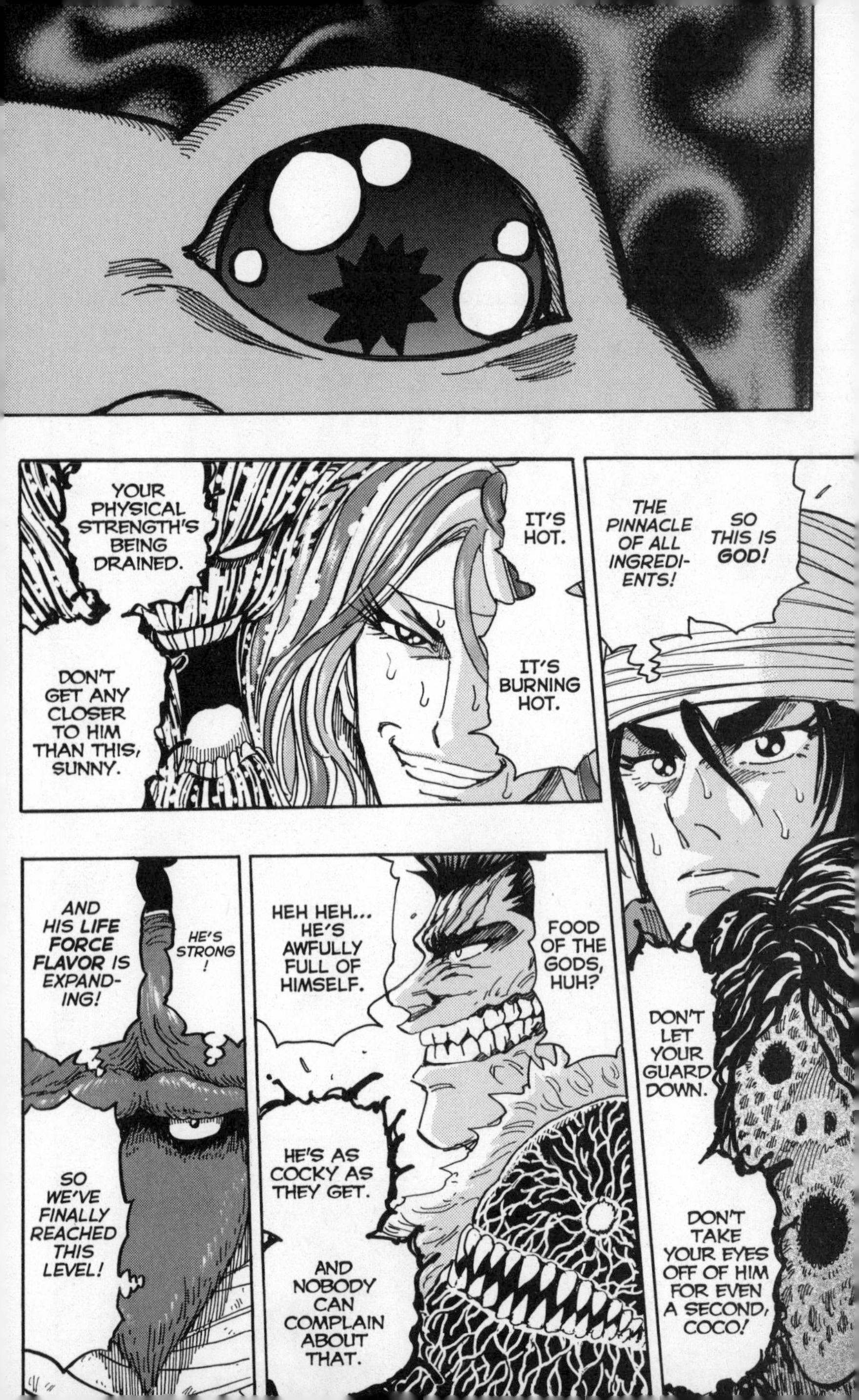
SO THIS IS GOD!
THE PINNACLE OF ALL INGREDI-ENTS!
DON'T LET YOUR GUARD DOWN.
DON'T TAKE YOUR EYES OFF OF HIM FOR EVEN A SECOND, COCO!
IT'S HOT.
IT'S BURNING HOT.
YOUR PHYSICAL STRENGTH'S BEING DRAINED.
DON'T GET ANY CLOSER TO HIM THAN THIS, SUNNY.
FOOD OF THE GODS, HUH?
HEH HEH... HE'S AWFULLY FULL OF HIMSELF.
HE'S AS COCKY AS THEY GET.
AND NOBODY CAN COMPLAIN ABOUT THAT.
HE'S STRONG!
AND HIS LIFE FORCE FLAVOR IS EXPAND-ING!
SO WE'VE FINALLY REACHED THIS LEVEL!

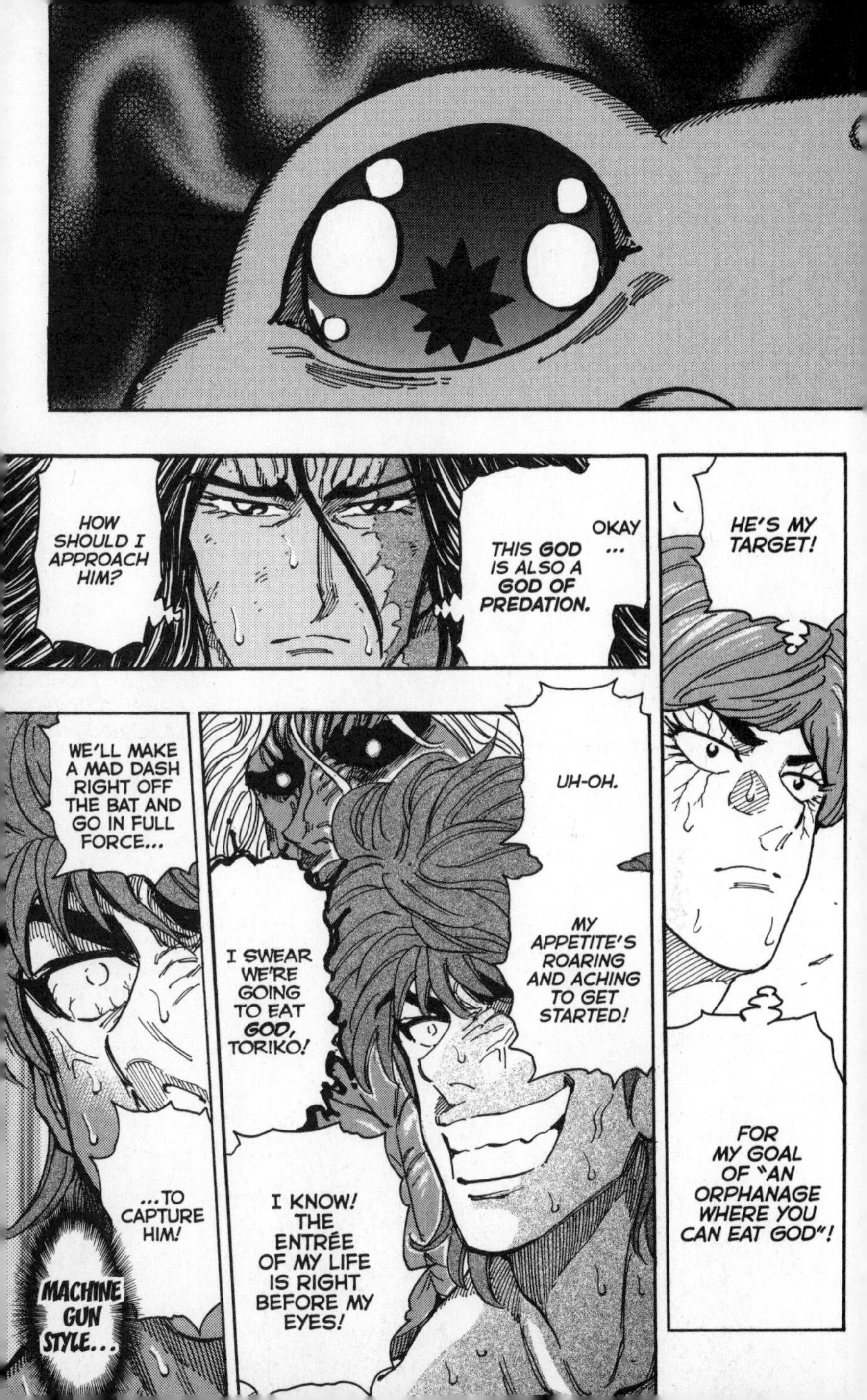
HE'S MY TARGET!
FOR MY GOAL OF "AN ORPHANAGE WHERE YOU CAN EAT GOD"!
OKAY ...
THIS GOD IS ALSO A GOD OF PREDATION.
HOW SHOULD I APPROACH HIM?
UH-OH.
MY APPETITE'S ROARING AND ACHING TO GET STARTED!
I SWEAR WE'RE GOING TO EAT GOD, TORIKO!
I KNOW! THE ENTRÉE OF MY LIFE IS RIGHT BEFORE MY EYES!
WE'LL MAKE A MAD DASH RIGHT OFF THE BAT AND GO IN FULL FORCE...
...TO CAPTURE HIM!
MACHINE GUN STYLE...

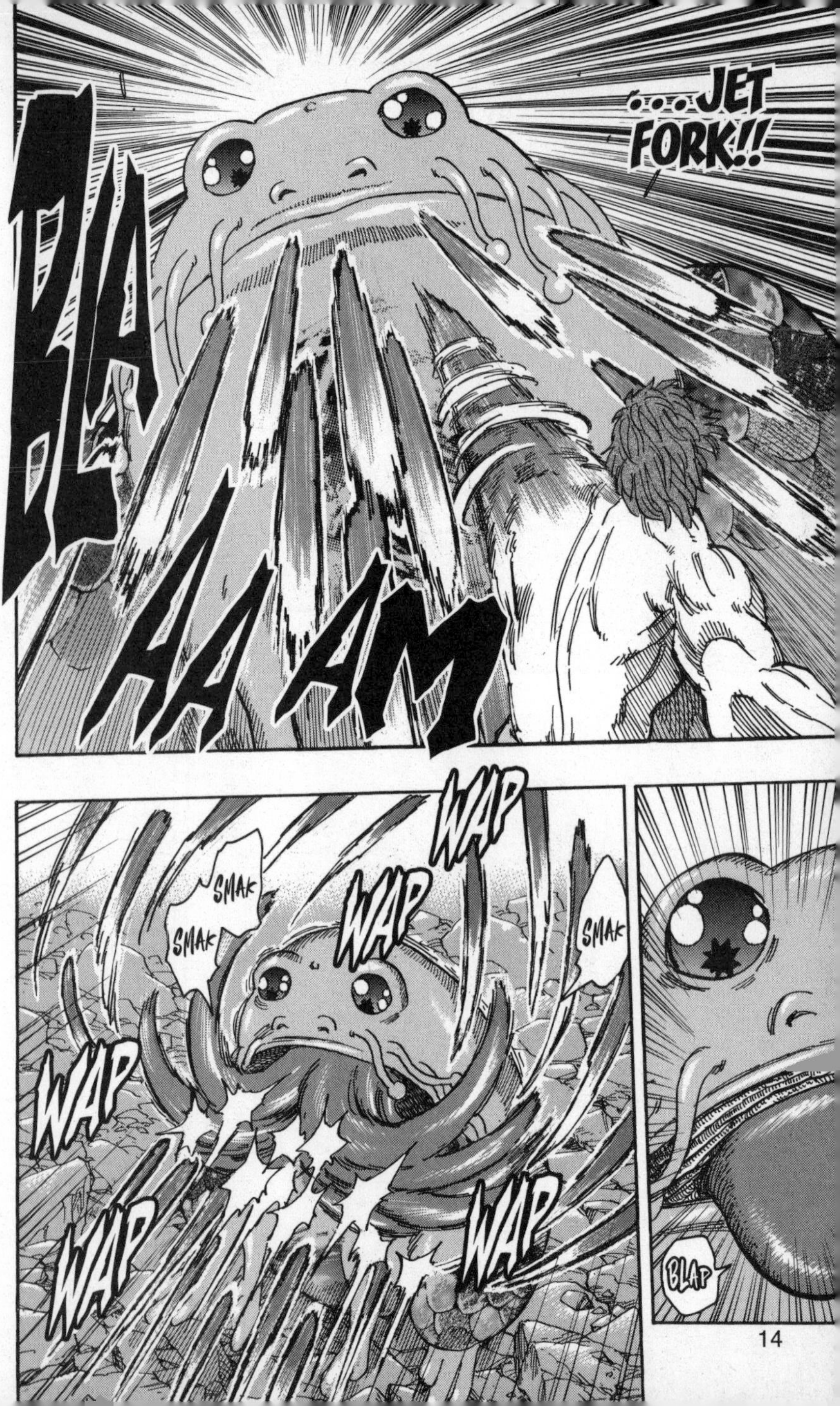
...JET FORK!!
BLAAAAM
BLAP
WAP
WAP
SMAK
SMAK
SMAK
WAP
WAP
WAP

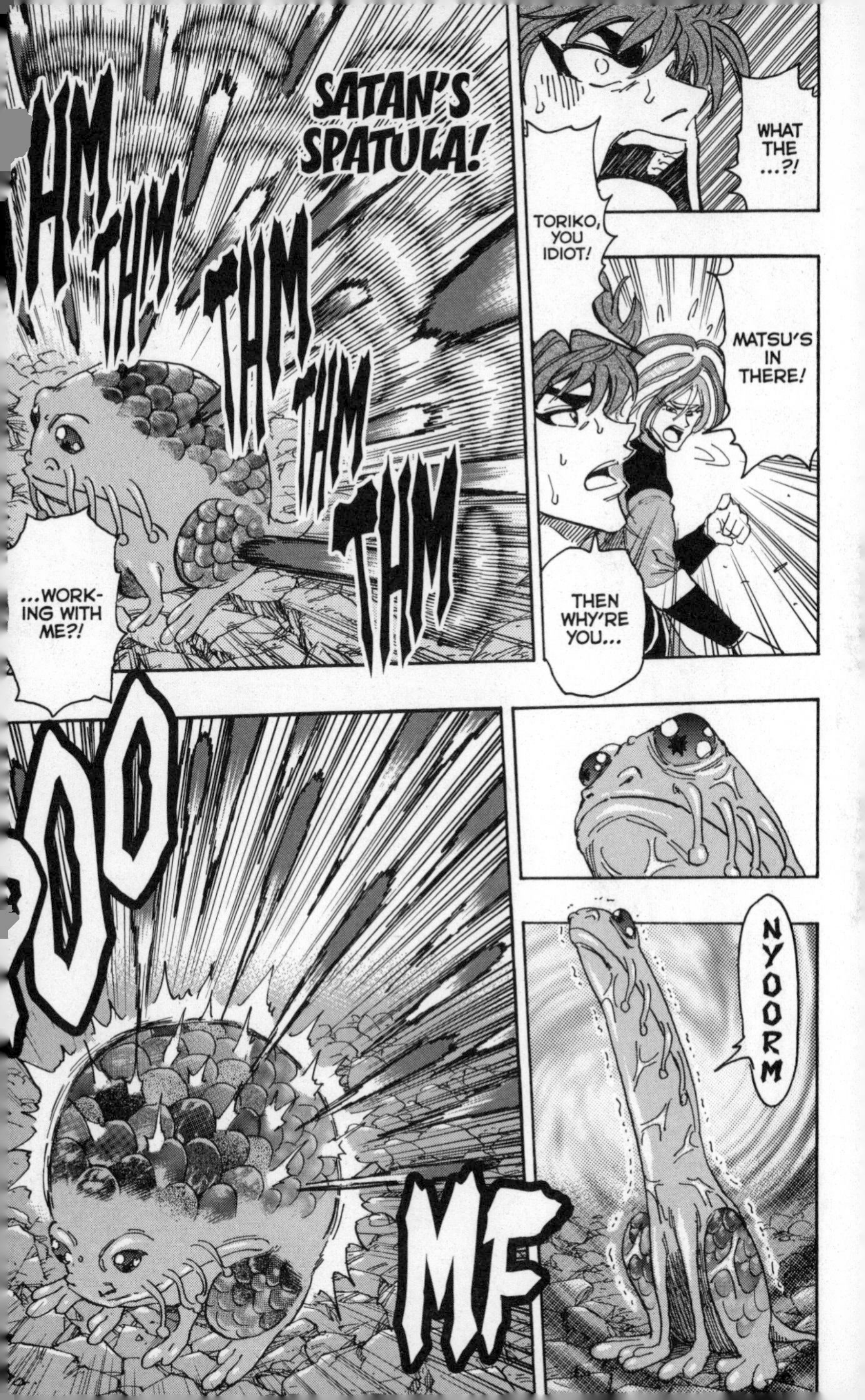
WHAT THE ...?!
TORIKO, YOU IDIOT!
MATSU'S IN THERE!
THEN WHY'RE YOU...
SATAN'S SPATULA!
THM-THM
THM THM THM
...WORKING WITH ME?!
NYOORM
MF

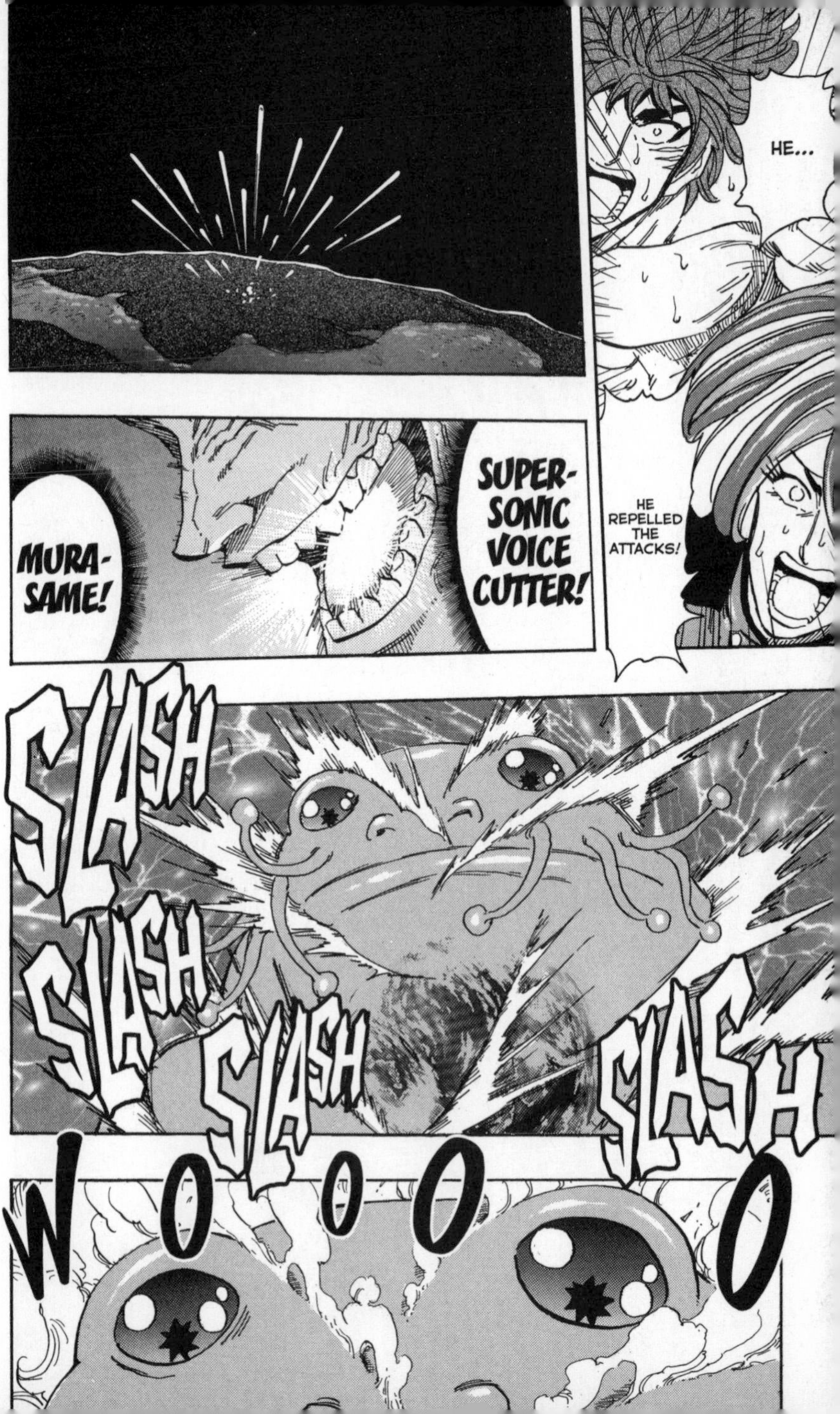
HE...
HE REPELLED THE ATTACKS!
SUPER-SONIC VOICE CUTTER!
MURA-SAME!
SLASH
SLASH
SLASH
SLASH
WOOOOO

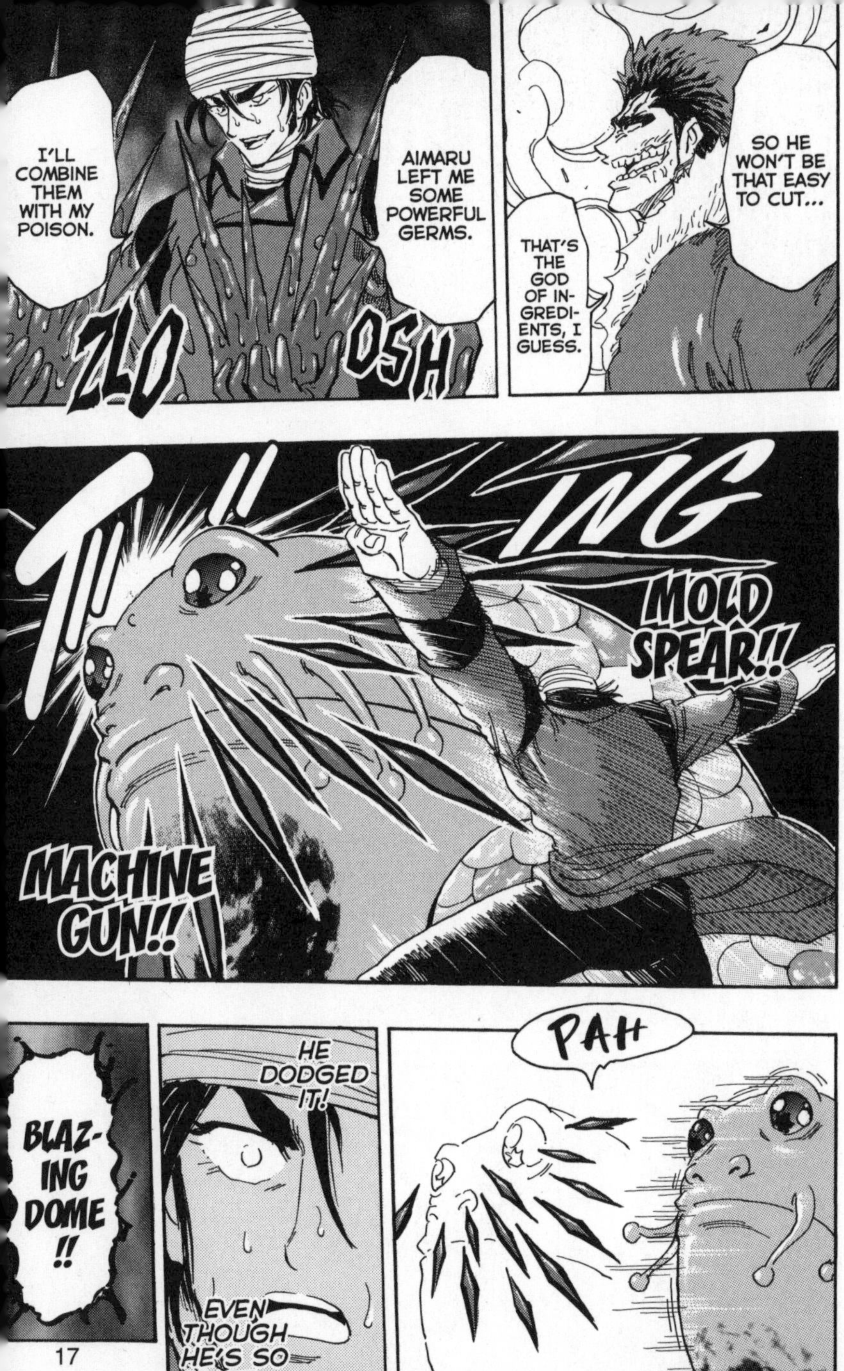
SO HE WON'T BE THAT EASY TO CUT...
THAT'S THE GOD OF INGREDIENTS, I GUESS.
AIMARU LEFT ME SOME POWERFUL GERMS.
I'LL COMBINE THEM WITH MY POISON.
ZLOOSH
TING
MOLD SPEAR!!
MACHINE GUN!!
PAH
HE DODGED IT!
EVEN THOUGH HE'S SO HUGE...
BLAZING DOME!!

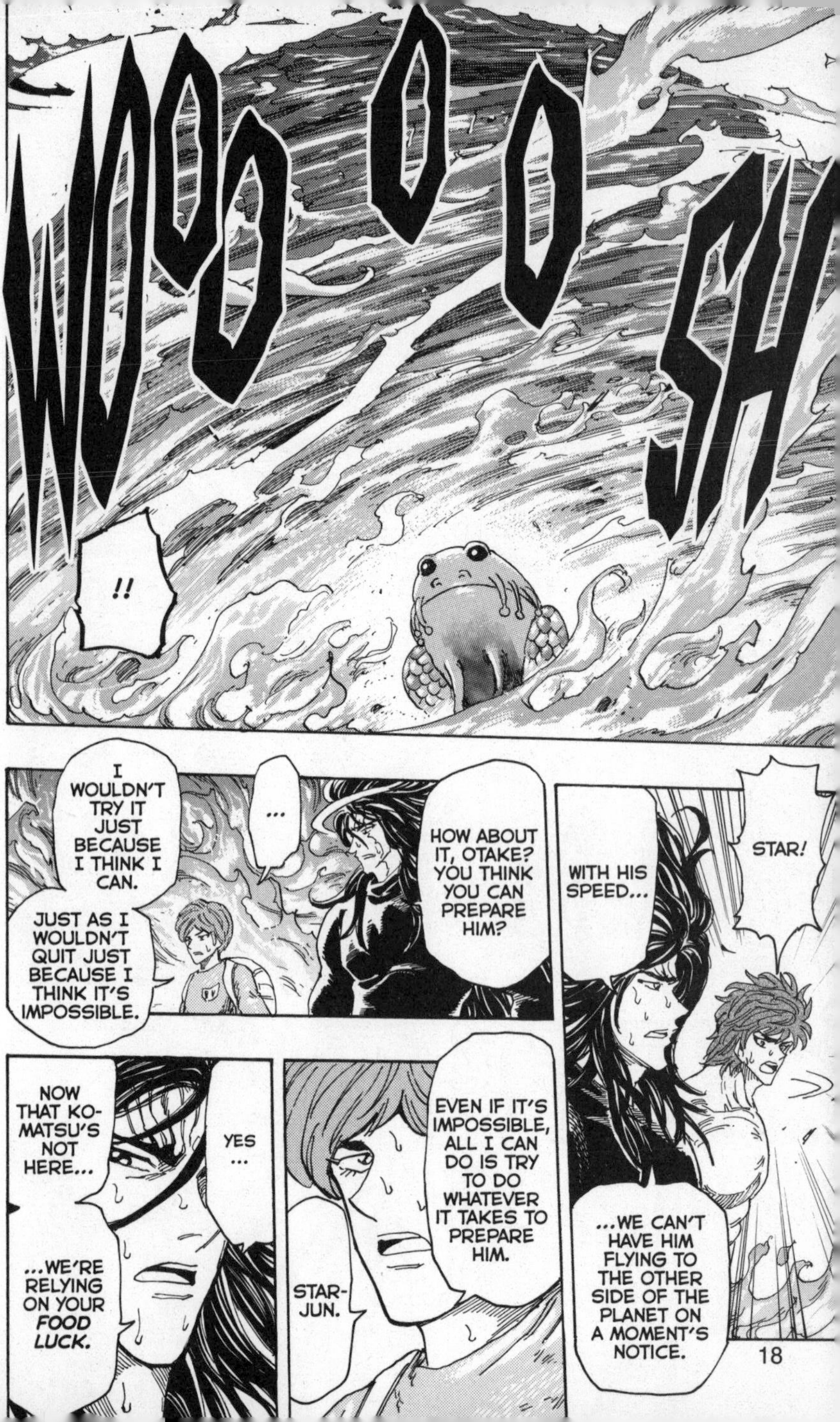
WOOOOSH
!!
STAR!
WITH HIS SPEED...
...WE CAN'T HAVE HIM FLYING TO THE OTHER SIDE OF THE PLANET ON A MOMENT'S NOTICE.
HOW ABOUT IT, OTAKE? YOU THINK YOU CAN PREPARE HIM?
...
I WOULDN'T TRY IT JUST BECAUSE I THINK I CAN.
JUST AS I WOULDN'T QUIT JUST BECAUSE I THINK IT'S IMPOSSIBLE.
EVEN IF IT'S IMPOSSIBLE, ALL I CAN DO IS TRY TO DO WHATEVER IT TAKES TO PREPARE HIM.
STAR-JUN.
NOW THAT KOMATSU'S NOT HERE...
YES...
...WE'RE RELYING ON YOUR *FOOD LUCK.*

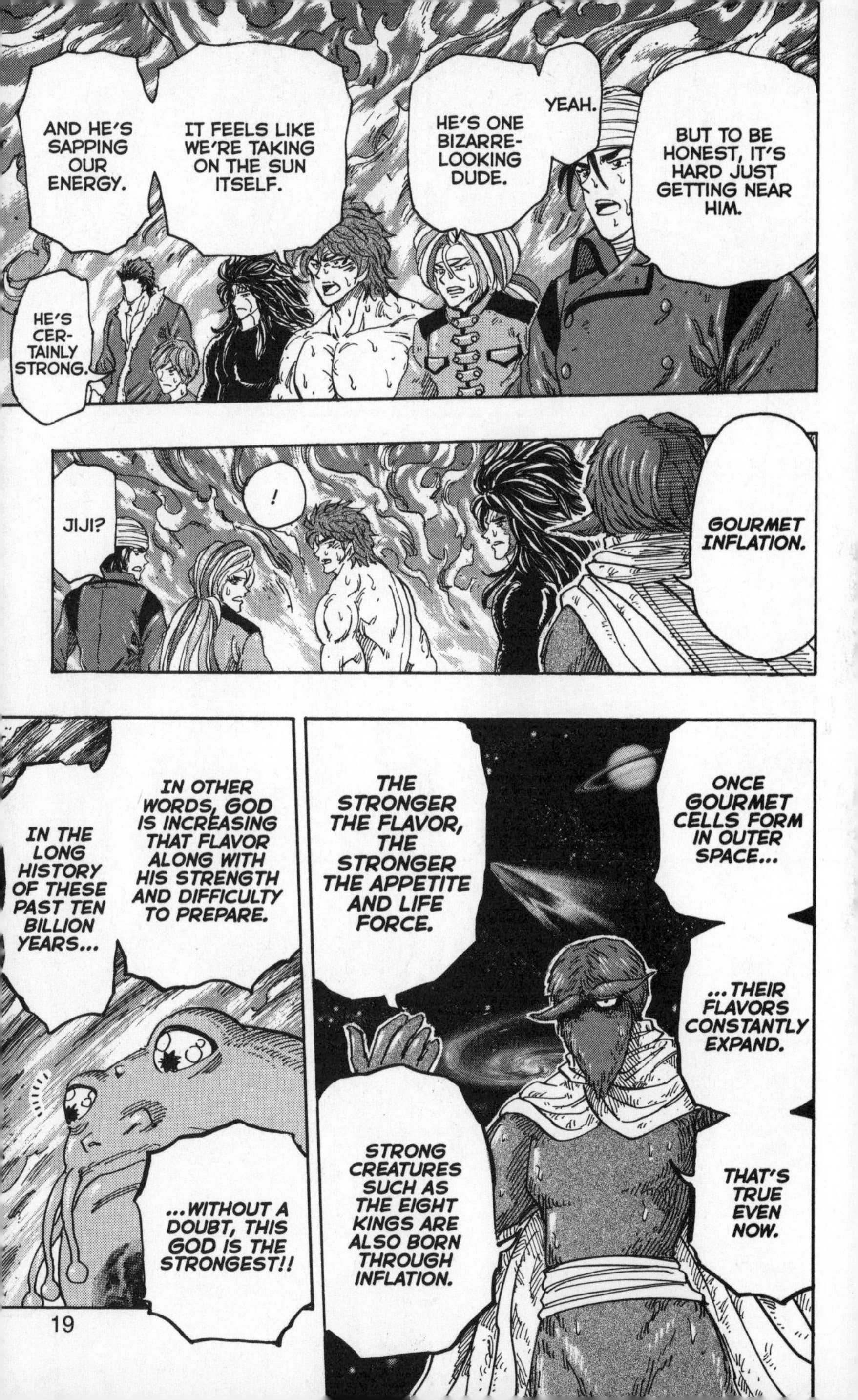

BUT TO BE HONEST, IT'S HARD JUST GETTING NEAR HIM.
YEAH.
HE'S ONE BIZARRE-LOOKING DUDE.
IT FEELS LIKE WE'RE TAKING ON THE SUN ITSELF.
AND HE'S SAPPING OUR ENERGY.
HE'S CER-TAINLY STRONG.
GOURMET INFLATION.
!
JIJI?
ONCE GOURMET CELLS FORM IN OUTER SPACE...
...THEIR FLAVORS CONSTANTLY EXPAND.
THAT'S TRUE EVEN NOW.
THE STRONGER THE FLAVOR, THE STRONGER THE APPETITE AND LIFE FORCE.
STRONG CREATURES SUCH AS THE EIGHT KINGS ARE ALSO BORN THROUGH INFLATION.
IN OTHER WORDS, GOD IS INCREASING THAT FLAVOR ALONG WITH HIS STRENGTH AND DIFFICULTY TO PREPARE.
IN THE LONG HISTORY OF THESE PAST TEN BILLION YEARS...
...WITHOUT A DOUBT, THIS GOD IS THE STRONGEST!!

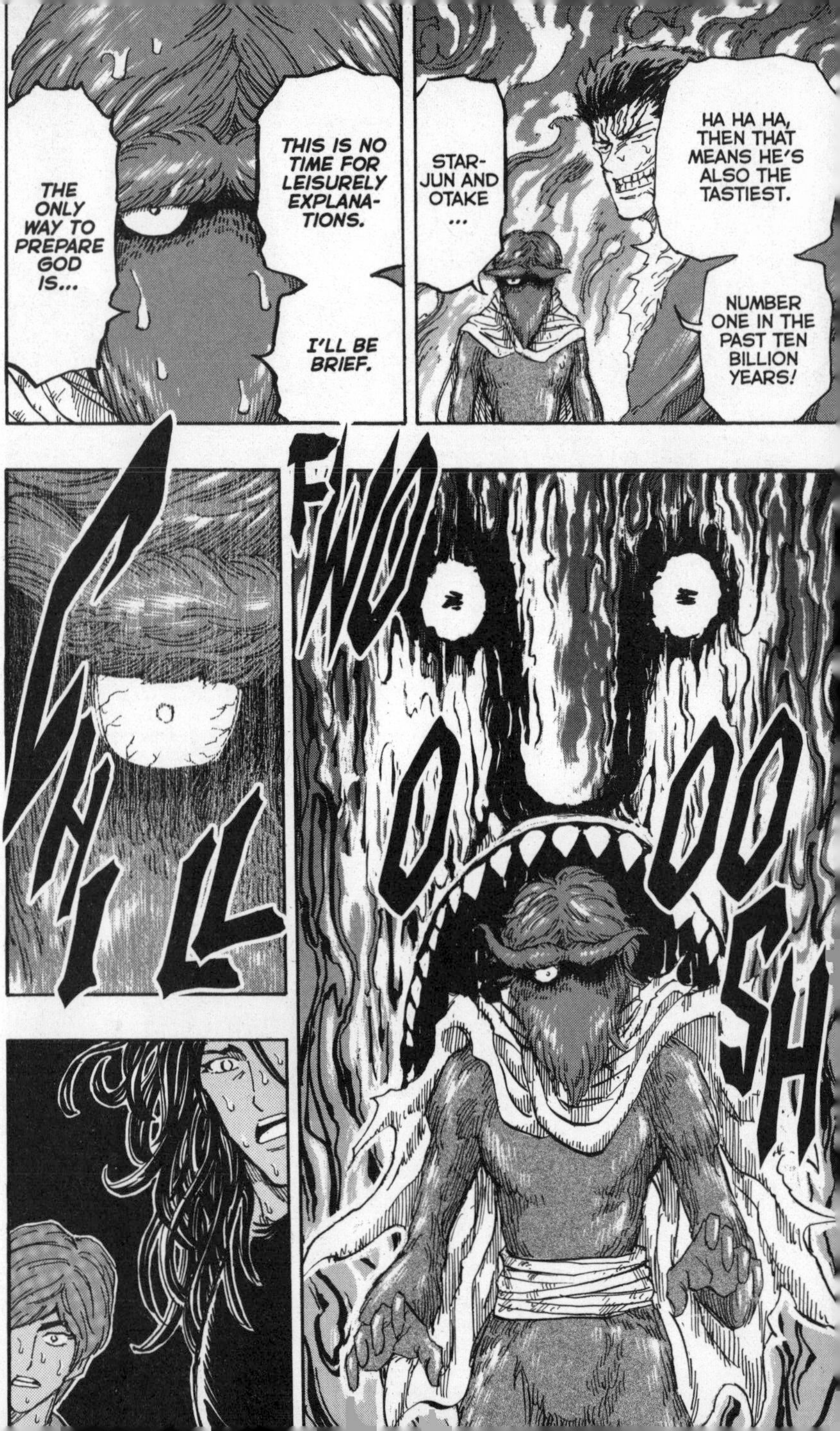
HA HA HA, THEN THAT MEANS HE'S ALSO THE TASTIEST.
NUMBER ONE IN THE PAST TEN BILLION YEARS!
STAR-JUN AND OTAKE...
THIS IS NO TIME FOR LEISURELY EXPLANA-TIONS.
I'LL BE BRIEF.
THE ONLY WAY TO PREPARE GOD IS...
FWOOOOSH
CHILL

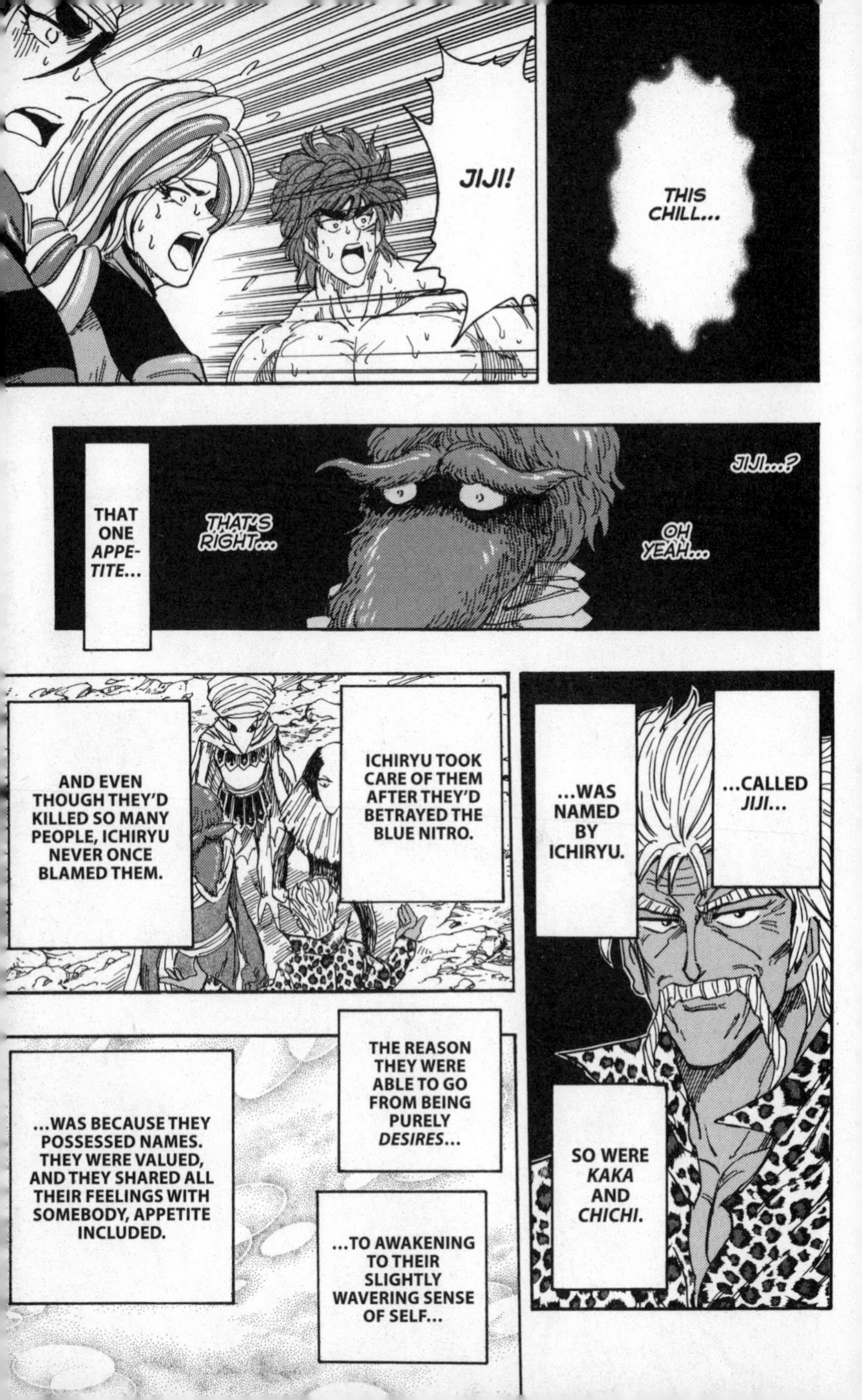
THIS CHILL...
JIJI!
JIJI...?
OH YEAH...
THAT'S RIGHT...
THAT ONE *APPETITE*...
...CALLED *JIJI*...
...WAS NAMED BY ICHIRYU.
SO WERE *KAKA* AND *CHICHI*.
ICHIRYU TOOK CARE OF THEM AFTER THEY'D BETRAYED THE BLUE NITRO.
AND EVEN THOUGH THEY'D KILLED SO MANY PEOPLE, ICHIRYU NEVER ONCE BLAMED THEM.
THE REASON THEY WERE ABLE TO GO FROM BEING PURELY *DESIRES*...
...TO AWAKENING TO THEIR SLIGHTLY WAVERING SENSE OF SELF...
...WAS BECAUSE THEY POSSESSED NAMES. THEY WERE VALUED, AND THEY SHARED ALL THEIR FEELINGS WITH SOMEBODY, APPETITE INCLUDED.

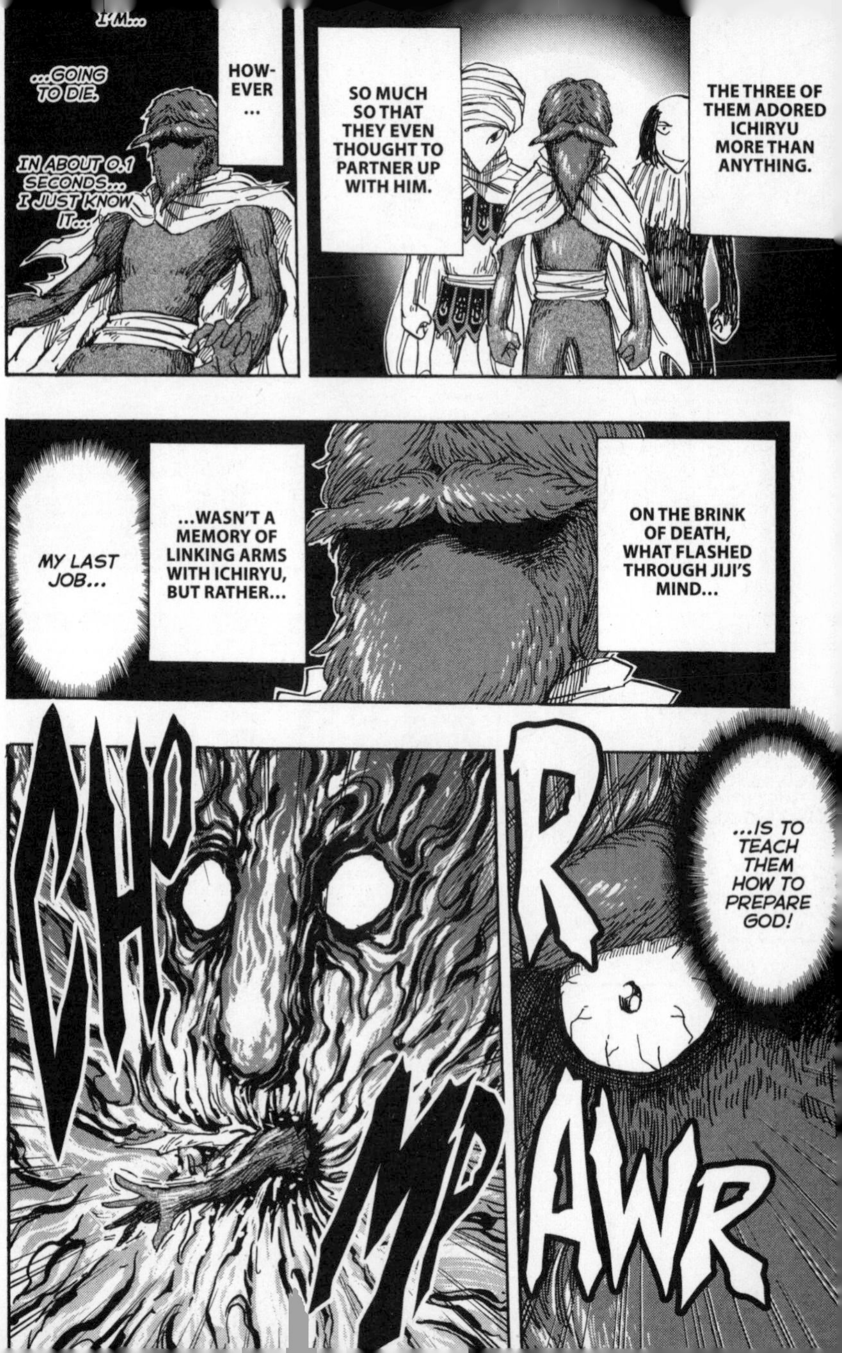
THE THREE OF THEM ADORED ICHIRYU MORE THAN ANYTHING.
SO MUCH SO THAT THEY EVEN THOUGHT TO PARTNER UP WITH HIM.
HOW-EVER ...
I'M...
...GOING TO DIE.
IN ABOUT 0.1 SECONDS... I JUST KNOW IT...
ON THE BRINK OF DEATH, WHAT FLASHED THROUGH JIJI'S MIND...
...WASN'T A MEMORY OF LINKING ARMS WITH ICHIRYU, BUT RATHER...
MY LAST JOB...
RAWR
...IS TO TEACH THEM HOW TO PREPARE GOD!
CHOMP

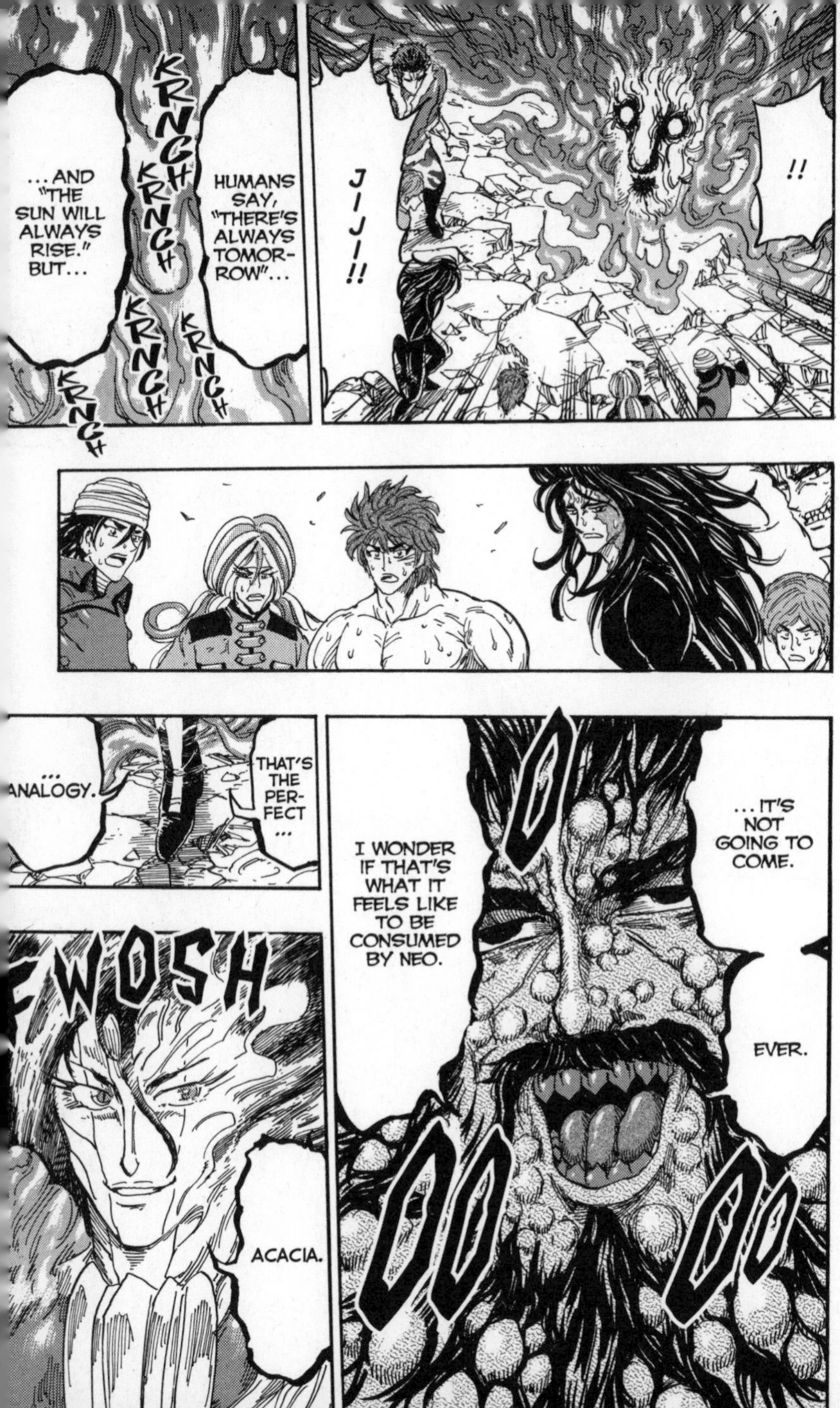
JIJI!!
!!
HUMANS SAY, "THERE'S ALWAYS TOMORROW"...
...AND "THE SUN WILL ALWAYS RISE." BUT...
KRNCH
KRNCH
KRNCH
KRNCH
KRNCH
KRNCH
...IT'S NOT GOING TO COME.
I WONDER IF THAT'S WHAT IT FEELS LIKE TO BE CONSUMED BY NEO.
EVER.
OOO
THAT'S THE PERFECT...
...ANALOGY.
FWOSH
ACACIA.

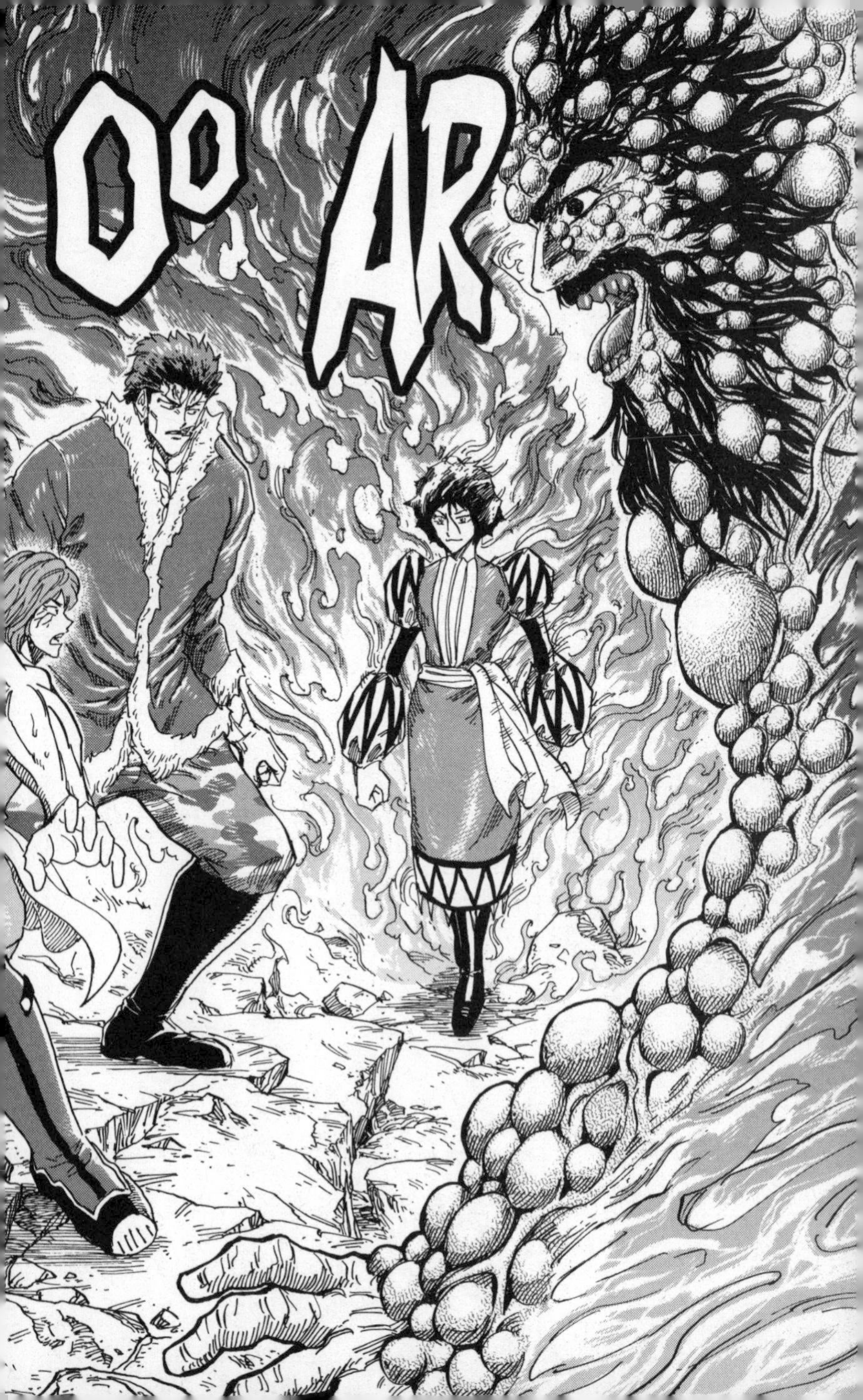
ROAR

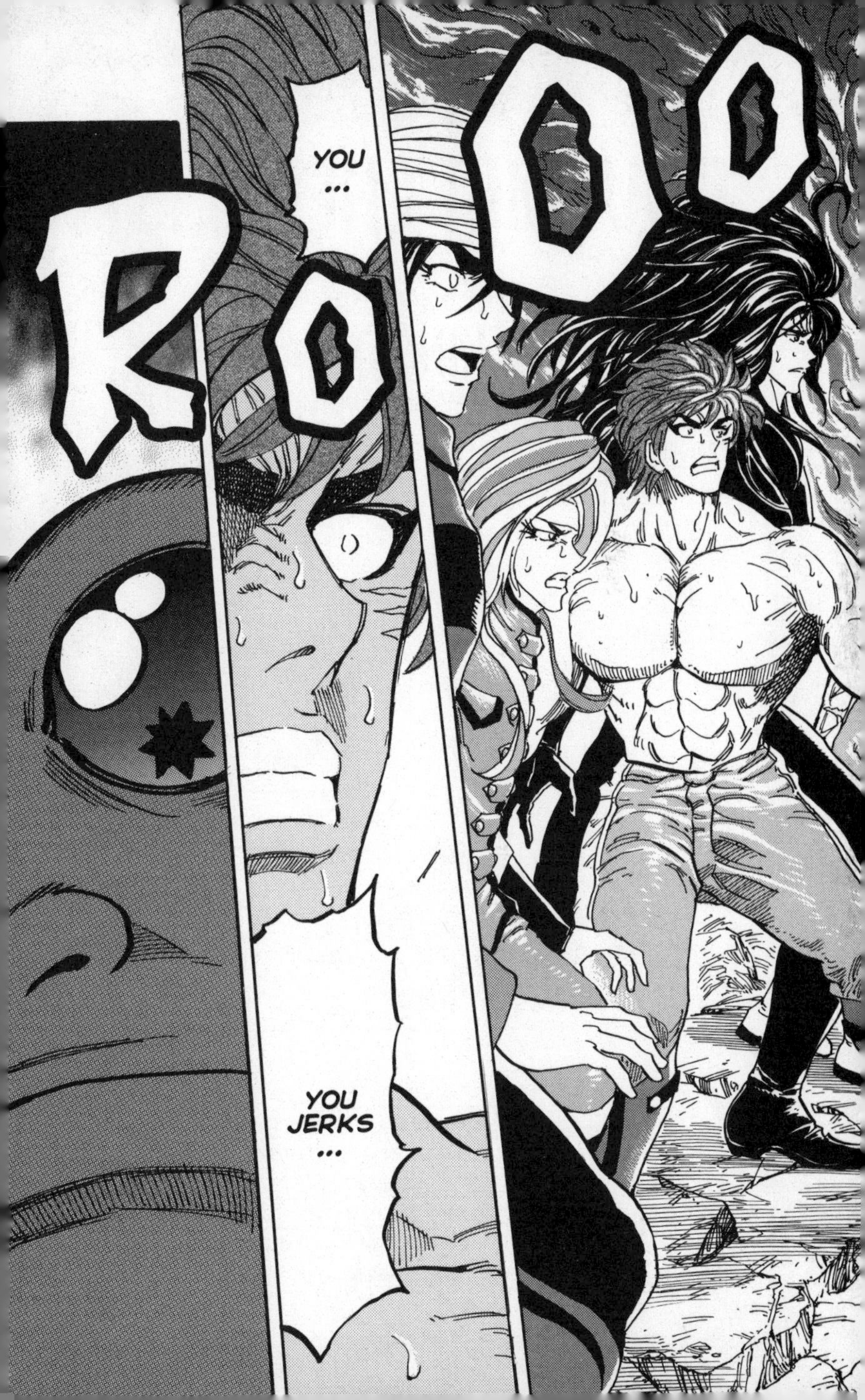
ROOOO
YOU ...
YOU JERKS ...

TORIKO

GOURMET CHECKLIST

Vol. 402

 ## SEA KING OCEAN
(GIANT MARINE MONSTER)

CAPTURE LEVEL: 4,390

HABITAT: GOURMET WORLD AREA 6

SIZE:: ---

HEIGHT: ---

WEIGHT: ---

PRICE: INEDIBLE

THE *APRON* WILL COME FROM THE SKIN OF THE *SEA KING, OCEAN.* *

SCALE

THE SEA KING WHOSE SKIN IS USED TO MAKE THE APRON COMPONENT OF THE GOLDEN COOKWARE USED TO PREPARE THE FISH TREASURE, ANOTHER. THE MAJORITY OF ITS BODY IS MADE OF SEAWATER, AND UNLESS YOU ATTACK ITS CORE YOU WON'T BE ABLE TO DAMAGE IT. ALSO, BY REGULATING ITS BODY TEMPERATURE, IT CAN CHANGE ITS STATE OF BEING TO SUBLIMATION, COAGULATION OR LIQUEFACTION AT WILL. IT CAN ALSO CHANGE FROM REGULAR WATER TO BOILING WATER TO STEAM. IT'S TRULY A VERSATILE CREATURE.

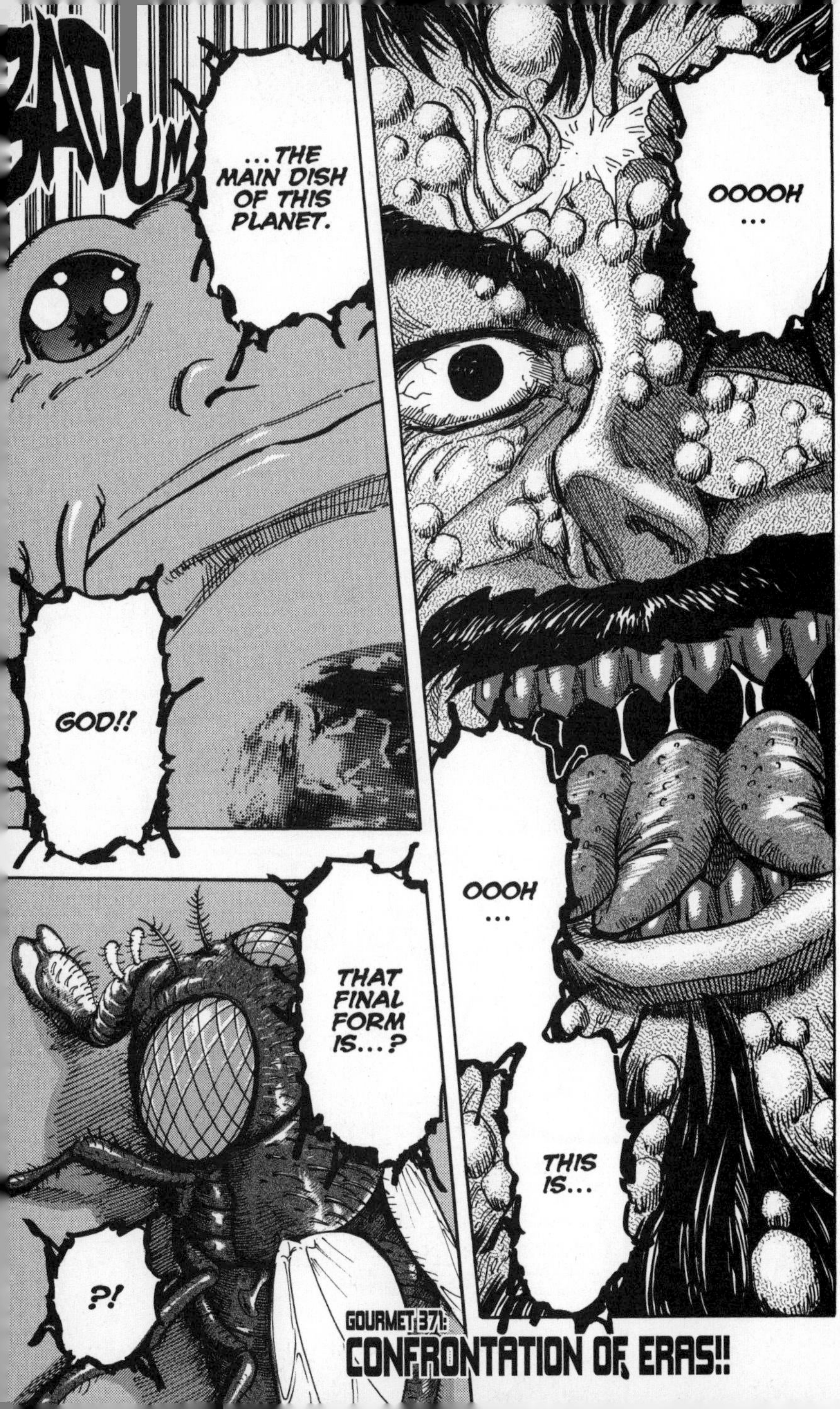
OOOOH ...
OOOH ...
THIS IS...
BADUM
...THE MAIN DISH OF THIS PLANET.
GOD!!
THAT FINAL FORM IS...?
?!

GOURMET 371: CONFRONTATION OF ERAS!!

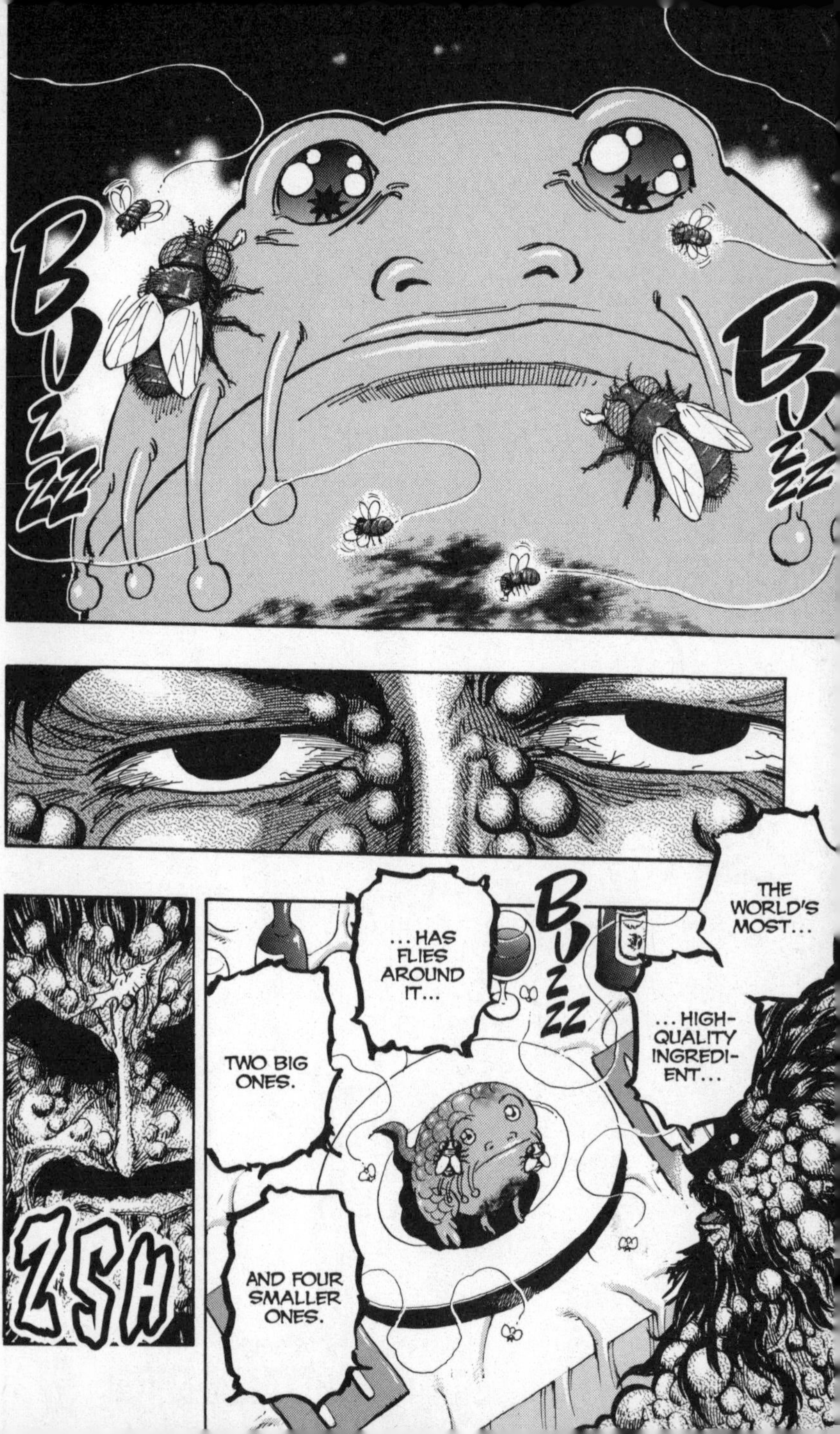
BUZZZ
BUZZZ
THE WORLD'S MOST...
...HIGH-QUALITY INGREDI-ENT...
BUZZZ
...HAS FLIES AROUND IT...
TWO BIG ONES.
AND FOUR SMALLER ONES.
ZSH

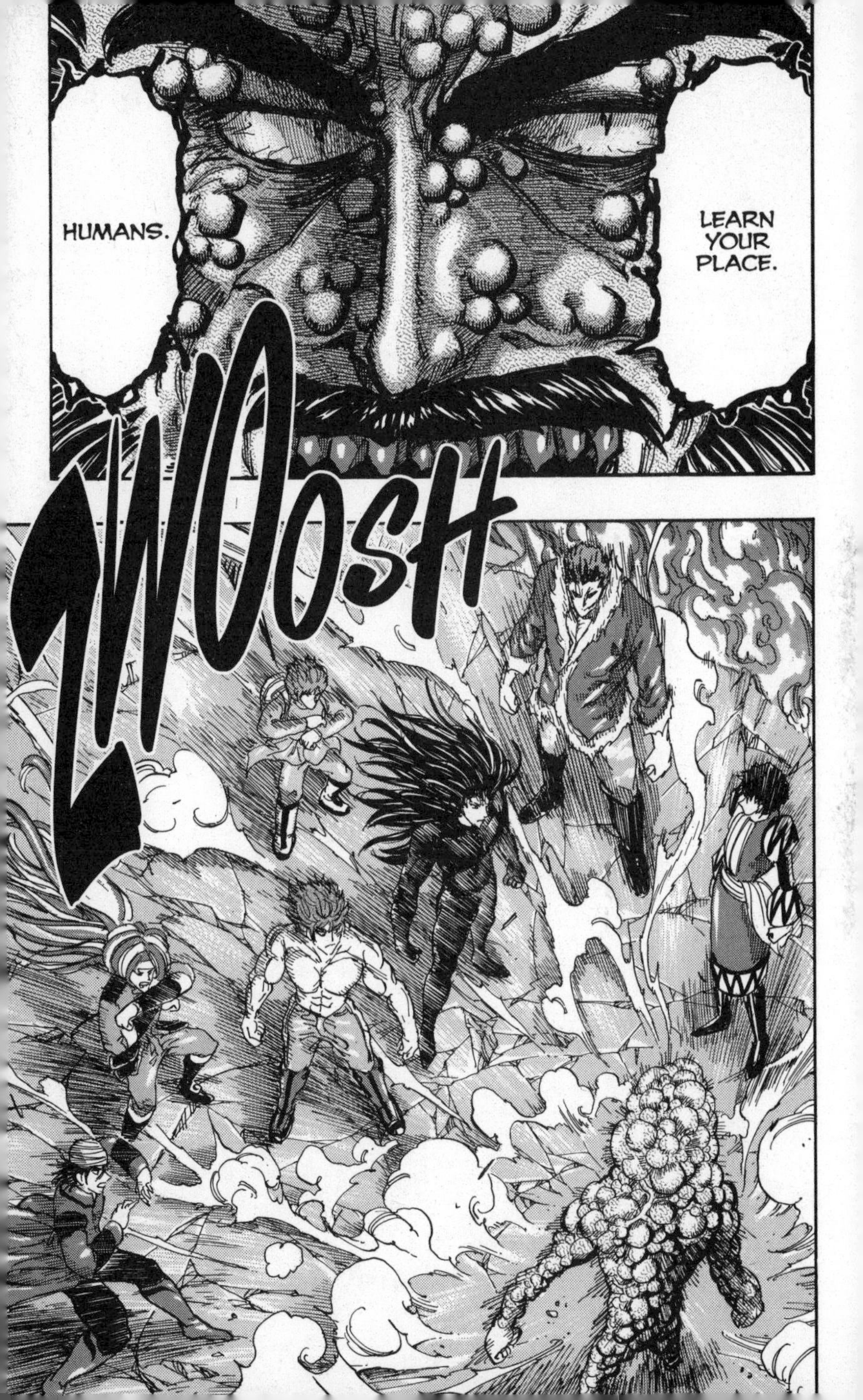
LEARN YOUR PLACE.
HUMANS.
WOOSH

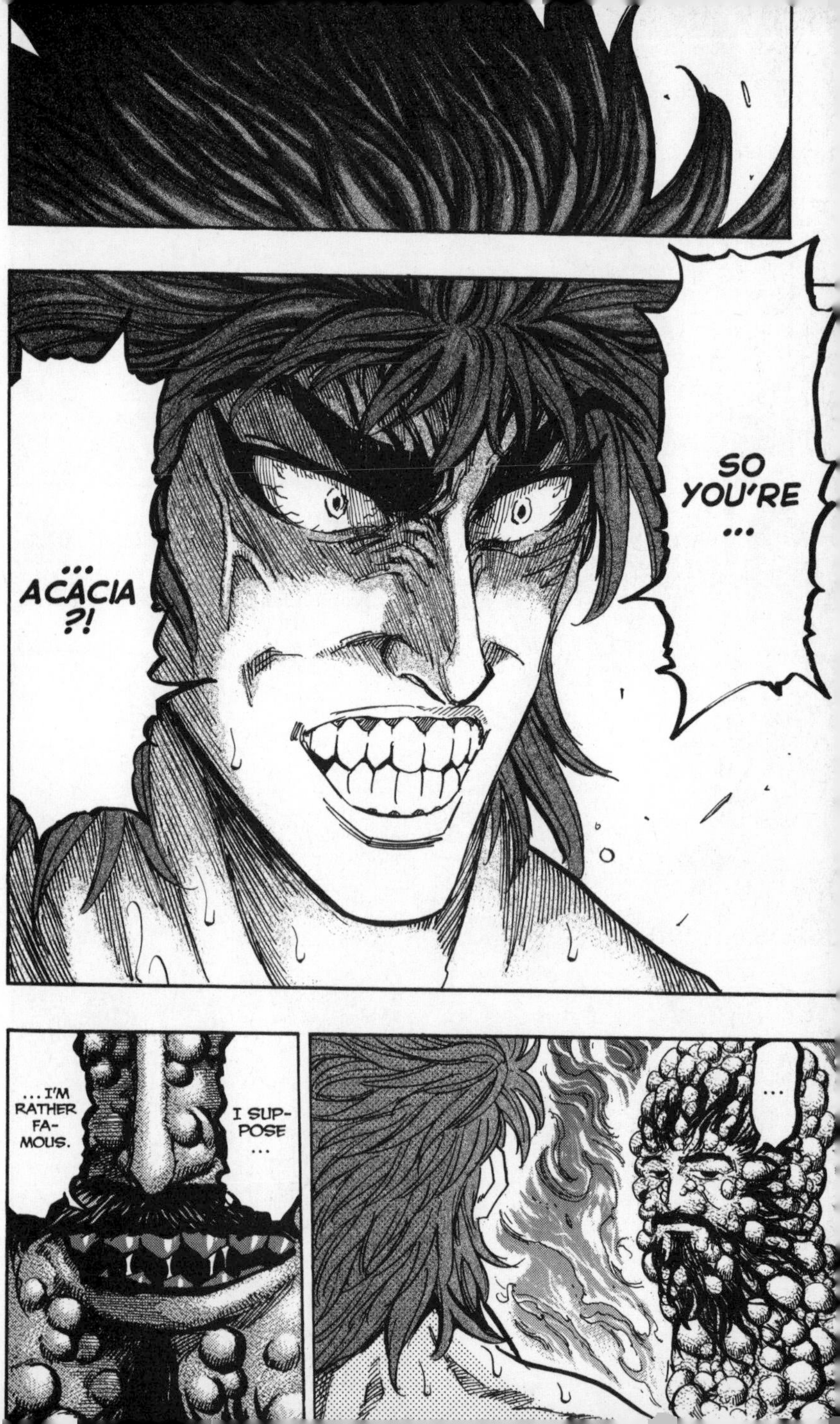
SO YOU'RE ...
... ACACIA ?!
...
I SUP-POSE ...
... I'M RATHER FA-MOUS.

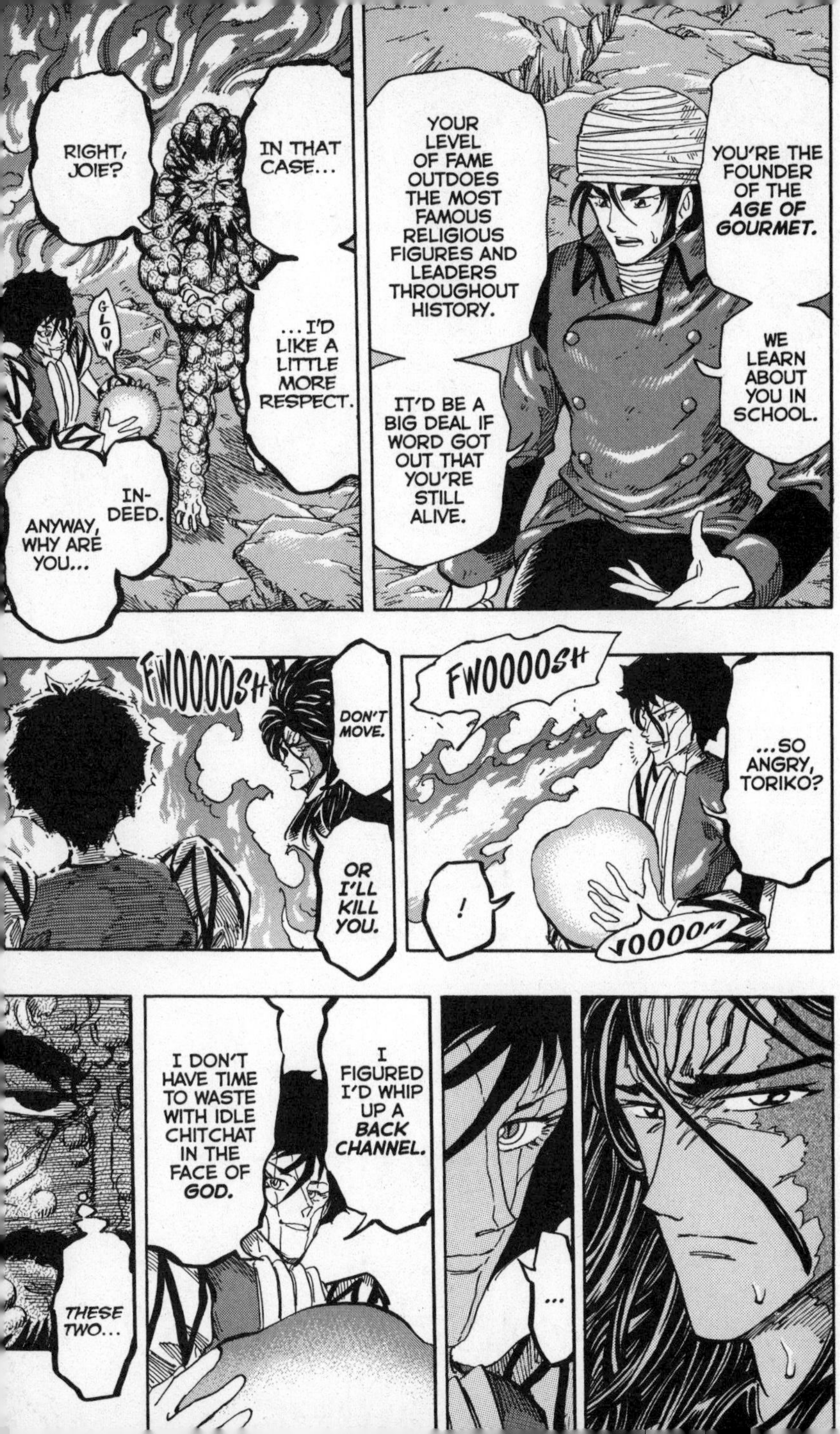
YOU'RE THE FOUNDER OF THE *AGE OF GOURMET.*
WE LEARN ABOUT YOU IN SCHOOL.
YOUR LEVEL OF FAME OUTDOES THE MOST FAMOUS RELIGIOUS FIGURES AND LEADERS THROUGHOUT HISTORY.
IT'D BE A BIG DEAL IF WORD GOT OUT THAT YOU'RE STILL ALIVE.
IN THAT CASE...
RIGHT, JOIE?
...I'D LIKE A LITTLE MORE RESPECT.
GLOW
IN-DEED.
ANYWAY, WHY ARE YOU...
FWOOOOSH
...SO ANGRY, TORIKO?
!
VOOOOM
FWOOOOSH
DON'T MOVE.
OR I'LL KILL YOU.
...
I FIGURED I'D WHIP UP A *BACK CHANNEL.*
I DON'T HAVE TIME TO WASTE WITH IDLE CHITCHAT IN THE FACE OF *GOD.*
THESE TWO...

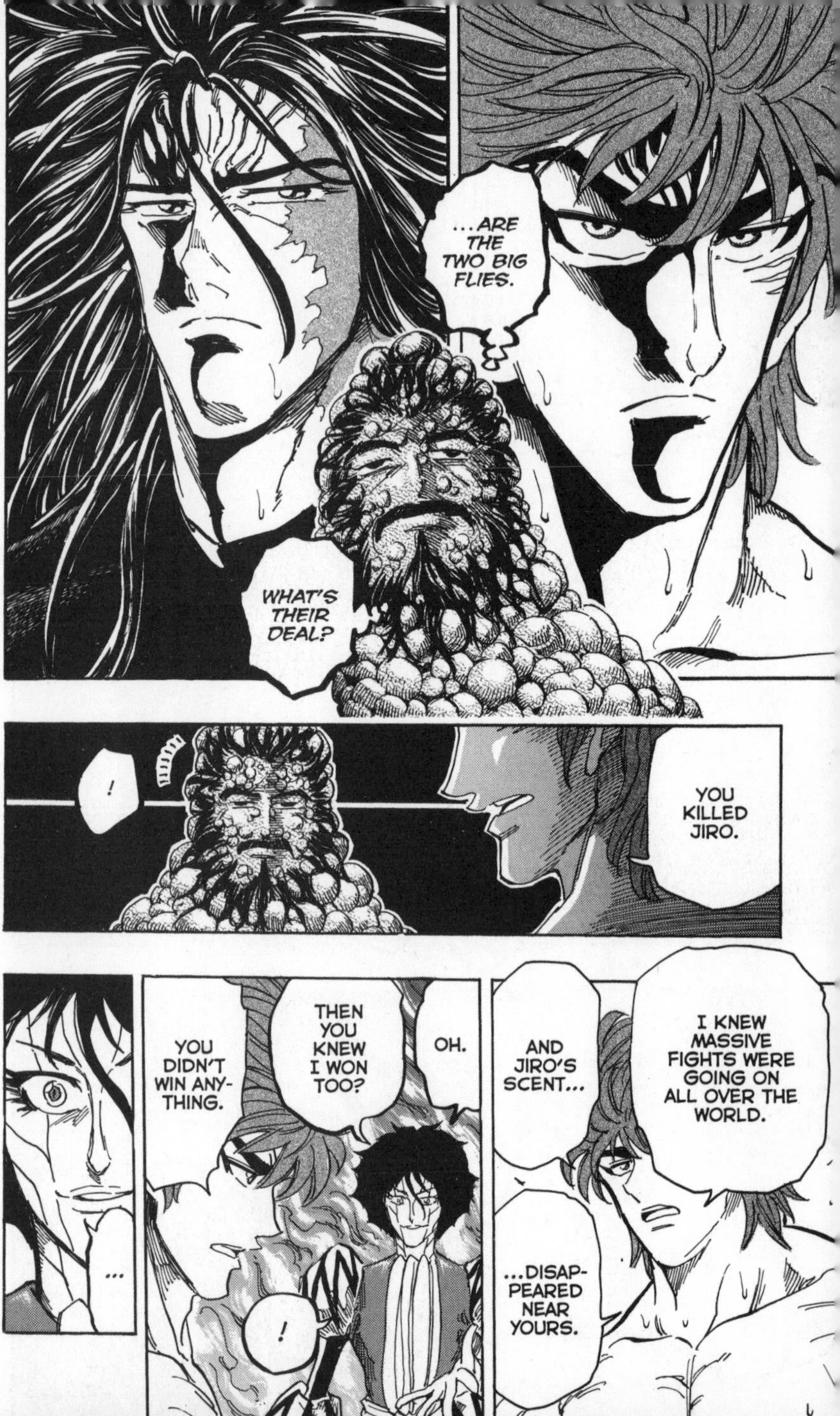
...ARE THE TWO BIG FLIES.
WHAT'S THEIR DEAL?
YOU KILLED JIRO.
!
I KNEW MASSIVE FIGHTS WERE GOING ON ALL OVER THE WORLD.
AND JIRO'S SCENT...
...DISAPPEARED NEAR YOURS.
OH.
THEN YOU KNEW I WON TOO?
YOU DIDN'T WIN ANYTHING.
!
...

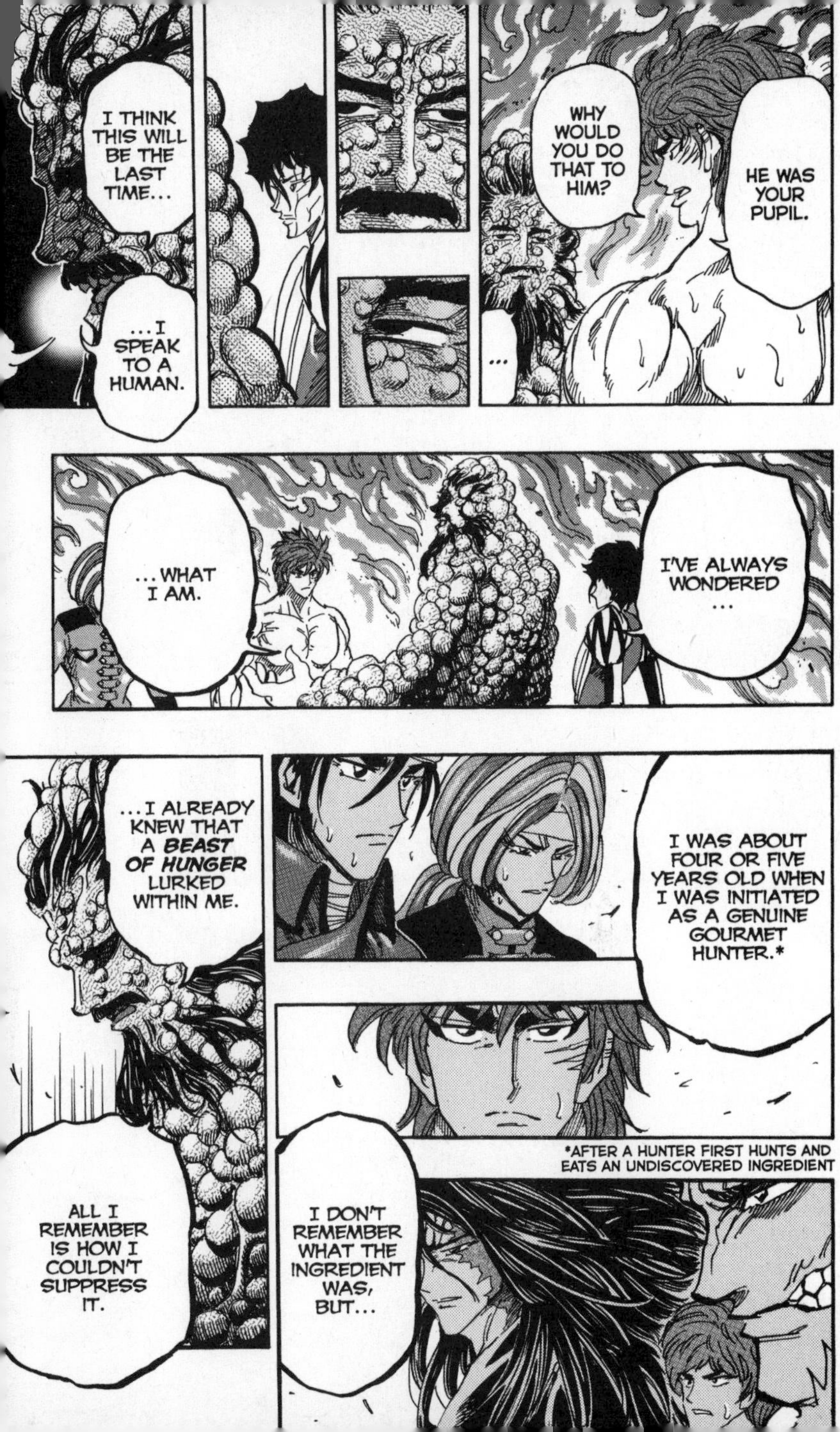
HE WAS YOUR PUPIL.
WHY WOULD YOU DO THAT TO HIM?
...
I THINK THIS WILL BE THE LAST TIME...
...I SPEAK TO A HUMAN.
I'VE ALWAYS WONDERED ...
...WHAT I AM.
I WAS ABOUT FOUR OR FIVE YEARS OLD WHEN I WAS INITIATED AS A GENUINE GOURMET HUNTER.*
...I ALREADY KNEW THAT A *BEAST OF HUNGER* LURKED WITHIN ME.
*AFTER A HUNTER FIRST HUNTS AND EATS AN UNDISCOVERED INGREDIENT
I DON'T REMEMBER WHAT THE INGREDIENT WAS, BUT...
ALL I REMEMBER IS HOW I COULDN'T SUPPRESS IT.

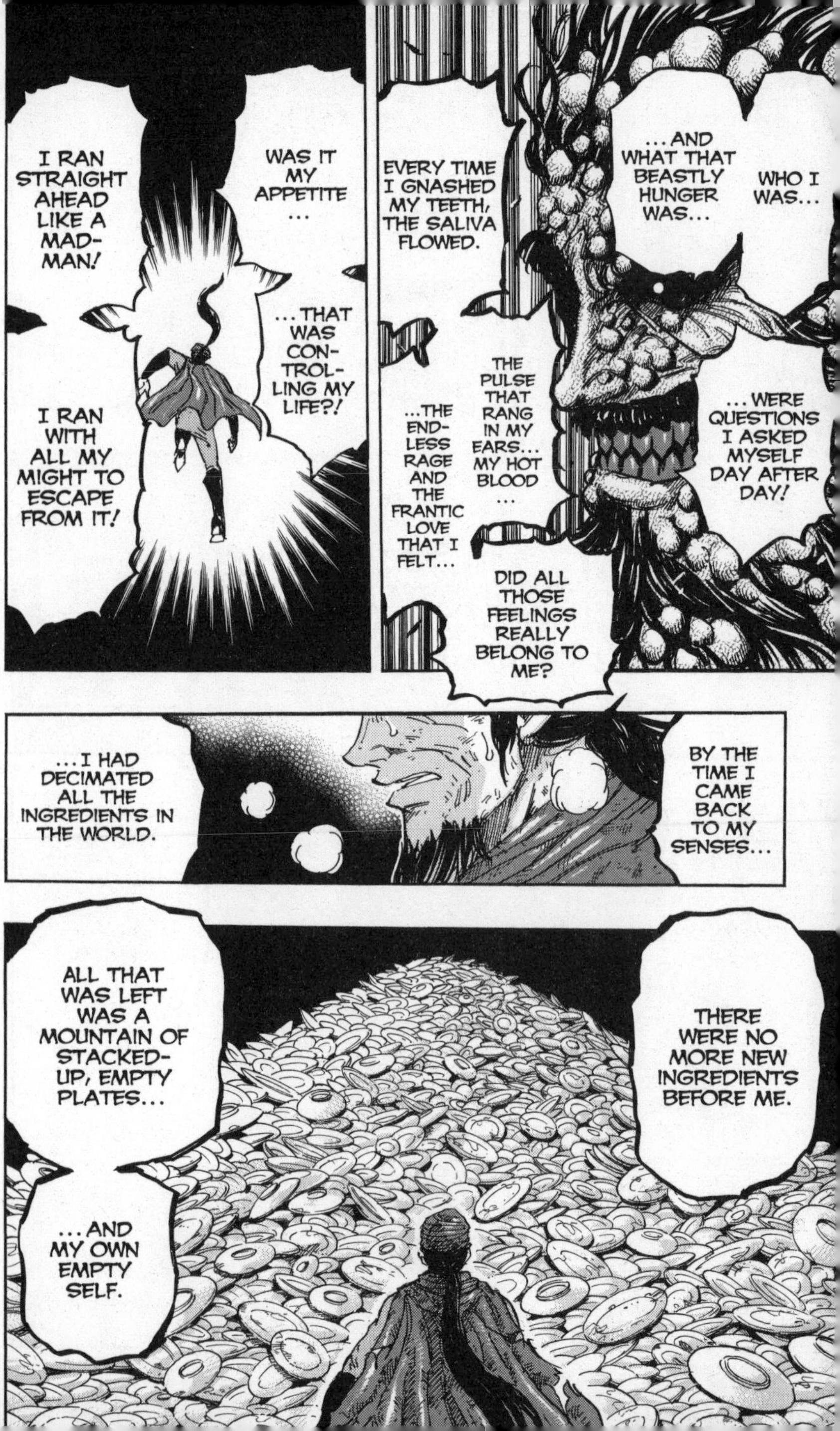
WHO I WAS...
...AND WHAT THAT BEASTLY HUNGER WAS...
EVERY TIME I GNASHED MY TEETH, THE SALIVA FLOWED.
...WERE QUESTIONS I ASKED MYSELF DAY AFTER DAY!
THE PULSE THAT RANG IN MY EARS... MY HOT BLOOD ...
...THE ENDLESS RAGE AND THE FRANTIC LOVE THAT I FELT...
DID ALL THOSE FEELINGS REALLY BELONG TO ME?
WAS IT MY APPETITE ...
I RAN STRAIGHT AHEAD LIKE A MADMAN!
...THAT WAS CONTROLLING MY LIFE?!
I RAN WITH ALL MY MIGHT TO ESCAPE FROM IT!
BY THE TIME I CAME BACK TO MY SENSES...
...I HAD DECIMATED ALL THE INGREDIENTS IN THE WORLD.
THERE WERE NO MORE NEW INGREDIENTS BEFORE ME.
ALL THAT WAS LEFT WAS A MOUNTAIN OF STACKED-UP, EMPTY PLATES...
...AND MY OWN EMPTY SELF.

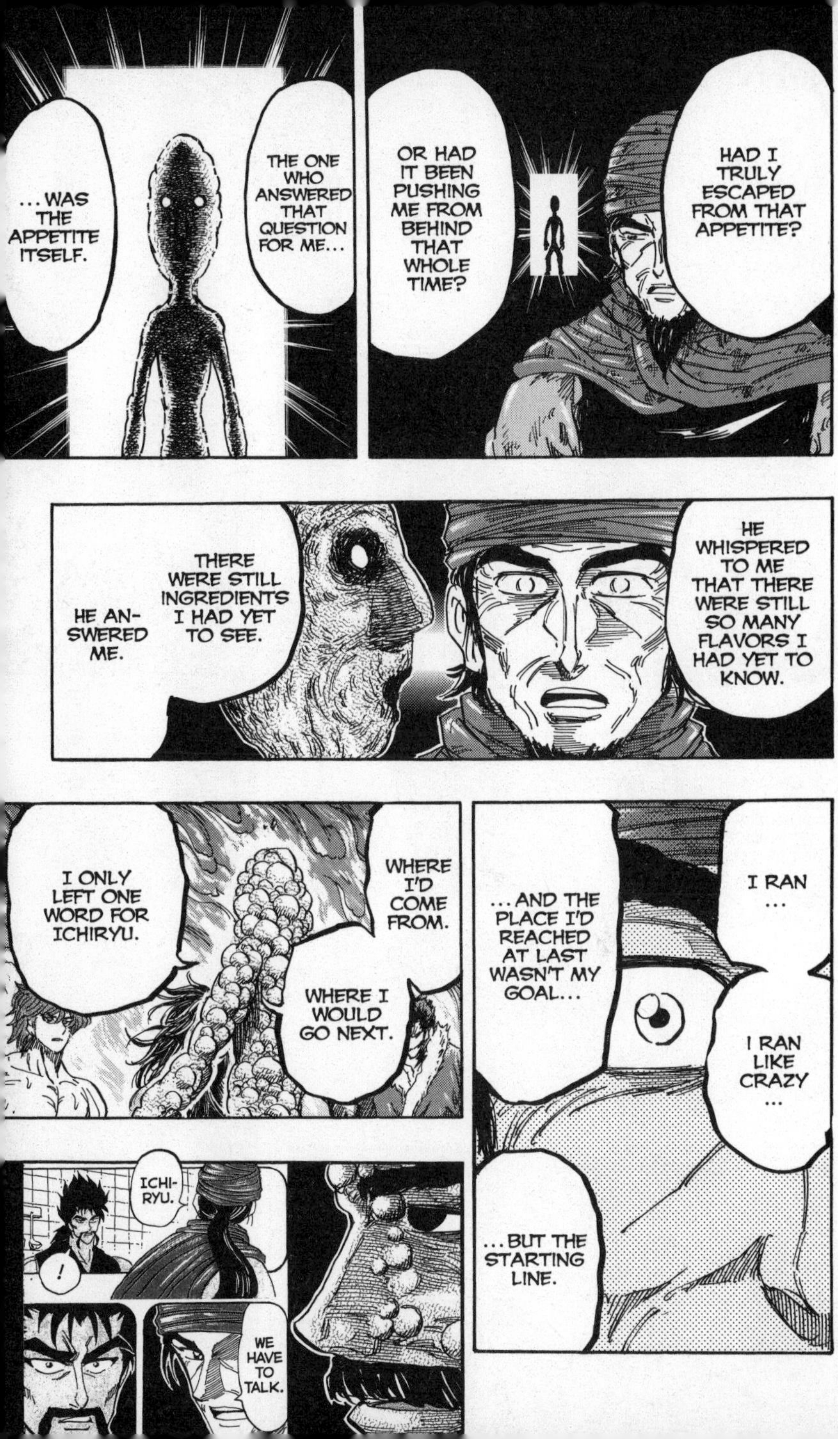
HAD I TRULY ESCAPED FROM THAT APPETITE?
OR HAD IT BEEN PUSHING ME FROM BEHIND THAT WHOLE TIME?
THE ONE WHO ANSWERED THAT QUESTION FOR ME...
...WAS THE APPETITE ITSELF.
HE WHISPERED TO ME THAT THERE WERE STILL SO MANY FLAVORS I HAD YET TO KNOW.
THERE WERE STILL INGREDIENTS I HAD YET TO SEE.
HE ANSWERED ME.
I RAN...
I RAN LIKE CRAZY...
...AND THE PLACE I'D REACHED AT LAST WASN'T MY GOAL...
...BUT THE STARTING LINE.
WHERE I'D COME FROM.
WHERE I WOULD GO NEXT.
I ONLY LEFT ONE WORD FOR ICHIRYU.
ICHI-RYU.
!
WE HAVE TO TALK.

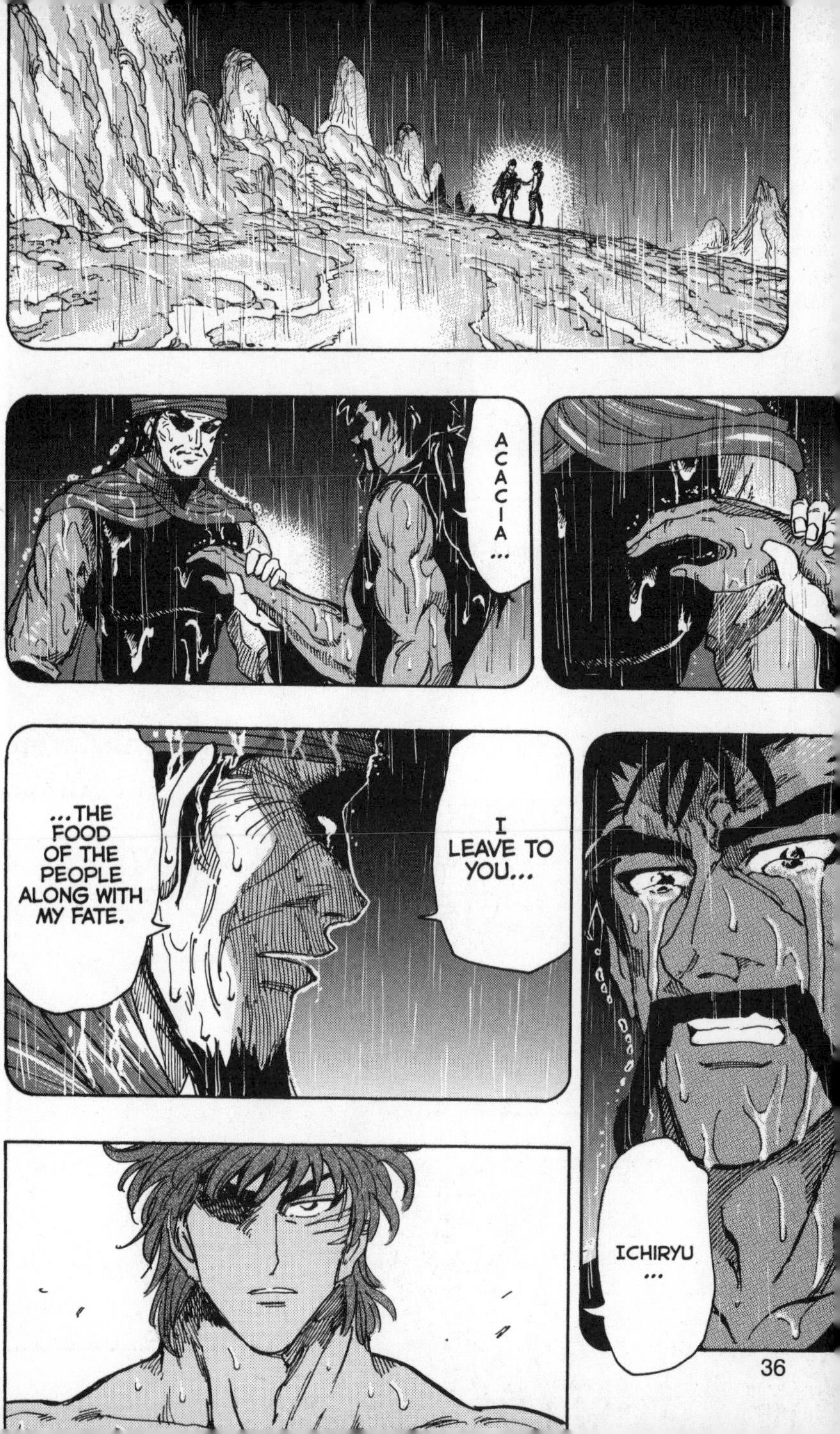
ACACIA...
ICHIRYU...
I LEAVE TO YOU...
...THE FOOD OF THE PEOPLE ALONG WITH MY FATE.

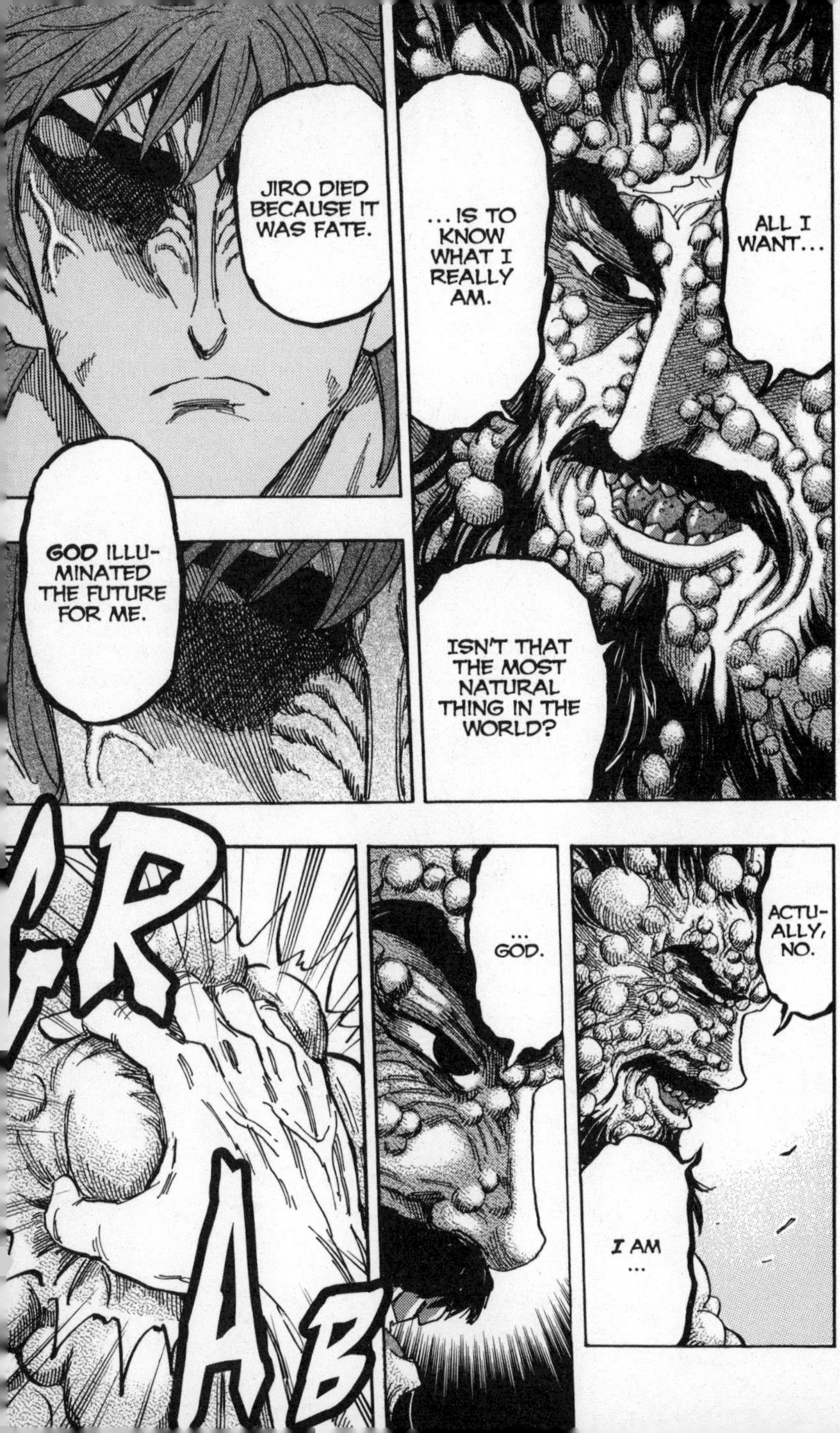
ALL I WANT...
...IS TO KNOW WHAT I REALLY AM.
ISN'T THAT THE MOST NATURAL THING IN THE WORLD?
JIRO DIED BECAUSE IT WAS FATE.
GOD ILLUMINATED THE FUTURE FOR ME.
ACTUALLY, NO.
I AM ...
... GOD.

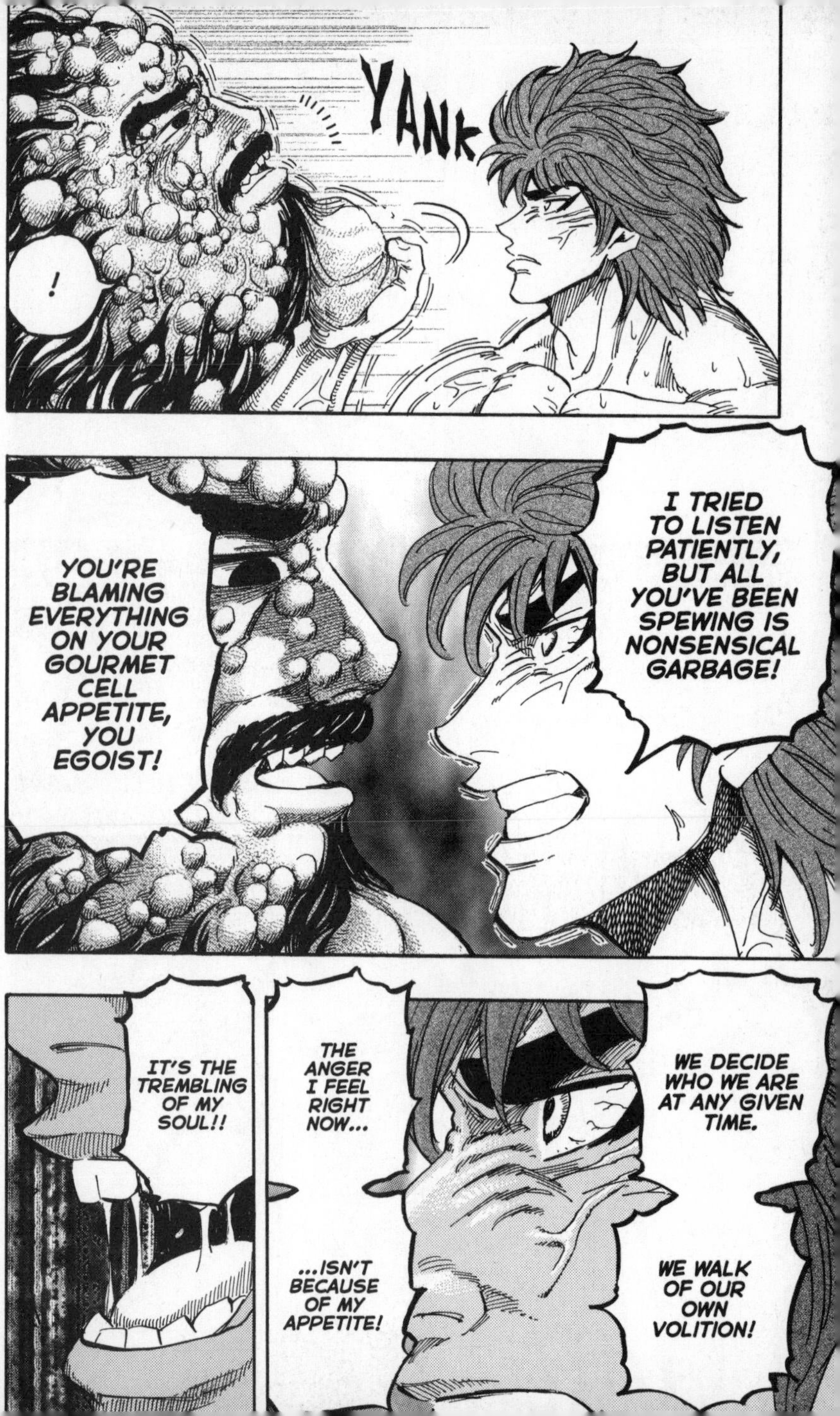
YANK
!
I TRIED TO LISTEN PATIENTLY, BUT ALL YOU'VE BEEN SPEWING IS NONSENSICAL GARBAGE!
YOU'RE BLAMING EVERYTHING ON YOUR GOURMET CELL APPETITE, YOU EGOIST!
WE DECIDE WHO WE ARE AT ANY GIVEN TIME.
WE WALK OF OUR OWN VOLITION!
THE ANGER I FEEL RIGHT NOW...
...ISN'T BECAUSE OF MY APPETITE!
IT'S THE TREMBLING OF MY SOUL!!

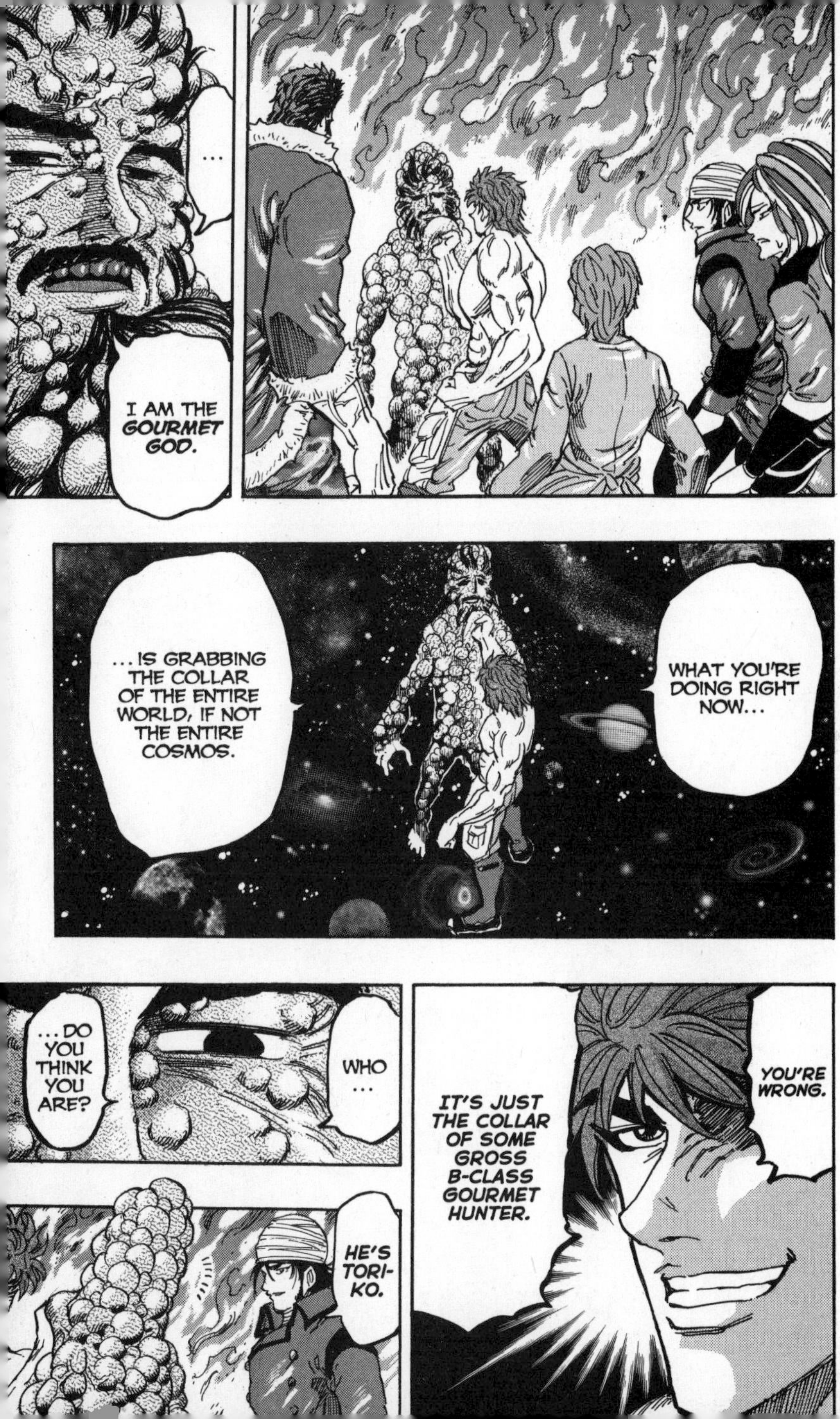
...
I AM THE GOURMET GOD.
WHAT YOU'RE DOING RIGHT NOW...
...IS GRABBING THE COLLAR OF THE ENTIRE WORLD, IF NOT THE ENTIRE COSMOS.
YOU'RE WRONG.
IT'S JUST THE COLLAR OF SOME GROSS B-CLASS GOURMET HUNTER.
WHO...
...DO YOU THINK YOU ARE?
HE'S TORIKO.

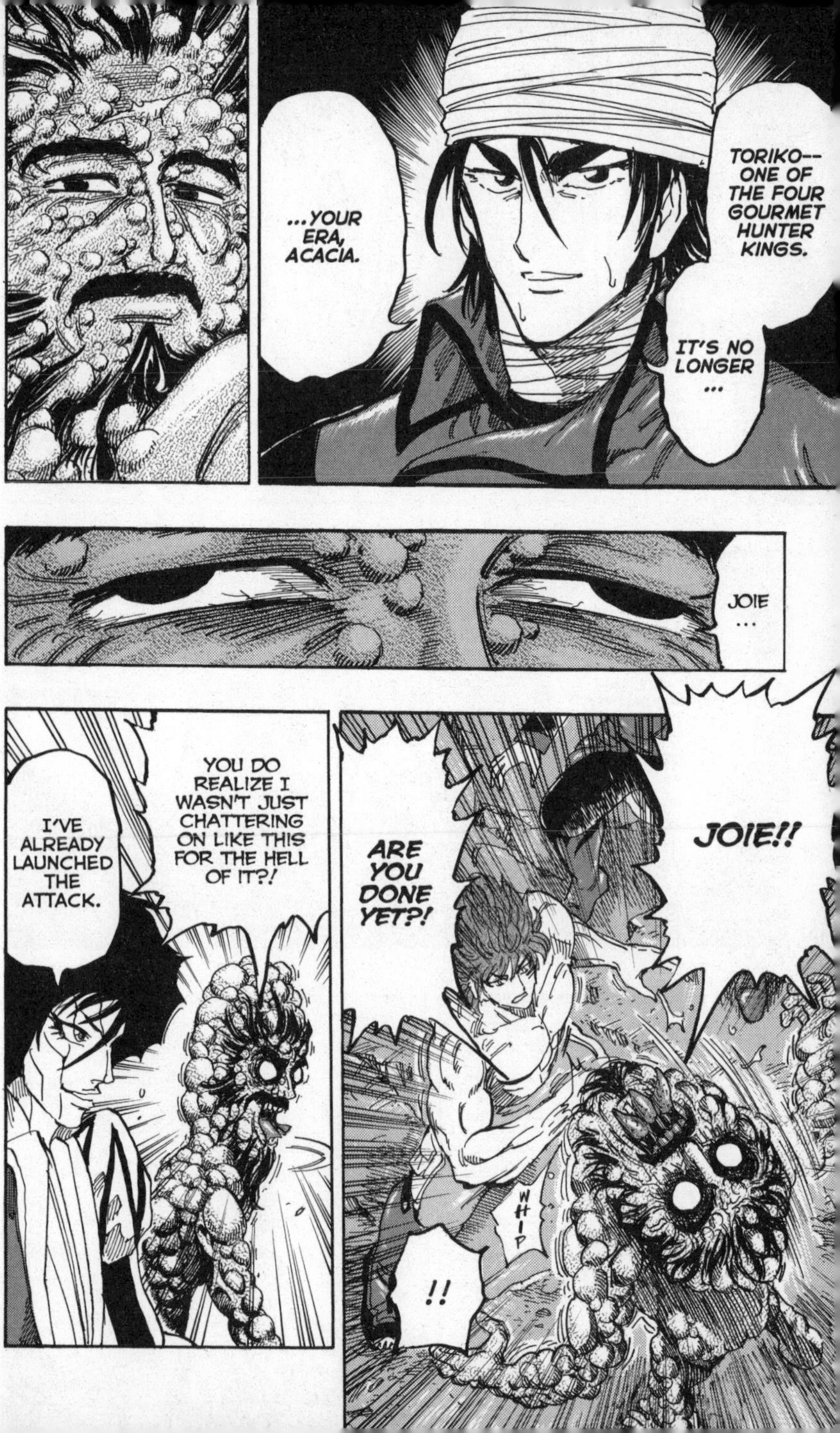
TORIKO--ONE OF THE FOUR GOURMET HUNTER KINGS.
IT'S NO LONGER ...
...YOUR ERA, ACACIA.
JOIE ...
JOIE!!
ARE YOU DONE YET?!
WHIP
!!
YOU DO REALIZE I WASN'T JUST CHATTERING ON LIKE THIS FOR THE HELL OF IT?!
I'VE ALREADY LAUNCHED THE ATTACK.

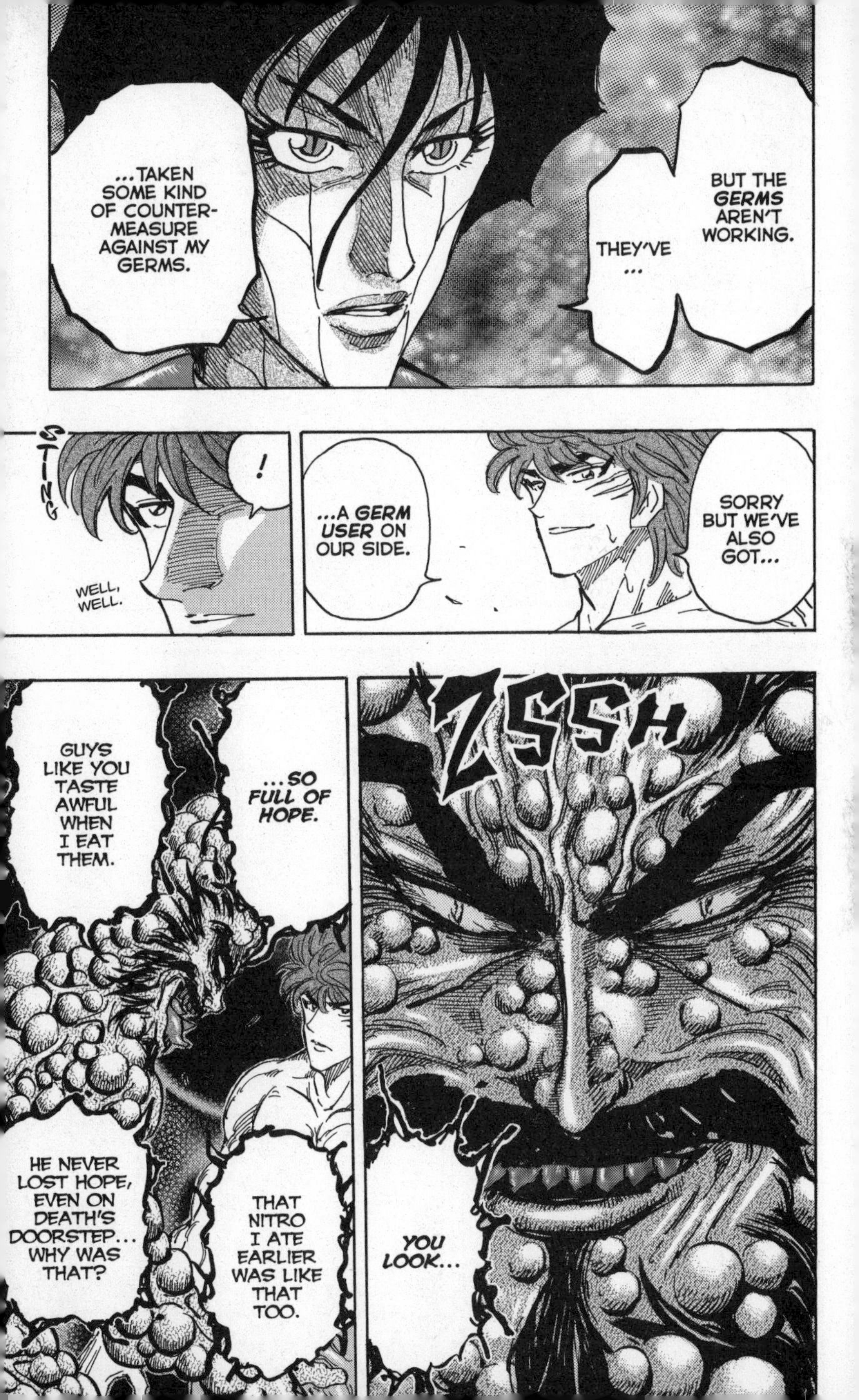
BUT THE GERMS AREN'T WORKING.
THEY'VE ...
...TAKEN SOME KIND OF COUNTER-MEASURE AGAINST MY GERMS.
SORRY BUT WE'VE ALSO GOT...
...A GERM USER ON OUR SIDE.
!
STING
WELL, WELL.
ZSSH
YOU LOOK...
...SO FULL OF HOPE.
GUYS LIKE YOU TASTE AWFUL WHEN I EAT THEM.
THAT NITRO I ATE EARLIER WAS LIKE THAT TOO.
HE NEVER LOST HOPE, EVEN ON DEATH'S DOORSTEP... WHY WAS THAT?

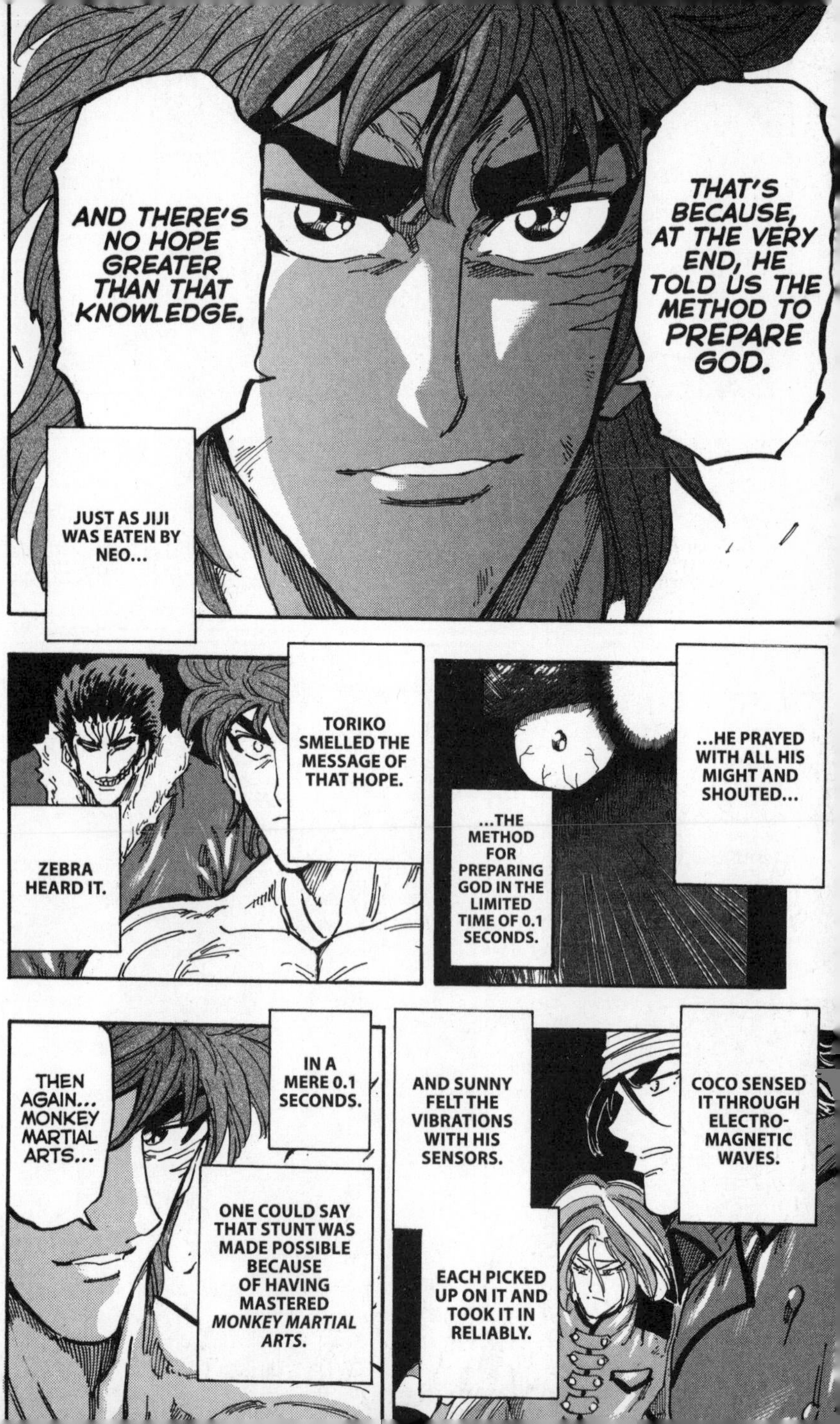
THAT'S BECAUSE, AT THE VERY END, HE TOLD US THE METHOD TO PREPARE GOD.
AND THERE'S NO HOPE GREATER THAN THAT KNOWLEDGE.
JUST AS JIJI WAS EATEN BY NEO...
...HE PRAYED WITH ALL HIS MIGHT AND SHOUTED...
...THE METHOD FOR PREPARING GOD IN THE LIMITED TIME OF 0.1 SECONDS.
TORIKO SMELLED THE MESSAGE OF THAT HOPE.
ZEBRA HEARD IT.
COCO SENSED IT THROUGH ELECTRO-MAGNETIC WAVES.
AND SUNNY FELT THE VIBRATIONS WITH HIS SENSORS.
EACH PICKED UP ON IT AND TOOK IT IN RELIABLY.
IN A MERE 0.1 SECONDS.
THEN AGAIN... MONKEY MARTIAL ARTS...
ONE COULD SAY THAT STUNT WAS MADE POSSIBLE BECAUSE OF HAVING MASTERED *MONKEY MARTIAL ARTS*.

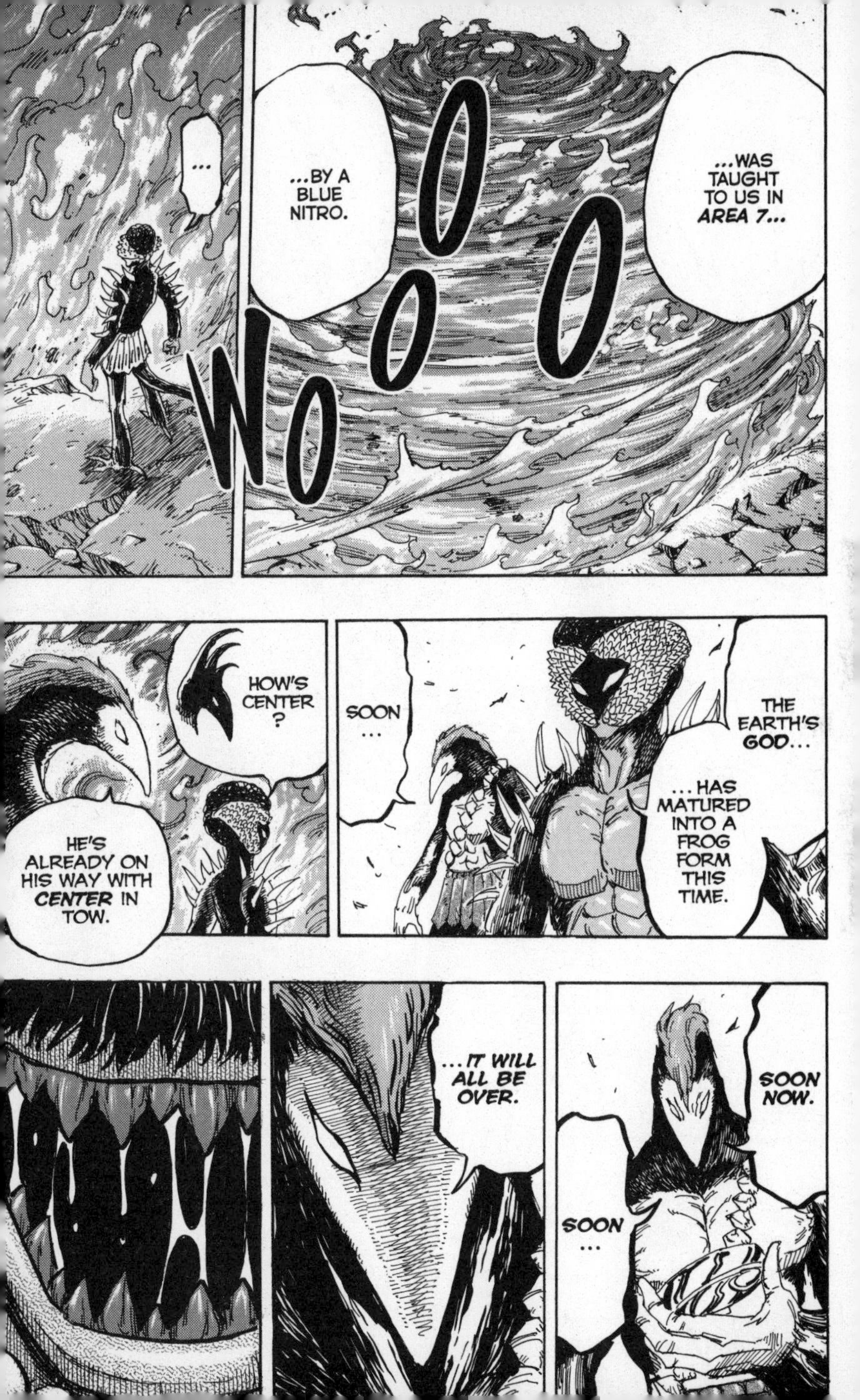
...WAS TAUGHT TO US IN AREA 7...
...BY A BLUE NITRO.
WOOOOO
...
THE EARTH'S GOD...
...HAS MATURED INTO A FROG FORM THIS TIME.
SOON ...
HOW'S CENTER?
HE'S ALREADY ON HIS WAY WITH CENTER IN TOW.
SOON NOW.
SOON ...
...IT WILL ALL BE OVER.

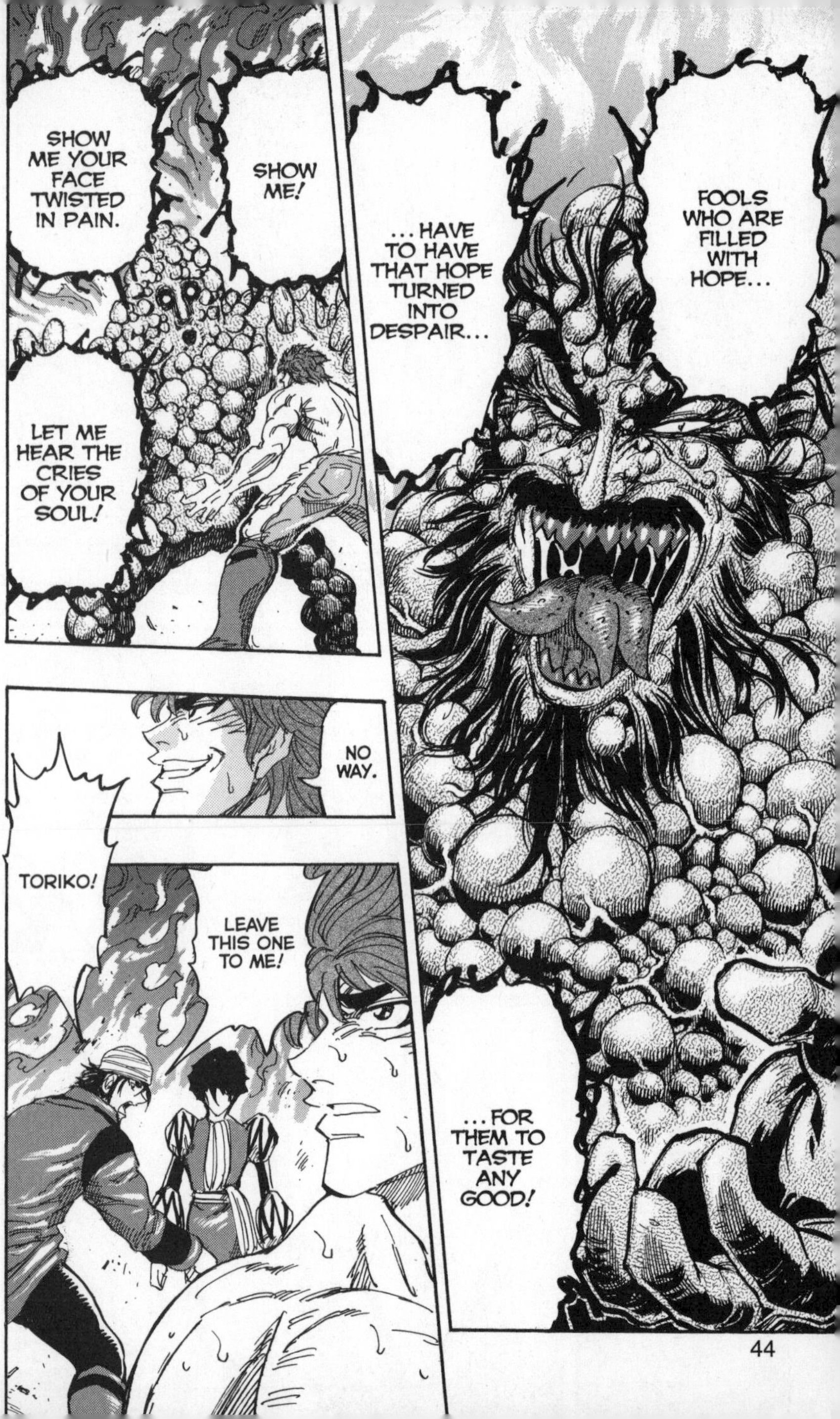
FOOLS WHO ARE FILLED WITH HOPE...
...HAVE TO HAVE THAT HOPE TURNED INTO DESPAIR...
...FOR THEM TO TASTE ANY GOOD!
SHOW ME!
SHOW ME YOUR FACE TWISTED IN PAIN.
LET ME HEAR THE CRIES OF YOUR SOUL!
NO WAY.
TORIKO!
LEAVE THIS ONE TO ME!

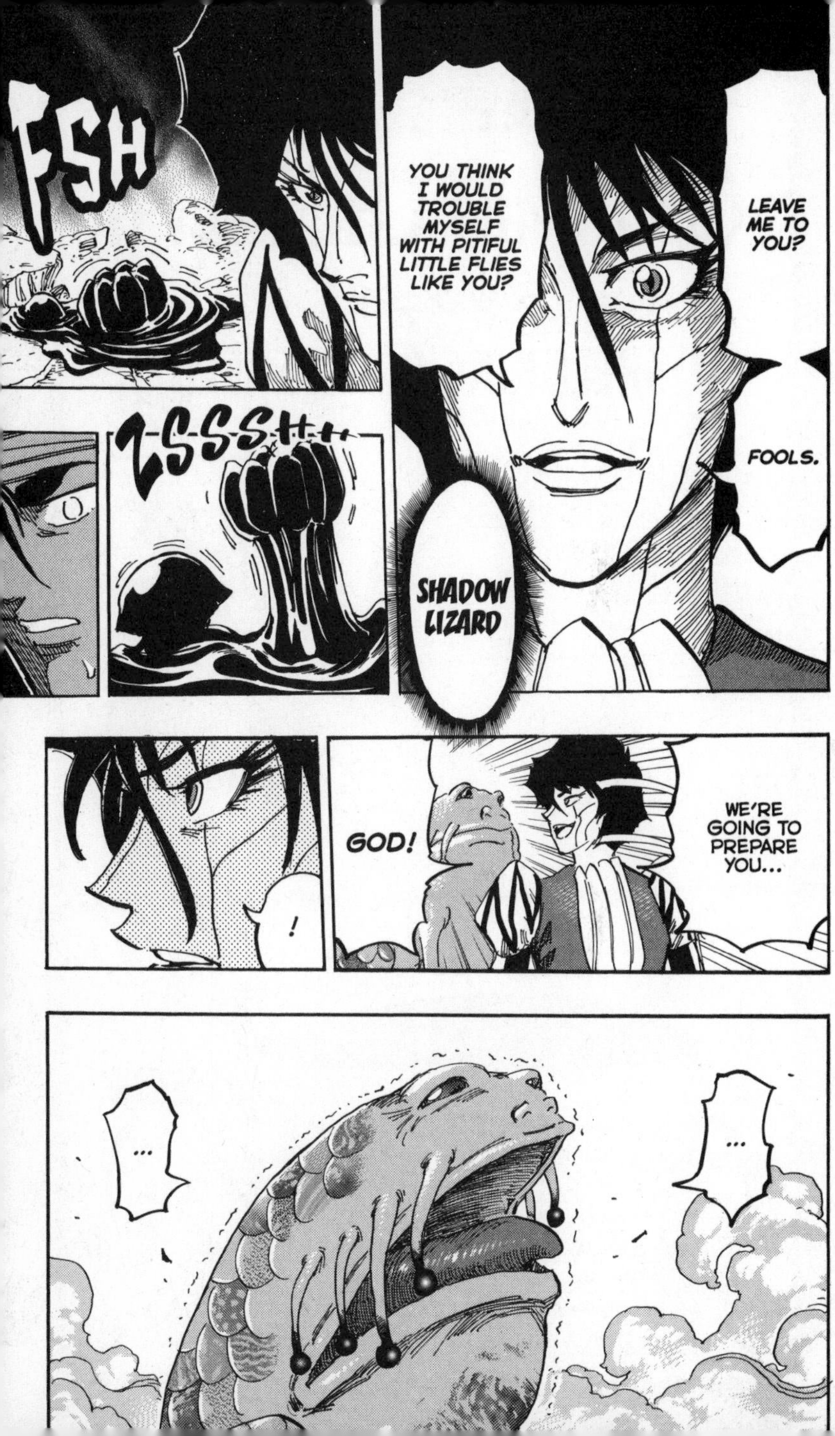
LEAVE ME TO YOU?
YOU THINK I WOULD TROUBLE MYSELF WITH PITIFUL LITTLE FLIES LIKE YOU?
FOOLS.
SHADOW LIZARD
FSH
ZSSSH...
WE'RE GOING TO PREPARE YOU...
GOD!
!
...
...

TORIKO

GOURMET CHECKLIST

Vol. 403

SHELL KING GIANT SHELL
(GIANT SHELL MONSTER)

CAPTURE LEVEL: UNKNOWN

HABITAT: GOURMET WORLD AREA 6

SIZE: 10 MILLION KM

HEIGHT: 3,500 M

WEIGHT: ---

PRICE: INEDIBLE

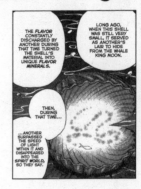

LONG AGO, WHEN THIS SHELL WAS STILL VERY SMALL, IT SERVED AS ANOTHER'S LAIR TO HIDE FROM THE WHALE KING MOON.
THE *FLAVOR* CONSTANTLY DISCHARGED BY ANOTHER DURING THAT TIME TURNED THE SHELL'S MATERIAL INTO UNIQUE *FLAVOR MINERALS.*
THEN, DURING THAT TIME...
...ANOTHER SURPASSED THE SPEED OF LIGHT WITHIN IT AND DISAPPEARED INTO THE *SPIRIT WORLD,* SO THEY SAY.

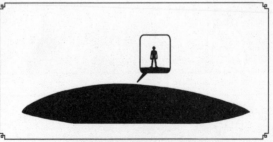

SCALE

THE SHELL KING WHOSE BODY IS USED TO MAKE THE FRYING PAN OF THE GOLDEN COOKWARE USED TO PREPARE THE FISH TREASURE, ANOTHER. IT'S NOT ONLY ONE OF THE SEVEN BEASTS, BUT IT'S ALSO HOME TO THE GIANT UNDERWATER CIVILIZATION, BLUE GRILL IN AREA 6. LONG AGO, WHEN IT WAS USED TO KEEP ANOTHER SAFE FROM THE WHALE KING MOON, IT WAS SAID THAT ANOTHER WOULD TURN ITS SHELL A UNIQUE FLAVOR. EVENTUALLY, ANOTHER SURPASSED THE SPEED OF LIGHT AND DISAPPEARED INTO THE SPIRIT WORLD, RESULTING IN A TIME WARP. BEFORE LONG, THE OTHER SEVEN BEASTS ALSO ENDED UP POSSESSING THEIR OWN BACK CHANNELS IN THE SAME WAY.

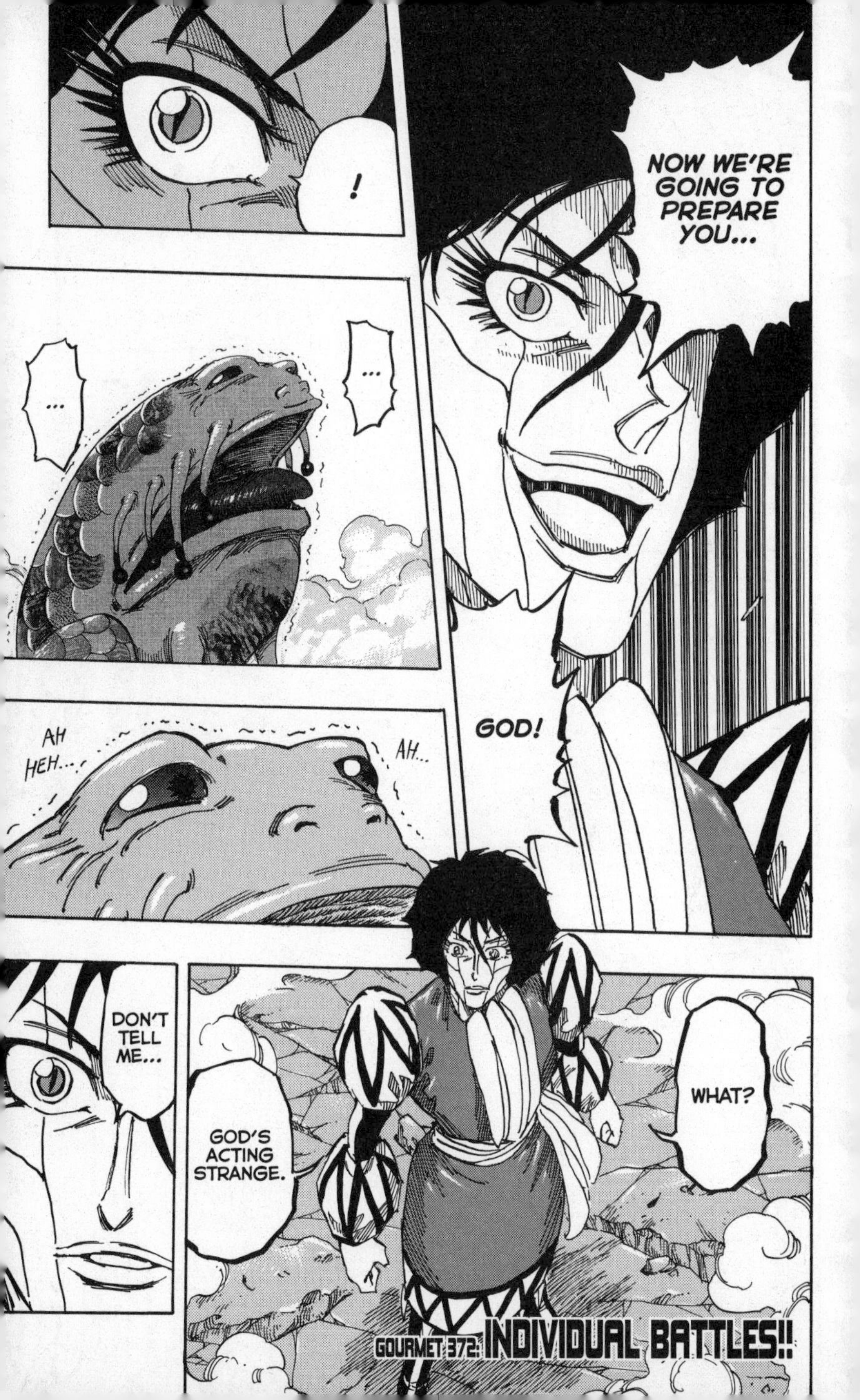
NOW WE'RE GOING TO PREPARE YOU...
GOD!
!
...
...
AH...
AH HEH...
WHAT?
GOD'S ACTING STRANGE.
DON'T TELL ME...
GOURMET 372: INDIVIDUAL BATTLES!!

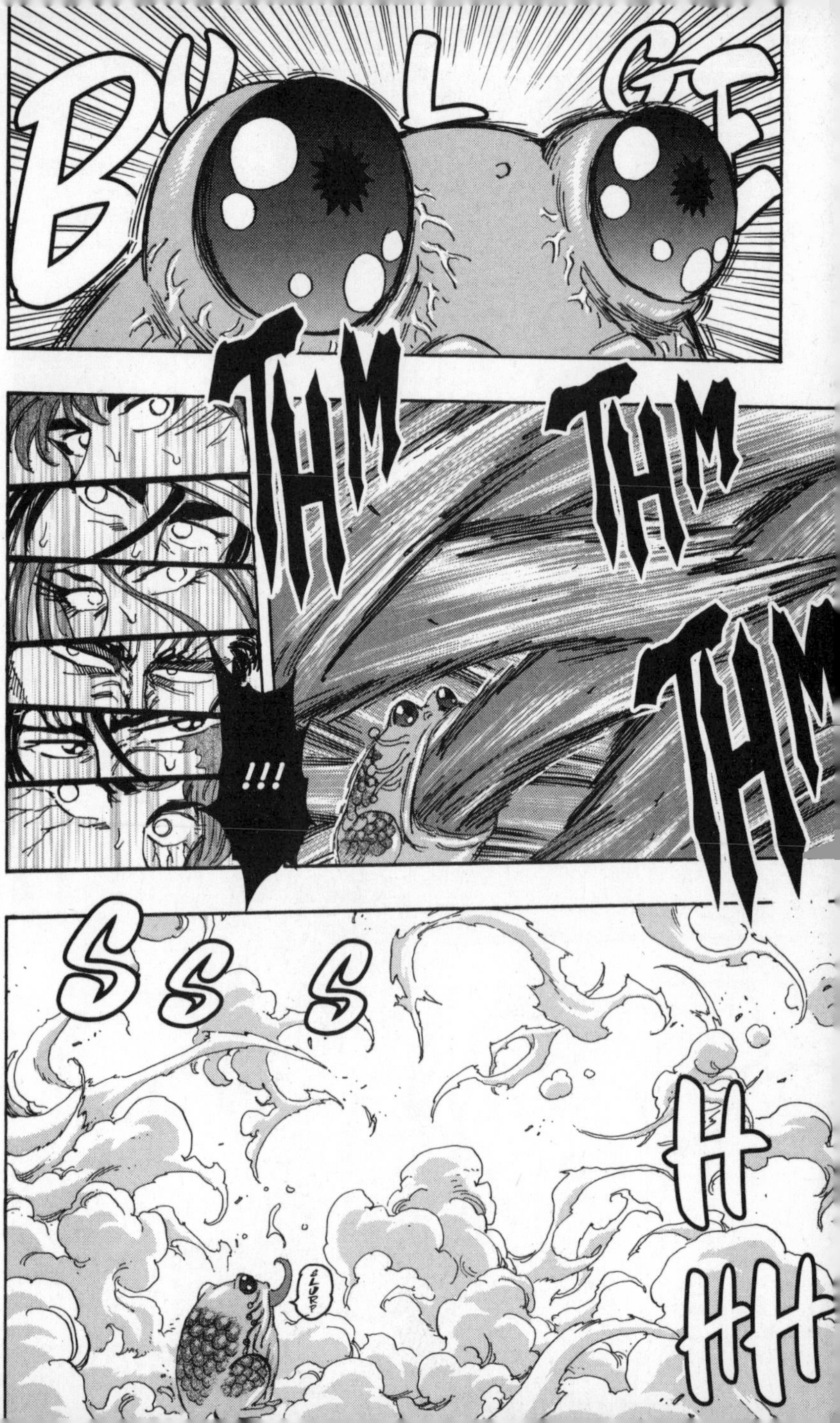
BULGE
THM
THM
THM
!!!
SSSHHH
SLURP

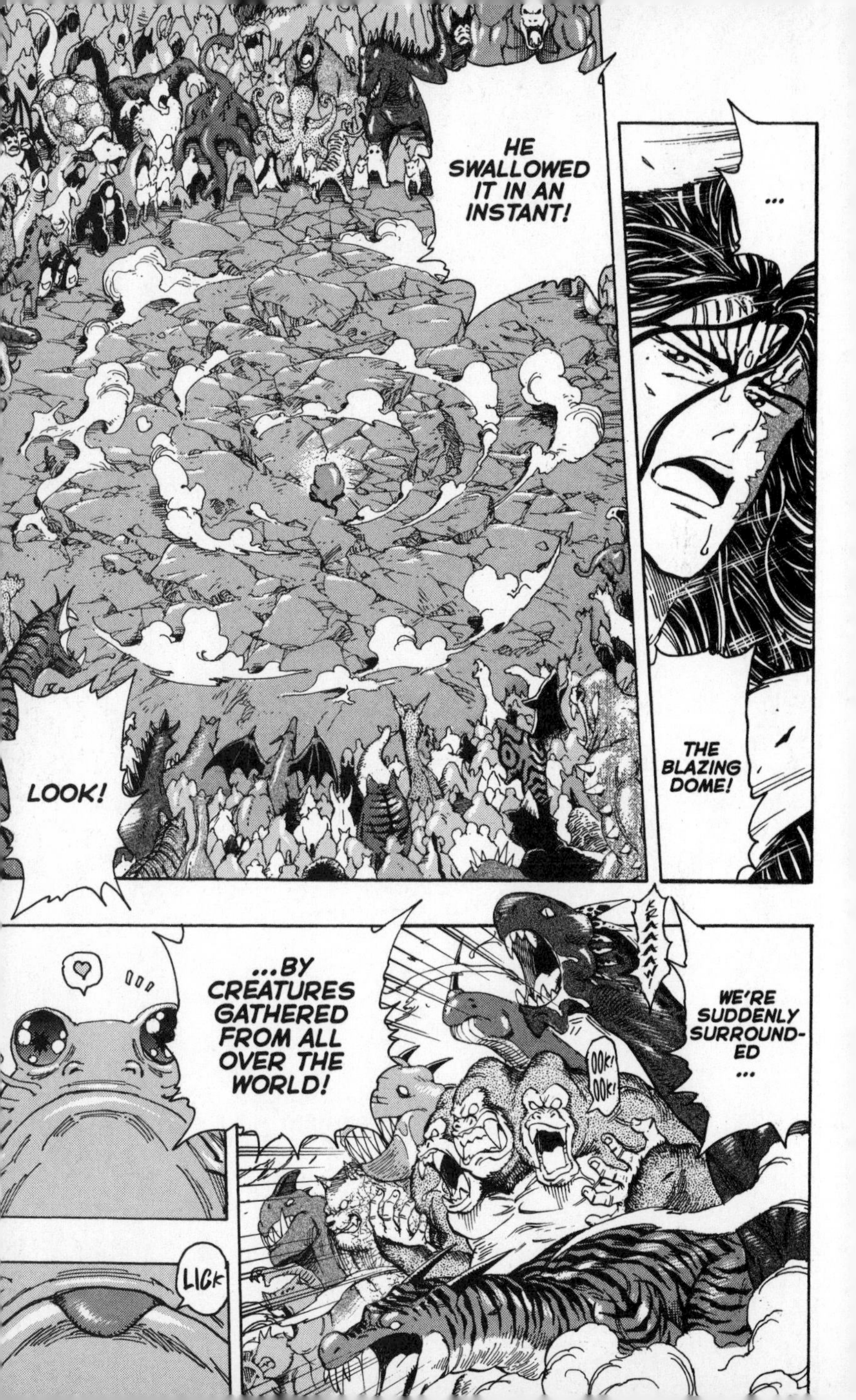
...
THE BLAZING DOME!
HE SWALLOWED IT IN AN INSTANT!
LOOK!
KRAAAAAW!
WE'RE SUDDENLY SURROUND-ED ...
OOK! OOK!
...BY CREATURES GATHERED FROM ALL OVER THE WORLD!
LICK

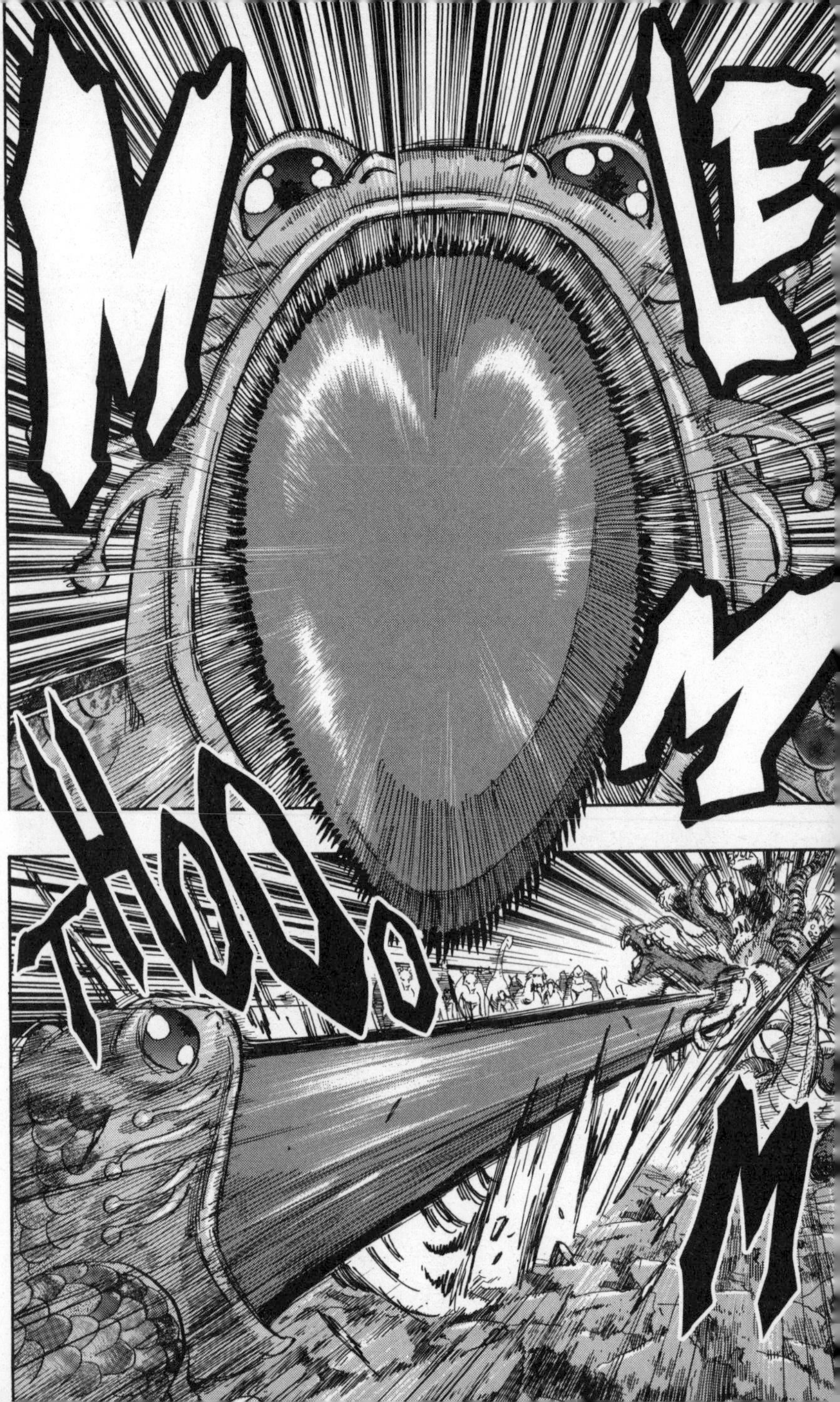
MLEM
THOOOM

WAAH!

STICk

!

...

HUH
?!

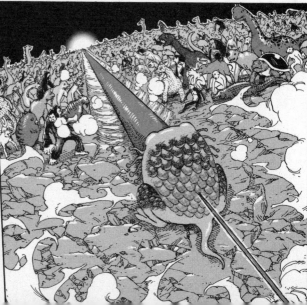

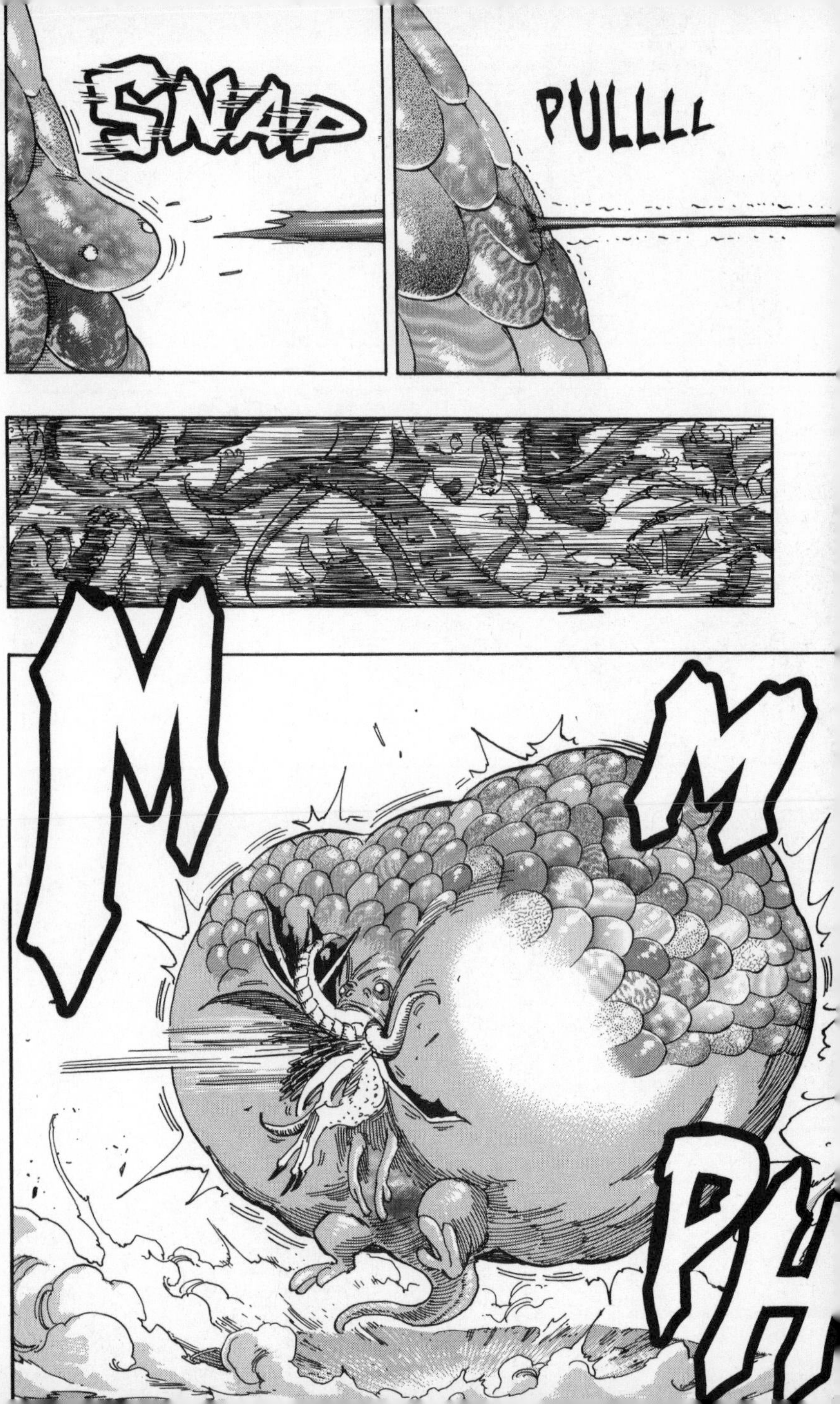
PULLLL
SNAP
M
M
PH

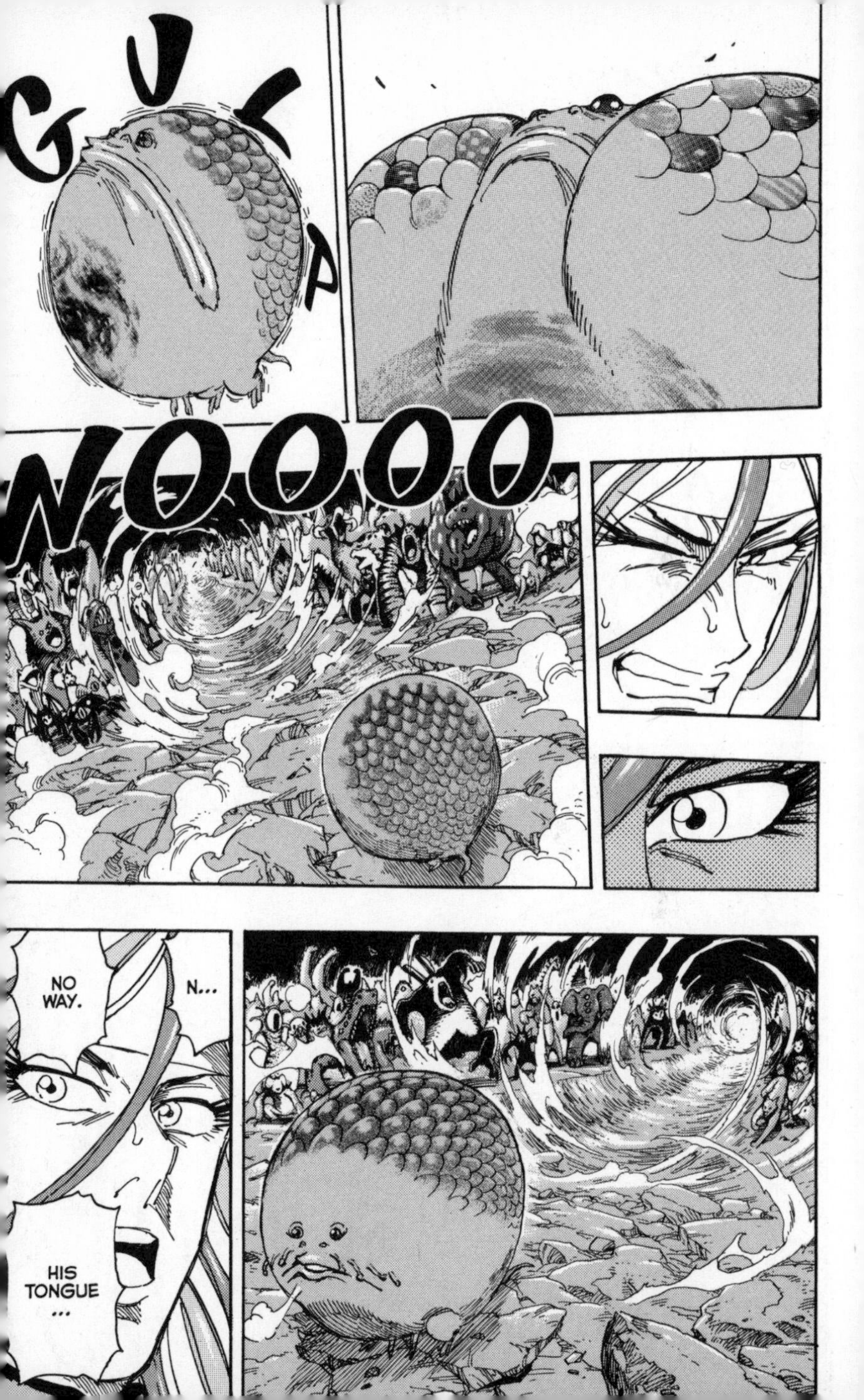
GULP
NOOOO
N...
NO WAY.
HIS TONGUE ...

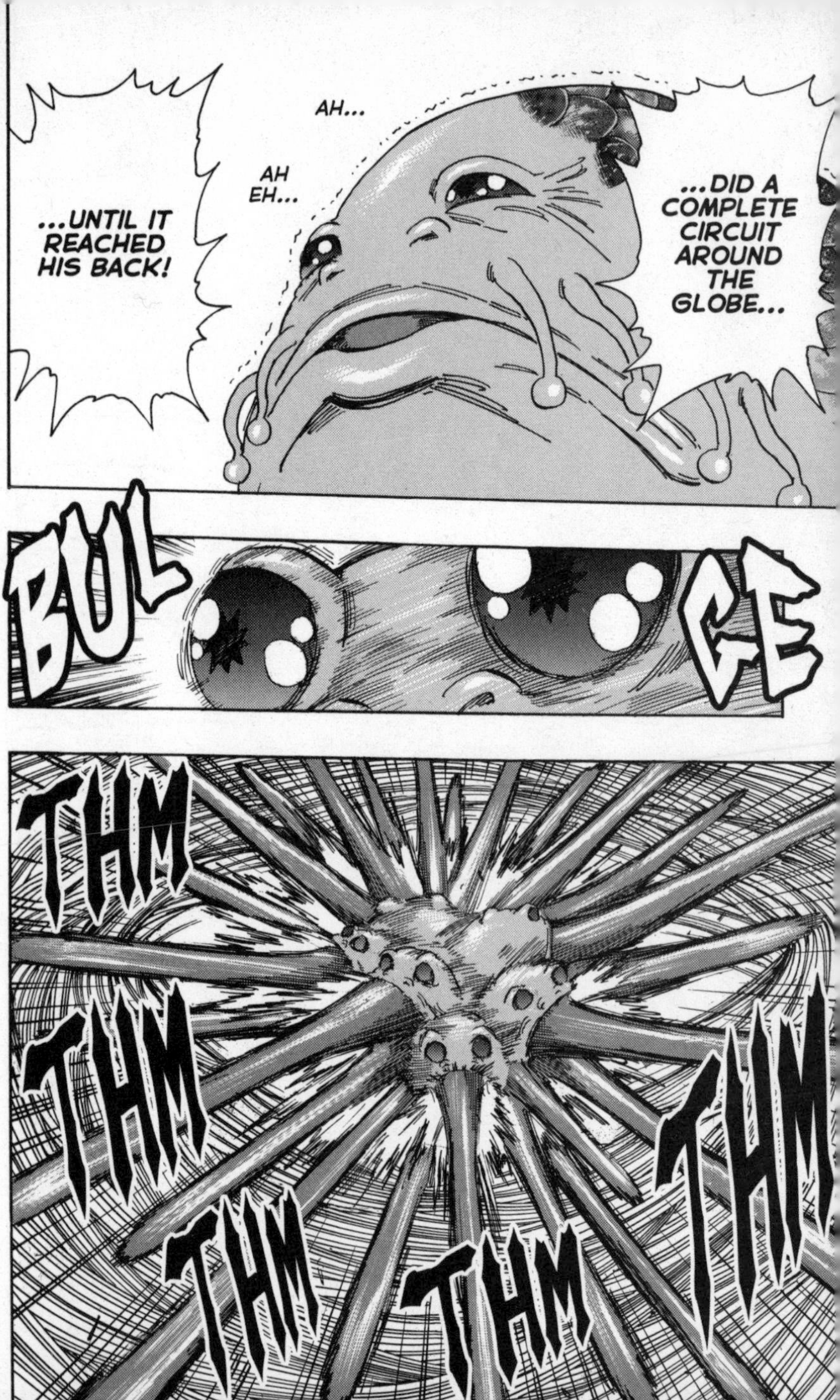
...DID A COMPLETE CIRCUIT AROUND THE GLOBE...
AH...
AH EH...
...UNTIL IT REACHED HIS BACK!
BULGE
THM
THM
THM
THM
THM

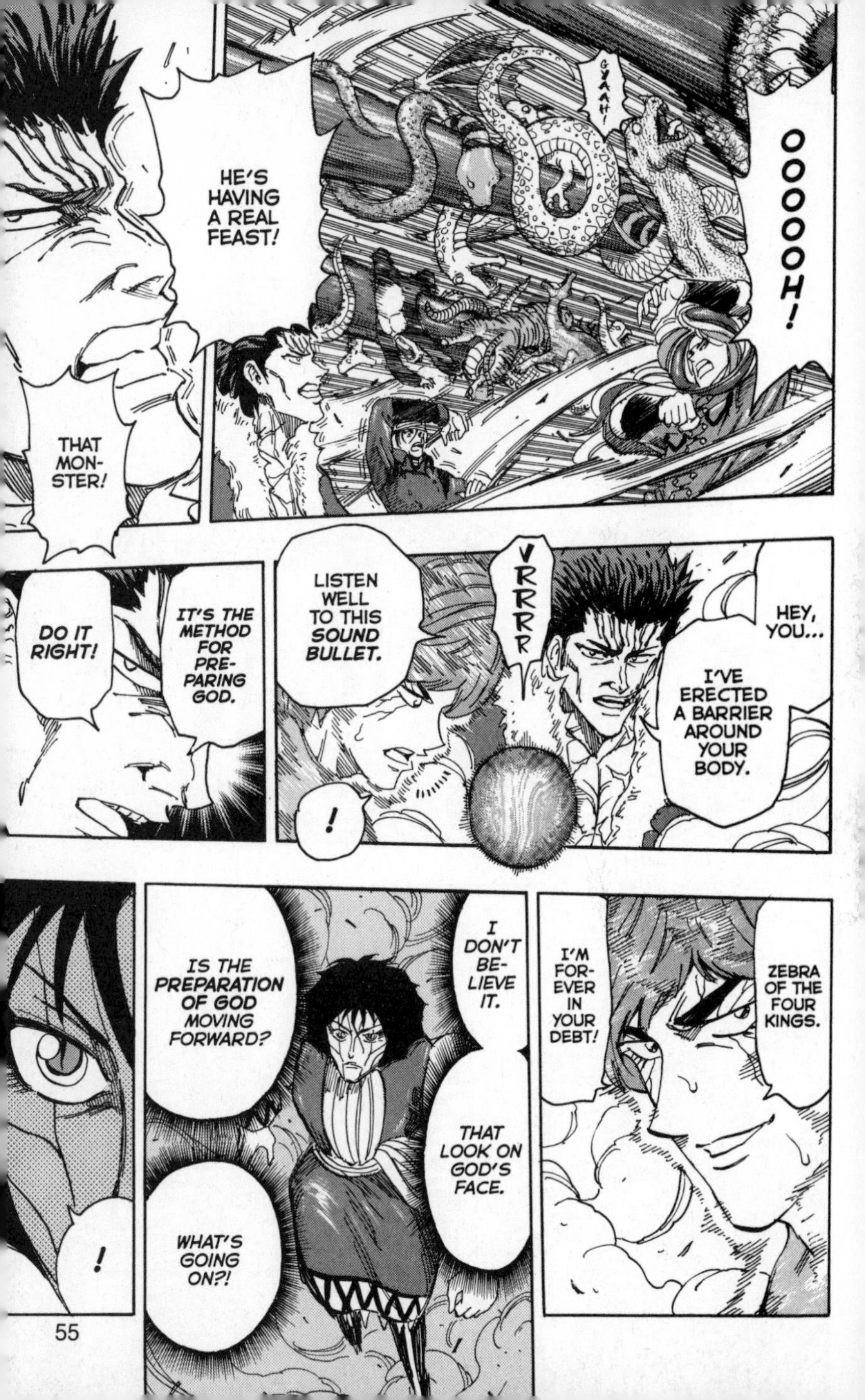
GYAAH!
OOOOOOH!
HE'S HAVING A REAL FEAST!
THAT MONSTER!
HEY, YOU...
I'VE ERECTED A BARRIER AROUND YOUR BODY.
VRRRR
LISTEN WELL TO THIS SOUND BULLET.
!
IT'S THE METHOD FOR PREPARING GOD.
DO IT RIGHT!
ZEBRA OF THE FOUR KINGS.
I'M FOREVER IN YOUR DEBT!
I DON'T BELIEVE IT.
THAT LOOK ON GOD'S FACE.
IS THE PREPARATION OF GOD MOVING FORWARD?
WHAT'S GOING ON?!
!

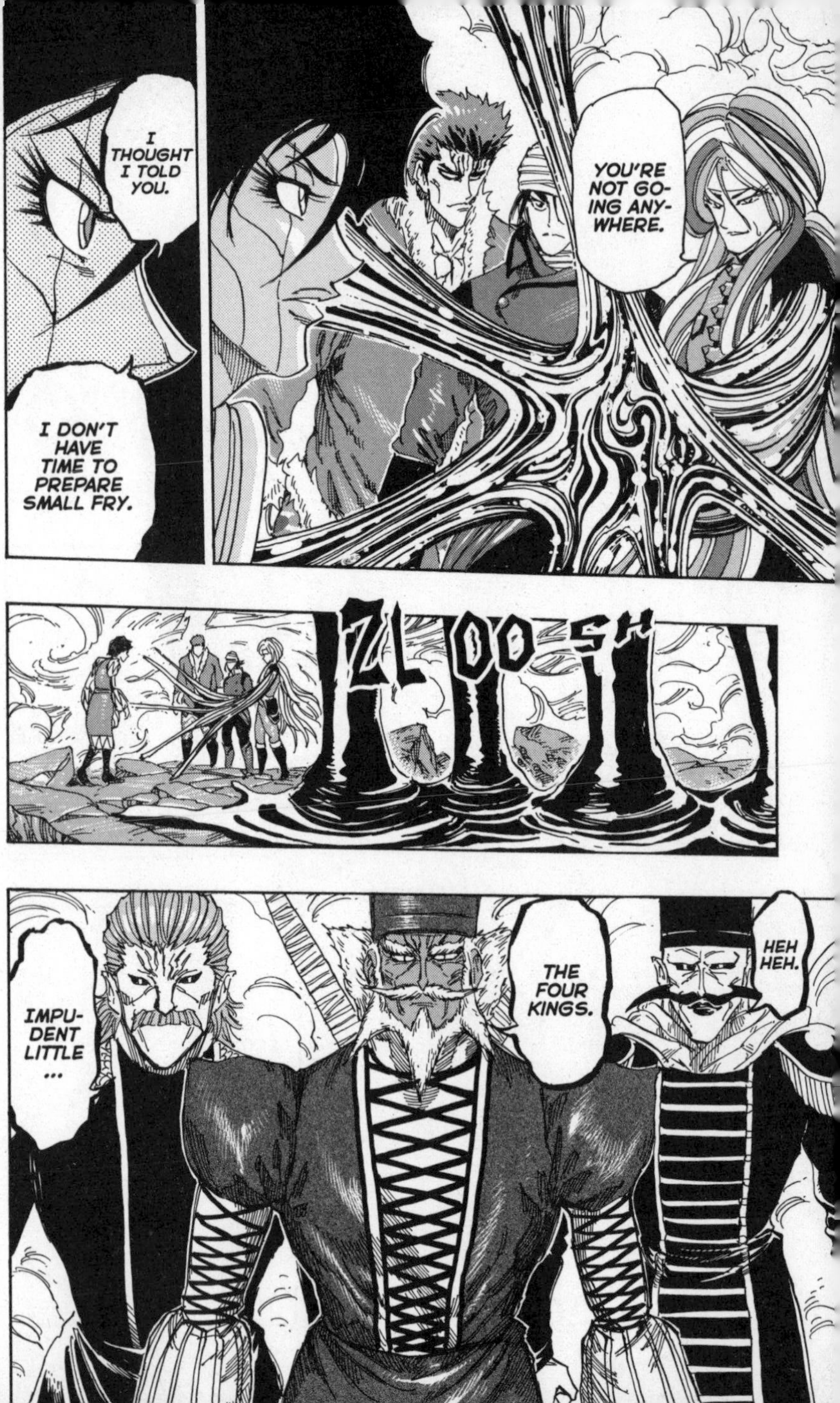

YOU'RE NOT GOING ANYWHERE.
I THOUGHT I TOLD YOU.
I DON'T HAVE TIME TO PREPARE SMALL FRY.
ZLOOSH
HEH HEH.
THE FOUR KINGS.
IMPUDENT LITTLE...

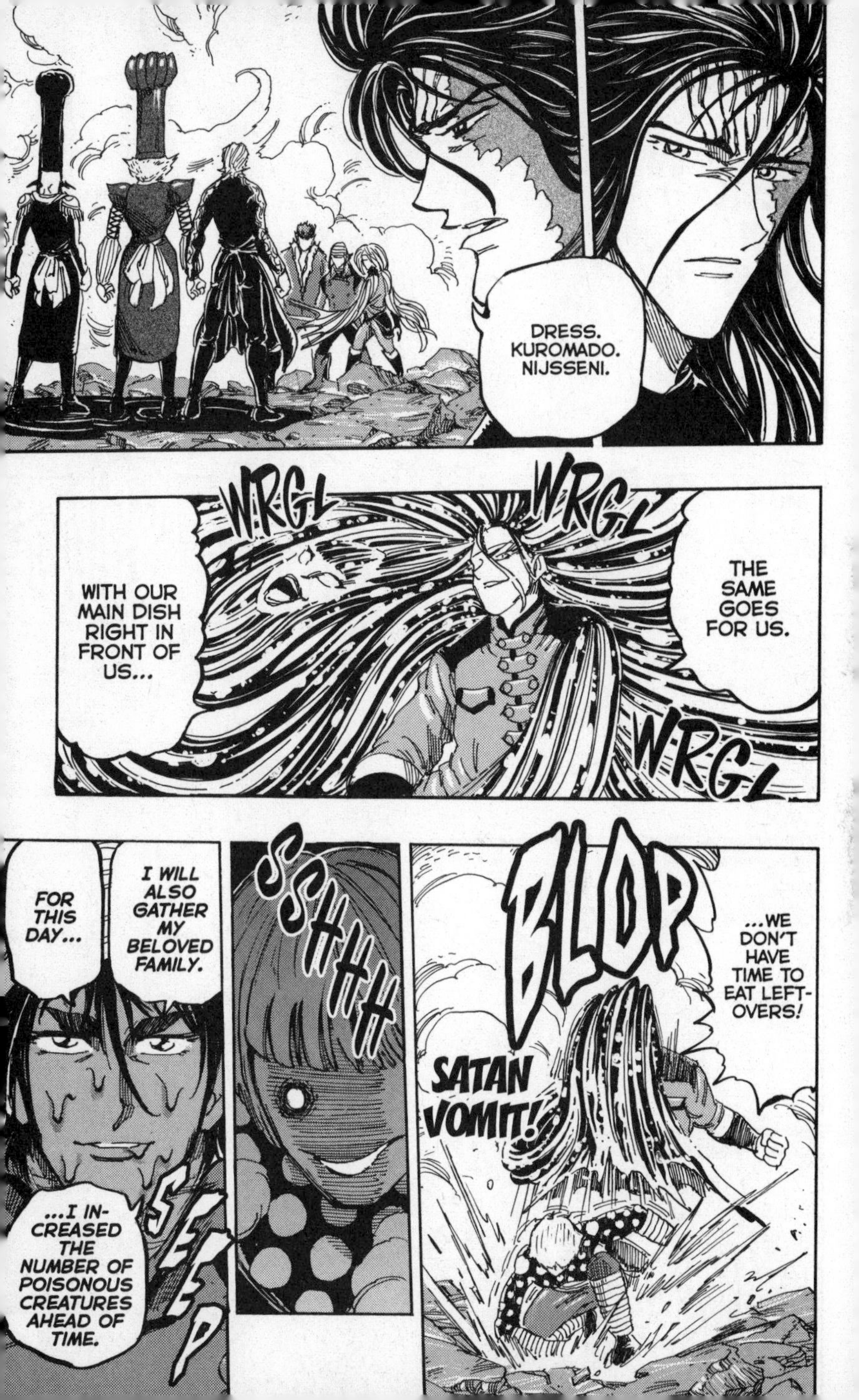
DRESS. KUROMADO. NIJSSENI.
THE SAME GOES FOR US.
WRGL
WRGL
WITH OUR MAIN DISH RIGHT IN FRONT OF US...
WRGL
BLOP
...WE DON'T HAVE TIME TO EAT LEFT-OVERS!
SATAN VOMIT!
SSHHH
I WILL ALSO GATHER MY BELOVED FAMILY.
FOR THIS DAY...
...I IN-CREASED THE NUMBER OF POISONOUS CREATURES AHEAD OF TIME.
SEEP

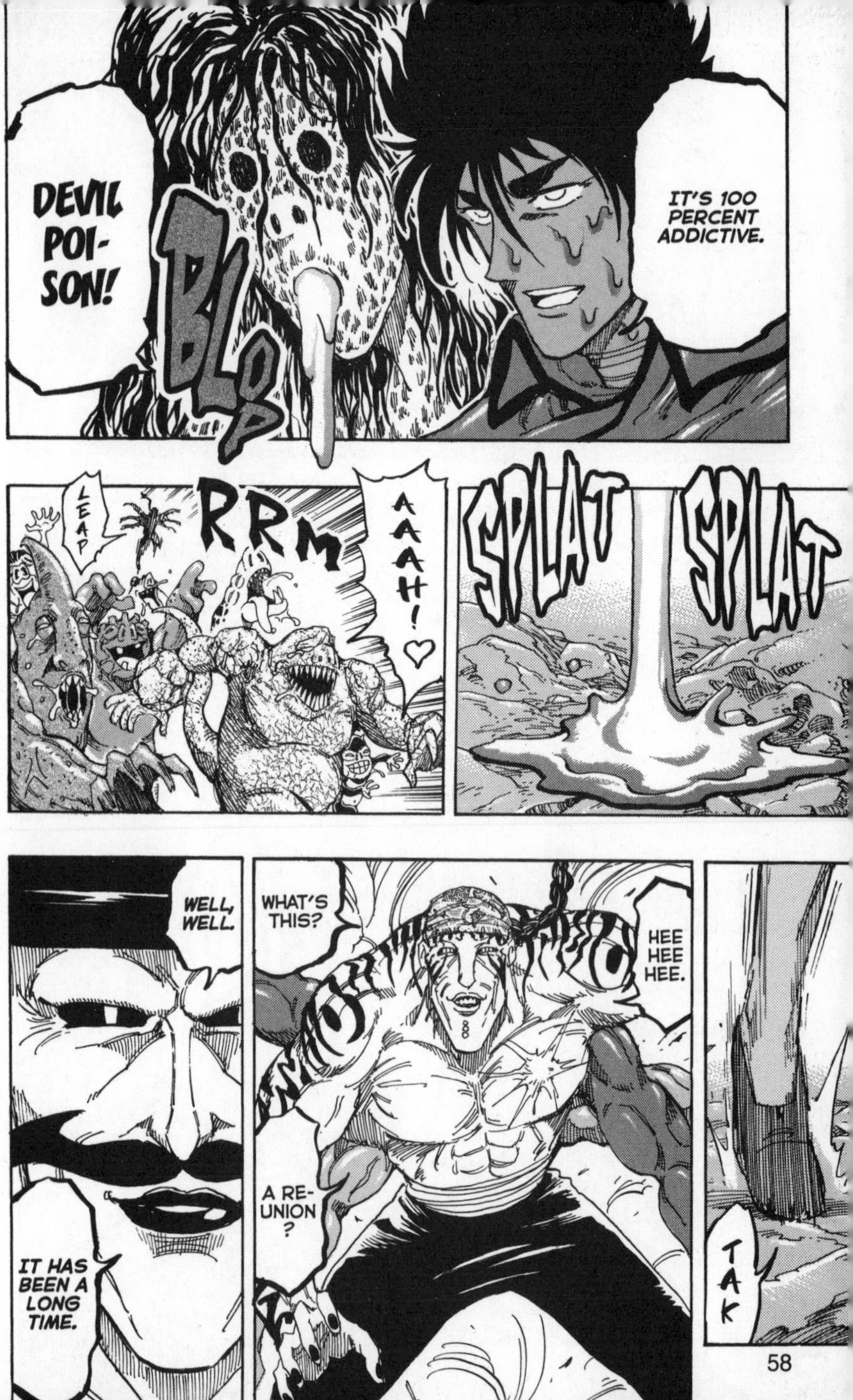
IT'S 100 PERCENT ADDICTIVE.
DEVIL POI-SON!
BLOB
SPLAT
SPLAT
AAAAH! ♡
RRM
LEAP
TAK
HEE HEE HEE.
WHAT'S THIS?
A RE-UNION?
WELL, WELL.
IT HAS BEEN A LONG TIME.

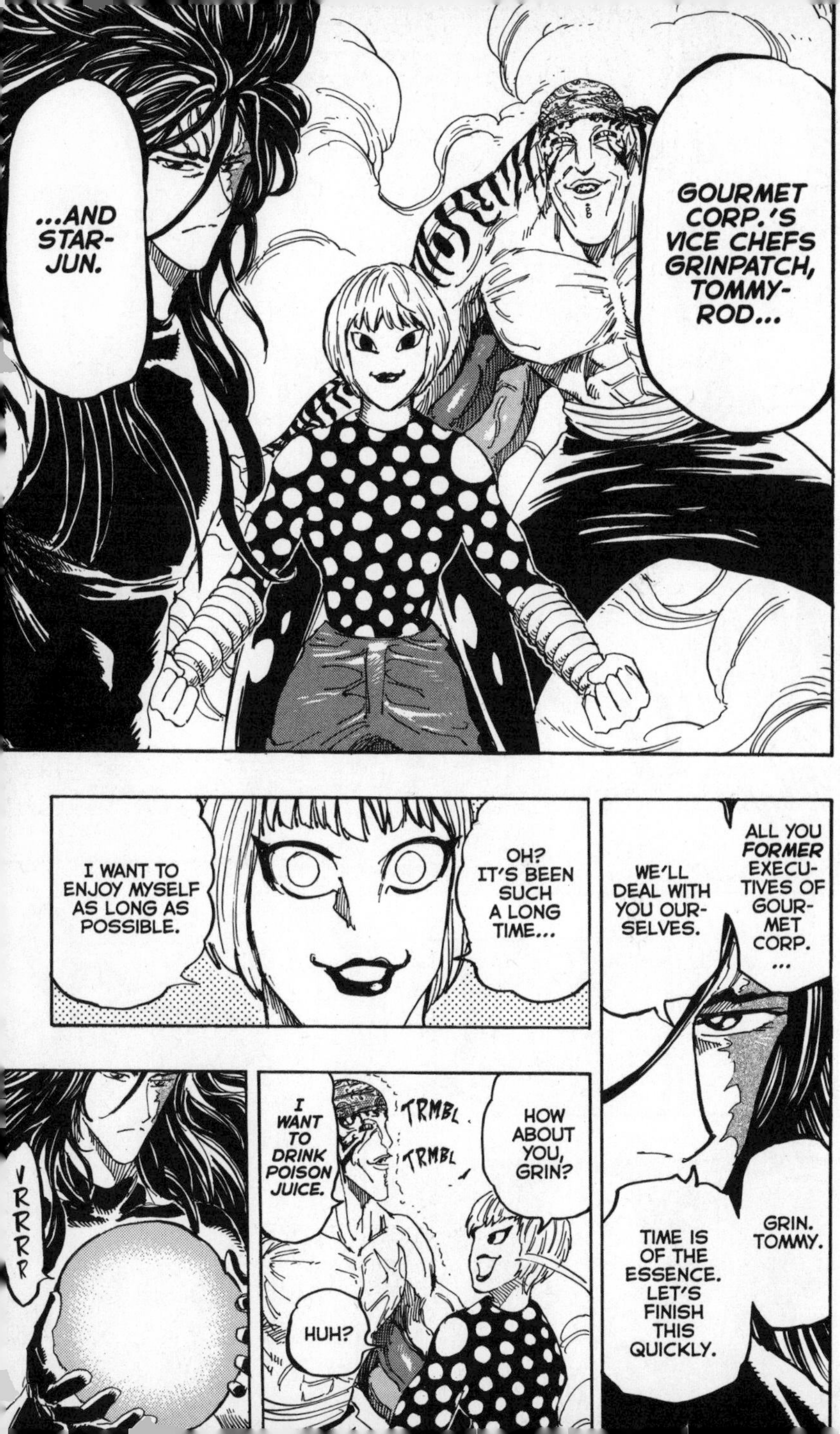
GOURMET CORP.'S VICE CHEFS GRINPATCH, TOMMYROD...
...AND STAR-JUN.
ALL YOU FORMER EXECUTIVES OF GOURMET CORP. ...
WE'LL DEAL WITH YOU OURSELVES.
GRIN. TOMMY.
TIME IS OF THE ESSENCE. LET'S FINISH THIS QUICKLY.
OH? IT'S BEEN SUCH A LONG TIME...
I WANT TO ENJOY MYSELF AS LONG AS POSSIBLE.
HOW ABOUT YOU, GRIN?
TRMBL
TRMBL
I WANT TO DRINK POISON JUICE.
HUH?
VRRRR

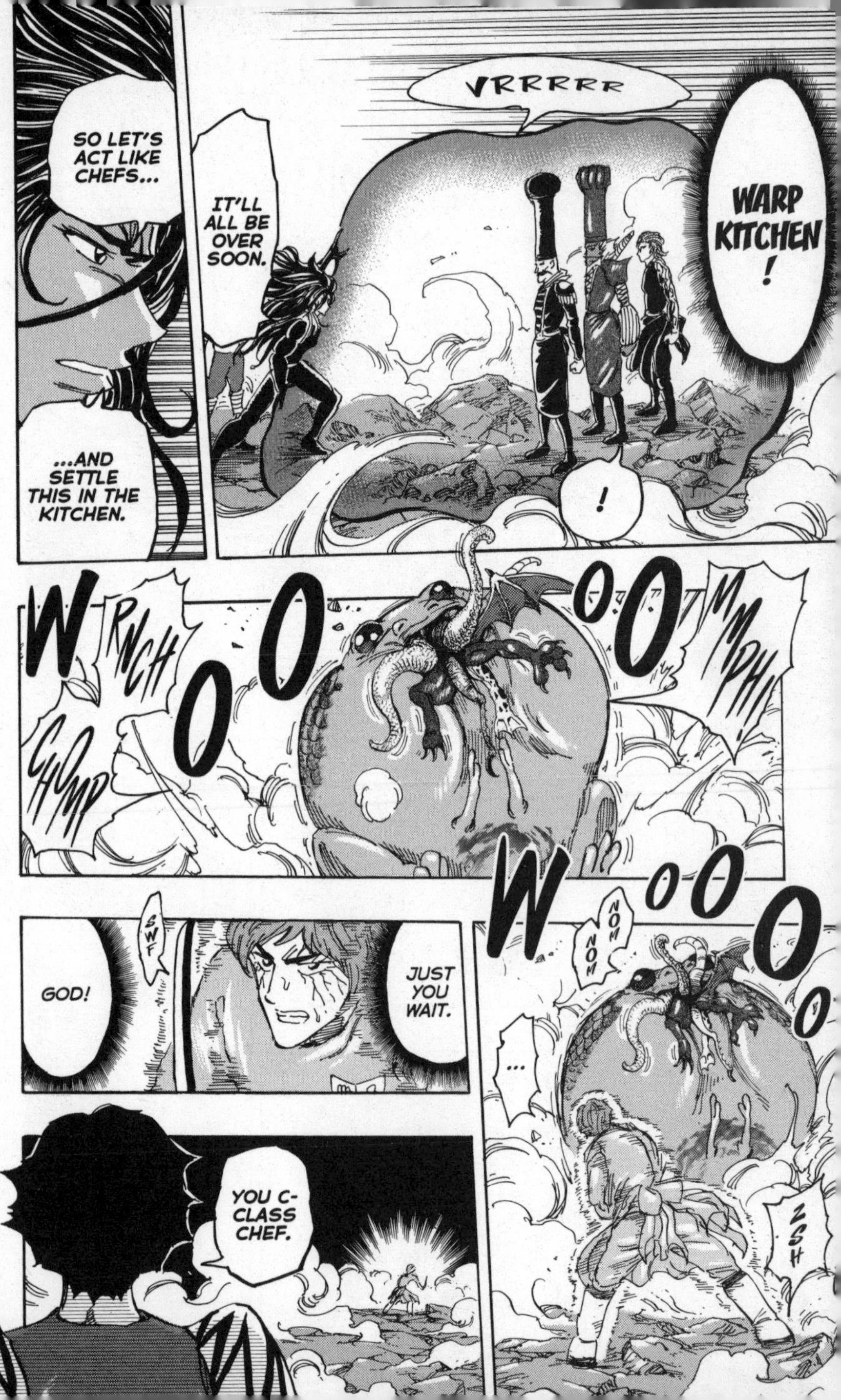

WARP KITCHEN!
VRRRRR
IT'LL ALL BE OVER SOON.
!
SO LET'S ACT LIKE CHEFS...
...AND SETTLE THIS IN THE KITCHEN.
WOOOOMMPH!
RNCH
CHOMP
WOOOO
NOM NOM
...
ZSH
JUST YOU WAIT.
SWF
GOD!
YOU C-CLASS CHEF.

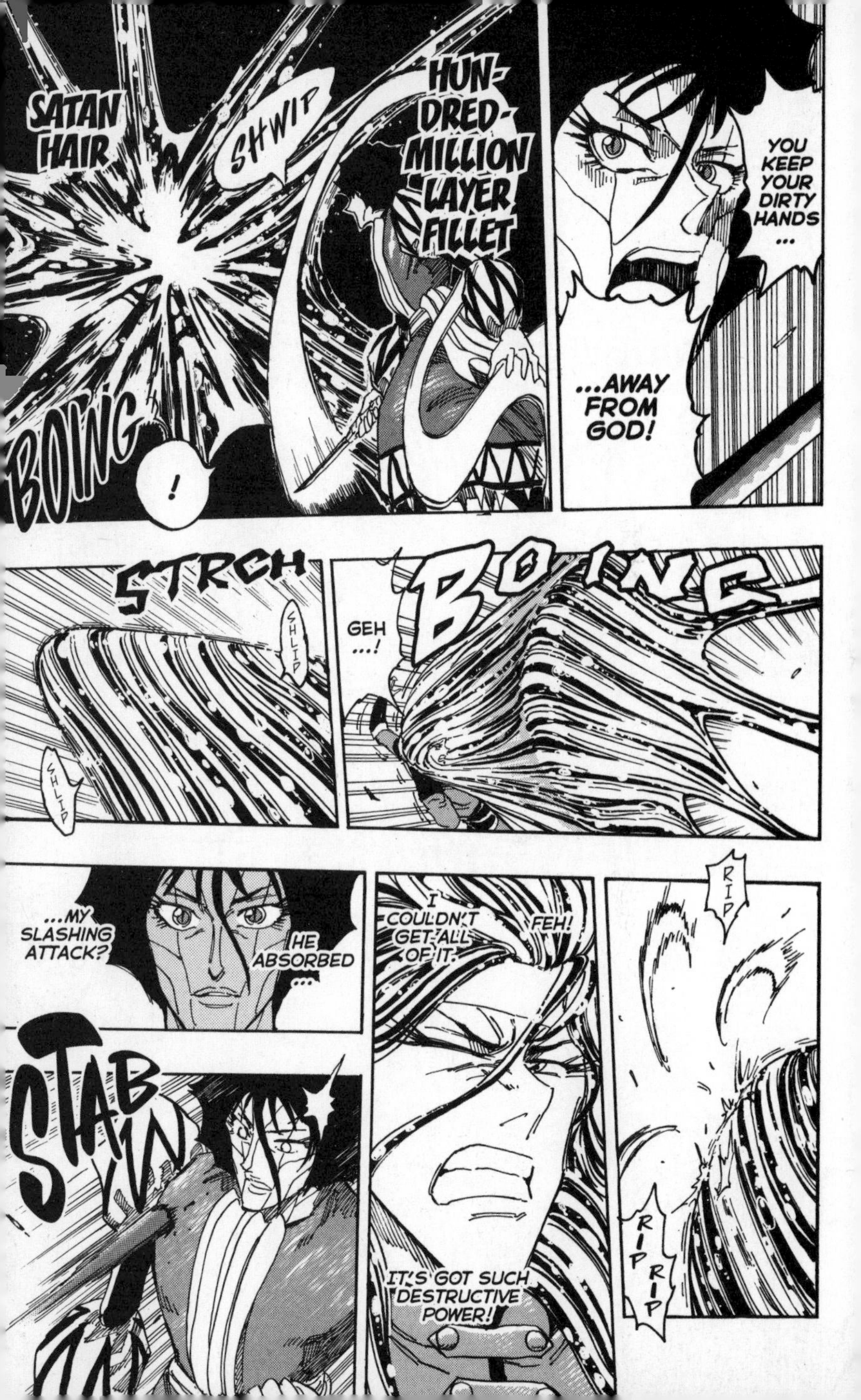
YOU KEEP YOUR DIRTY HANDS...
...AWAY FROM GOD!
HUNDRED-MILLION LAYER FILLET
SHWIP
SATAN HAIR
BOING
!
BOING
GEH...!
STRCH
SHLIP
SHLIP
RIP
RIP
RIP
FEH!
I COULDN'T GET ALL OF IT.
IT'S GOT SUCH DESTRUCTIVE POWER!
HE ABSORBED...
...MY SLASHING ATTACK?
STAB

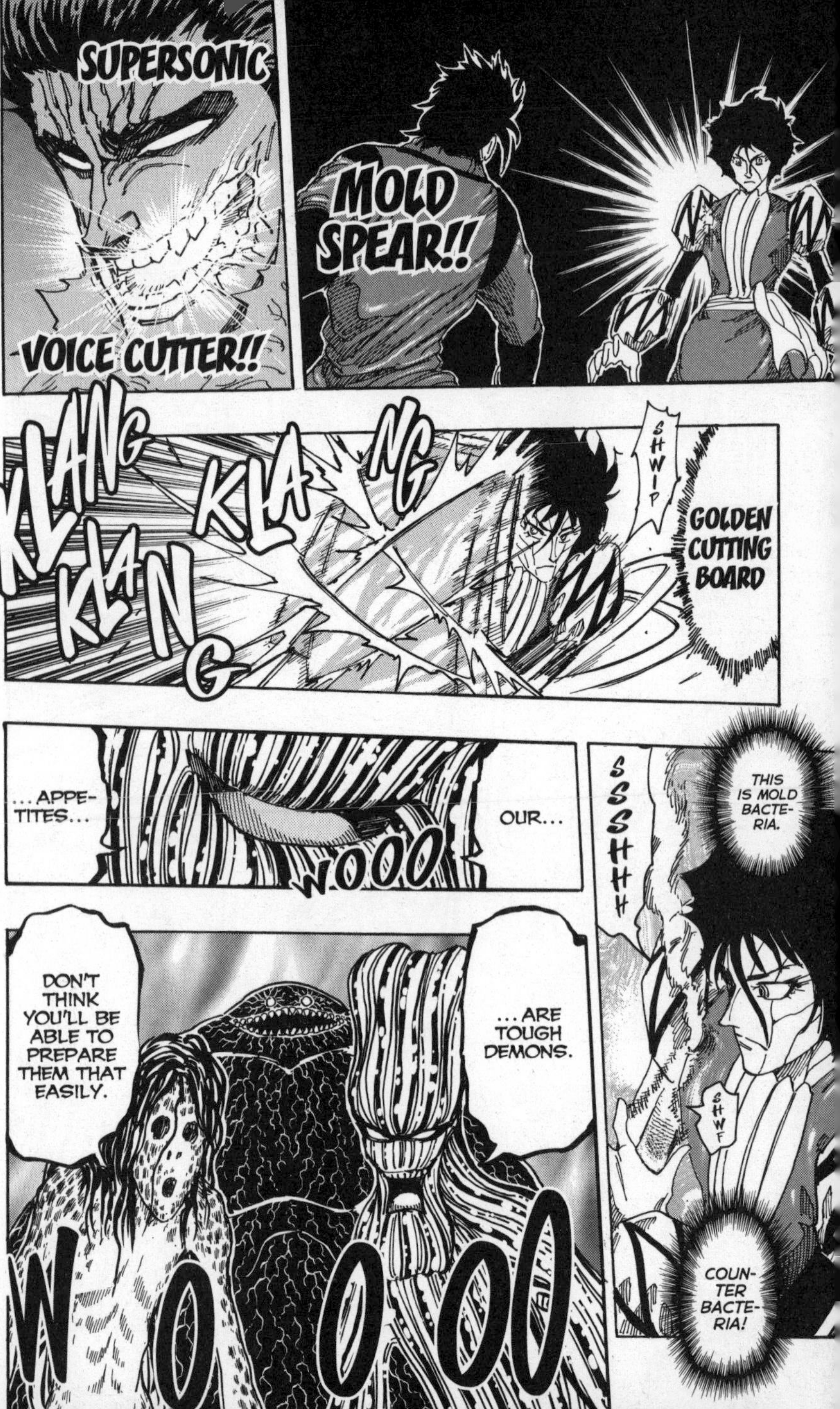
MOLD SPEAR!!
SUPERSONIC
VOICE CUTTER!!
SHWIP
GOLDEN CUTTING BOARD
KLANG
KLANG
KLANG
THIS IS MOLD BACTERIA.
SSSHHH
SHWF
COUNTER BACTERIA!
OUR...
...APPETITES...
WOOO
...ARE TOUGH DEMONS.
DON'T THINK YOU'LL BE ABLE TO PREPARE THEM THAT EASILY.
WOOOO

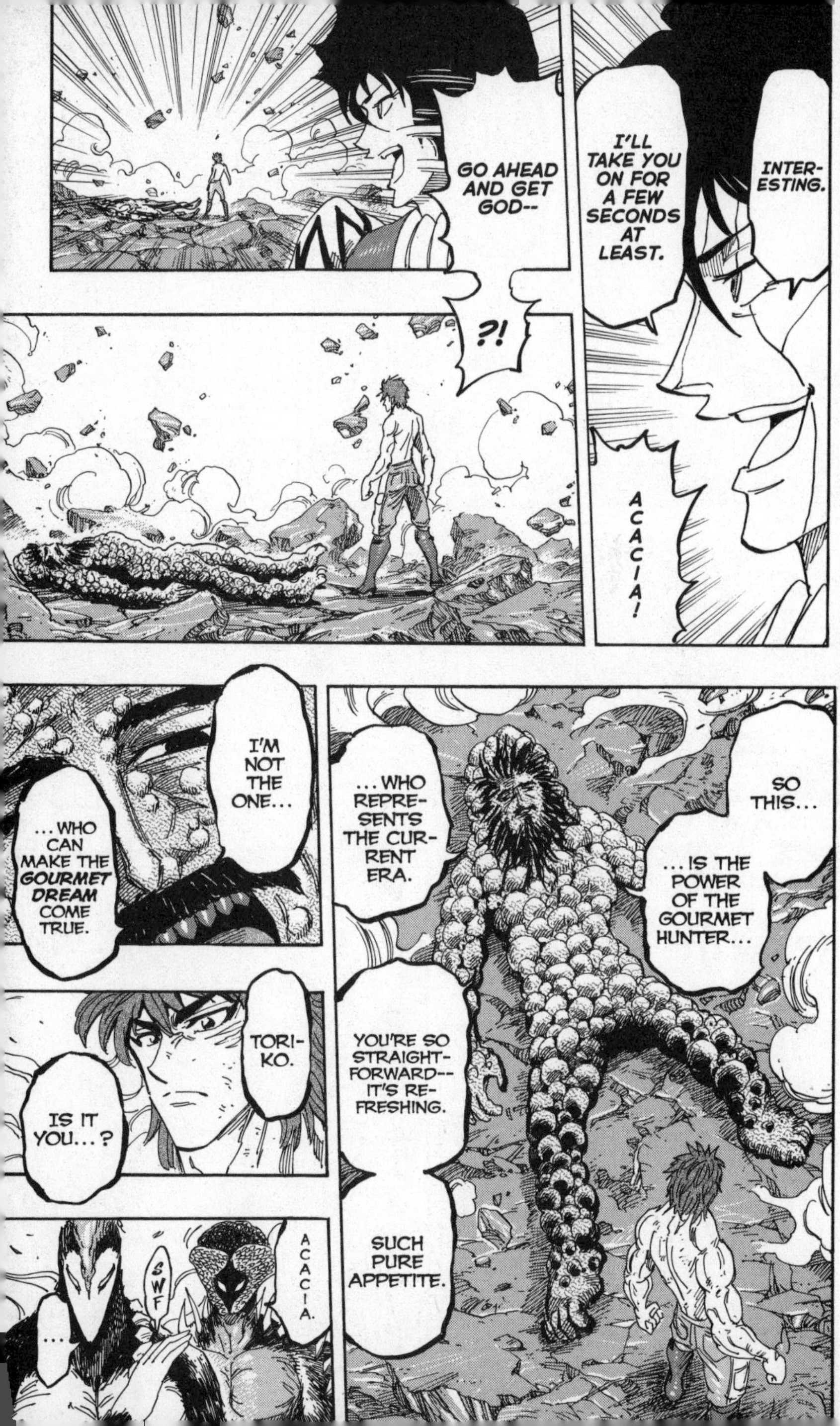
INTERESTING.
I'LL TAKE YOU ON FOR A FEW SECONDS AT LEAST.
ACACIA!
GO AHEAD AND GET GOD--
?!
SO THIS...
...IS THE POWER OF THE GOURMET HUNTER...
...WHO REPRESENTS THE CURRENT ERA.
YOU'RE SO STRAIGHTFORWARD-- IT'S REFRESHING.
SUCH PURE APPETITE.
I'M NOT THE ONE...
...WHO CAN MAKE THE *GOURMET DREAM* COME TRUE.
TORIKO.
IS IT YOU...?
ACACIA.
SWF
...

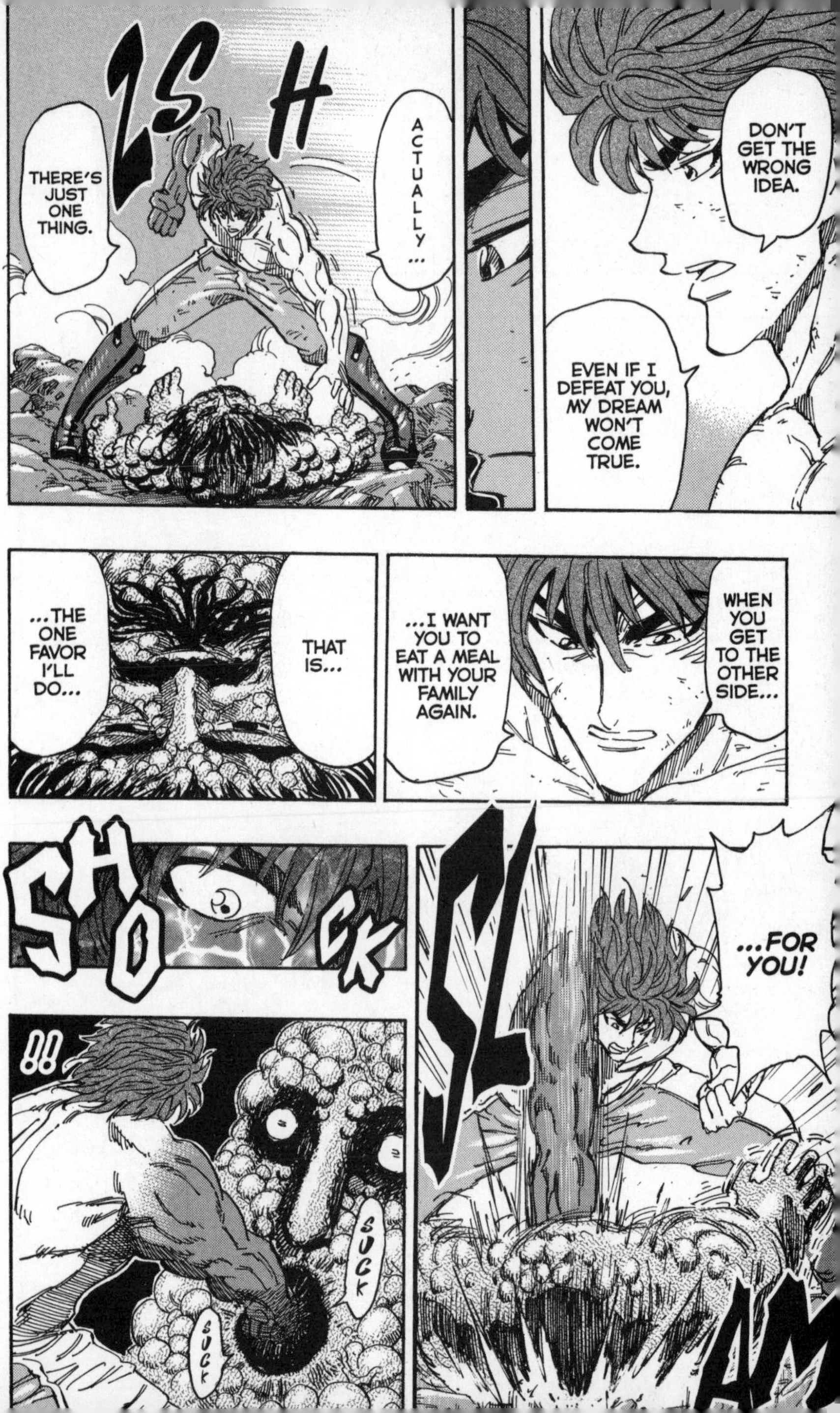
DON'T GET THE WRONG IDEA.
EVEN IF I DEFEAT YOU, MY DREAM WON'T COME TRUE.
ACTUALLY...
THERE'S JUST ONE THING.
ZSH
WHEN YOU GET TO THE OTHER SIDE...
...I WANT YOU TO EAT A MEAL WITH YOUR FAMILY AGAIN.
THAT IS...
...THE ONE FAVOR I'LL DO...
...FOR YOU!
SL
AM
SHOCK
!!
SUCK
SUCK

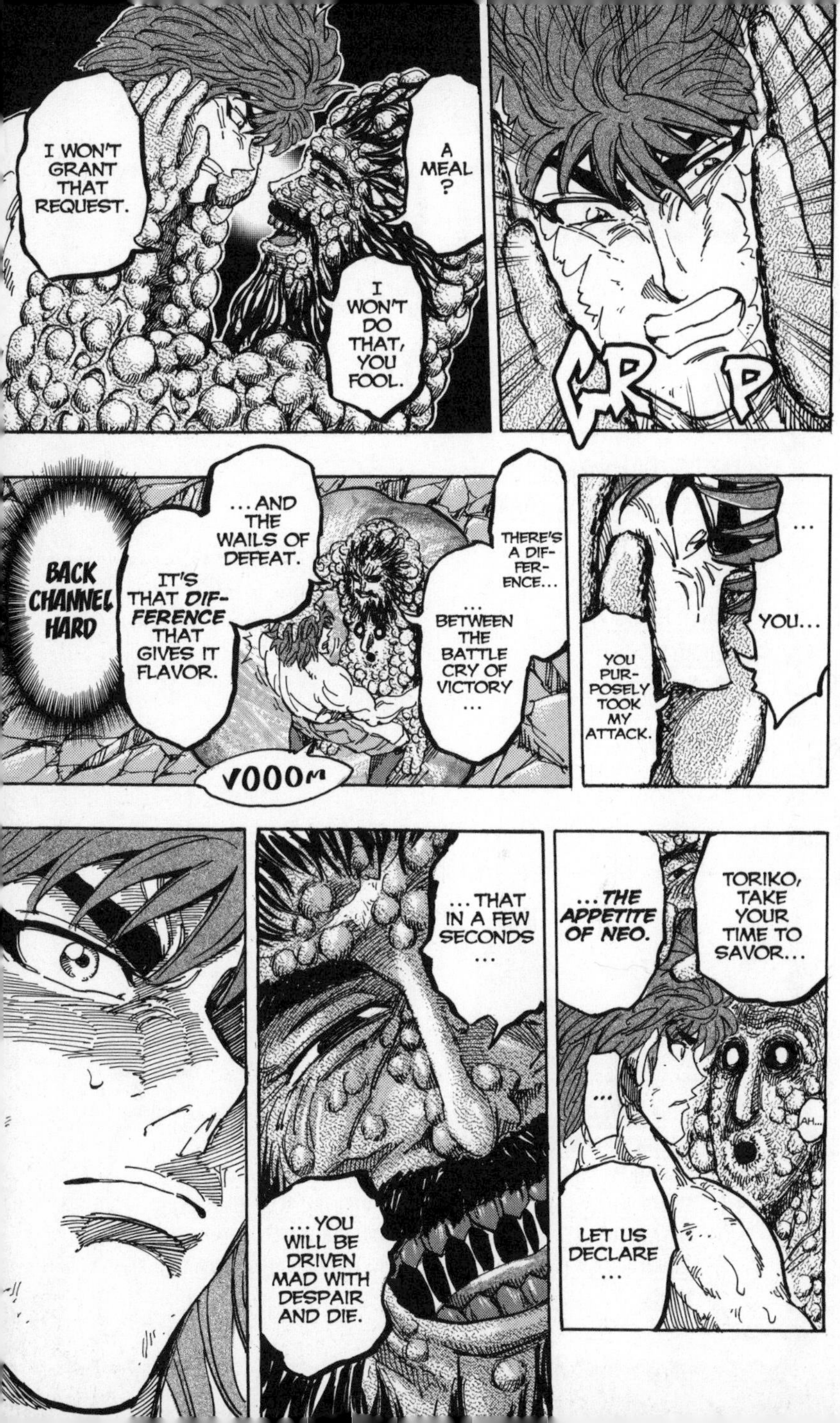
CR P
A MEAL?
I WON'T DO THAT, YOU FOOL.
I WON'T GRANT THAT REQUEST.
...
YOU...
YOU PURPOSELY TOOK MY ATTACK.
THERE'S A DIFFERENCE...
...BETWEEN THE BATTLE CRY OF VICTORY...
...AND THE WAILS OF DEFEAT.
IT'S THAT *DIFFERENCE* THAT GIVES IT FLAVOR.
BACK CHANNEL HARD
VOOOM
TORIKO, TAKE YOUR TIME TO SAVOR...
...*THE APPETITE OF NEO.*
AH...
...
LET US DECLARE...
...THAT IN A FEW SECONDS...
...YOU WILL BE DRIVEN MAD WITH DESPAIR AND DIE.

TORIKO

GOURMET CHECKLIST

Vol. 404

MAYLE
(CHEF)

CAPTURE LEVEL: UNKNOWN
HABITAT: GOURMET WORLD AREA 6, BLUE GRILL
SIZE: ---
HEIGHT: 192 CM
WEIGHT: 105 KG
PRICE: INEDIBLE

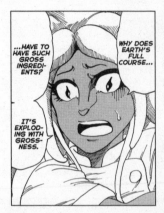

WHY DOES EARTH'S FULL COURSE...
...HAVE TO HAVE SUCH GROSS INGREDI-ENTS?
IT'S EXPLOD-ING WITH GROSS-NESS.

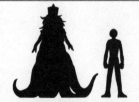

SCALE

AS THE HEAD CHEF OF BLUE GRILL, SHE WAS TASKED WITH THE RESURRECTION AND PREPARATION OF ACACIA'S FULL-COURSE MEAL AT DON SLIME AND GREAT KING ENMA SQUID'S ORDERS. DESPITE HER GOOFY APPEARANCE AND HABIT OF CALLING EVERYTHING GROSS, SHE DOES NOT BRING SHAME TO HER TITLE AS THE HEAD CHEF AND WAS ABLE TO GATHER THE FIVE LONE WOLF TEN-SHELL MASTER CHEFS. ALSO, EVEN THOUGH THEY DON'T LOOK ALIKE, APPARENTLY THE GREAT KING ENMA SQUID IS HER FATHER.

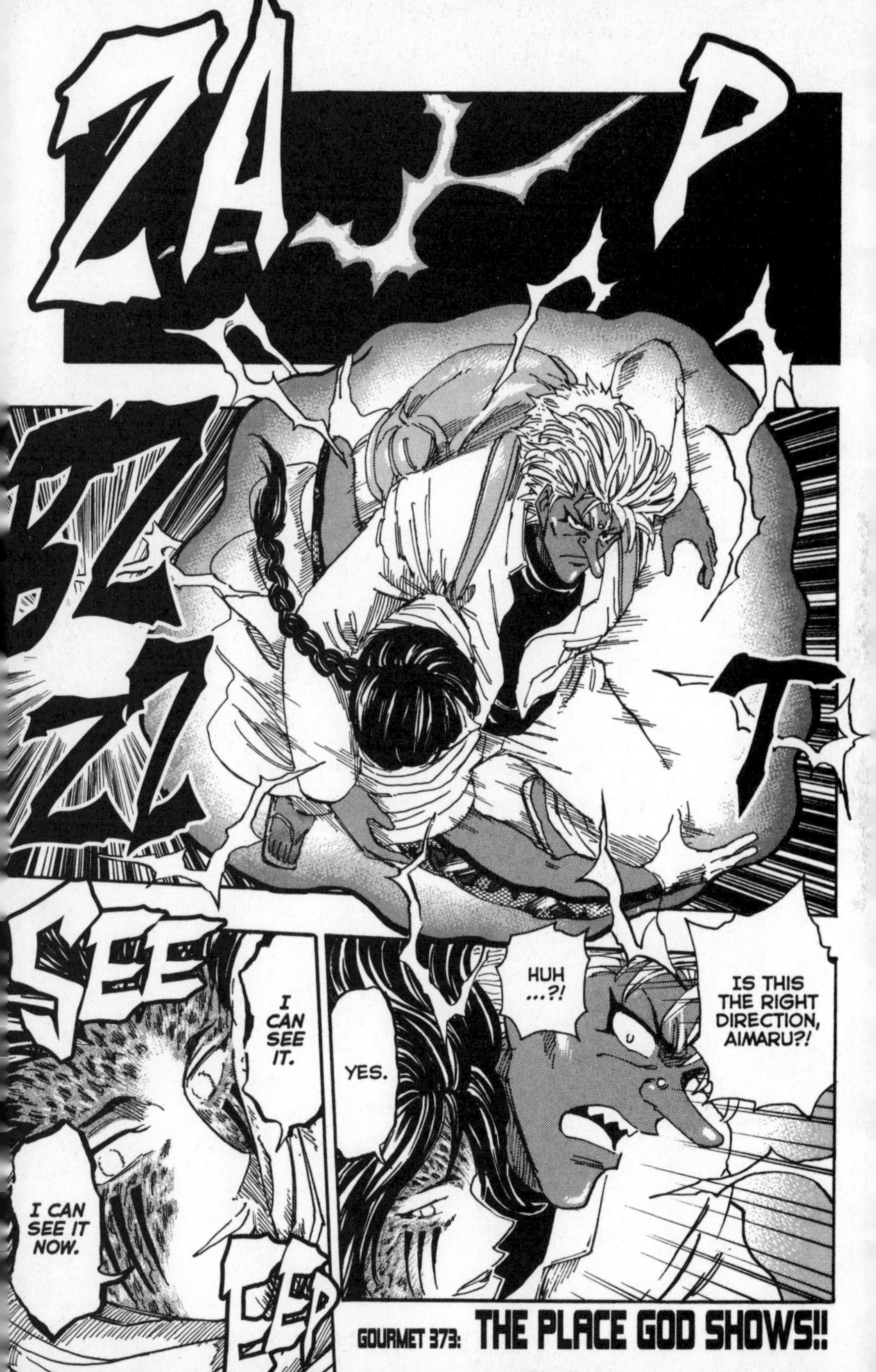
ZAP
BZZZT
IS THIS THE RIGHT DIRECTION, AIMARU?!
HUH ...?!
YES.
I CAN SEE IT.
SEE
I CAN SEE IT NOW.
GOURMET 373: THE PLACE GOD SHOWS!!

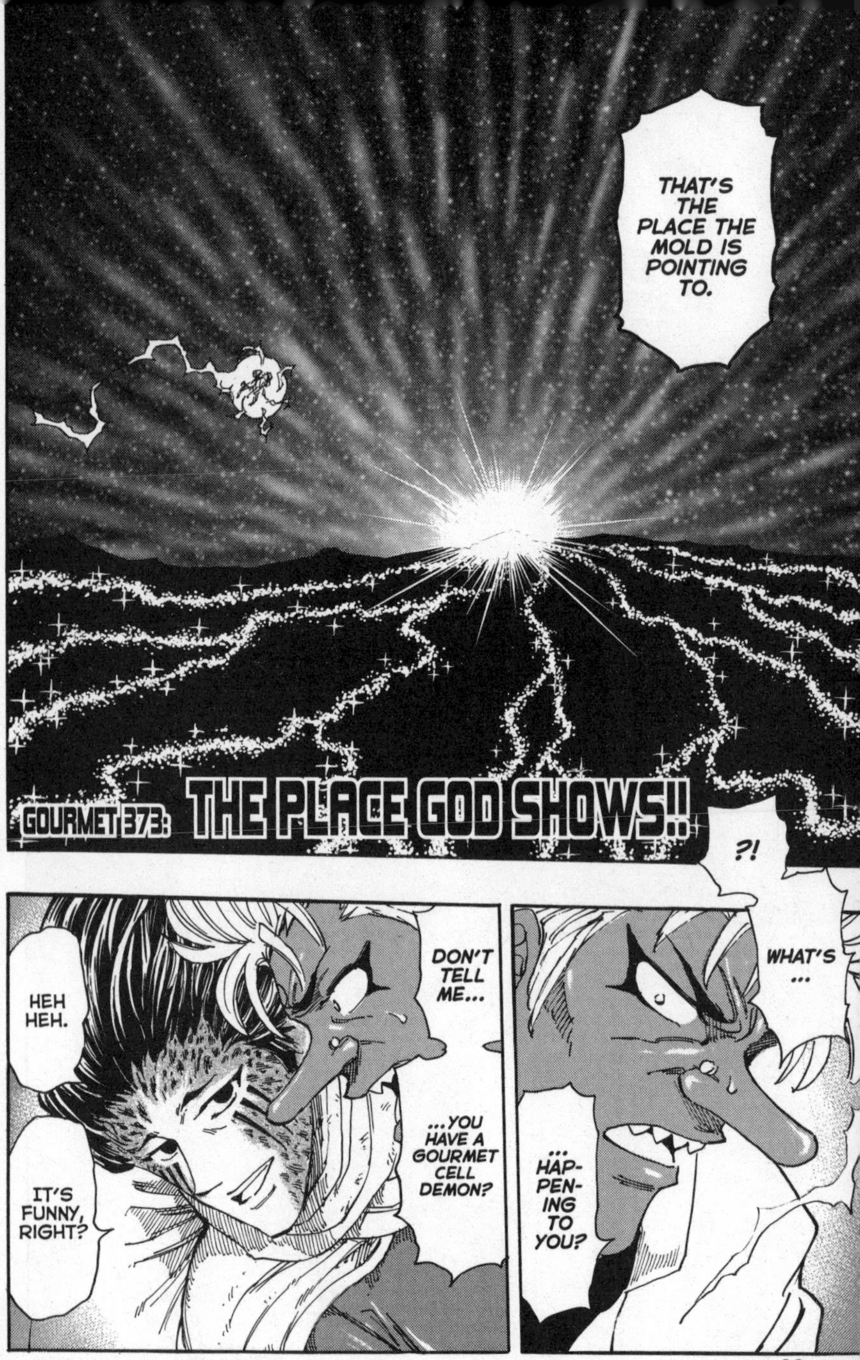
THAT'S THE PLACE THE MOLD IS POINTING TO.
GOURMET 373: THE PLACE GOD SHOWS!!
?!
WHAT'S...
...HAPPENING TO YOU?
DON'T TELL ME...
...YOU HAVE A GOURMET CELL DEMON?
HEH HEH.
IT'S FUNNY, RIGHT?

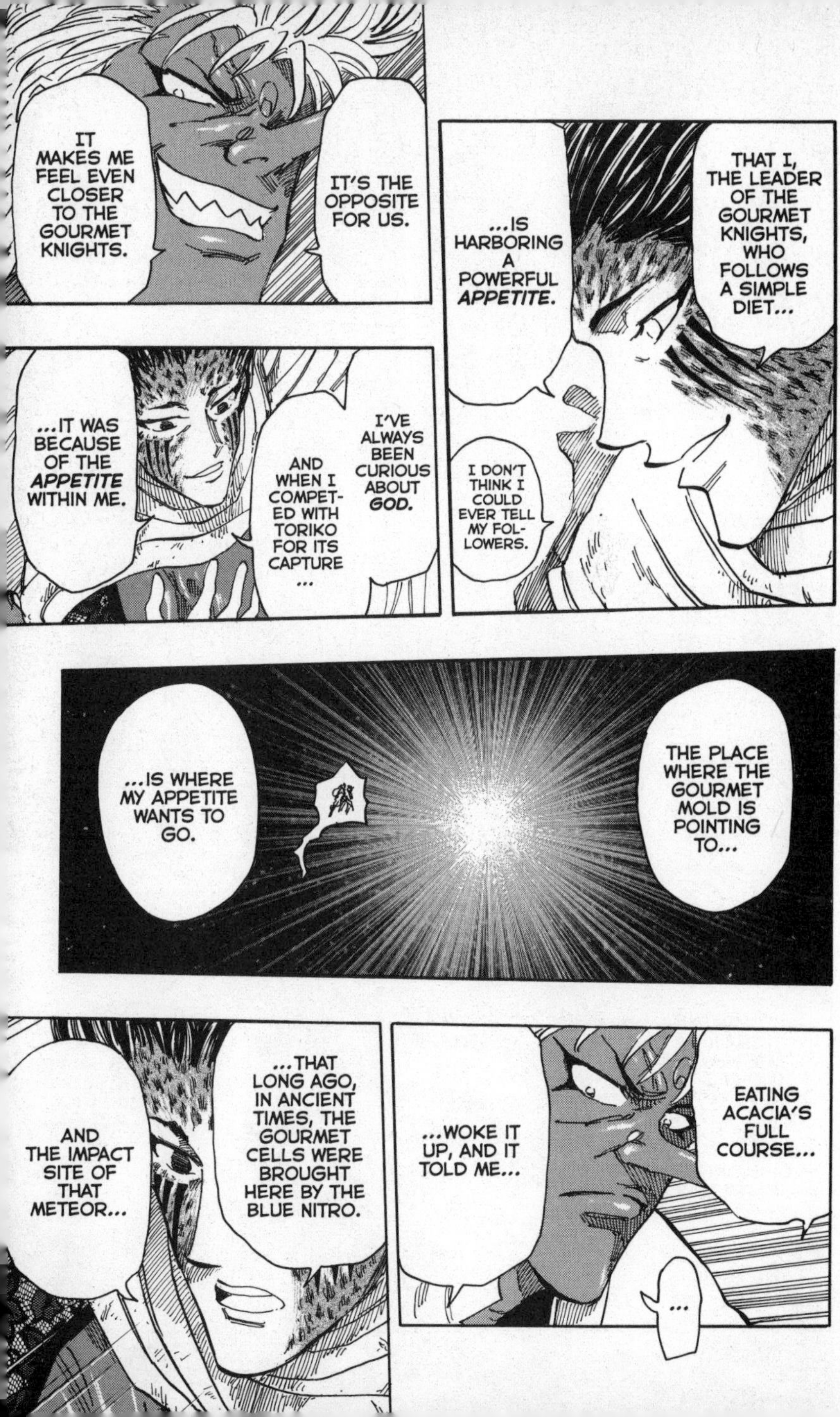
THAT I, THE LEADER OF THE GOURMET KNIGHTS, WHO FOLLOWS A SIMPLE DIET...
...IS HARBORING A POWERFUL *APPETITE*.
I DON'T THINK I COULD EVER TELL MY FOL-LOWERS.
IT'S THE OPPOSITE FOR US.
IT MAKES ME FEEL EVEN CLOSER TO THE GOURMET KNIGHTS.
I'VE ALWAYS BEEN CURIOUS ABOUT *GOD.*
AND WHEN I COMPET-ED WITH TORIKO FOR ITS CAPTURE...
...IT WAS BECAUSE OF THE *APPETITE* WITHIN ME.
THE PLACE WHERE THE GOURMET MOLD IS POINTING TO...
...IS WHERE MY APPETITE WANTS TO GO.
EATING ACACIA'S FULL COURSE...
...WOKE IT UP, AND IT TOLD ME...
...
...THAT LONG AGO, IN ANCIENT TIMES, THE GOURMET CELLS WERE BROUGHT HERE BY THE BLUE NITRO.
AND THE IMPACT SITE OF THAT METEOR...

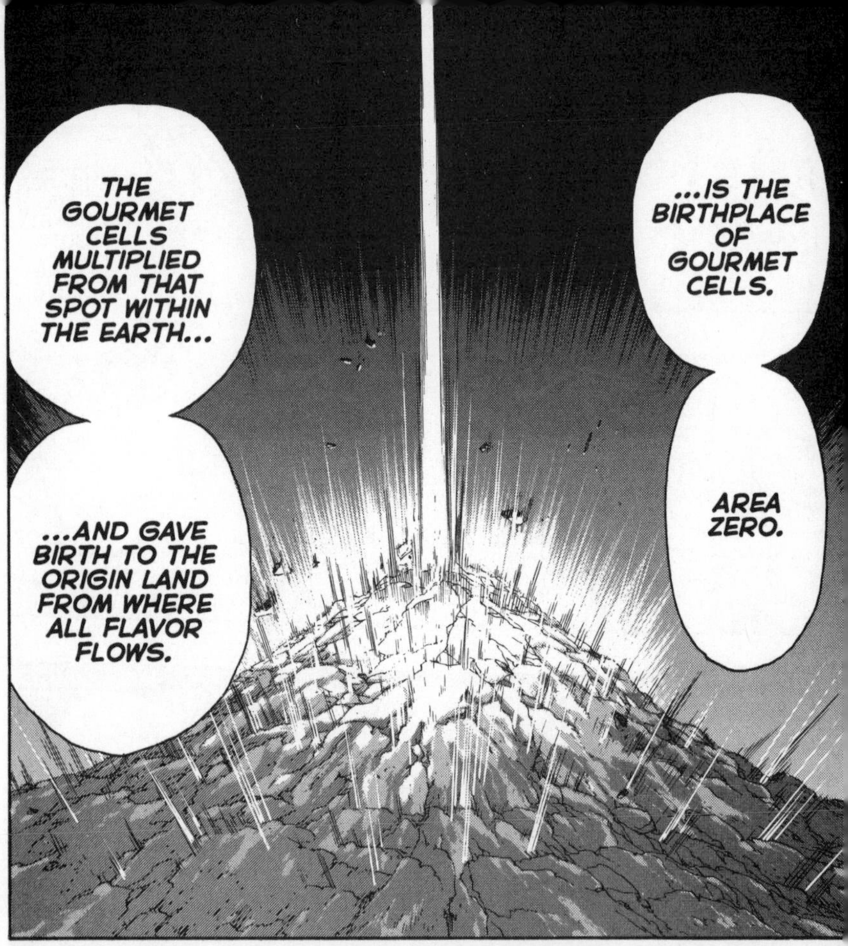
...IS THE BIRTHPLACE OF GOURMET CELLS.
AREA ZERO.
THE GOURMET CELLS MULTIPLIED FROM THAT SPOT WITHIN THE EARTH...
...AND GAVE BIRTH TO THE ORIGIN LAND FROM WHERE ALL FLAVOR FLOWS.

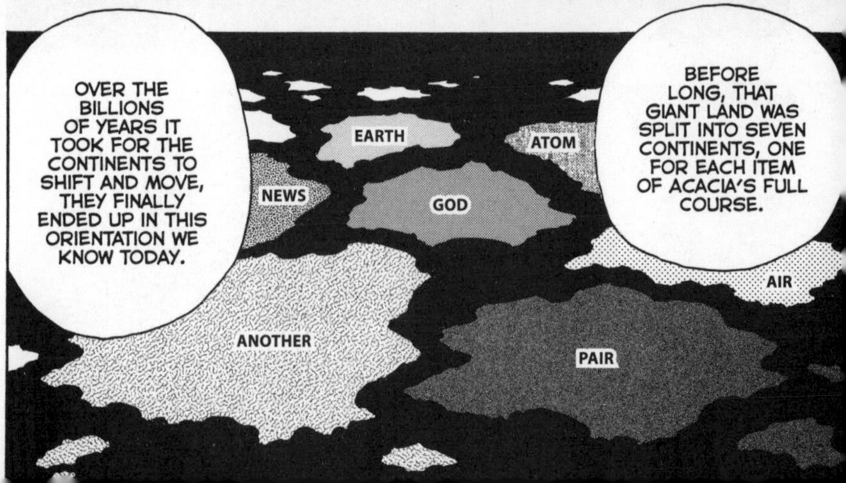
BEFORE LONG, THAT GIANT LAND WAS SPLIT INTO SEVEN CONTINENTS, ONE FOR EACH ITEM OF ACACIA'S FULL COURSE.
OVER THE BILLIONS OF YEARS IT TOOK FOR THE CONTINENTS TO SHIFT AND MOVE, THEY FINALLY ENDED UP IN THIS ORIENTATION WE KNOW TODAY.
ATOM
EARTH
AIR
GOD
NEWS
PAIR
ANOTHER

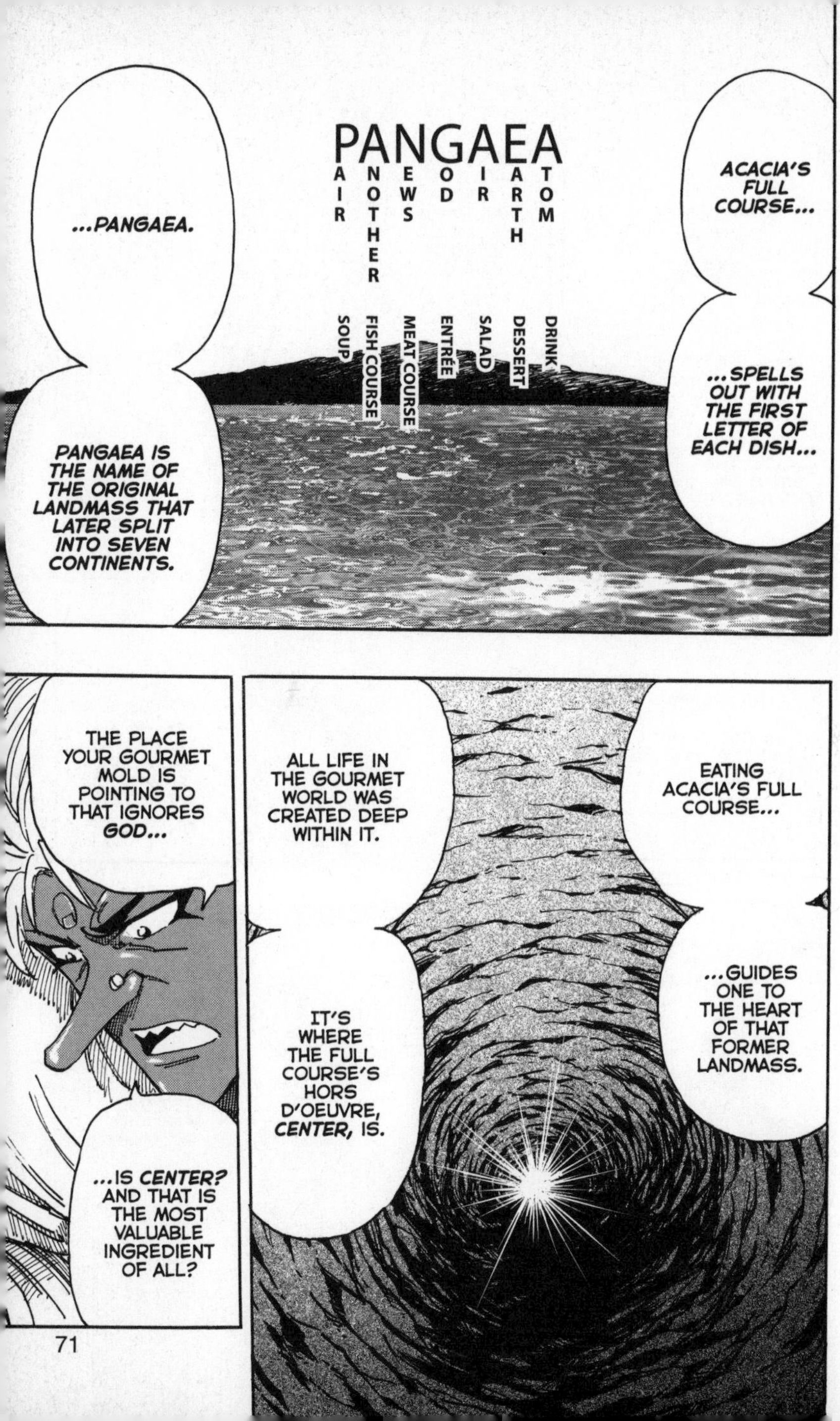
ACACIA'S FULL COURSE...
...SPELLS OUT WITH THE FIRST LETTER OF EACH DISH...
PANGAEA
PAIR
ANOTHER
NEWS
GOD
AIR
EARTH
ATOM
SOUP
FISH COURSE
MEAT COURSE
ENTRÉE
SALAD
DESSERT
DRINK
...PANGAEA.
PANGAEA IS THE NAME OF THE ORIGINAL LANDMASS THAT LATER SPLIT INTO SEVEN CONTINENTS.
EATING ACACIA'S FULL COURSE...
...GUIDES ONE TO THE HEART OF THAT FORMER LANDMASS.
ALL LIFE IN THE GOURMET WORLD WAS CREATED DEEP WITHIN IT.
IT'S WHERE THE FULL COURSE'S HORS D'OEUVRE, *CENTER*, IS.
THE PLACE YOUR GOURMET MOLD IS POINTING TO THAT IGNORES *GOD*...
...IS *CENTER*? AND THAT IS THE MOST VALUABLE INGREDIENT OF ALL?

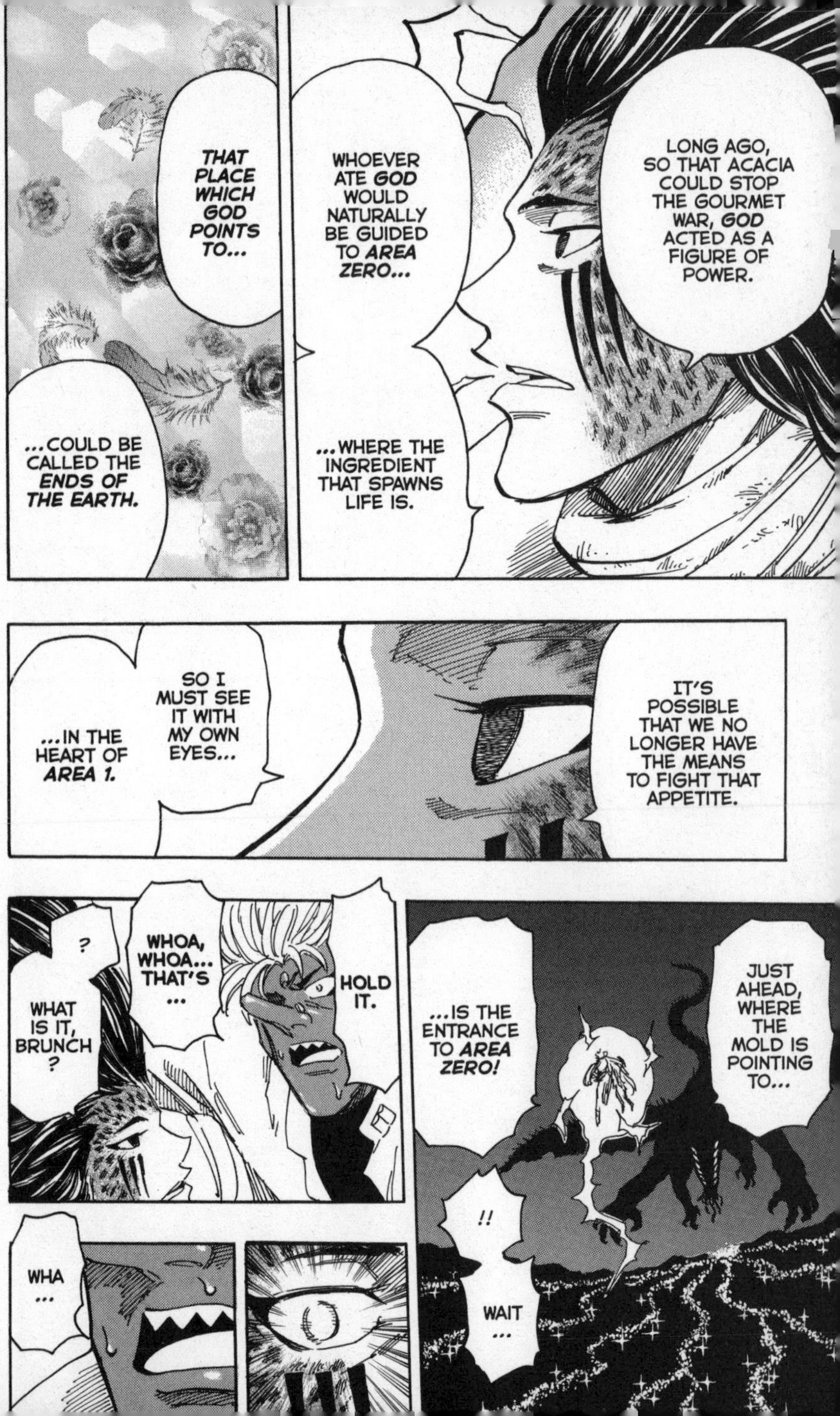
LONG AGO, SO THAT ACACIA COULD STOP THE GOURMET WAR, GOD ACTED AS A FIGURE OF POWER.
WHOEVER ATE GOD WOULD NATURALLY BE GUIDED TO AREA ZERO...
...WHERE THE INGREDIENT THAT SPAWNS LIFE IS.
THAT PLACE WHICH GOD POINTS TO...
...COULD BE CALLED THE ENDS OF THE EARTH.
IT'S POSSIBLE THAT WE NO LONGER HAVE THE MEANS TO FIGHT THAT APPETITE.
SO I MUST SEE IT WITH MY OWN EYES...
...IN THE HEART OF AREA 1.
JUST AHEAD, WHERE THE MOLD IS POINTING TO...
...IS THE ENTRANCE TO AREA ZERO!
!!
WAIT ...
HOLD IT.
WHOA, WHOA... THAT'S ...
?
WHAT IS IT, BRUNCH ?
WHA ...

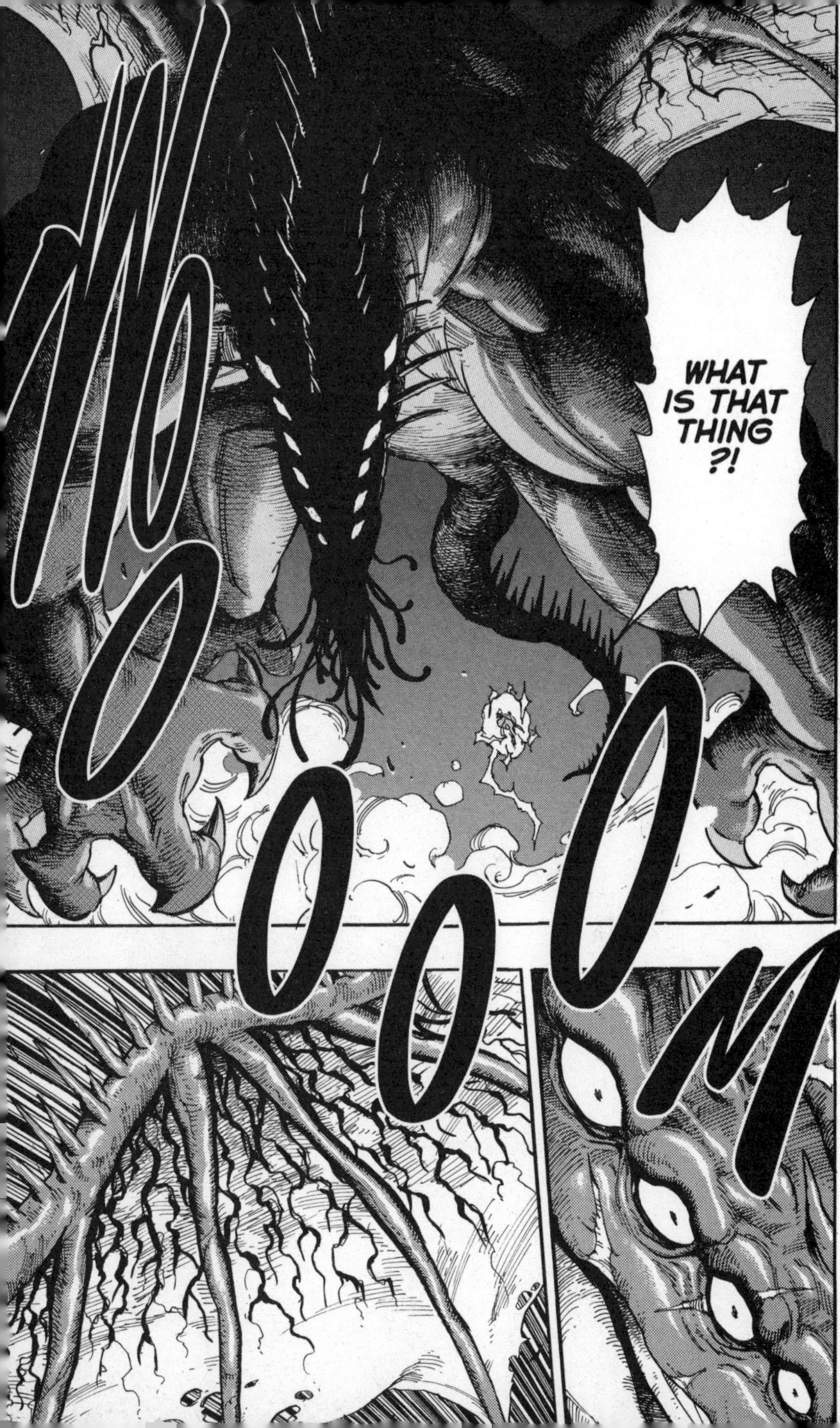
WHAT IS THAT THING ?!

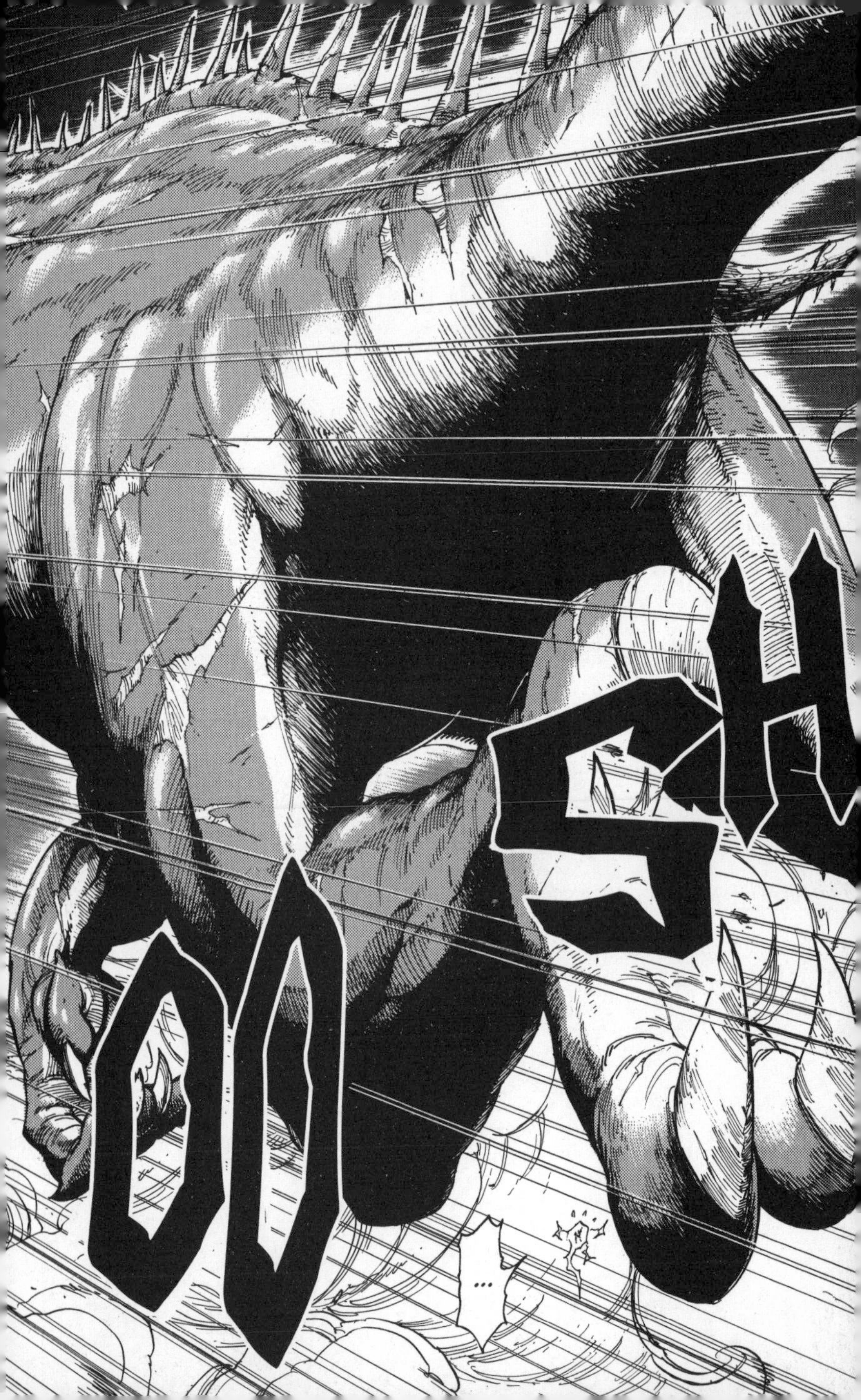
OOSH
...

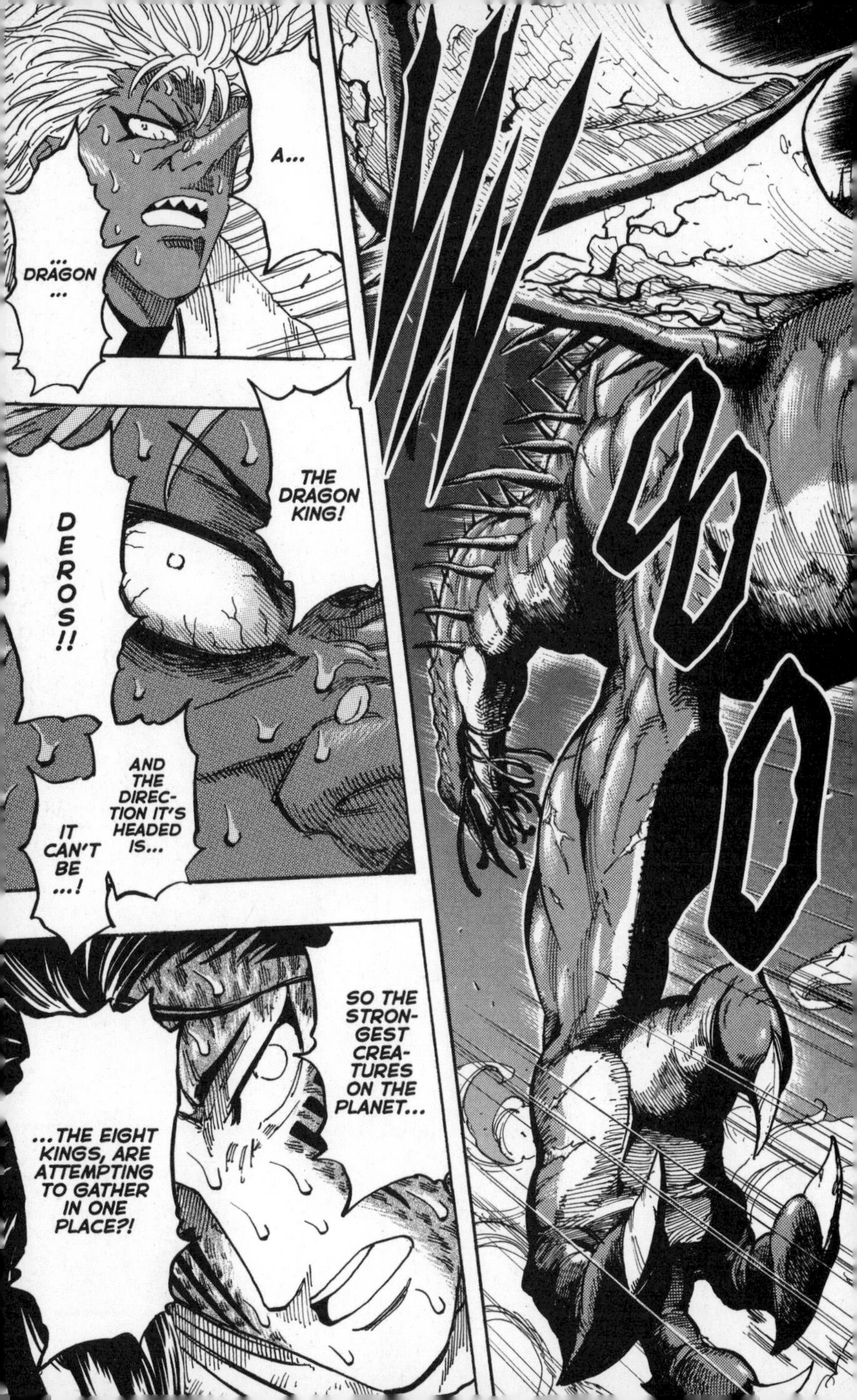
A...
...DRAGON...
THE DRAGON KING!
DEROS!!
AND THE DIRECTION IT'S HEADED IS...
IT CAN'T BE...!
SO THE STRONGEST CREATURES ON THE PLANET...
...THE EIGHT KINGS, ARE ATTEMPTING TO GATHER IN ONE PLACE?!

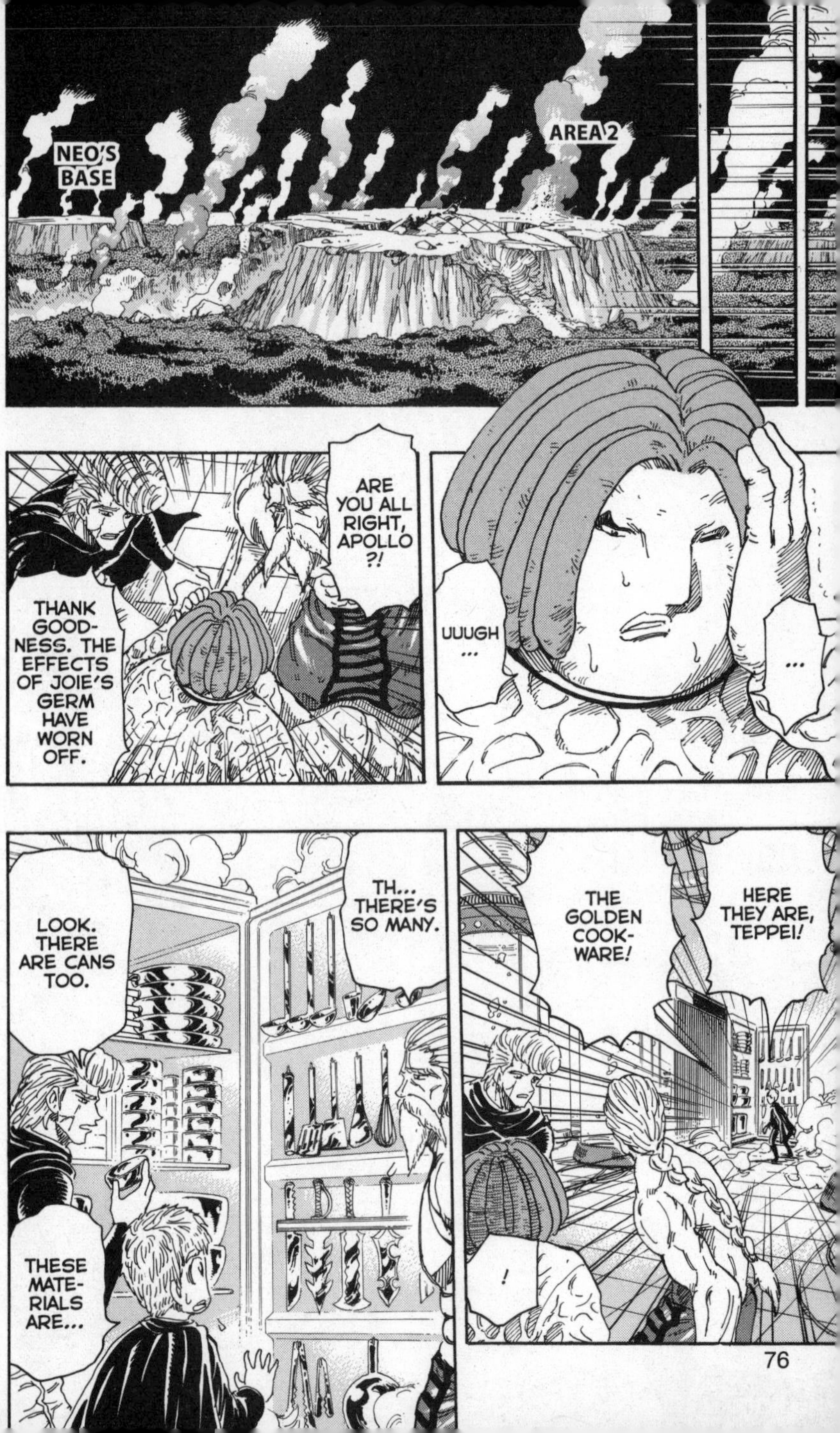
AREA 2
NEO'S BASE
...
UUUGH ...
ARE YOU ALL RIGHT, APOLLO?!
THANK GOODNESS. THE EFFECTS OF JOIE'S GERM HAVE WORN OFF.
HERE THEY ARE, TEPPEI!
THE GOLDEN COOKWARE!
!
TH... THERE'S SO MANY.
LOOK. THERE ARE CANS TOO.
THESE MATERIALS ARE...

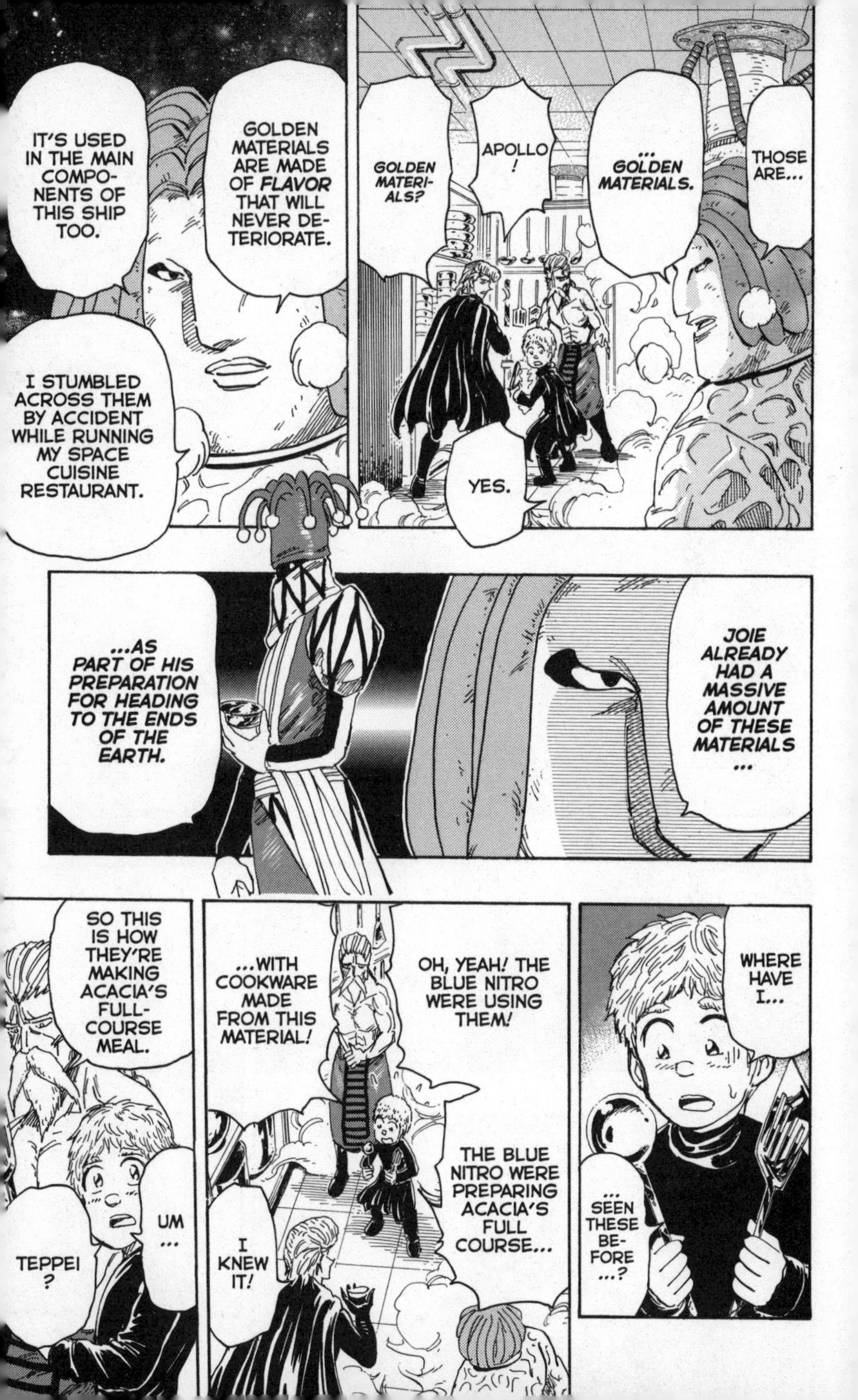
THOSE ARE...
...GOLDEN MATERIALS.
APOLLO!
GOLDEN MATERIALS?
YES.
GOLDEN MATERIALS ARE MADE OF *FLAVOR* THAT WILL NEVER DETERIORATE.
IT'S USED IN THE MAIN COMPONENTS OF THIS SHIP TOO.
I STUMBLED ACROSS THEM BY ACCIDENT WHILE RUNNING MY SPACE CUISINE RESTAURANT.
JOIE ALREADY HAD A MASSIVE AMOUNT OF THESE MATERIALS...
...AS PART OF HIS PREPARATION FOR HEADING TO THE ENDS OF THE EARTH.
WHERE HAVE I...
...SEEN THESE BEFORE...?
OH, YEAH! THE BLUE NITRO WERE USING THEM!
...WITH COOKWARE MADE FROM THIS MATERIAL!
THE BLUE NITRO WERE PREPARING ACACIA'S FULL COURSE...
I KNEW IT!
SO THIS IS HOW THEY'RE MAKING ACACIA'S FULL-COURSE MEAL.
UM...
TEPPEI?

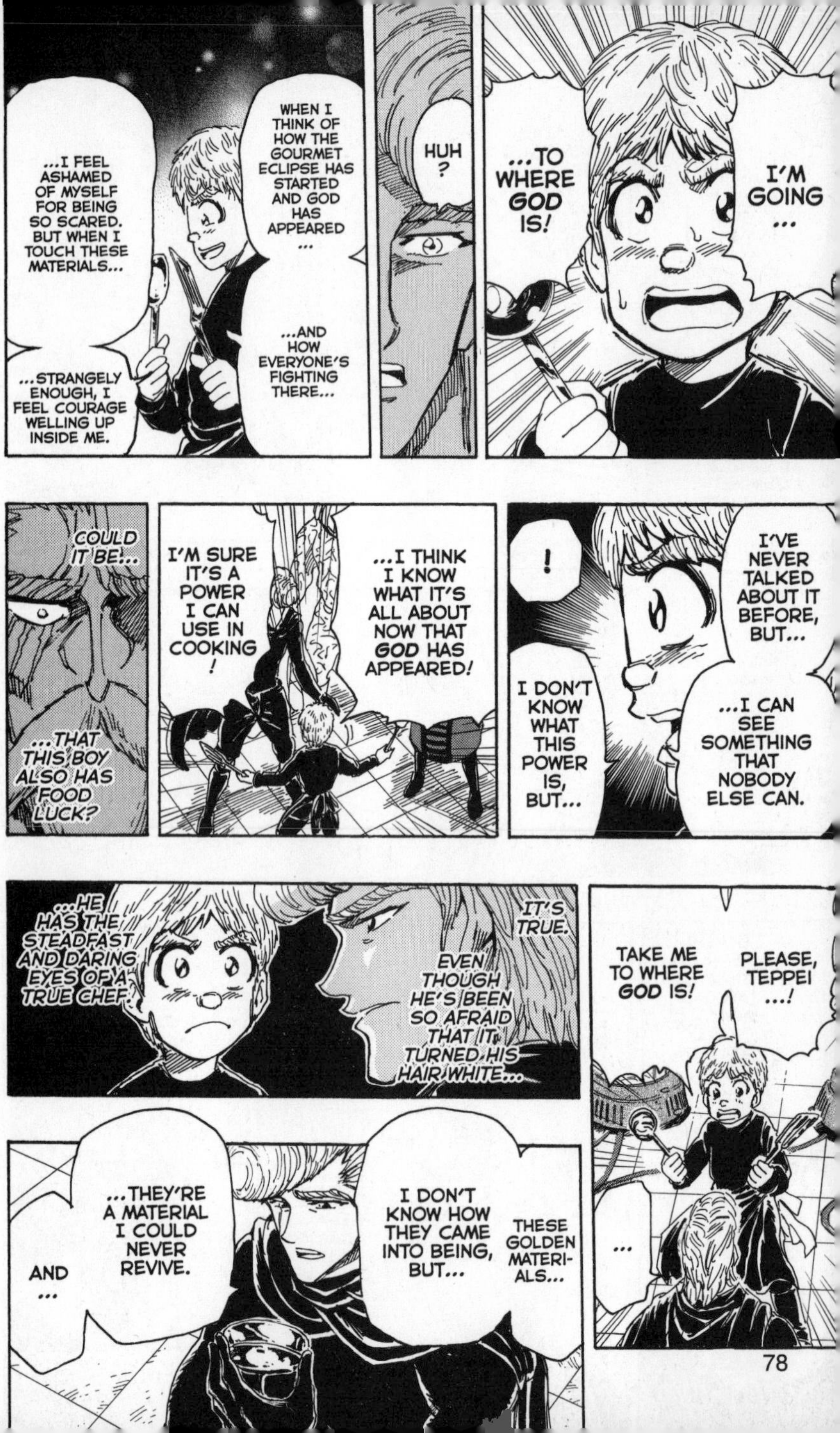
I'M GOING...
...TO WHERE GOD IS!
HUH?
WHEN I THINK OF HOW THE GOURMET ECLIPSE HAS STARTED AND GOD HAS APPEARED...
...AND HOW EVERYONE'S FIGHTING THERE...
...I FEEL ASHAMED OF MYSELF FOR BEING SO SCARED. BUT WHEN I TOUCH THESE MATERIALS...
...STRANGELY ENOUGH, I FEEL COURAGE WELLING UP INSIDE ME.
I'VE NEVER TALKED ABOUT IT BEFORE, BUT...
!
...I CAN SEE SOMETHING THAT NOBODY ELSE CAN.
I DON'T KNOW WHAT THIS POWER IS, BUT...
...I THINK I KNOW WHAT IT'S ALL ABOUT NOW THAT GOD HAS APPEARED!
I'M SURE IT'S A POWER I CAN USE IN COOKING!
COULD IT BE...
...THAT THIS BOY ALSO HAS FOOD LUCK?
PLEASE, TEPPEI...!
TAKE ME TO WHERE GOD IS!
...
IT'S TRUE.
EVEN THOUGH HE'S BEEN SO AFRAID THAT IT TURNED HIS HAIR WHITE...
...HE HAS THE STEADFAST AND DARING EYES OF A TRUE CHEF!
THESE GOLDEN MATERIALS...
I DON'T KNOW HOW THEY CAME INTO BEING, BUT...
...THEY'RE A MATERIAL I COULD NEVER REVIVE.
AND...

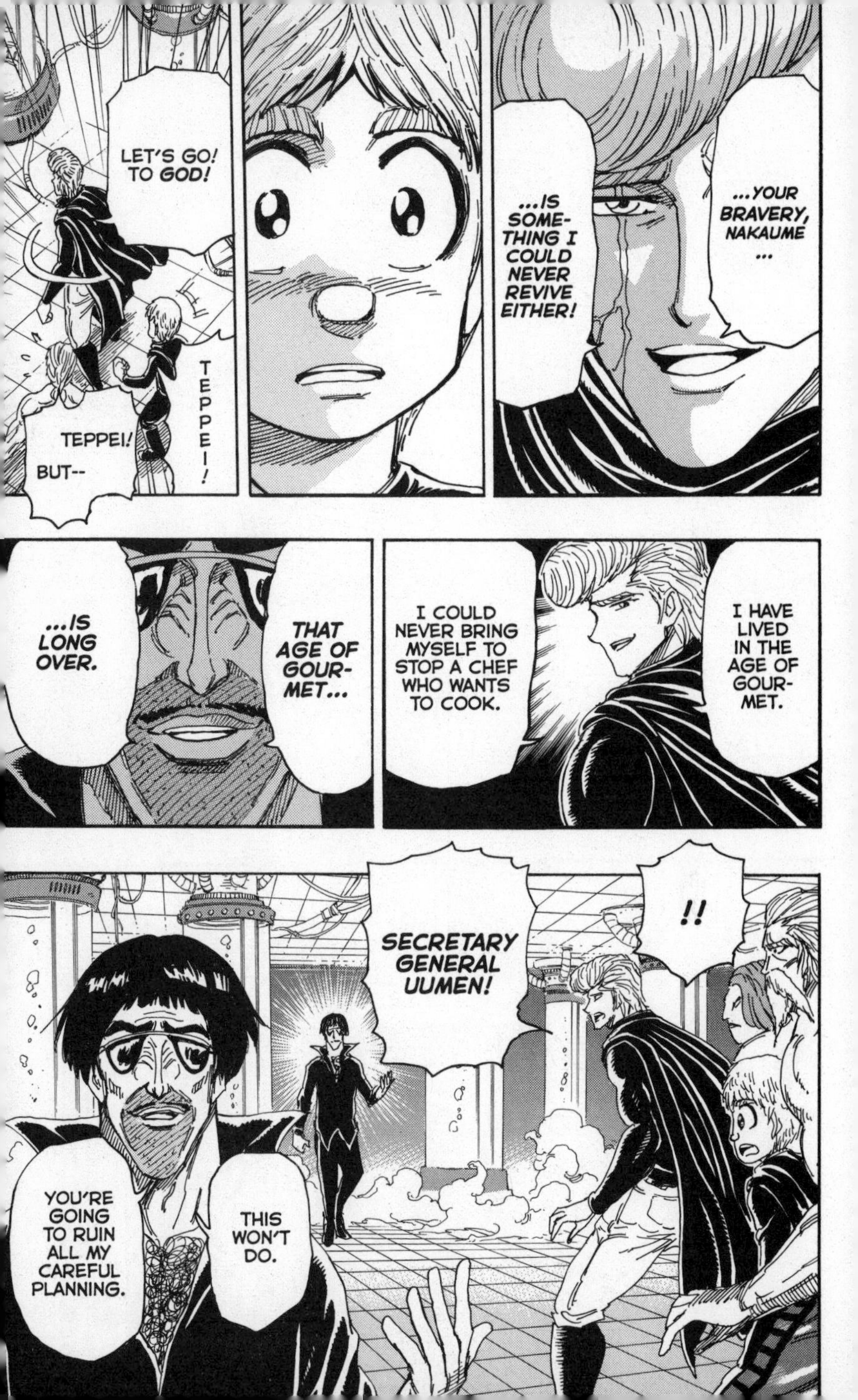
...YOUR BRAVERY, NAKAUME ...
...IS SOMETHING I COULD NEVER REVIVE EITHER!
LET'S GO! TO GOD!
TEPPEI!
TEPPEI! BUT--
I HAVE LIVED IN THE AGE OF GOURMET.
I COULD NEVER BRING MYSELF TO STOP A CHEF WHO WANTS TO COOK.
THAT AGE OF GOURMET...
...IS LONG OVER.
!!
SECRETARY GENERAL UUMEN!
THIS WON'T DO.
YOU'RE GOING TO RUIN ALL MY CAREFUL PLANNING.

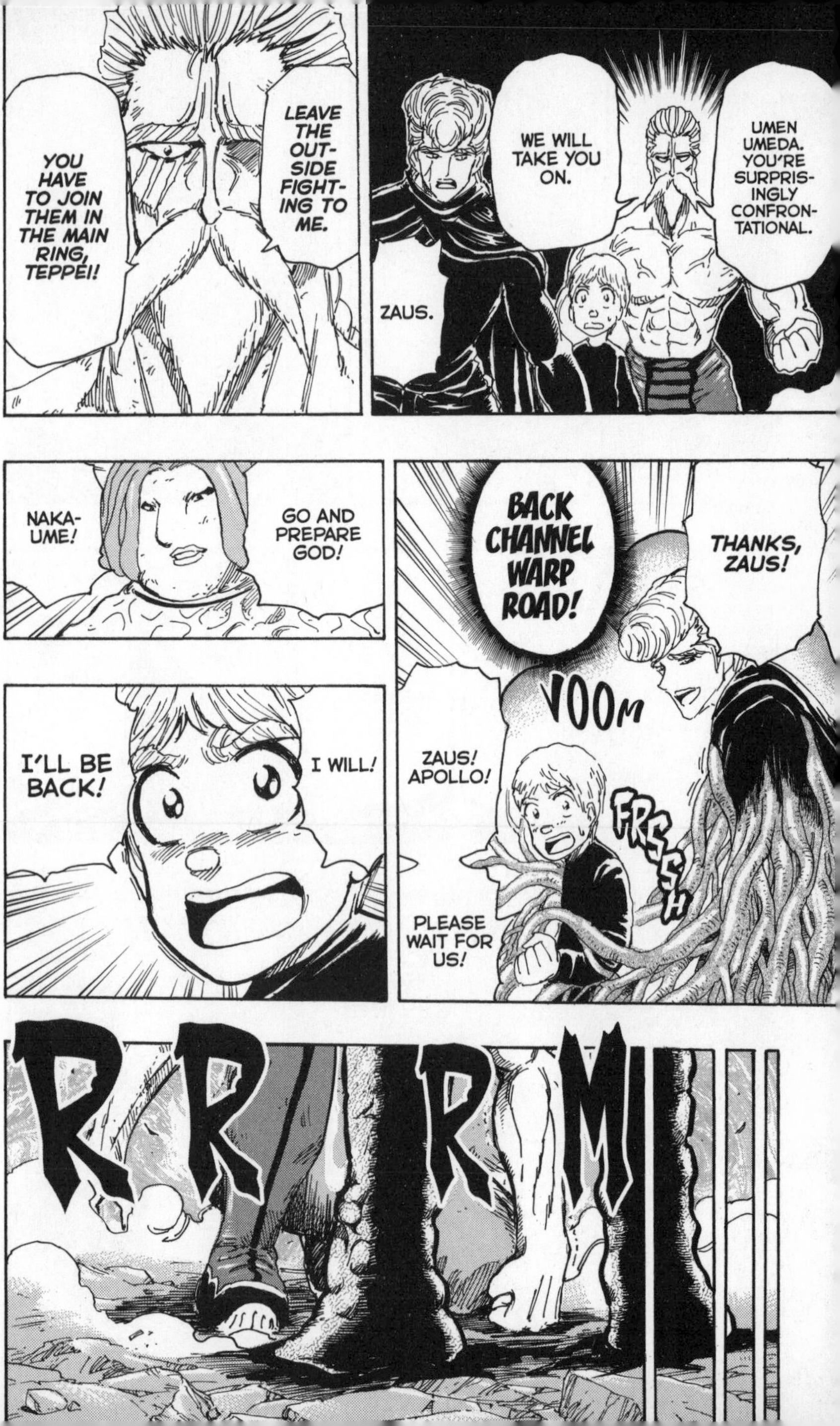
UMEN UMEDA. YOU'RE SURPRISINGLY CONFRONTATIONAL.
WE WILL TAKE YOU ON.
ZAUS.
LEAVE THE OUTSIDE FIGHTING TO ME.
YOU HAVE TO JOIN THEM IN THE MAIN RING, TEPPEI!
THANKS, ZAUS!
BACK CHANNEL WARP ROAD!
VOOM
FRSSH
ZAUS! APOLLO!
PLEASE WAIT FOR US!
GO AND PREPARE GOD!
NAKA-UME!
I WILL!
I'LL BE BACK!
RRRM

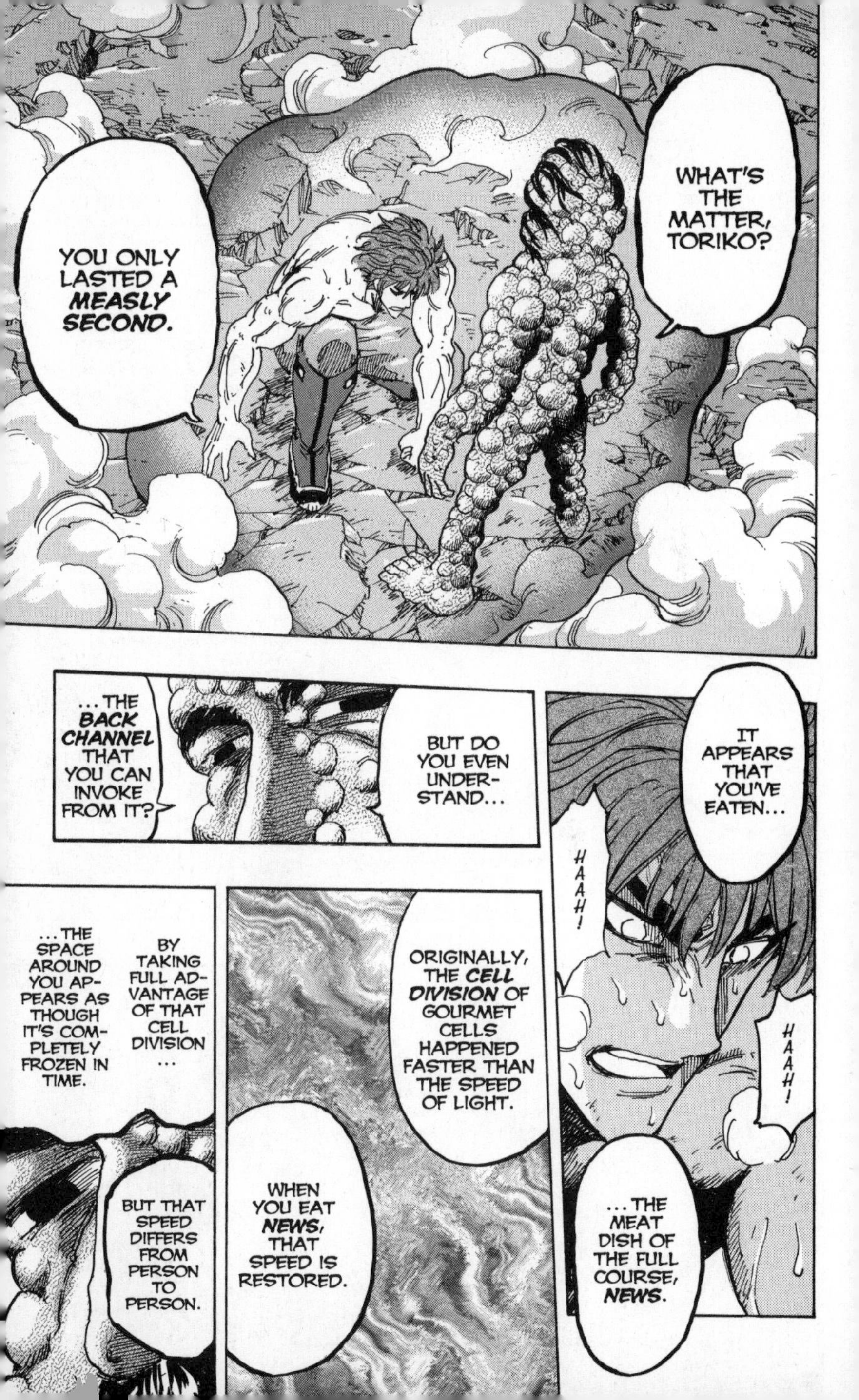

WHAT'S THE MATTER, TORIKO?
YOU ONLY LASTED A **MEASLY SECOND.**
IT APPEARS THAT YOU'VE EATEN...
HAAAH!
HAAH!
...THE MEAT DISH OF THE FULL COURSE, **NEWS**.
BUT DO YOU EVEN UNDERSTAND...
...THE **BACK CHANNEL** THAT YOU CAN INVOKE FROM IT?
ORIGINALLY, THE **CELL DIVISION** OF GOURMET CELLS HAPPENED FASTER THAN THE SPEED OF LIGHT.
WHEN YOU EAT **NEWS**, THAT SPEED IS RESTORED.
BY TAKING FULL ADVANTAGE OF THAT CELL DIVISION...
...THE SPACE AROUND YOU APPEARS AS THOUGH IT'S COMPLETELY FROZEN IN TIME.
BUT THAT SPEED DIFFERS FROM PERSON TO PERSON.

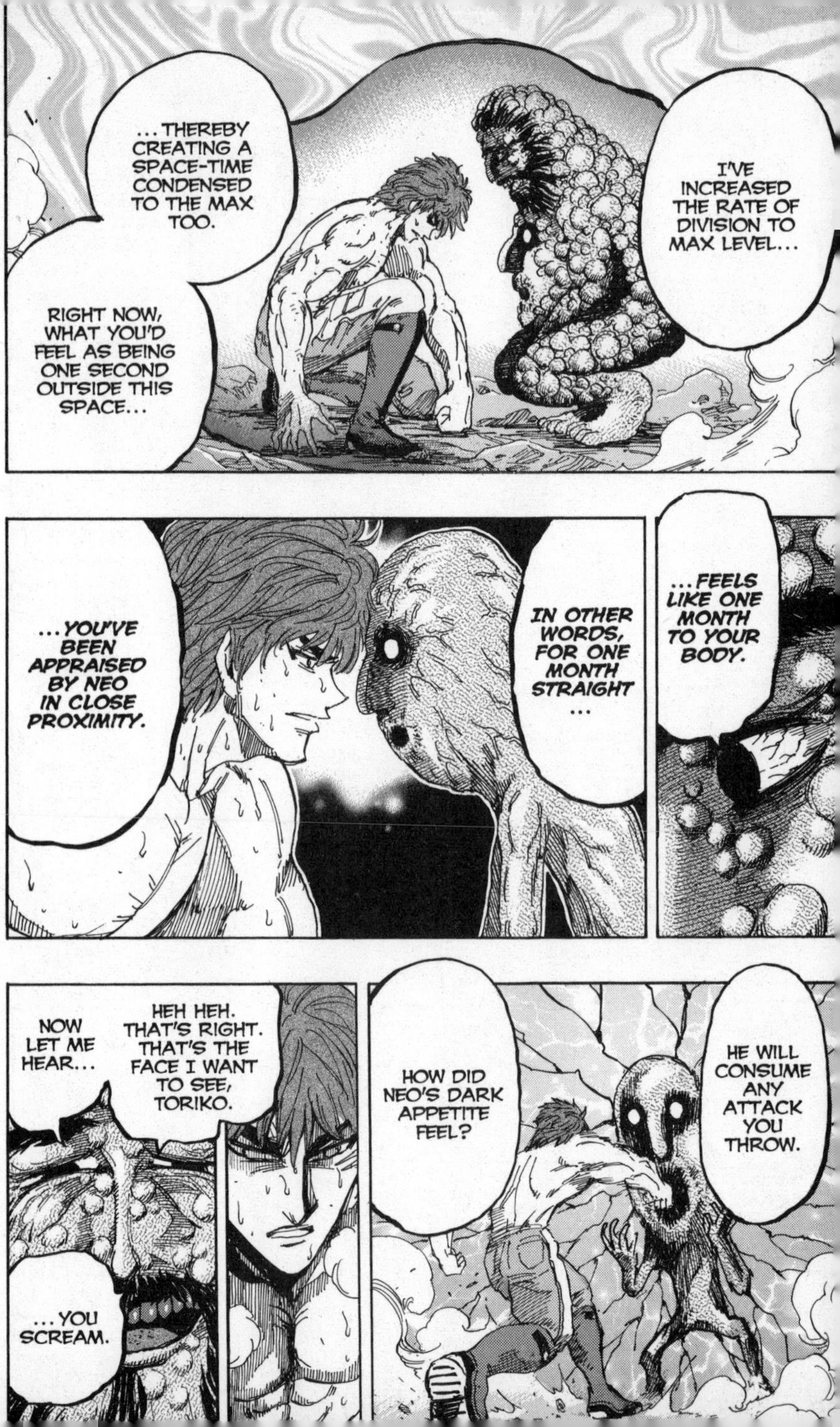
I'VE INCREASED THE RATE OF DIVISION TO MAX LEVEL...
...THEREBY CREATING A SPACE-TIME CONDENSED TO THE MAX TOO.
RIGHT NOW, WHAT YOU'D FEEL AS BEING ONE SECOND OUTSIDE THIS SPACE...
...FEELS LIKE ONE MONTH TO YOUR BODY.
IN OTHER WORDS, FOR ONE MONTH STRAIGHT...
...YOU'VE BEEN APPRAISED BY NEO IN CLOSE PROXIMITY.
HE WILL CONSUME ANY ATTACK YOU THROW.
HOW DID NEO'S DARK APPETITE FEEL?
HEH HEH. THAT'S RIGHT. THAT'S THE FACE I WANT TO SEE, TORIKO.
NOW LET ME HEAR...
...YOU SCREAM.

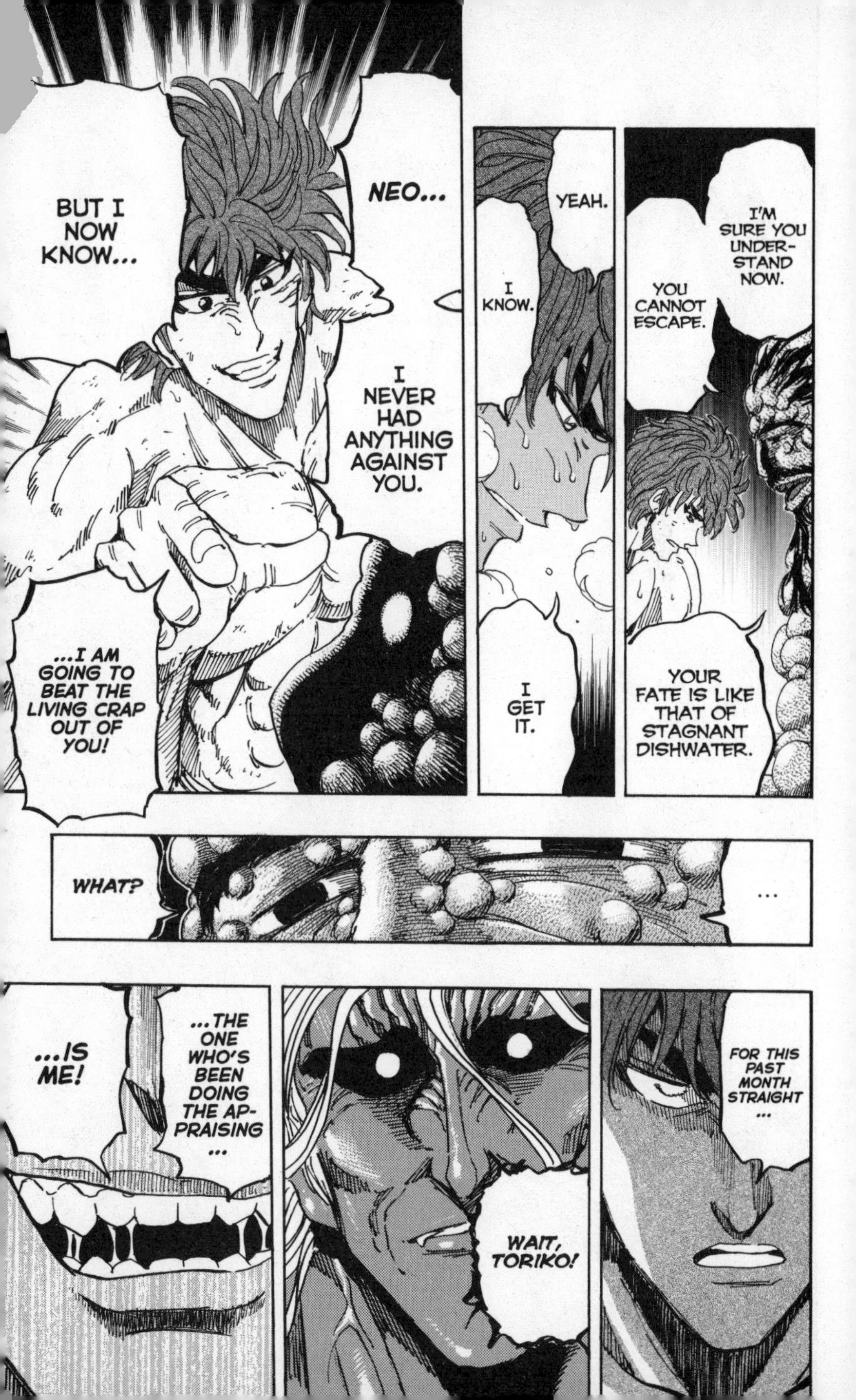
I'M SURE YOU UNDERSTAND NOW.
YOU CANNOT ESCAPE.
YOUR FATE IS LIKE THAT OF STAGNANT DISHWATER.
YEAH.
I KNOW.
I GET IT.
NEO...
I NEVER HAD ANYTHING AGAINST YOU.
BUT I NOW KNOW...
...I AM GOING TO BEAT THE LIVING CRAP OUT OF YOU!
...
WHAT?
FOR THIS PAST MONTH STRAIGHT...
WAIT, TORIKO!
...THE ONE WHO'S BEEN DOING THE APPRAISING...
...IS ME!

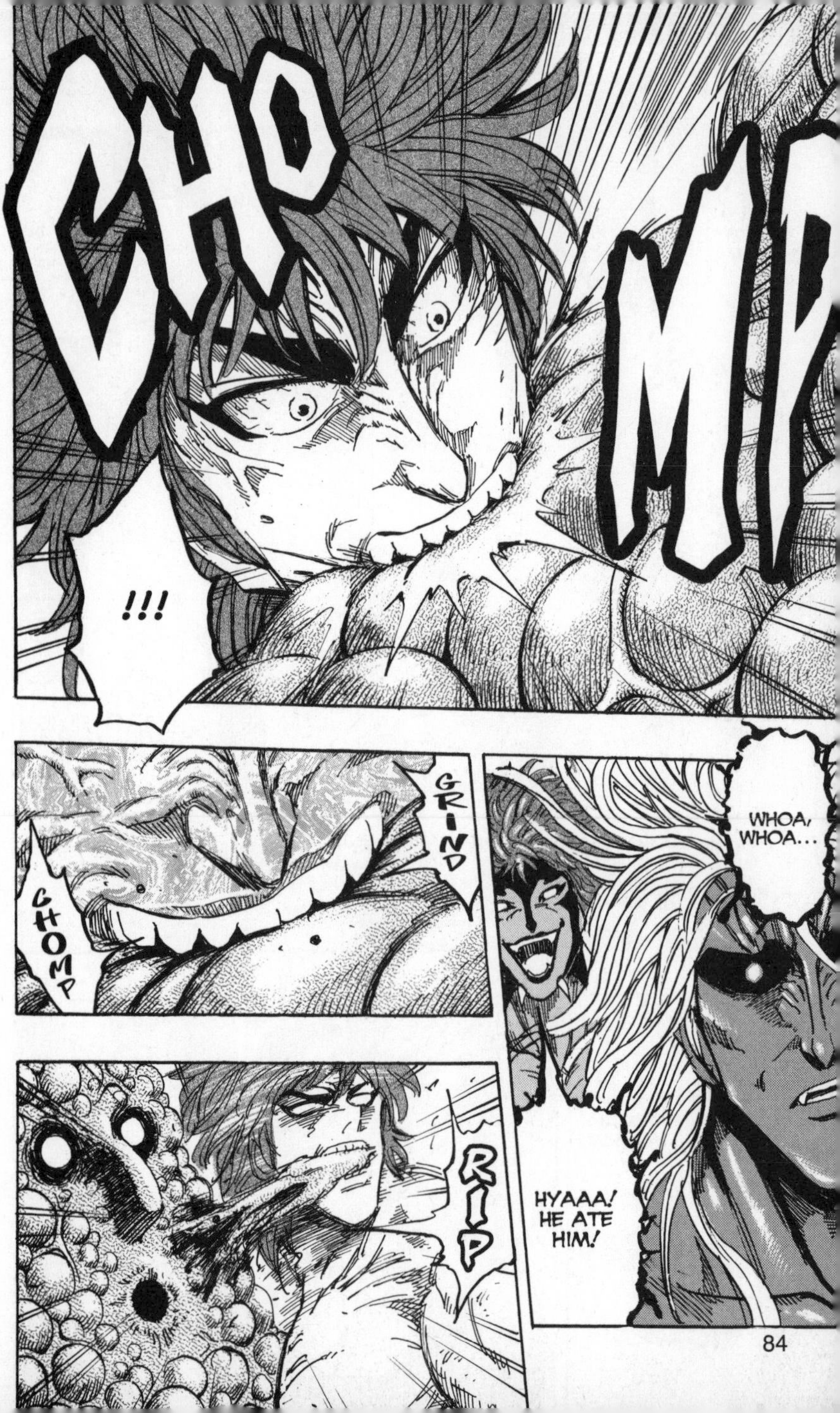
CHOMP
!!!
WHOA, WHOA...
HYAAA! HE ATE HIM!
GRIND
CHOMP
RIP

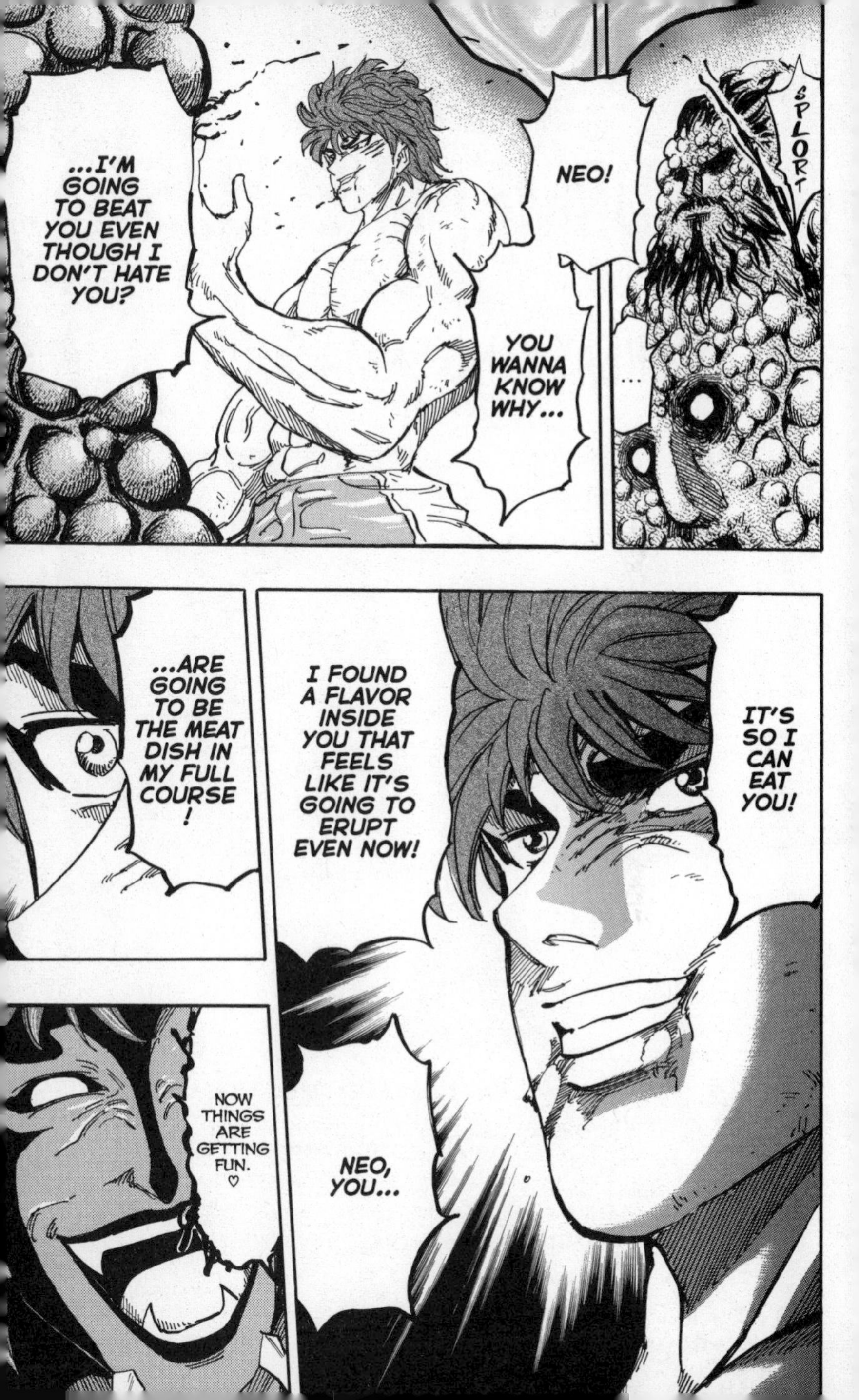
SPLORT
...
NEO!
YOU WANNA KNOW WHY...
...I'M GOING TO BEAT YOU EVEN THOUGH I DON'T HATE YOU?
IT'S SO I CAN EAT YOU!
I FOUND A FLAVOR INSIDE YOU THAT FEELS LIKE IT'S GOING TO ERUPT EVEN NOW!
NEO, YOU...
...ARE GOING TO BE THE MEAT DISH IN MY FULL COURSE!
NOW THINGS ARE GETTING FUN. ♡

TORIKO

GOURMET CHECKLIST

Vol. 405

GREAT KING ENMA SQUID
(FOOD SPIRIT)

CAPTURE LEVEL: UNKNOWN
HABITAT: GOURMET WORLD AREA 6, SPIRIT WORLD
SIZE: 40 M
HEIGHT: ---
WEIGHT: 2,500 TONS
PRICE: INEDIBLE

GREAT KING ENMA SQUID.

SO, YOU MADE IT.

I AM THE RULER OF THIS WORLD.

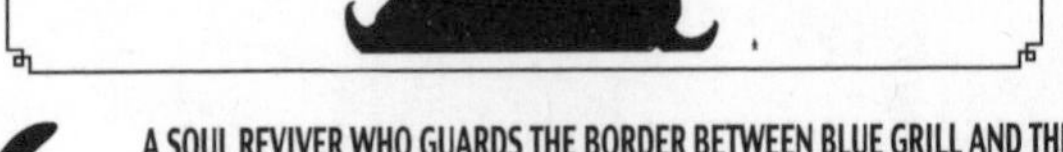

SCALE

A SOUL REVIVER WHO GUARDS THE BORDER BETWEEN BLUE GRILL AND THE SPIRIT WORLD'S BACK CHANNEL AT THE FOOD SPIRIT GATE. ALONG WITH DON SLIME, HE HAS SET HIS SIGHTS ON THE RESURRECTION AND PREPARATION OF ACACIA'S FULL COURSE AND HAS ALREADY SUCCEEDED IN THE RESURRECTION OF AIR. HE HAS AN UNUSUAL MANNER OF SPEECH, BUT IS DON SLIME'S SWORN FRIEND AND A CAPABLE FIGURE WHO WILL SUCCEED DON SLIME IN BLUE GRILL.

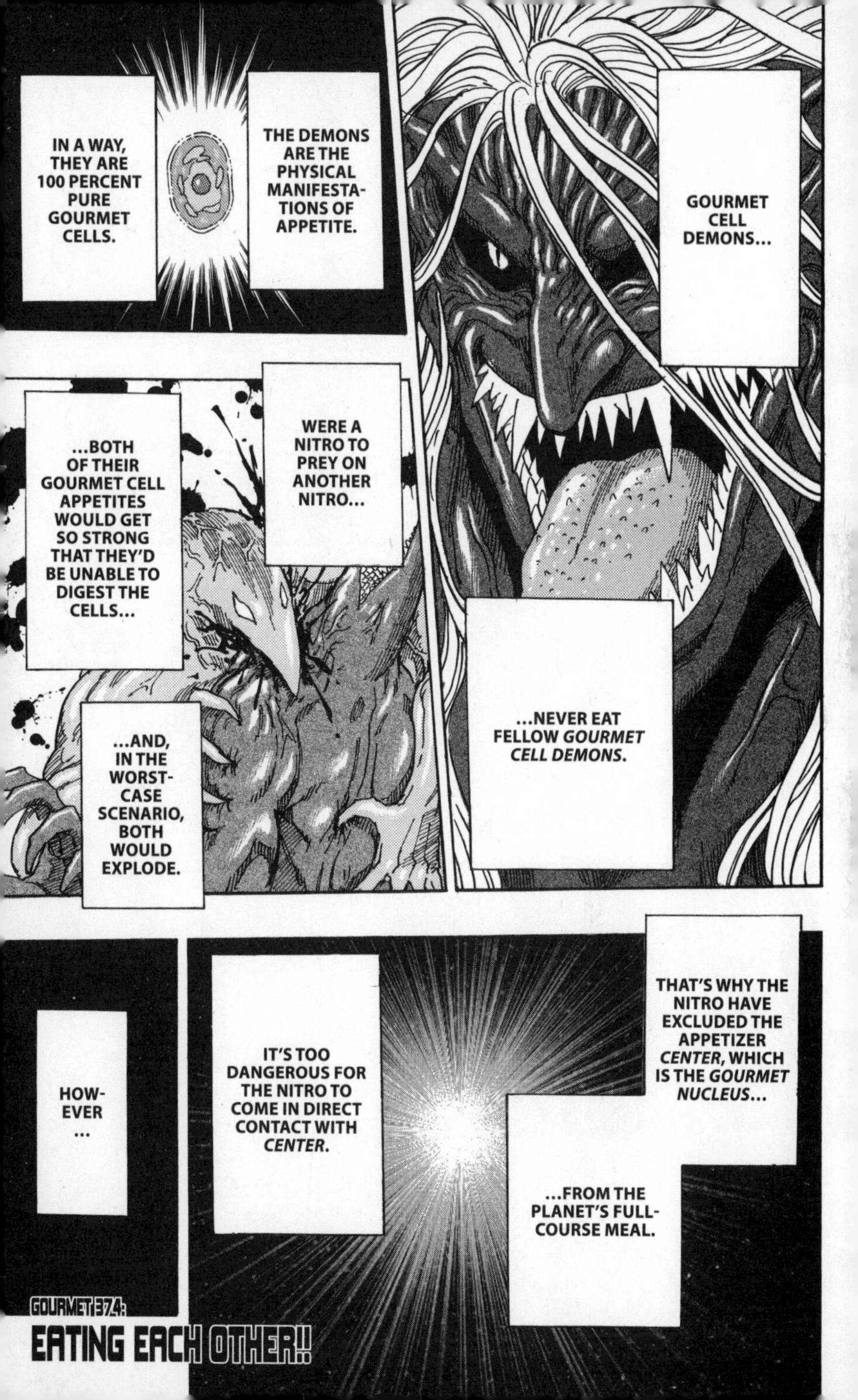
GOURMET CELL DEMONS...
...NEVER EAT FELLOW *GOURMET CELL DEMONS*.
THE DEMONS ARE THE PHYSICAL MANIFESTA-TIONS OF APPETITE.
IN A WAY, THEY ARE 100 PERCENT PURE GOURMET CELLS.
WERE A NITRO TO PREY ON ANOTHER NITRO...
...BOTH OF THEIR GOURMET CELL APPETITES WOULD GET SO STRONG THAT THEY'D BE UNABLE TO DIGEST THE CELLS...
...AND, IN THE WORST-CASE SCENARIO, BOTH WOULD EXPLODE.
THAT'S WHY THE NITRO HAVE EXCLUDED THE APPETIZER *CENTER*, WHICH IS THE *GOURMET NUCLEUS*...
...FROM THE PLANET'S FULL-COURSE MEAL.
IT'S TOO DANGEROUS FOR THE NITRO TO COME IN DIRECT CONTACT WITH *CENTER*.
HOW-EVER...
GOURMET 374:
EATING EACH OTHER!!

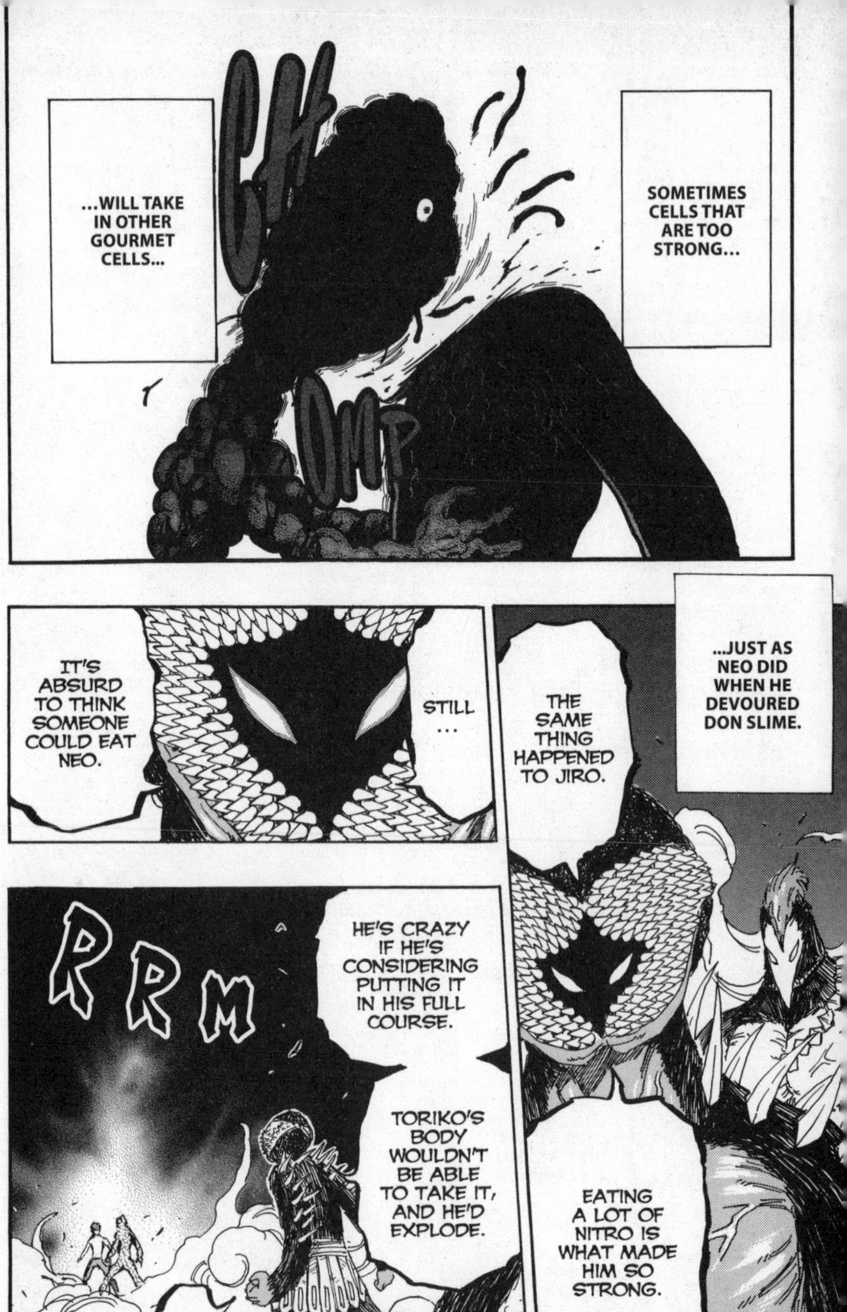

SOMETIMES CELLS THAT ARE TOO STRONG...
CHOMP
...WILL TAKE IN OTHER GOURMET CELLS...
...JUST AS NEO DID WHEN HE DEVOURED DON SLIME.
THE SAME THING HAPPENED TO JIRO.
EATING A LOT OF NITRO IS WHAT MADE HIM SO STRONG.
STILL...
IT'S ABSURD TO THINK SOMEONE COULD EAT NEO.
HE'S CRAZY IF HE'S CONSIDERING PUTTING IT IN HIS FULL COURSE.
TORIKO'S BODY WOULDN'T BE ABLE TO TAKE IT, AND HE'D EXPLODE.
RRM
!

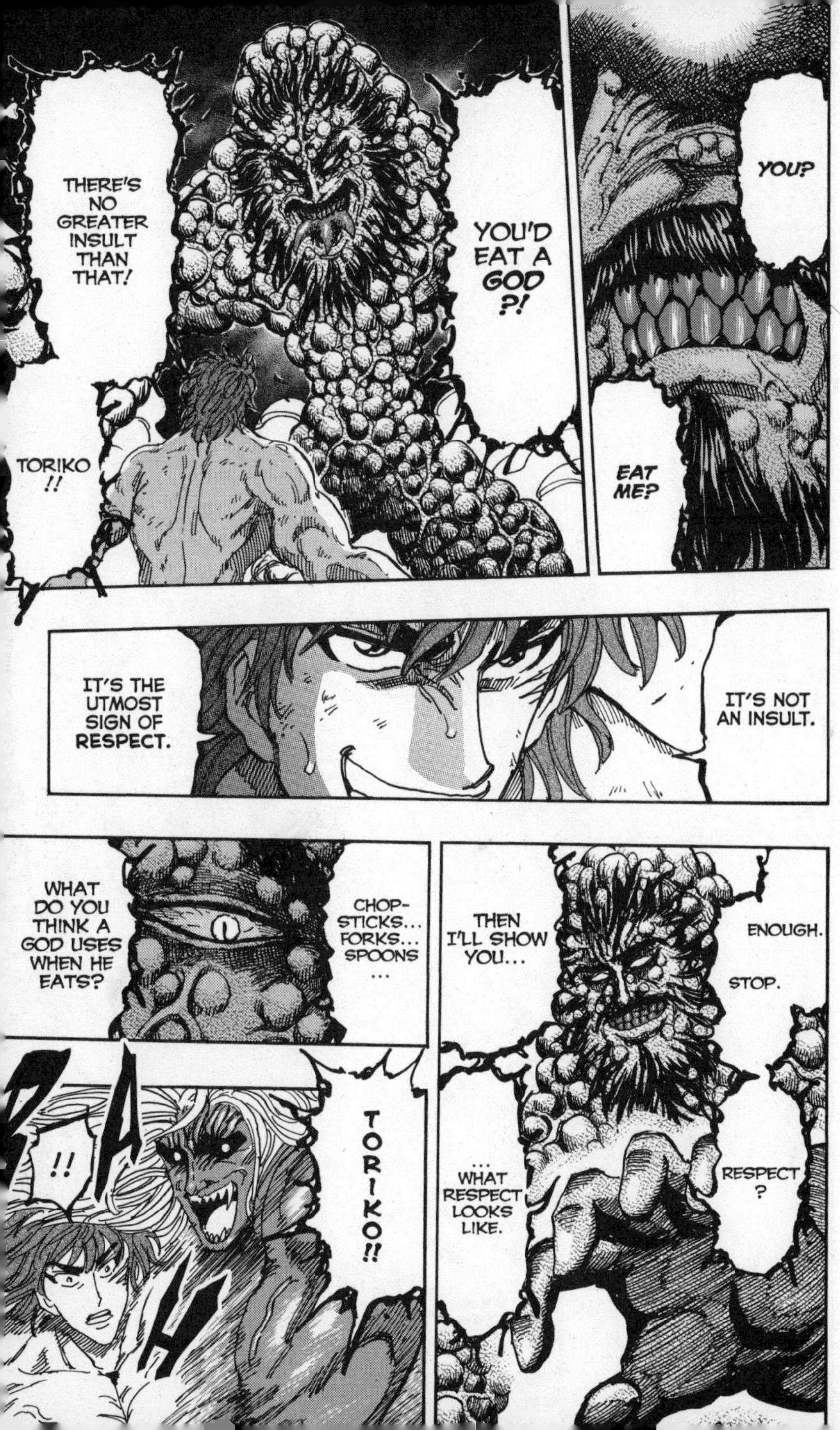
YOU?
EAT ME?
YOU'D EAT A GOD ?!
THERE'S NO GREATER INSULT THAN THAT!
TORIKO !!
IT'S NOT AN INSULT.
IT'S THE UTMOST SIGN OF RESPECT.
ENOUGH.
STOP.
RESPECT ?
THEN I'LL SHOW YOU...
...WHAT RESPECT LOOKS LIKE.
CHOP-STICKS... FORKS... SPOONS ...
WHAT DO YOU THINK A GOD USES WHEN HE EATS?
TORIKO!!
!!

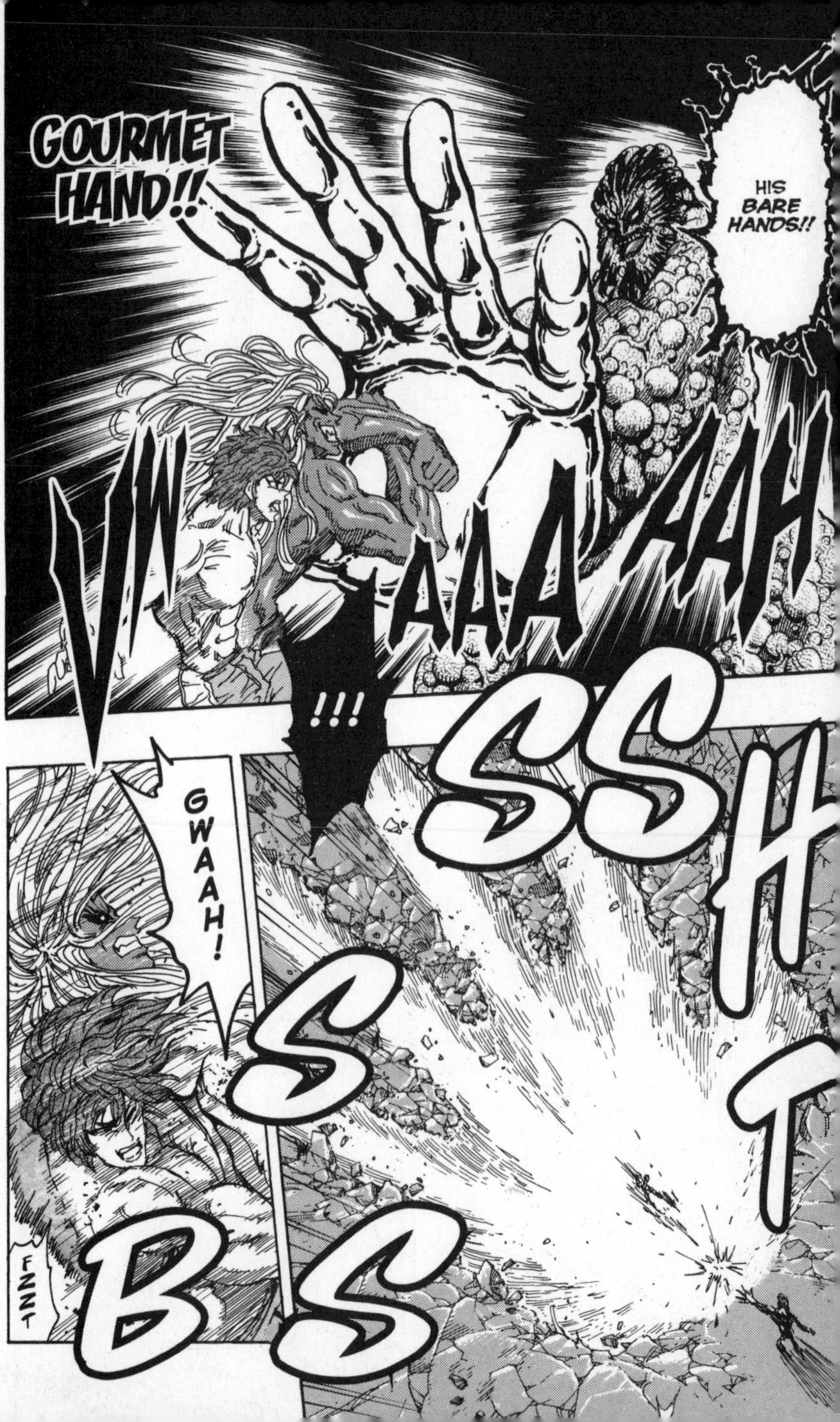
HIS BARE HANDS!!
GOURMET HAND!!
VWAAAAAH
!!!
BSSSSHT
GWAAH!
FZZT

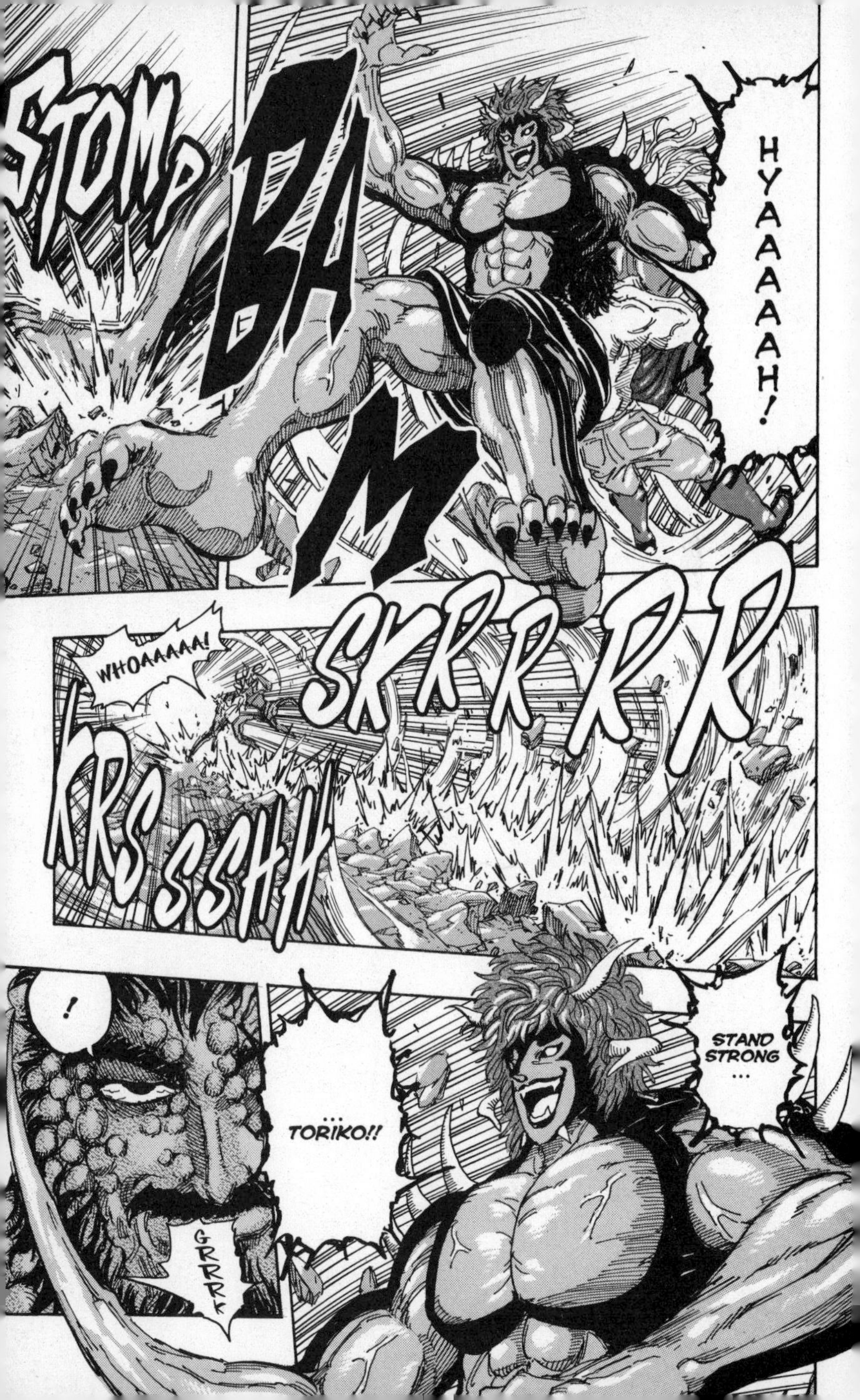
HYAAAAAAH!
BAM
STOMP
SKRRRRR
WHOAAAAA!
KRSSSHH
STAND STRONG...
...TORIKO!!
!
GRRRRK

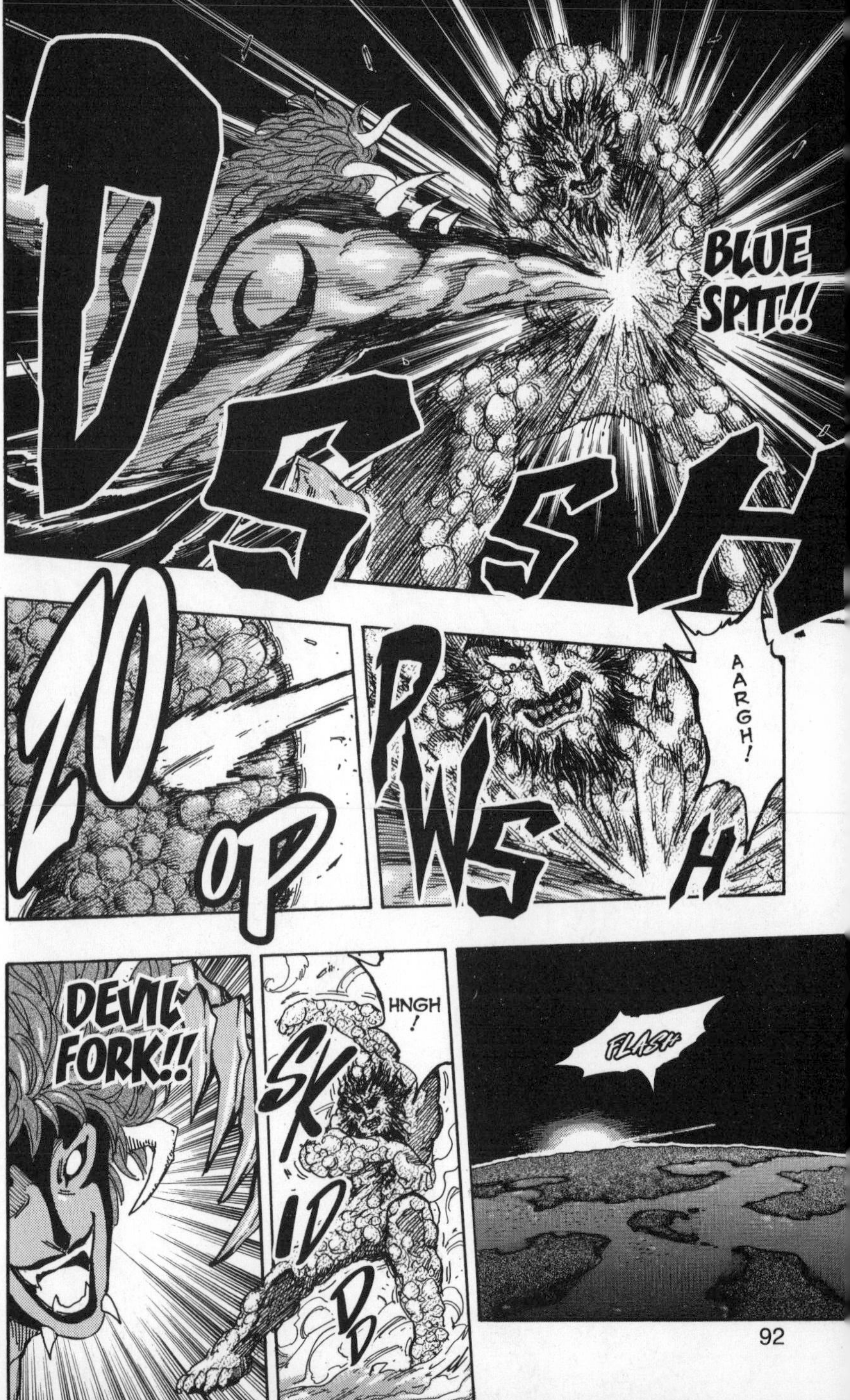
DSSH
BLUE SPIT!!
AARGH!
PWSH
ZOOP
FLASH
HNGH!
SKIDD
DEVIL FORK!!

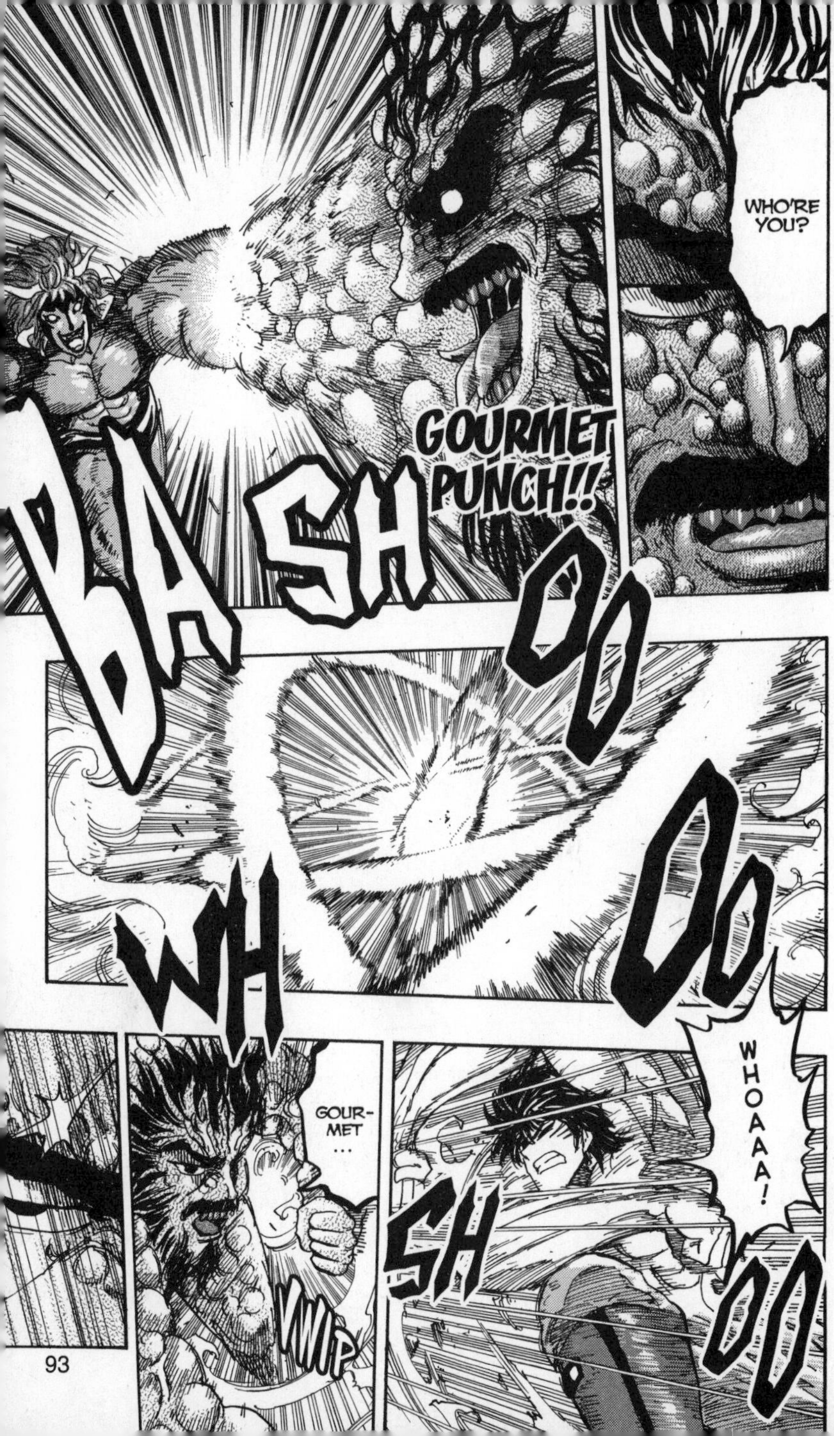
WHO'RE YOU?
GOURMET PUNCH!!
BASH
WHOOOO
WHOAAA!
SHOOO
GOURMET...
VWIP

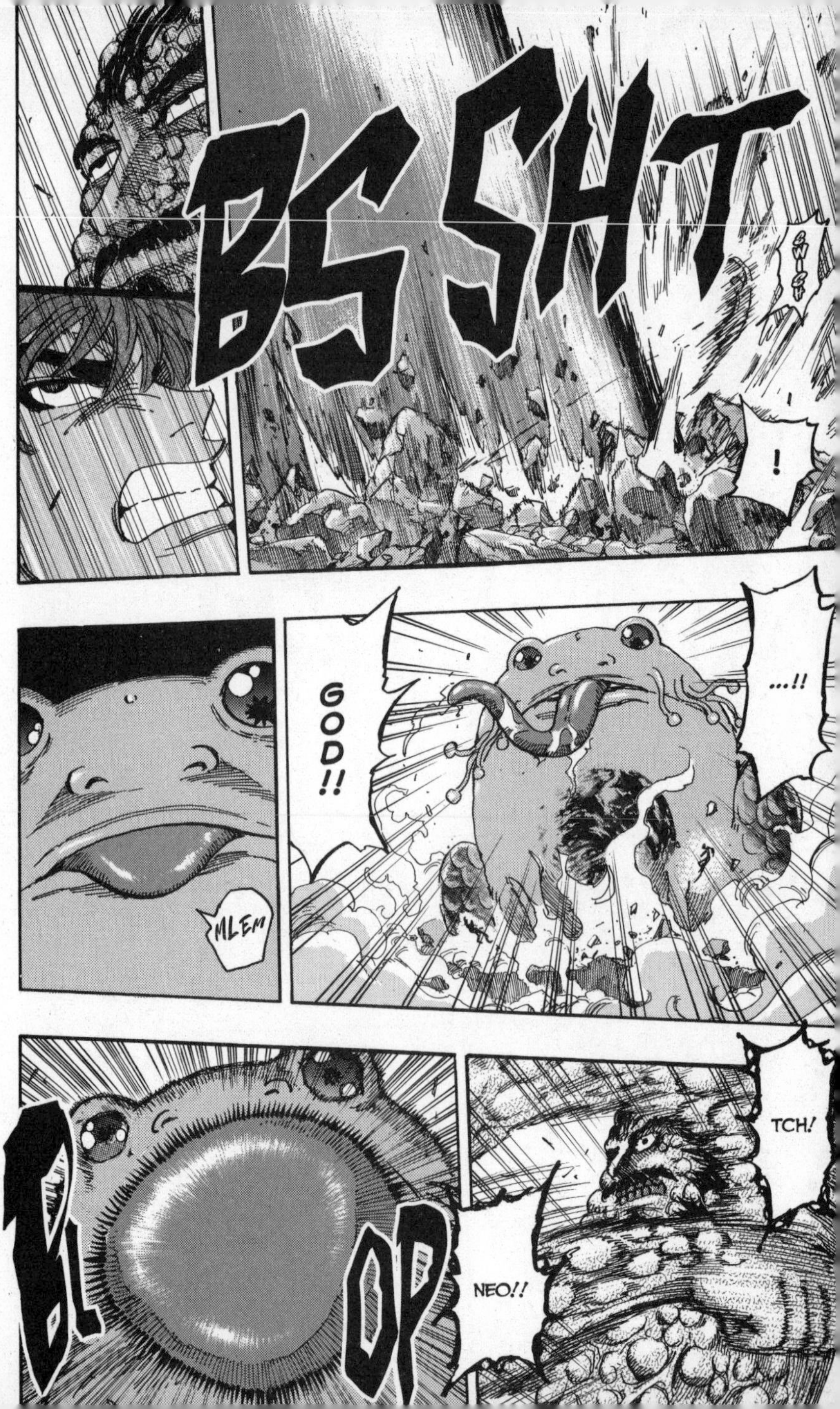
BSSHT
SWISH
!
...!!
GOD!!
MLEM
TCH!
NEO!!
BL
OP

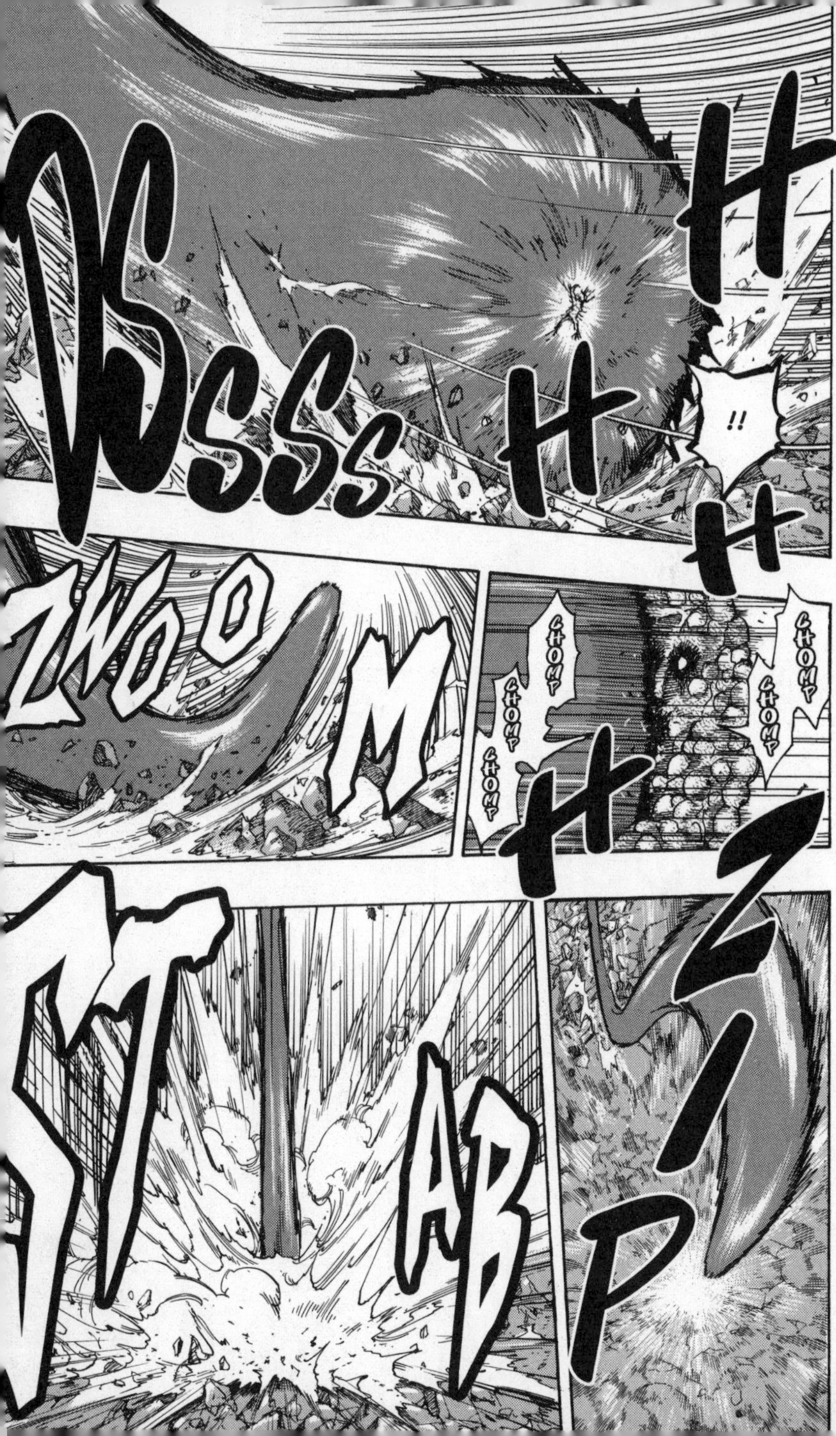
DSSSHHHH
!!
CHOMP
CHOMP
CHOMP
CHOMP
ZWOOOM
STAB

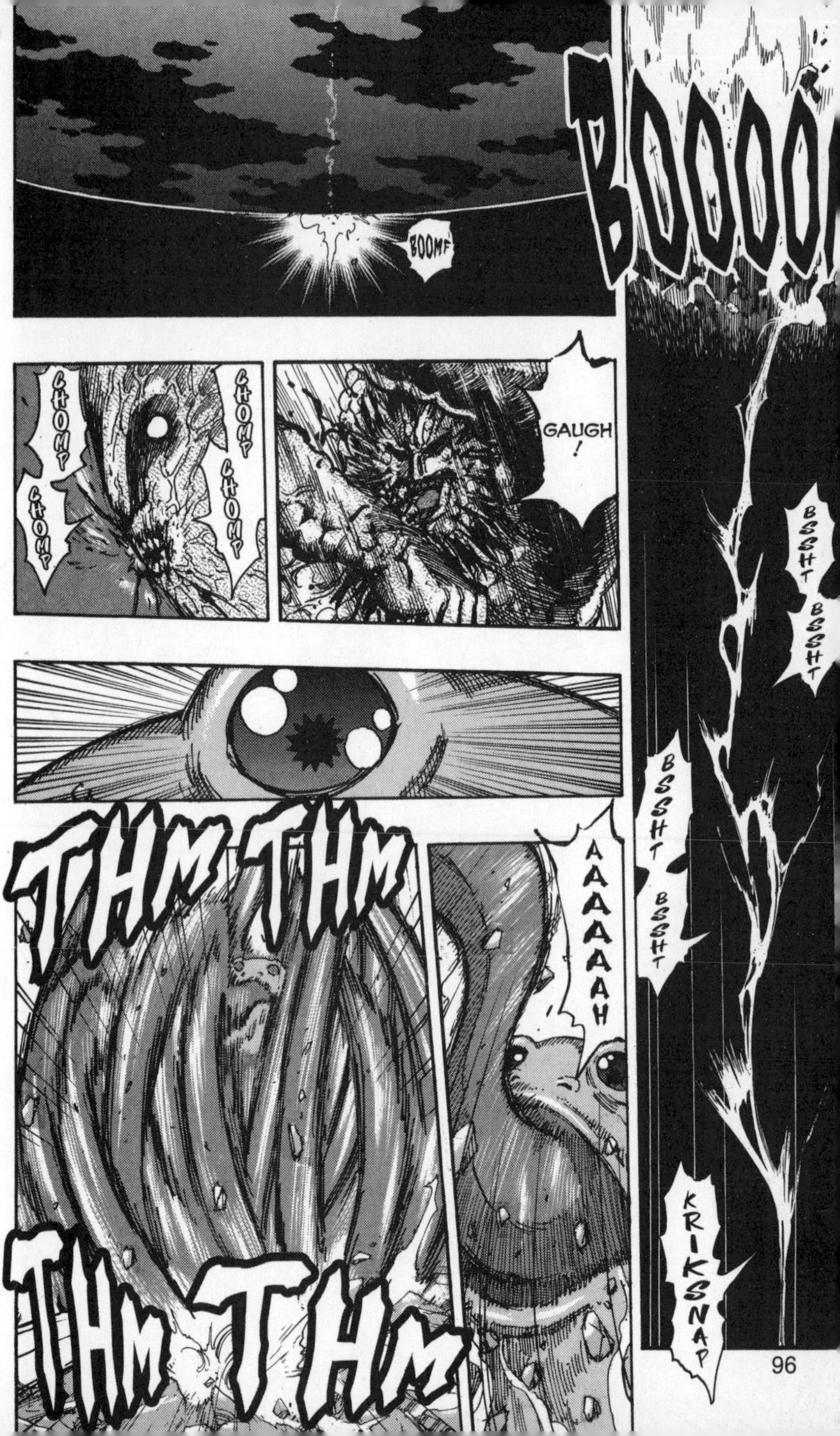

BOOOO
BSSHT BSSHT
BSSHT BSSHT
KRIKSNAP
BOOMF
GAUGH!
CHOMP CHOMP
CHOMP CHOMP
AAAAAAH
THM THM
THM THM

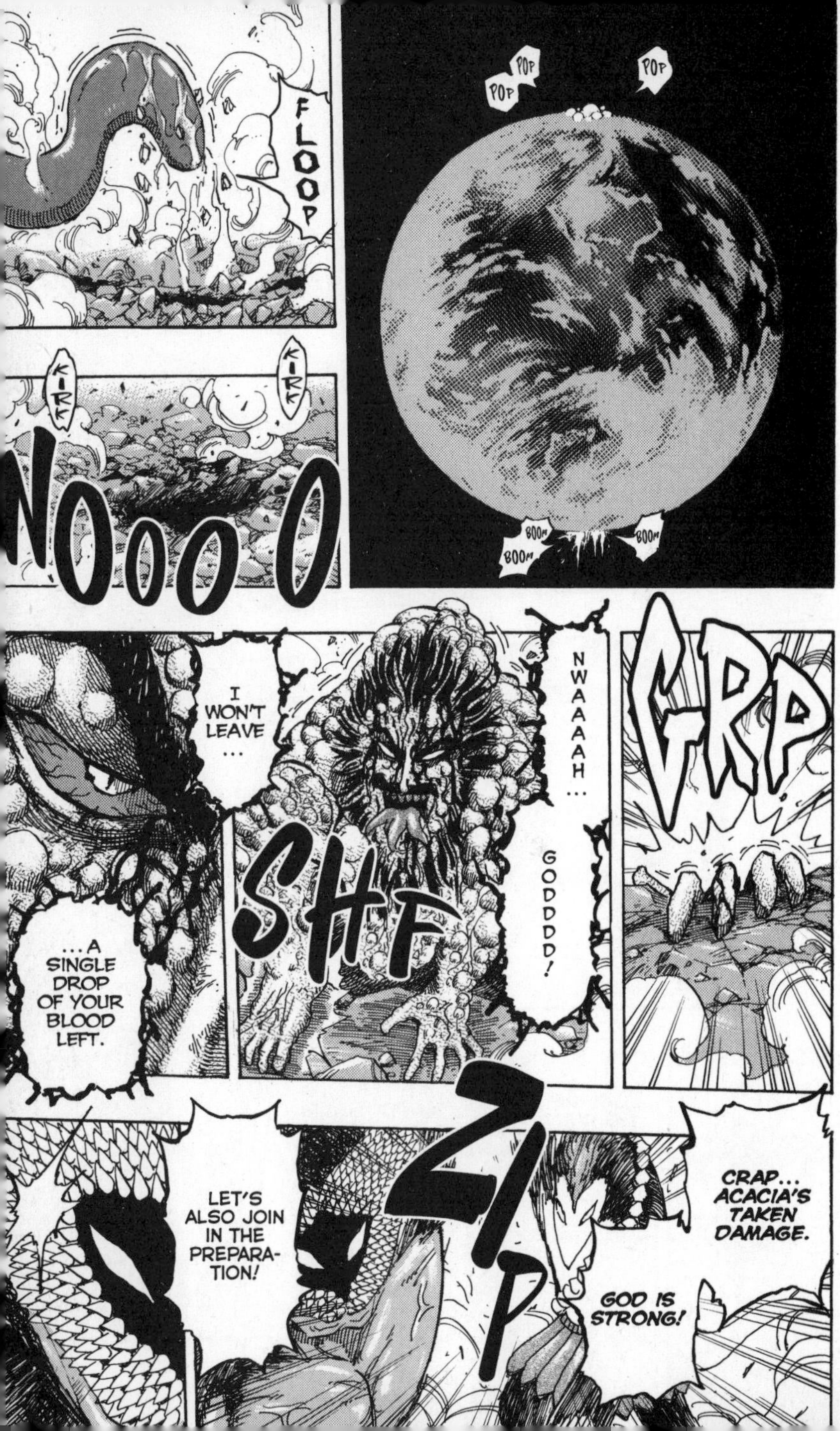
POP
POP
POP
BOOM
BOOM
BOOM
FLOOP
KIRK
KIRK
NOOOO
CRP
NWAAAAH... GODDDDD!
I WON'T LEAVE...
SHF
...A SINGLE DROP OF YOUR BLOOD LEFT.
CRAP... ACACIA'S TAKEN DAMAGE.
GOD IS STRONG!
ZIP
LET'S ALSO JOIN IN THE PREPARATION!

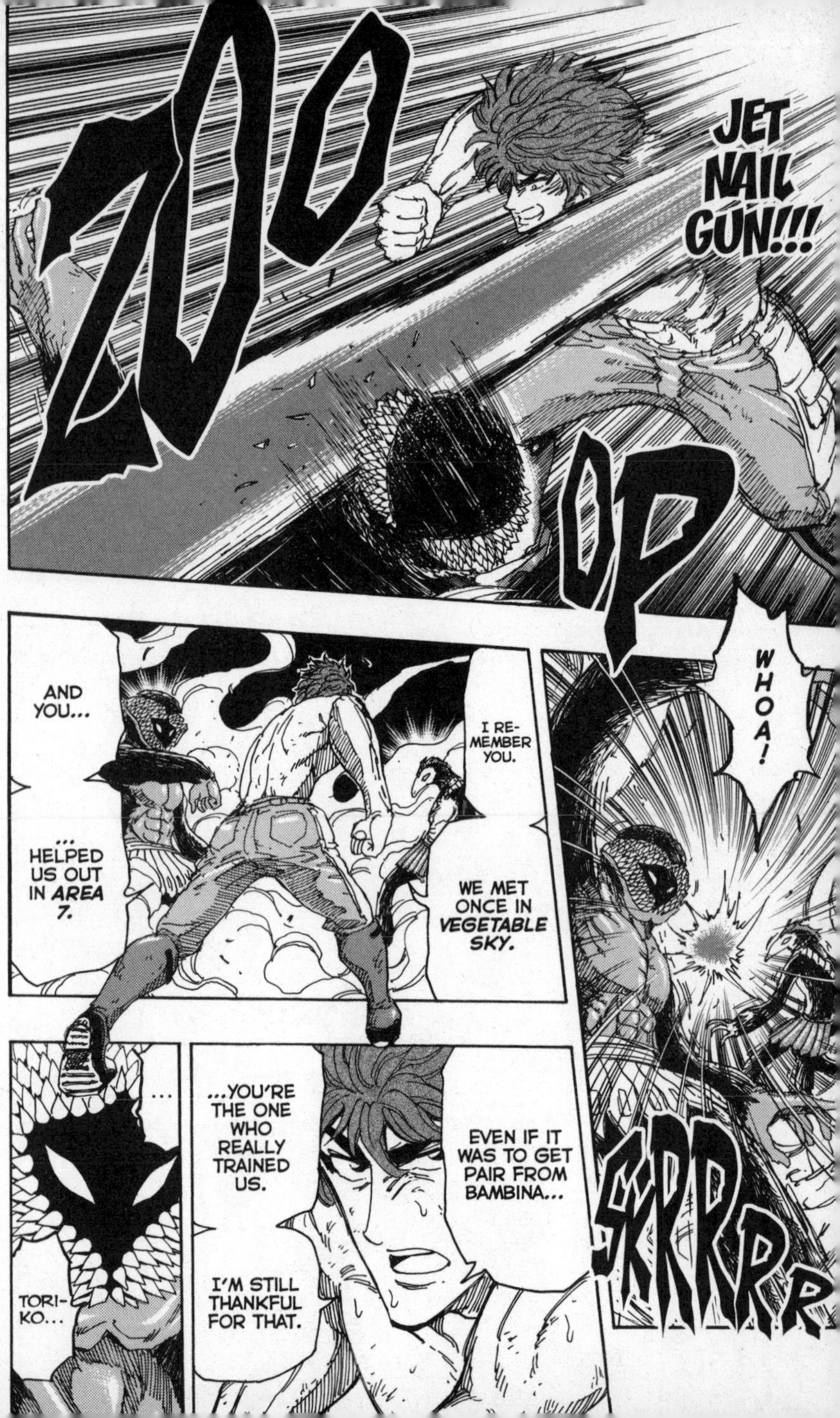
JET NAIL GUN!!!
ZOOOP
WHOA!
SKRRRR
I RE-MEMBER YOU.
WE MET ONCE IN *VEGETABLE SKY.*
AND YOU...
...HELPED US OUT IN *AREA 7.*
EVEN IF IT WAS TO GET PAIR FROM BAMBINA...
...YOU'RE THE ONE WHO REALLY TRAINED US.
I'M STILL THANKFUL FOR THAT.
...
TORI-KO...

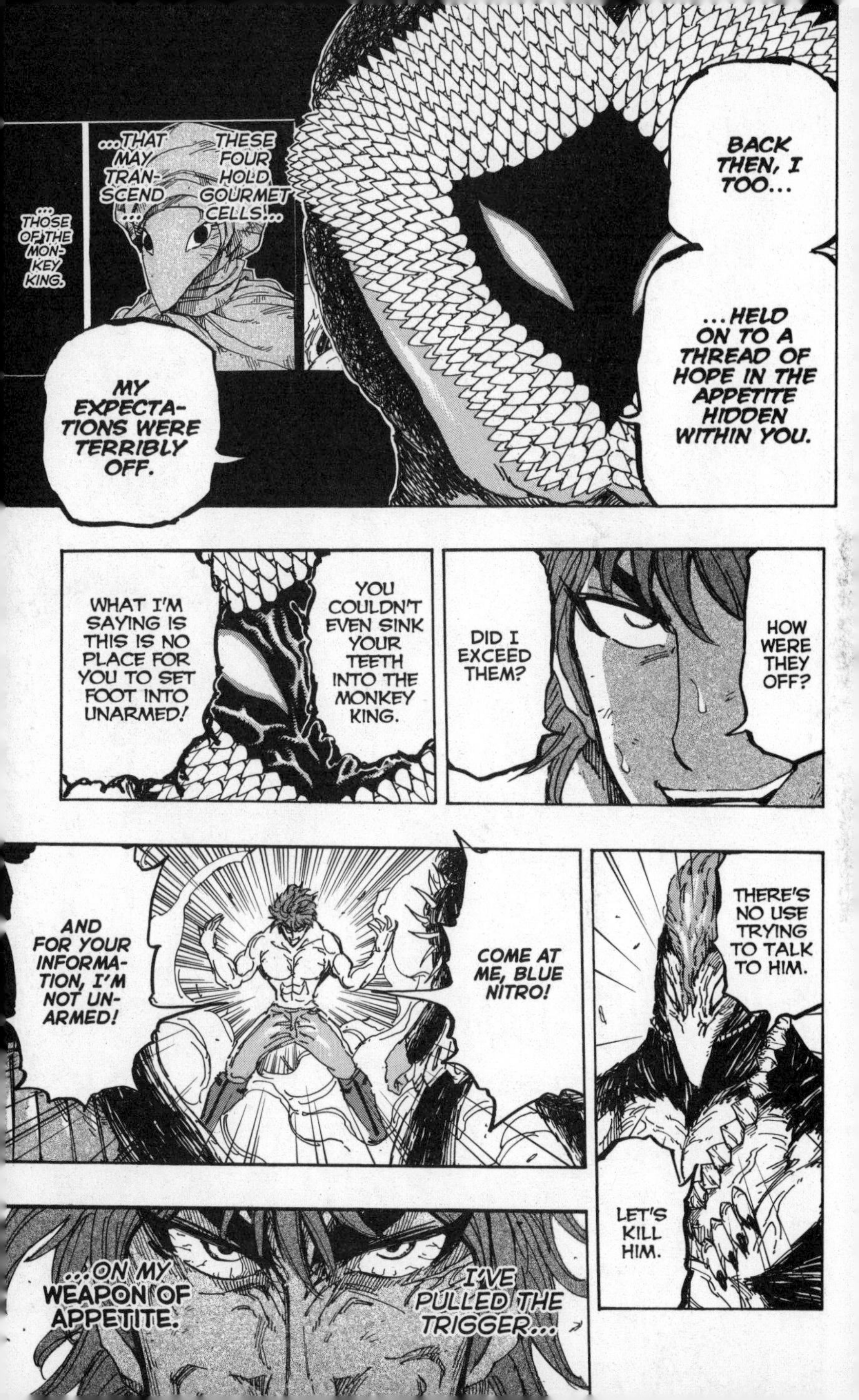
BACK THEN, I TOO...
...HELD ON TO A THREAD OF HOPE IN THE APPETITE HIDDEN WITHIN YOU.
THESE FOUR HOLD GOURMET CELLS...
...THAT MAY TRANSCEND...
...THOSE OF THE MONKEY KING.
MY EXPECTATIONS WERE TERRIBLY OFF.
HOW WERE THEY OFF?
DID I EXCEED THEM?
YOU COULDN'T EVEN SINK YOUR TEETH INTO THE MONKEY KING.
WHAT I'M SAYING IS THIS IS NO PLACE FOR YOU TO SET FOOT INTO UNARMED!
THERE'S NO USE TRYING TO TALK TO HIM.
LET'S KILL HIM.
COME AT ME, BLUE NITRO!
AND FOR YOUR INFORMATION, I'M NOT UNARMED!
I'VE PULLED THE TRIGGER...
...ON MY WEAPON OF APPETITE.

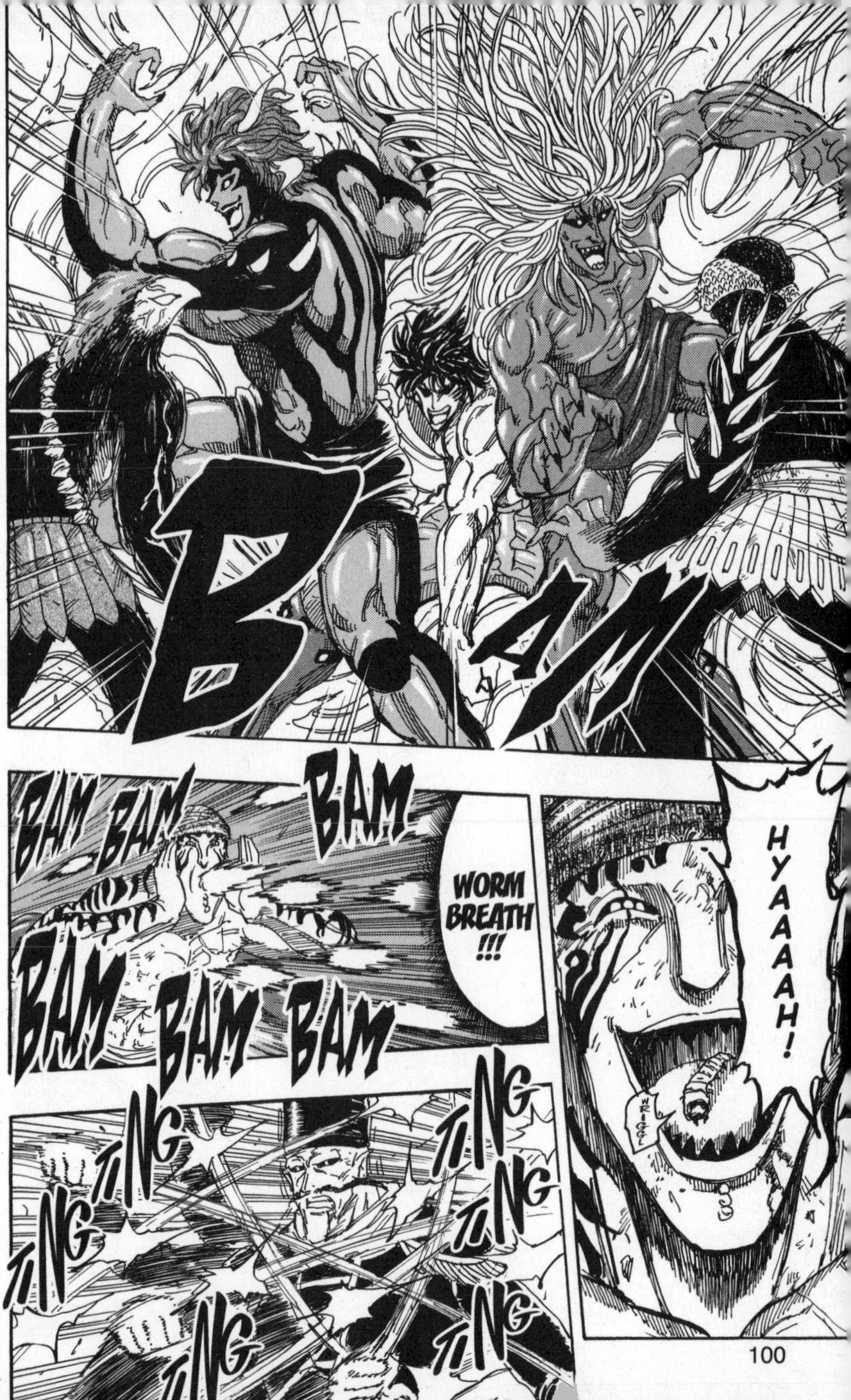
BAM
HYAAAAH!
WRIGGL
BAM BAM BAM
WORM BREATH!!!
BAM BAM BAM BAM
TING TING TING TING TING TING TING

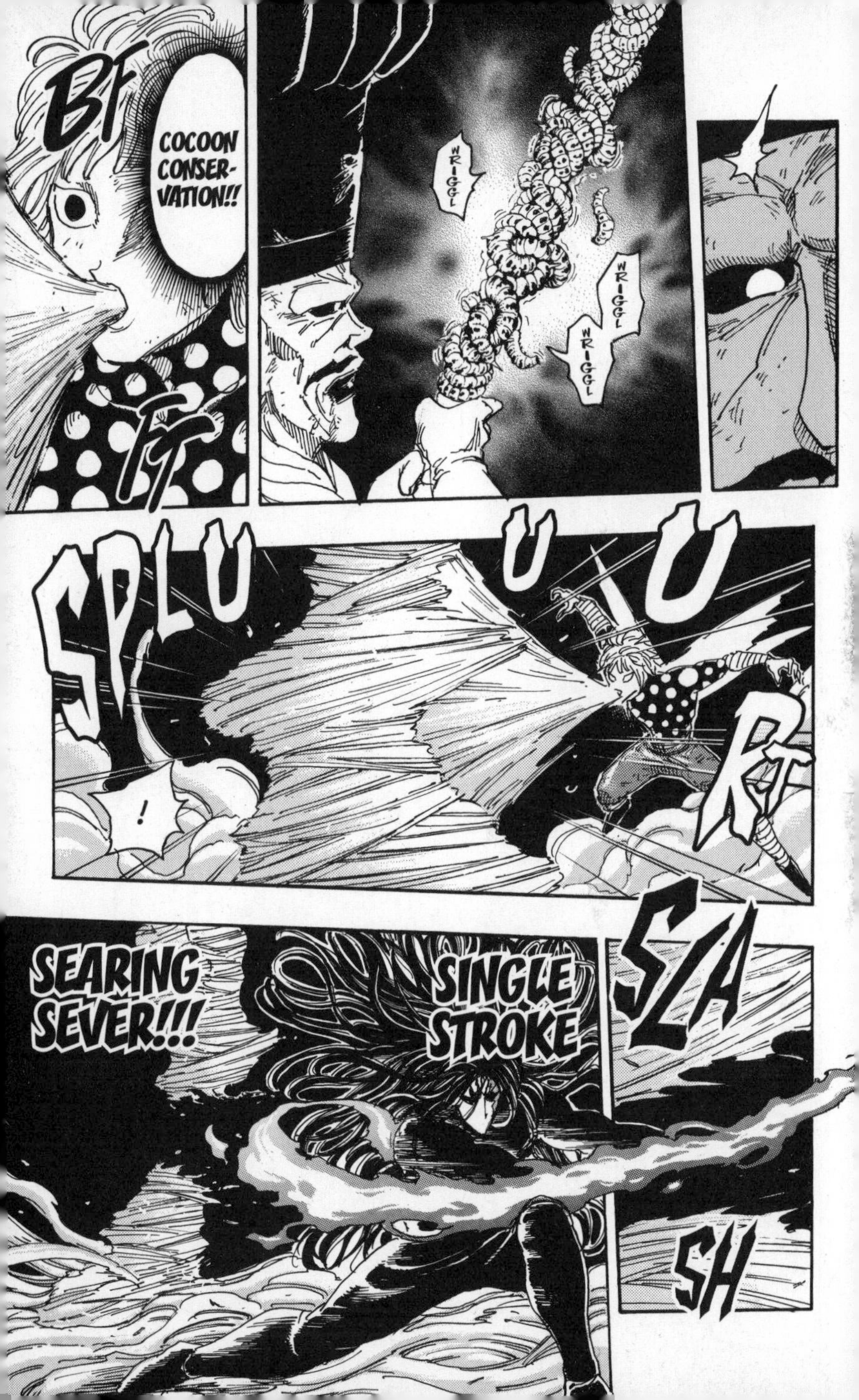

WRIGGL
WRIGGL
WRIGGL
BF
COCOON CONSERVATION!!
FT
SPLUUURT
!
SA
SH
SINGLE STROKE
SEARING SEVER!!!

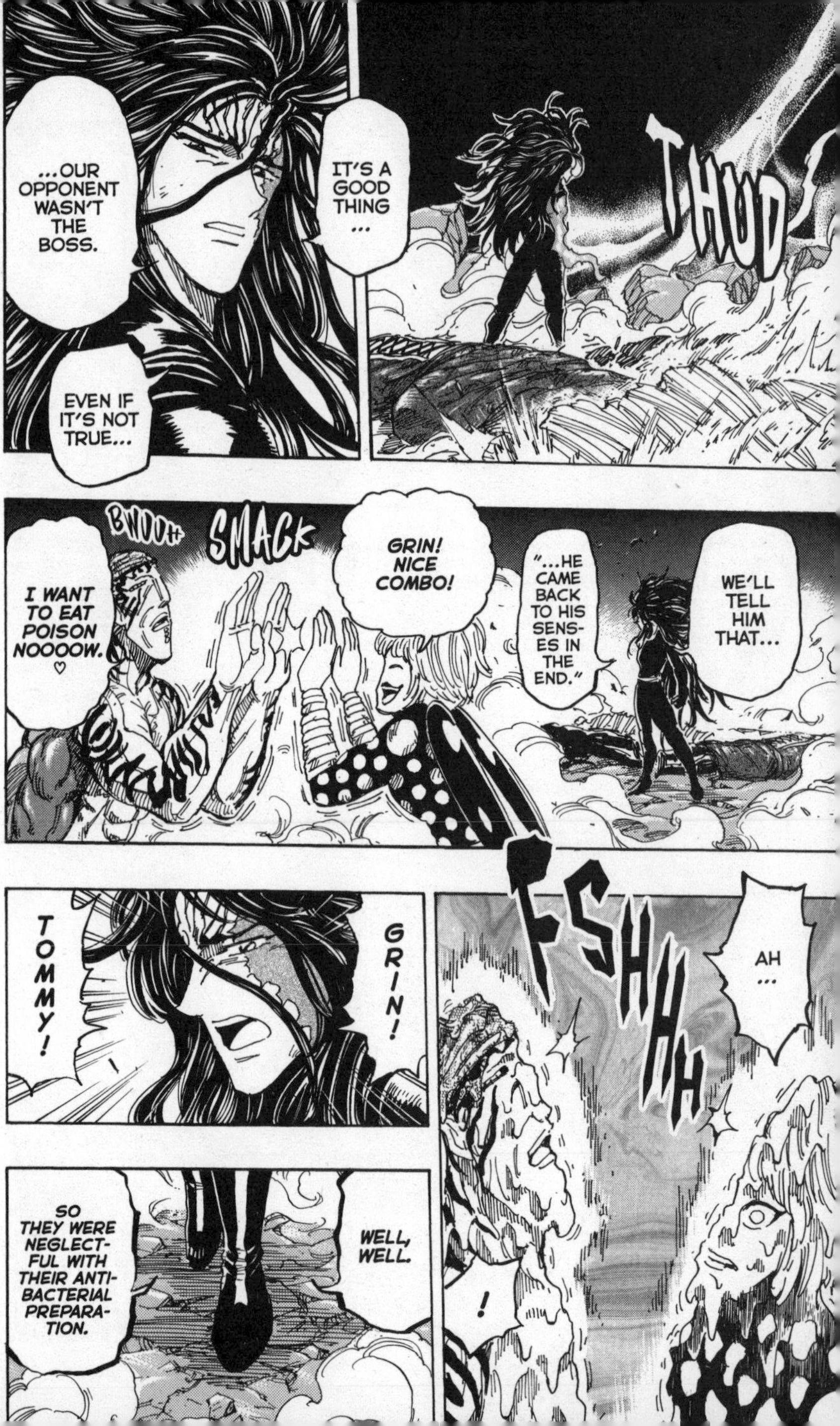
THUD
IT'S A GOOD THING ...
...OUR OPPONENT WASN'T THE BOSS.
EVEN IF IT'S NOT TRUE...
WE'LL TELL HIM THAT...
"...HE CAME BACK TO HIS SENSES IN THE END."
GRIN! NICE COMBO!
SMACK
BWOOH
I WANT TO EAT POISON NOOOOW. ♡
FSHHH
AH ...
!
GRIN!
TOMMY!
WELL, WELL.
SO THEY WERE NEGLECTFUL WITH THEIR ANTIBACTERIAL PREPARATION.

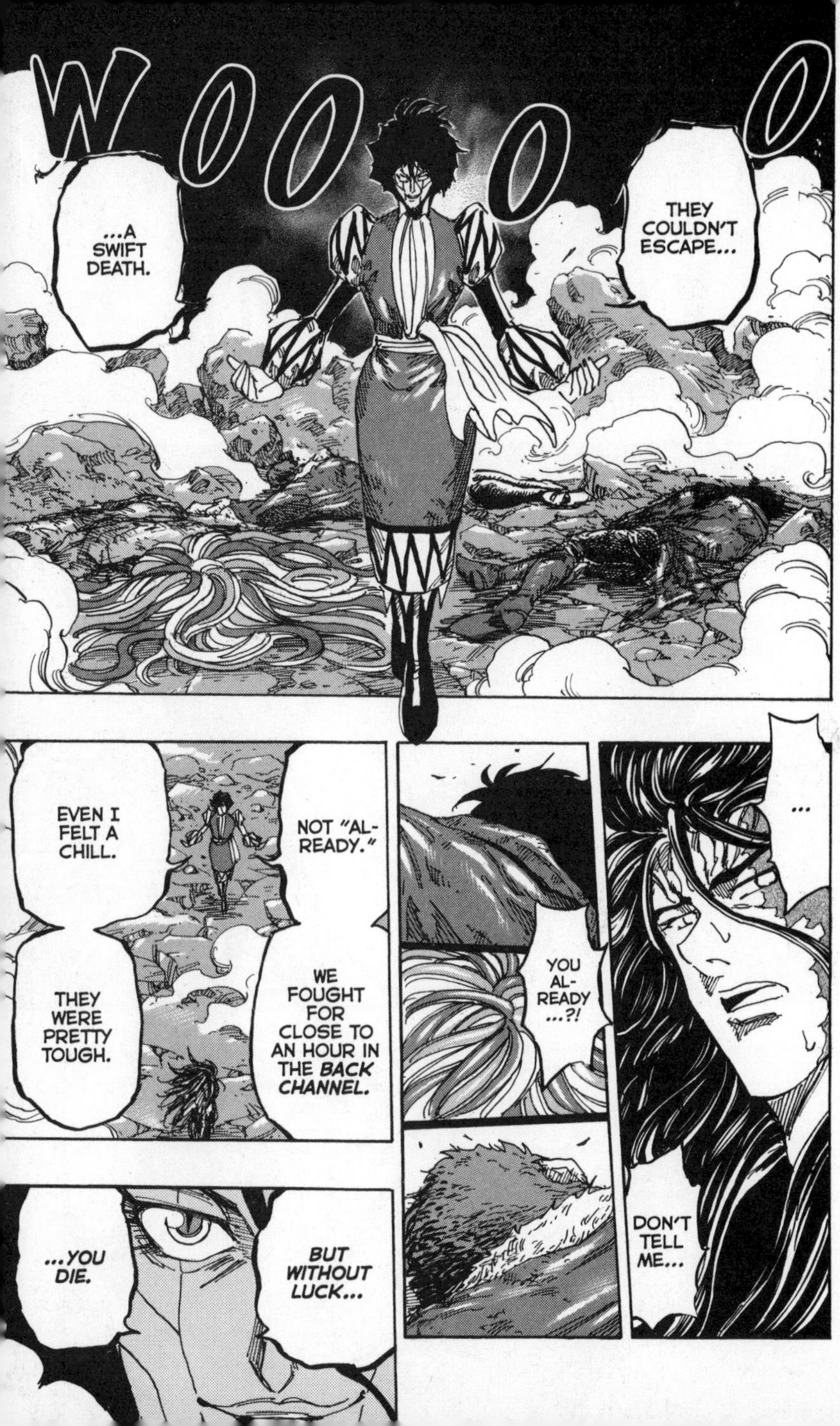
WOOOOO
THEY COULDN'T ESCAPE...
...A SWIFT DEATH.
...
YOU AL-READY ...?!
DON'T TELL ME...
NOT "AL-READY."
WE FOUGHT FOR CLOSE TO AN HOUR IN THE *BACK CHANNEL*.
EVEN I FELT A CHILL.
THEY WERE PRETTY TOUGH.
BUT WITHOUT LUCK...
...YOU DIE.

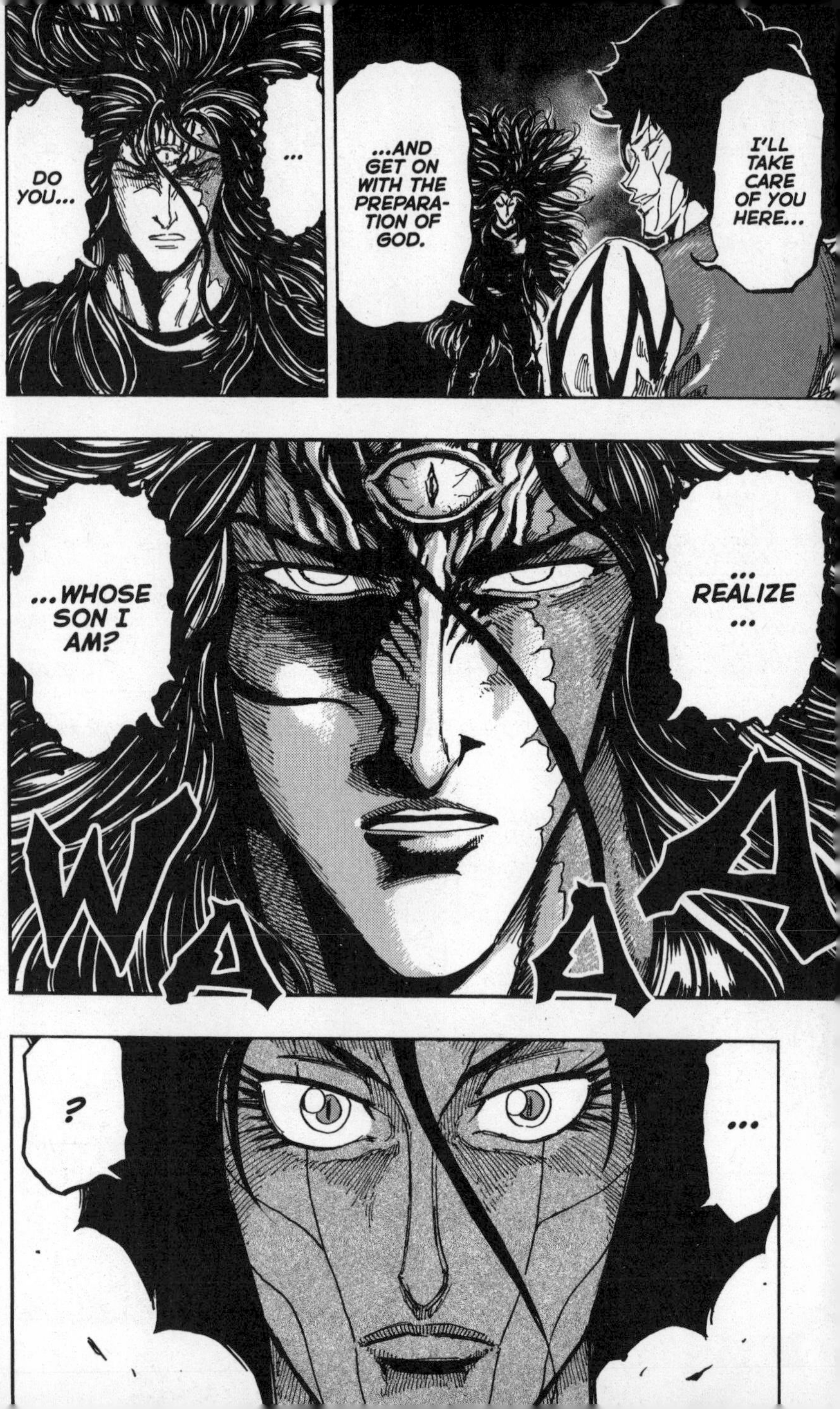
I'LL TAKE CARE OF YOU HERE...
...AND GET ON WITH THE PREPARATION OF GOD.
...
DO YOU...
... REALIZE ...
...WHOSE SON I AM?
WAAA
...
?

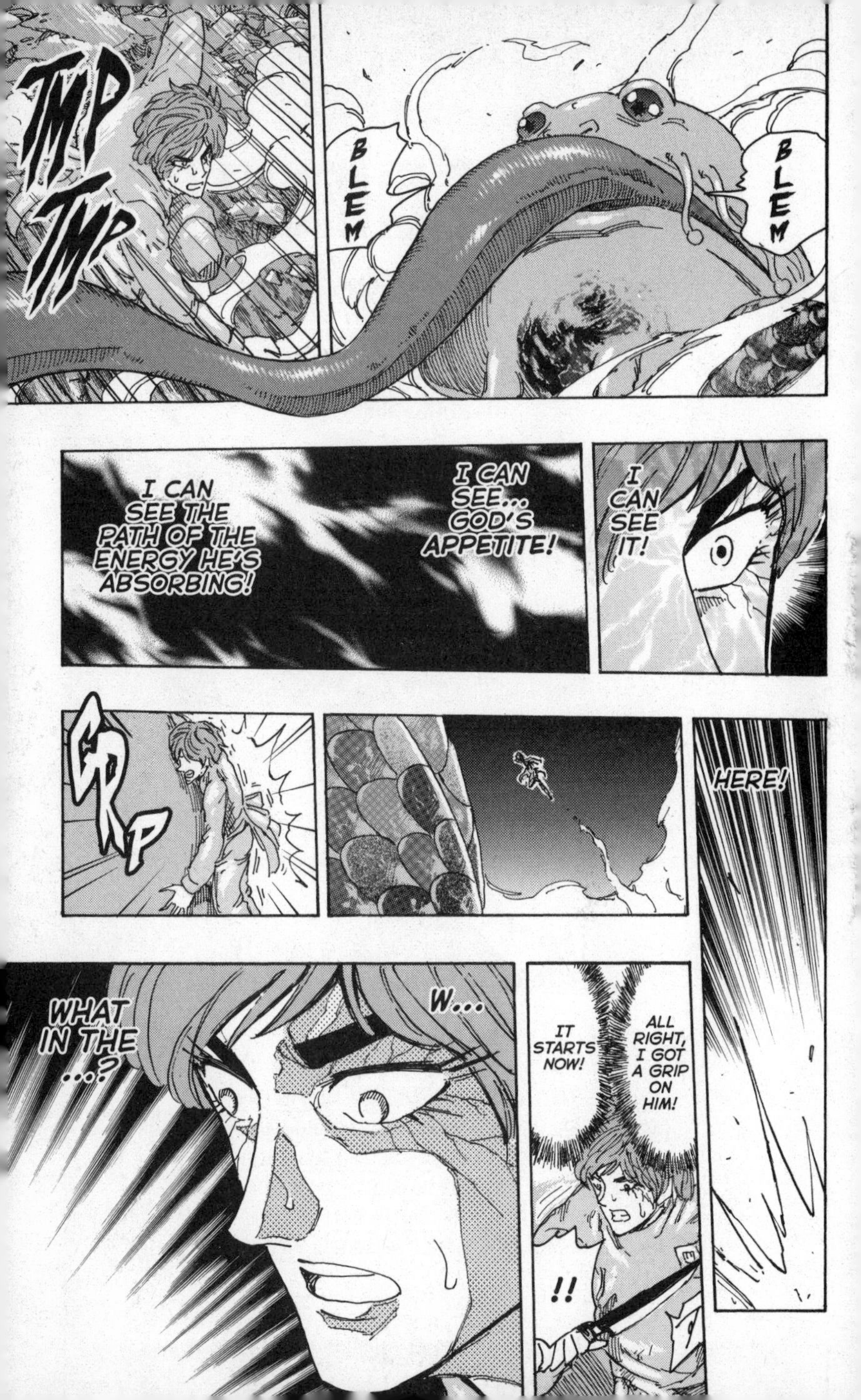
BLEM
BLEM
TMP TMP
I CAN SEE IT!
I CAN SEE... GOD'S APPETITE!
I CAN SEE THE PATH OF THE ENERGY HE'S ABSORBING!
HERE!
GRIP
ALL RIGHT, I GOT A GRIP ON HIM!
IT STARTS NOW!
!!
W...
WHAT IN THE ...?

TORIKO

GOURMET CHECKLIST

Vol. 406

ANOTHER
(FISH TREASURE)

CAPTURE LEVEL: 7,800
HABITAT: GOURMET WORLD: AREA 6
SIZE: 12 M
HEIGHT: ---
WEIGHT: 25 TONS
PRICE: 80 MILLION YEN PER 100 GRAMS

SCALE

THE FISH TREASURE IN ACACIA'S FULL-COURSE MEAL. ALL OF THE FLAVORS THAT FLOW THROUGHOUT THE ENTIRETY OF THE GOURMET WORLD'S OCEANS WERE BIRTHED BY ANOTHER AND, BY EATING ANOTHER, THEY SAY IT WILL AWAKEN A NEW SENSE OF TASTE. IT TAKES 600,000 YEARS TO PREPARE ANOTHER AND IT'S ONE OF THE HARDEST INGREDIENTS TO PREPARE IN ACACIA'S FULL-COURSE MEAL. KOMATSU WAS ABLE TO PREPARE IT IN THE RECORD TIME OF 65 YEARS.

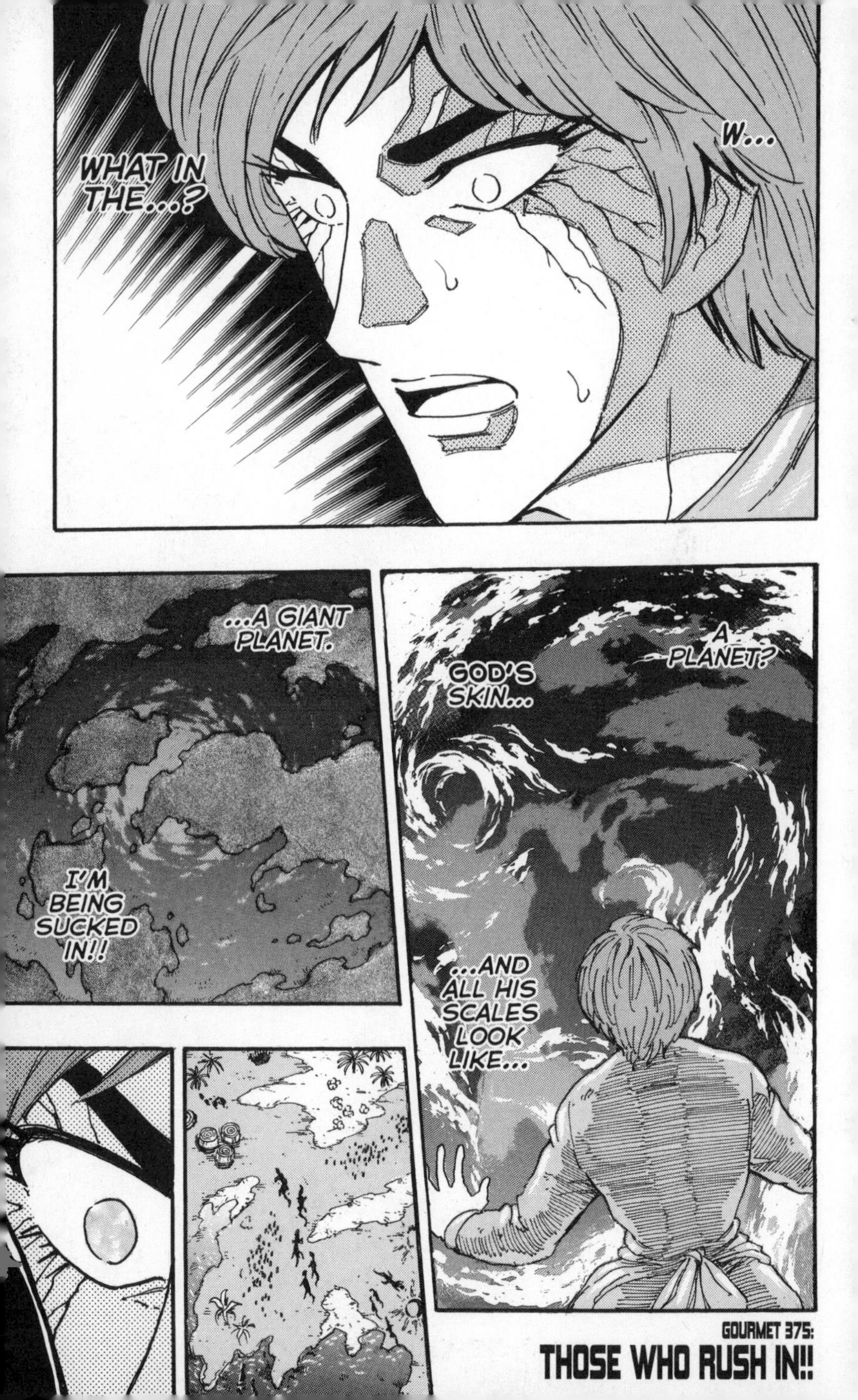
W...
WHAT IN THE...?
A PLANET?
GOD'S SKIN...
...AND ALL HIS SCALES LOOK LIKE...
...A GIANT PLANET.
I'M BEING SUCKED IN!!

GOURMET 375:

THOSE WHO RUSH IN!!

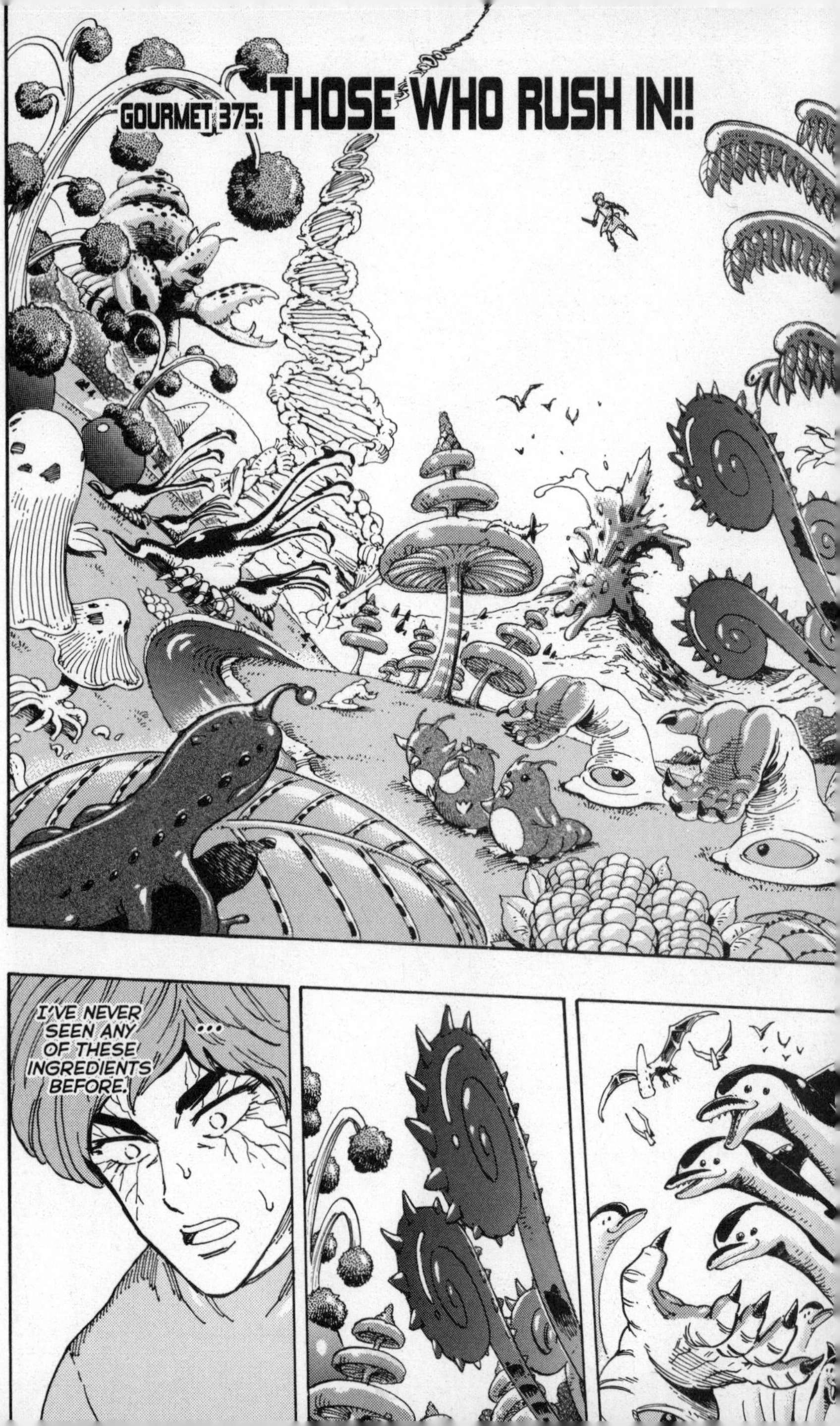
GOURMET 375: THOSE WHO RUSH IN!!
...
I'VE NEVER SEEN ANY OF THESE INGREDIENTS BEFORE.

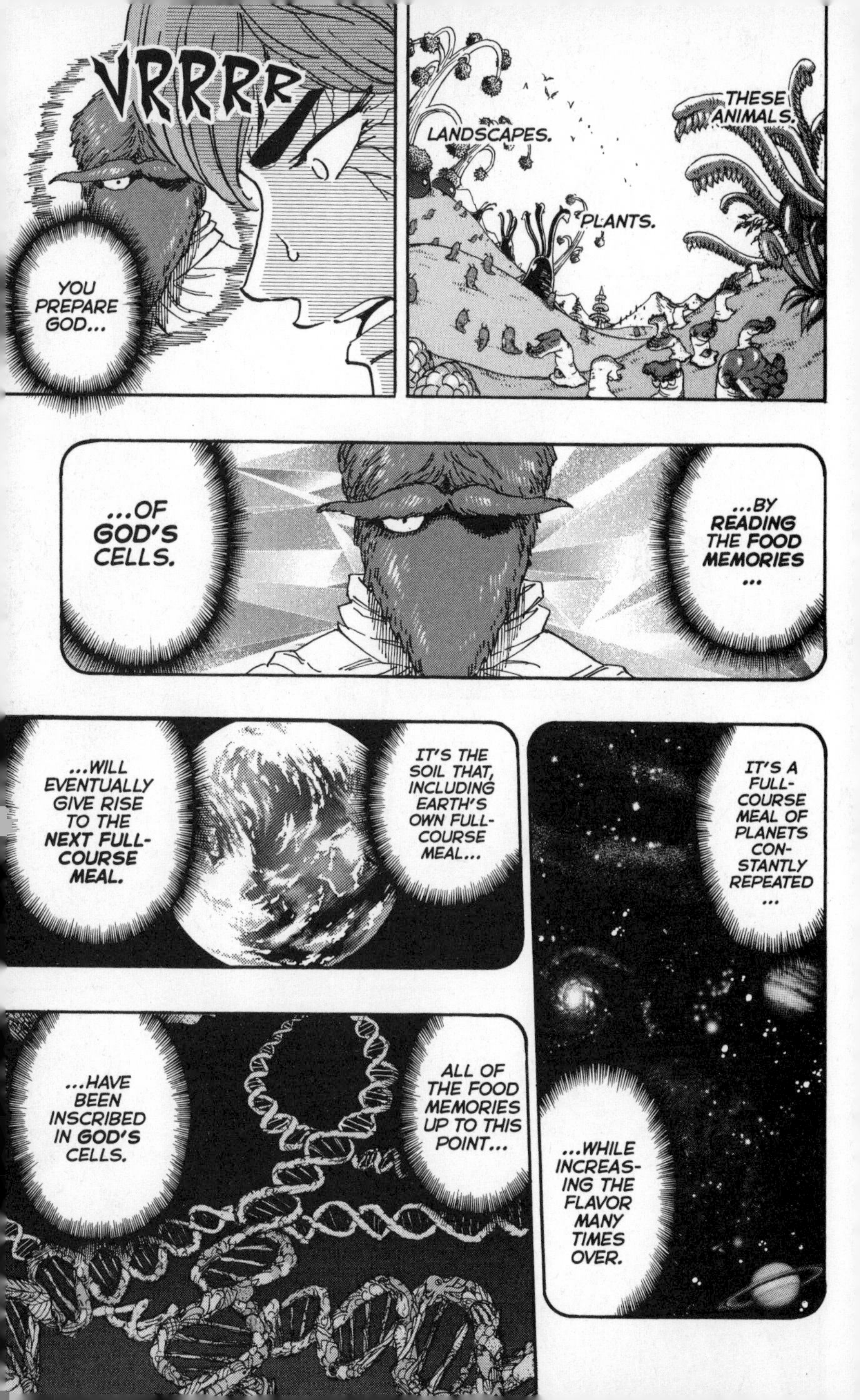
THESE ANIMALS.
LANDSCAPES.
PLANTS.
VRRRR
YOU PREPARE GOD...
...BY READING THE FOOD MEMORIES...
...OF GOD'S CELLS.
IT'S A FULL-COURSE MEAL OF PLANETS CON-STANTLY REPEATED...
...WHILE INCREAS-ING THE FLAVOR MANY TIMES OVER.
IT'S THE SOIL THAT, INCLUDING EARTH'S OWN FULL-COURSE MEAL...
...WILL EVENTUALLY GIVE RISE TO THE NEXT FULL-COURSE MEAL.
ALL OF THE FOOD MEMORIES UP TO THIS POINT...
...HAVE BEEN INSCRIBED IN GOD'S CELLS.

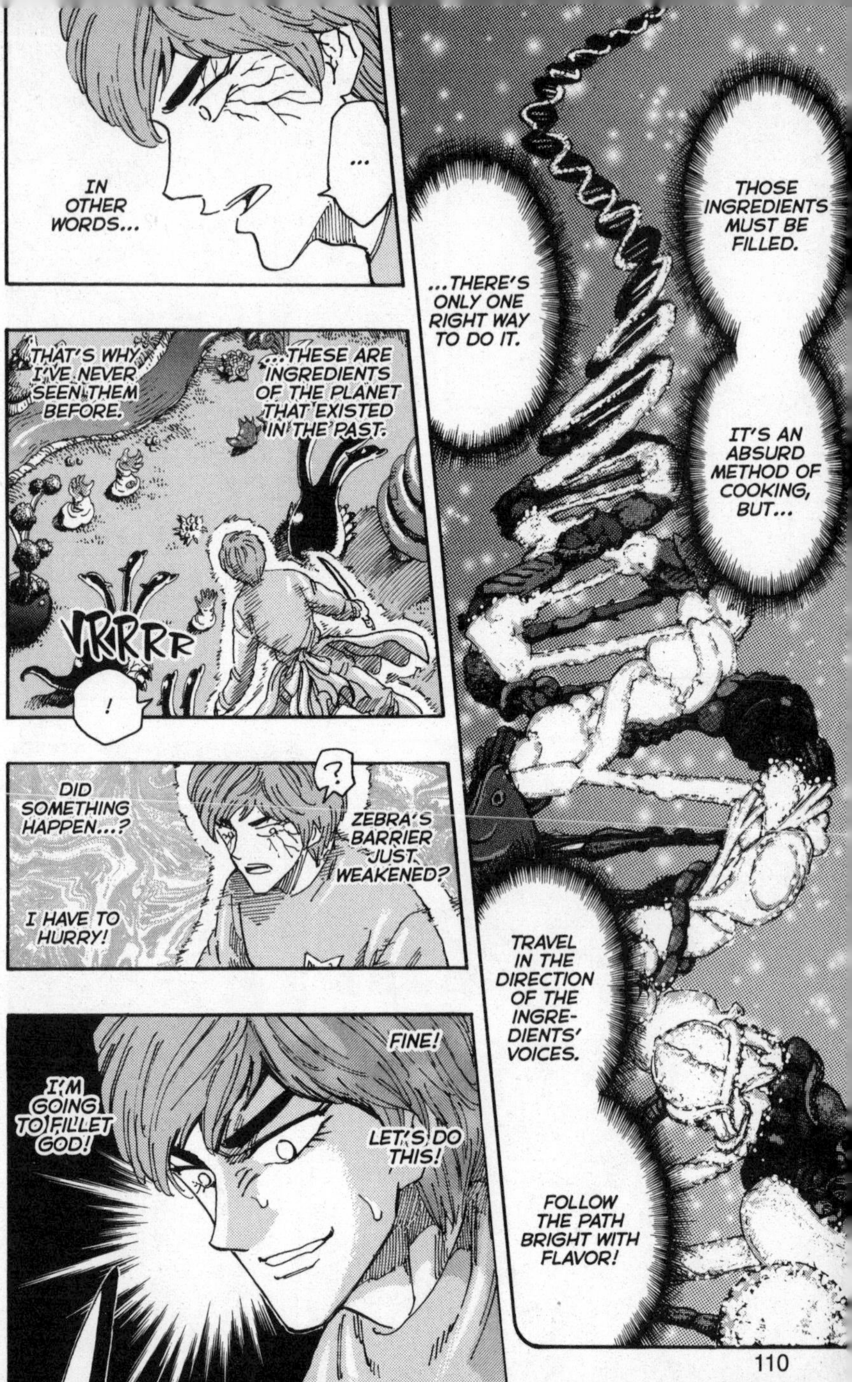
THOSE INGREDIENTS MUST BE FILLED.
...THERE'S ONLY ONE RIGHT WAY TO DO IT.
IT'S AN ABSURD METHOD OF COOKING, BUT...
TRAVEL IN THE DIRECTION OF THE INGRE-DIENTS' VOICES.
FOLLOW THE PATH BRIGHT WITH FLAVOR!
...
IN OTHER WORDS...
...THESE ARE INGREDIENTS OF THE PLANET THAT EXISTED IN THE PAST.
THAT'S WHY I'VE NEVER SEEN THEM BEFORE.
VRRRR
!
?
ZEBRA'S BARRIER JUST WEAKENED?
DID SOMETHING HAPPEN...?
I HAVE TO HURRY!
FINE!
LET'S DO THIS!
I'M GOING TO FILLET GOD!

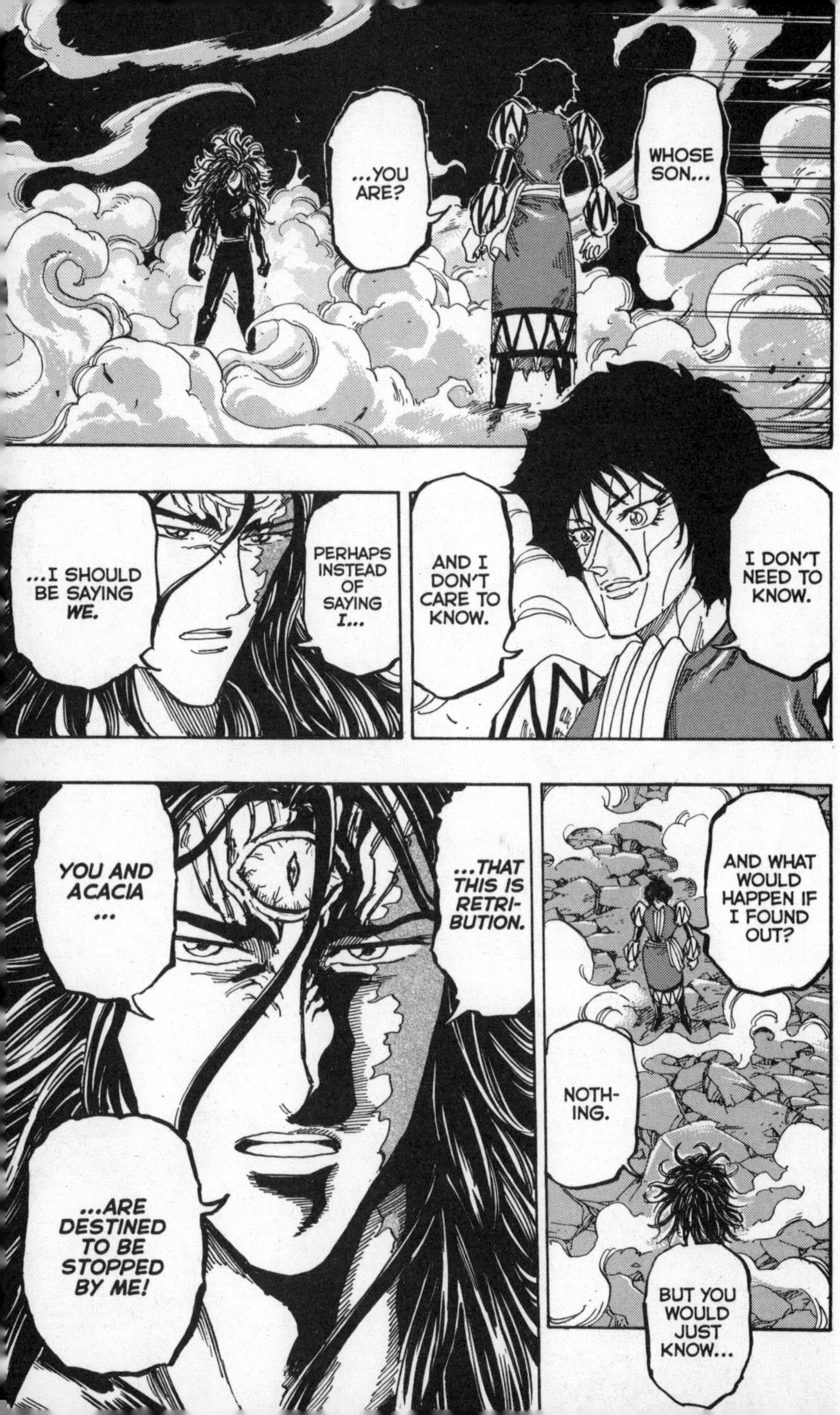
WHOSE SON...
...YOU ARE?
I DON'T NEED TO KNOW.
AND I DON'T CARE TO KNOW.
PERHAPS INSTEAD OF SAYING *I*...
...I SHOULD BE SAYING *WE*.
AND WHAT WOULD HAPPEN IF I FOUND OUT?
NOTH-ING.
BUT YOU WOULD JUST KNOW...
...THAT THIS IS RETRI-BUTION.
YOU AND ACACIA ...
...ARE DESTINED TO BE STOPPED BY ME!

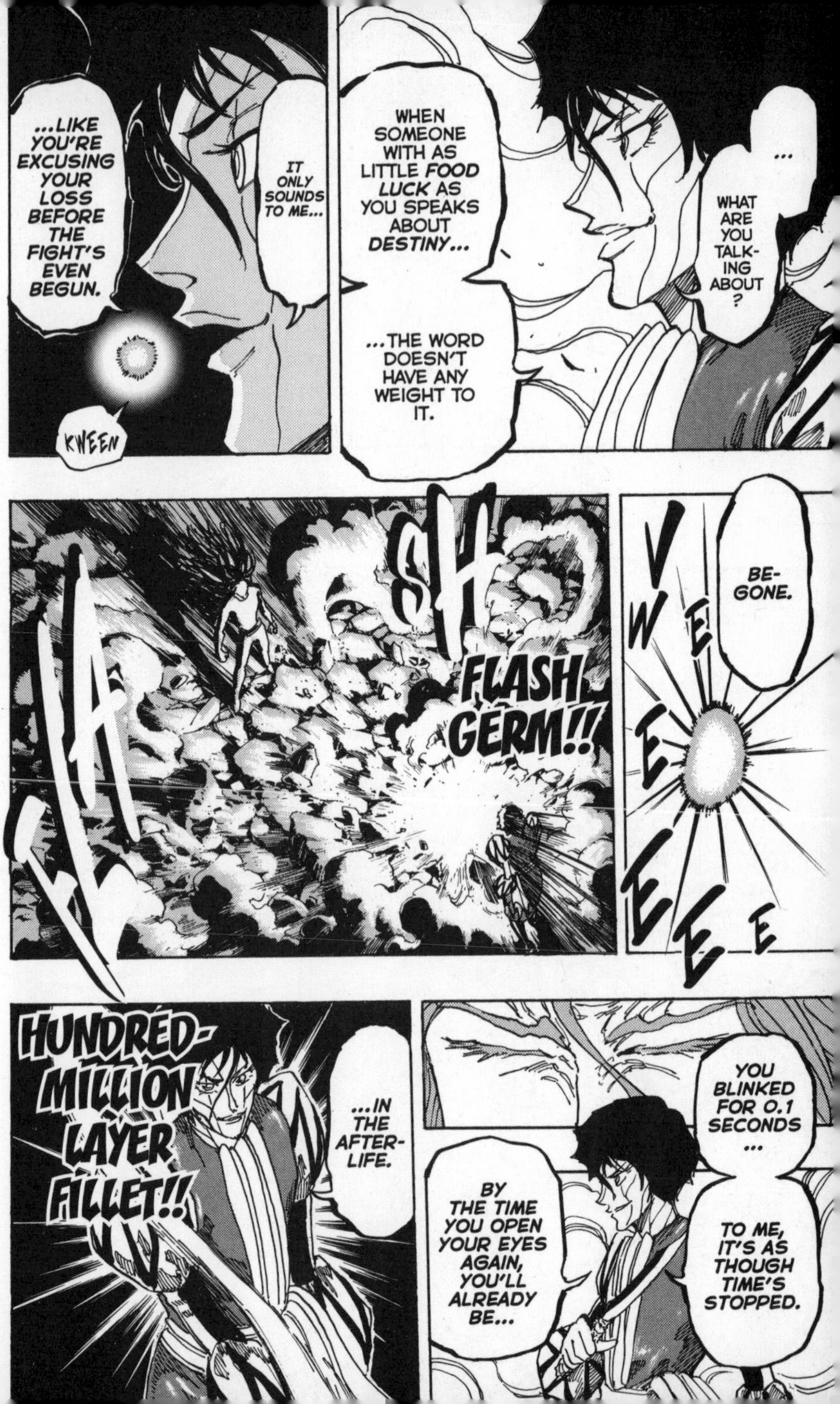
...
WHAT ARE YOU TALKING ABOUT?
WHEN SOMEONE WITH AS LITTLE *FOOD LUCK* AS YOU SPEAKS ABOUT *DESTINY*...
...THE WORD DOESN'T HAVE ANY WEIGHT TO IT.
IT ONLY SOUNDS TO ME...
...LIKE YOU'RE EXCUSING YOUR LOSS BEFORE THE FIGHT'S EVEN BEGUN.
KWEEN
BE-GONE.
VWEEEEEE
SH
FLASH GERM!!
YOU BLINKED FOR 0.1 SECONDS...
TO ME, IT'S AS THOUGH TIME'S STOPPED.
BY THE TIME YOU OPEN YOUR EYES AGAIN, YOU'LL ALREADY BE...
...IN THE AFTER-LIFE.
HUNDRED-MILLION LAYER FILLET!!

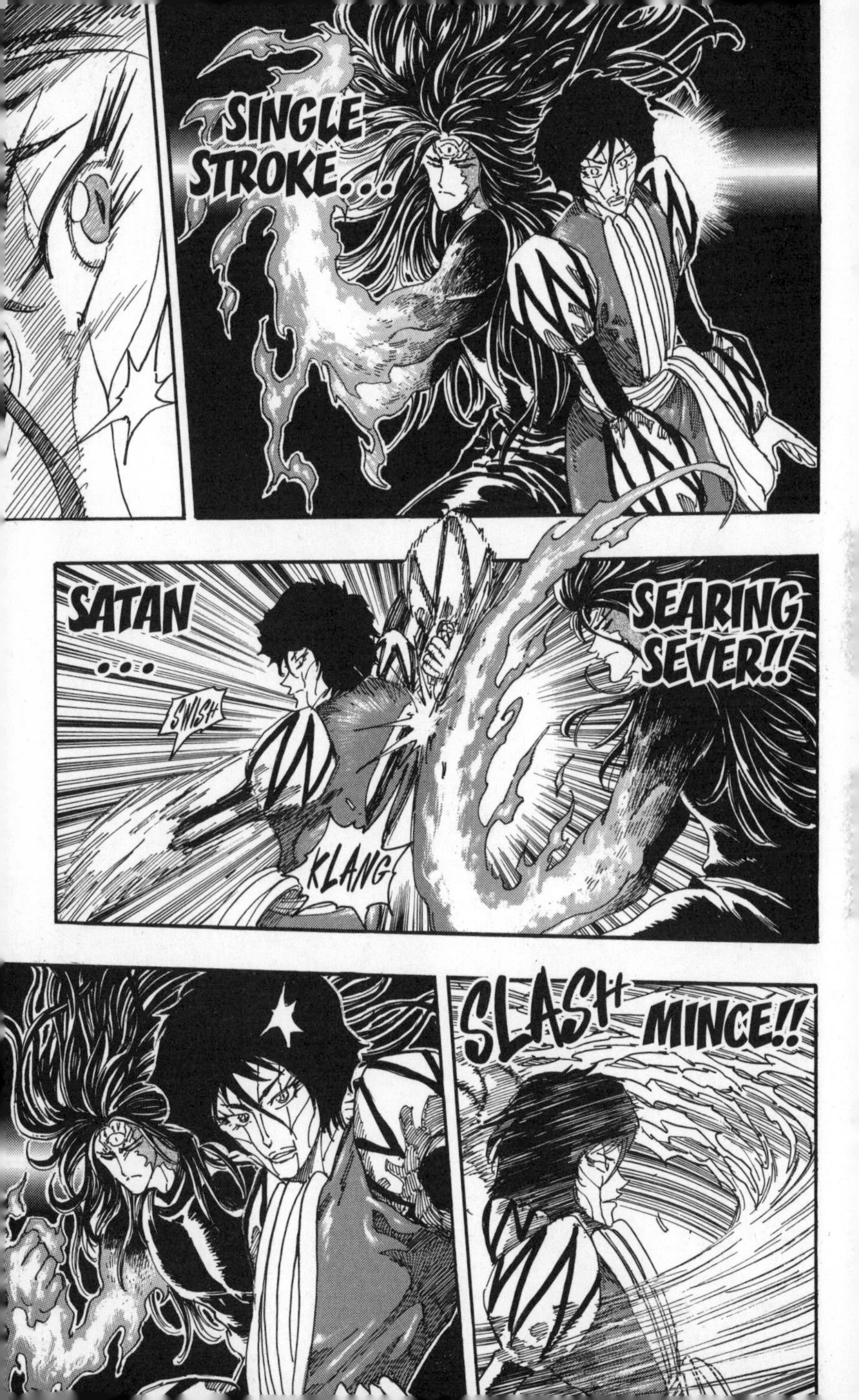
SINGLE STROKE...
SEARING SEVER!!
SATAN ...
SWISH
KLANG
MINCE!!
SLASH

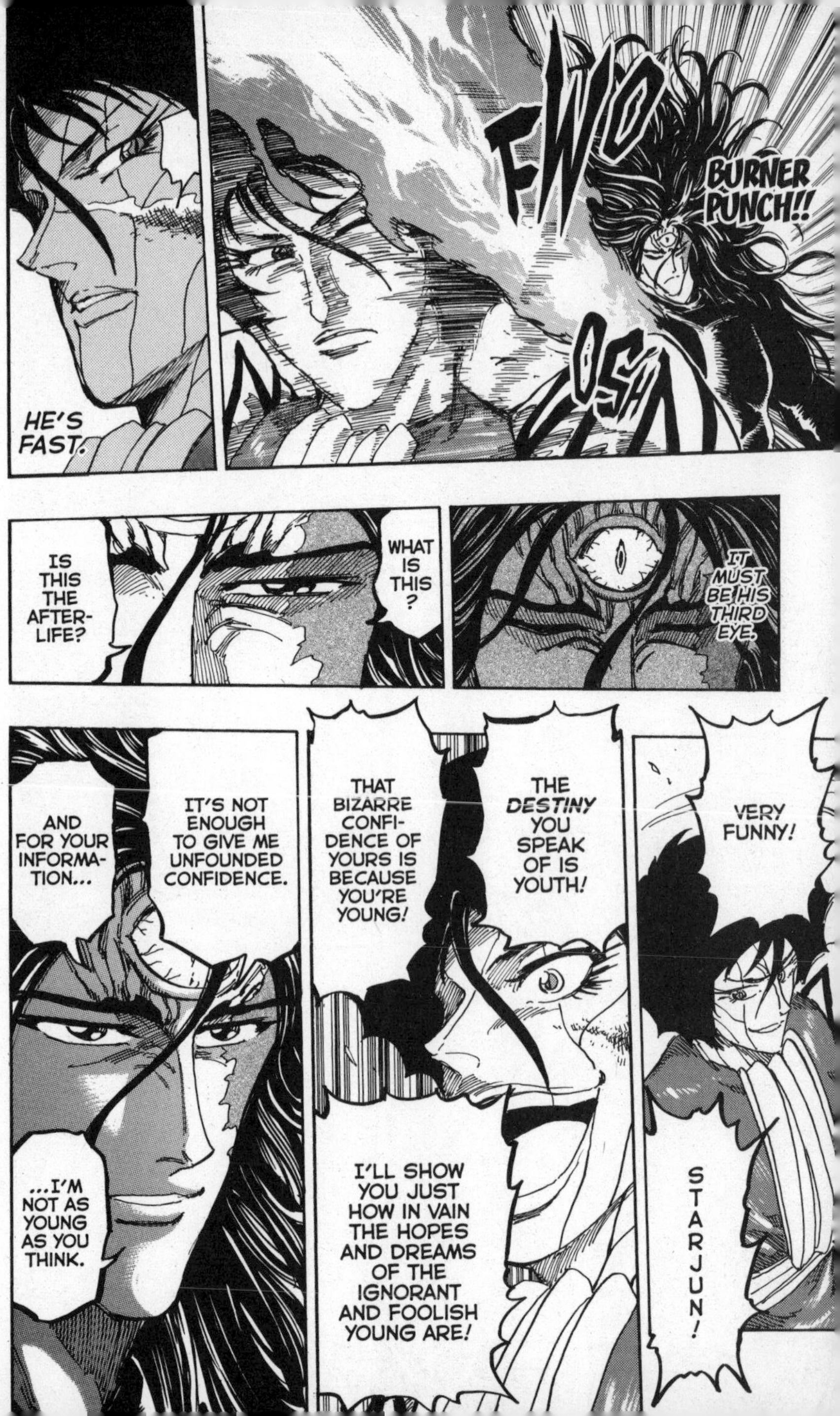
FWO
BURNER PUNCH!!
OSA
HE'S FAST.
IT MUST BE HIS THIRD EYE.
WHAT IS THIS?
IS THIS THE AFTER-LIFE?
VERY FUNNY!
STARJUN!
THE *DESTINY* YOU SPEAK OF IS YOUTH!
THAT BIZARRE CONFIDENCE OF YOURS IS BECAUSE YOU'RE YOUNG!
I'LL SHOW YOU JUST HOW IN VAIN THE HOPES AND DREAMS OF THE IGNORANT AND FOOLISH YOUNG ARE!
IT'S NOT ENOUGH TO GIVE ME UNFOUNDED CONFIDENCE.
AND FOR YOUR INFORMATION...
...I'M NOT AS YOUNG AS YOU THINK.

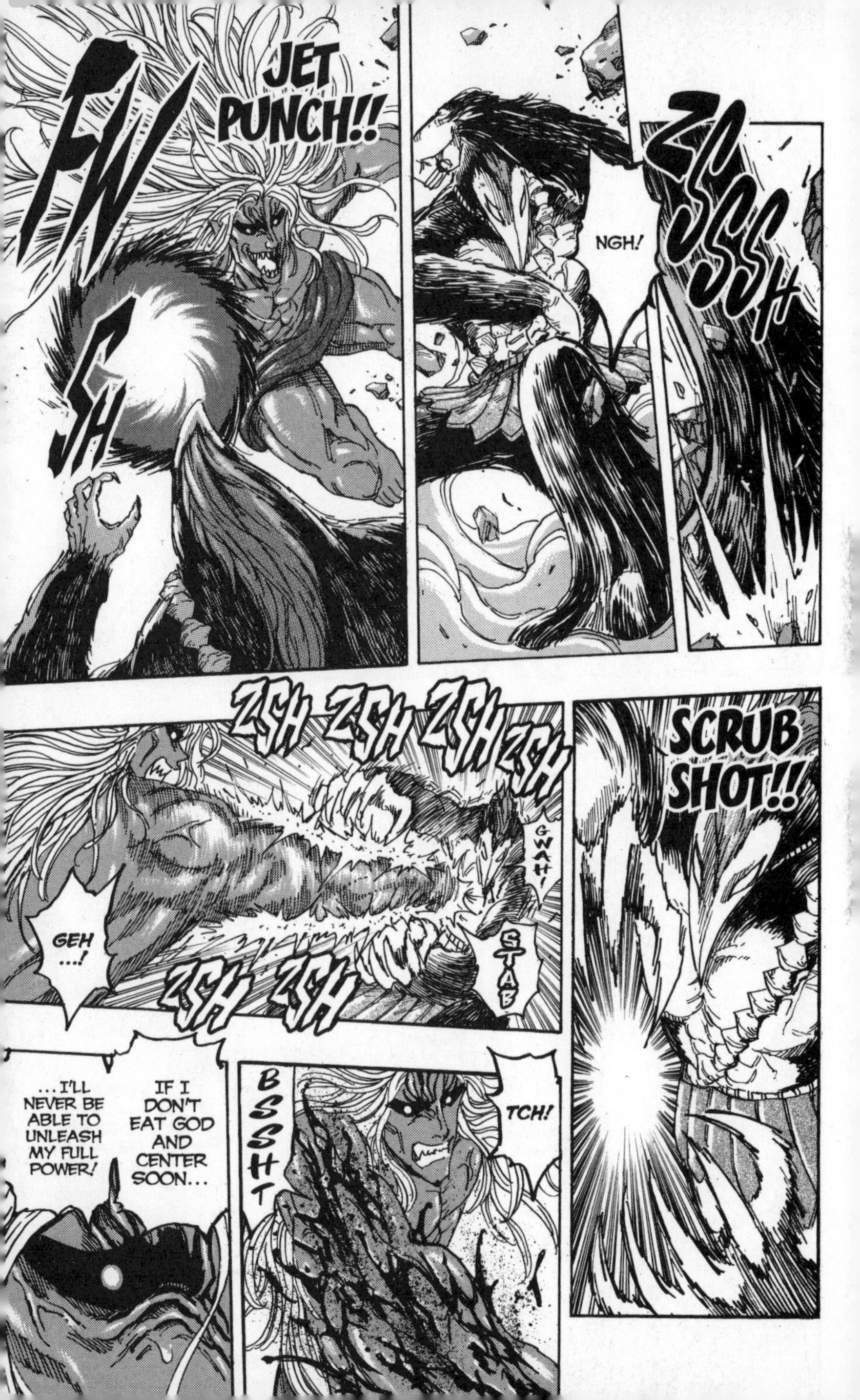
ZSSSH
NGH!
JET PUNCH!!
FWSH
SCRUB SHOT!!
ZSH ZSH ZSH ZSH ZSH
GWAH!
STAB
ZSH ZSH
GEH ...!
TCH!
BSSHT
IF I DON'T EAT GOD AND CENTER SOON...
...I'LL NEVER BE ABLE TO UNLEASH MY FULL POWER!

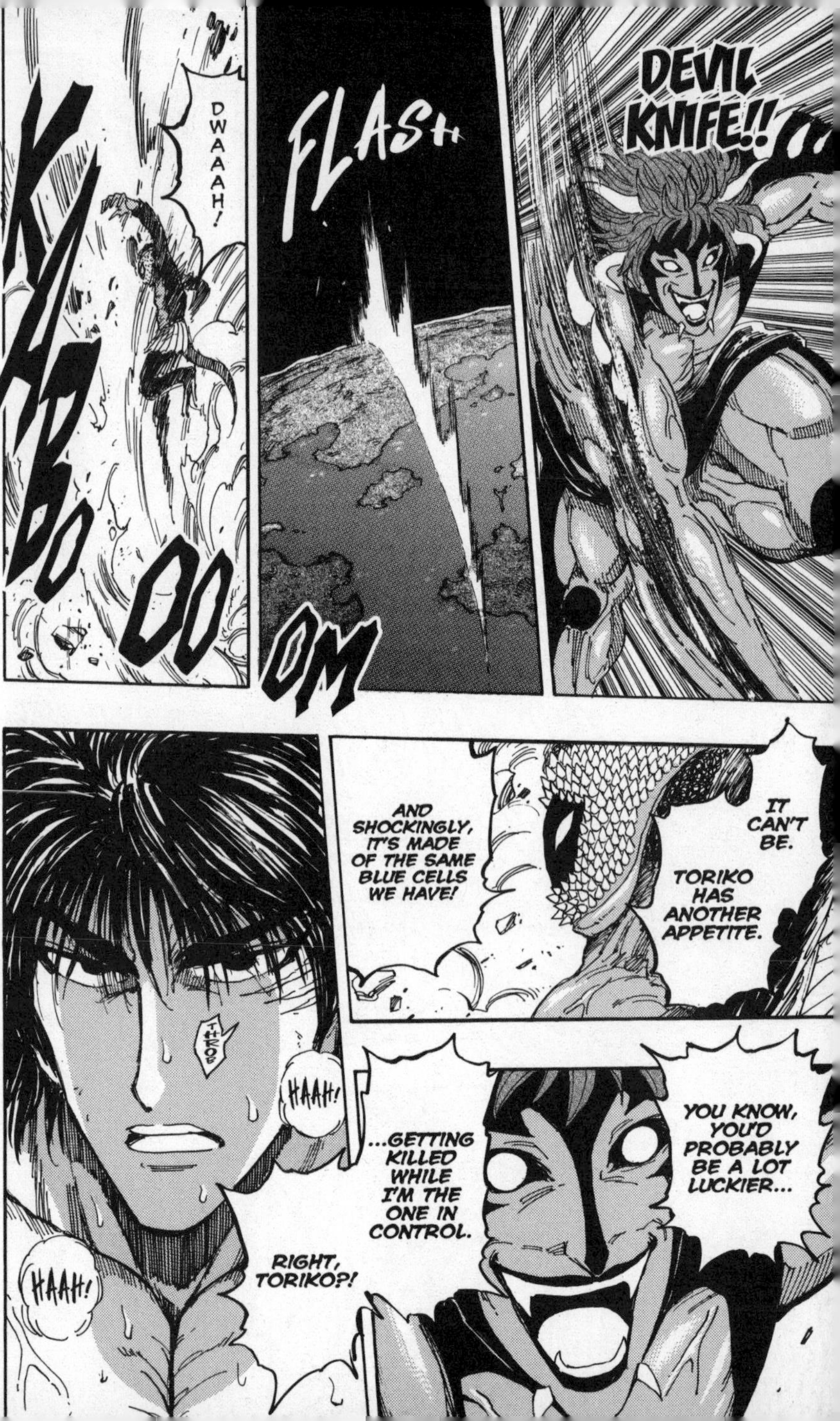
DEVIL KNIFE!!
FLASH
DWAAAAH!
KABOOOOM
IT CAN'T BE.
TORIKO HAS ANOTHER APPETITE.
AND SHOCKINGLY, IT'S MADE OF THE SAME BLUE CELLS WE HAVE!
YOU KNOW, YOU'D PROBABLY BE A LOT LUCKIER...
...GETTING KILLED WHILE I'M THE ONE IN CONTROL.
RIGHT, TORIKO?!
THROB
HAAH!
HAAH!

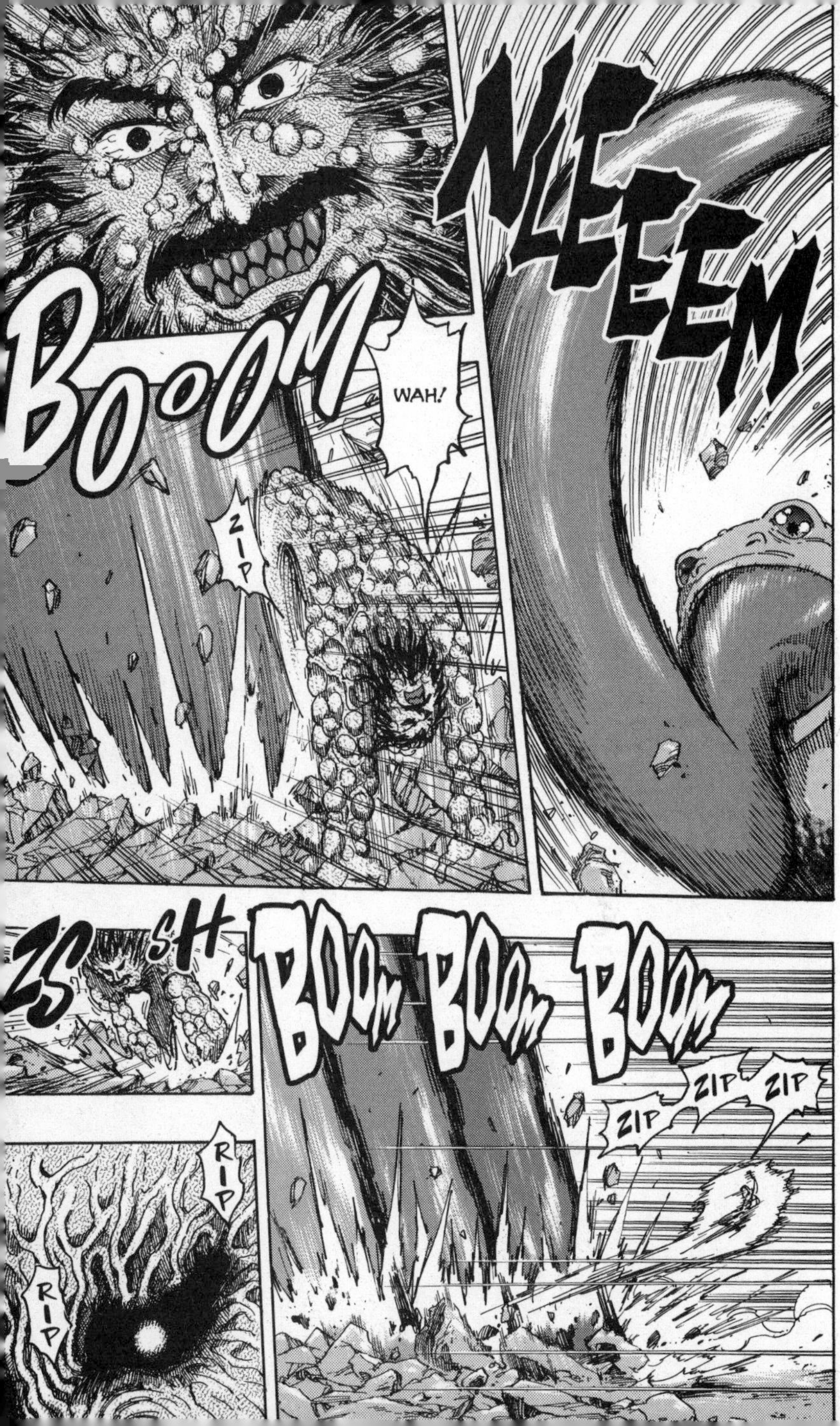
NIEEEM
BOOOM
WAH!
ZIP
BOOM BOOM BOOM
ZIP ZIP ZIP
ZSSH
RIP RIP

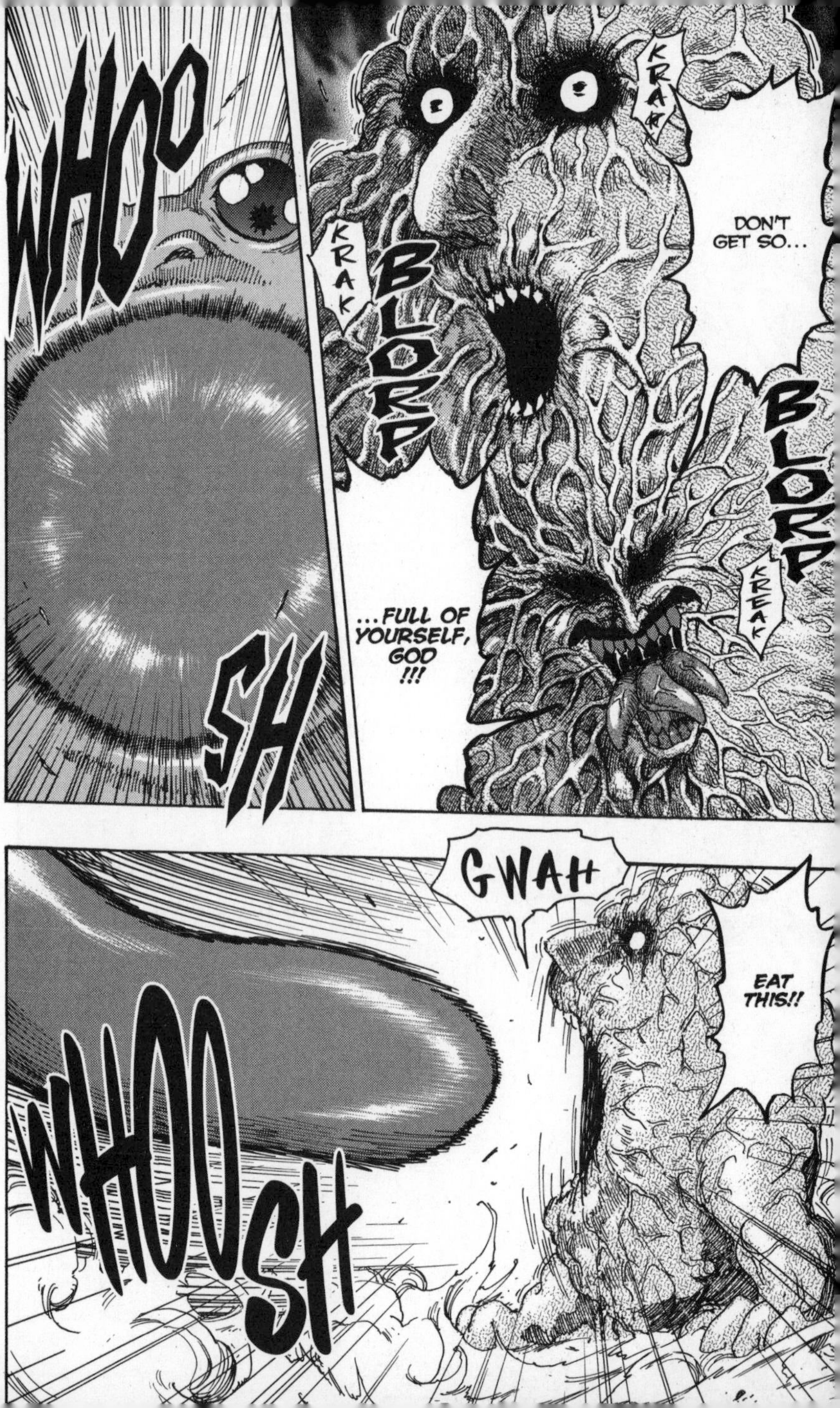
KRAK
DON'T GET SO...
BLORP
KREAK
BLORP
KRAK
...FULL OF YOURSELF, GOD !!!
WHOOSH
GWAH
EAT THIS!!
WHOOSH

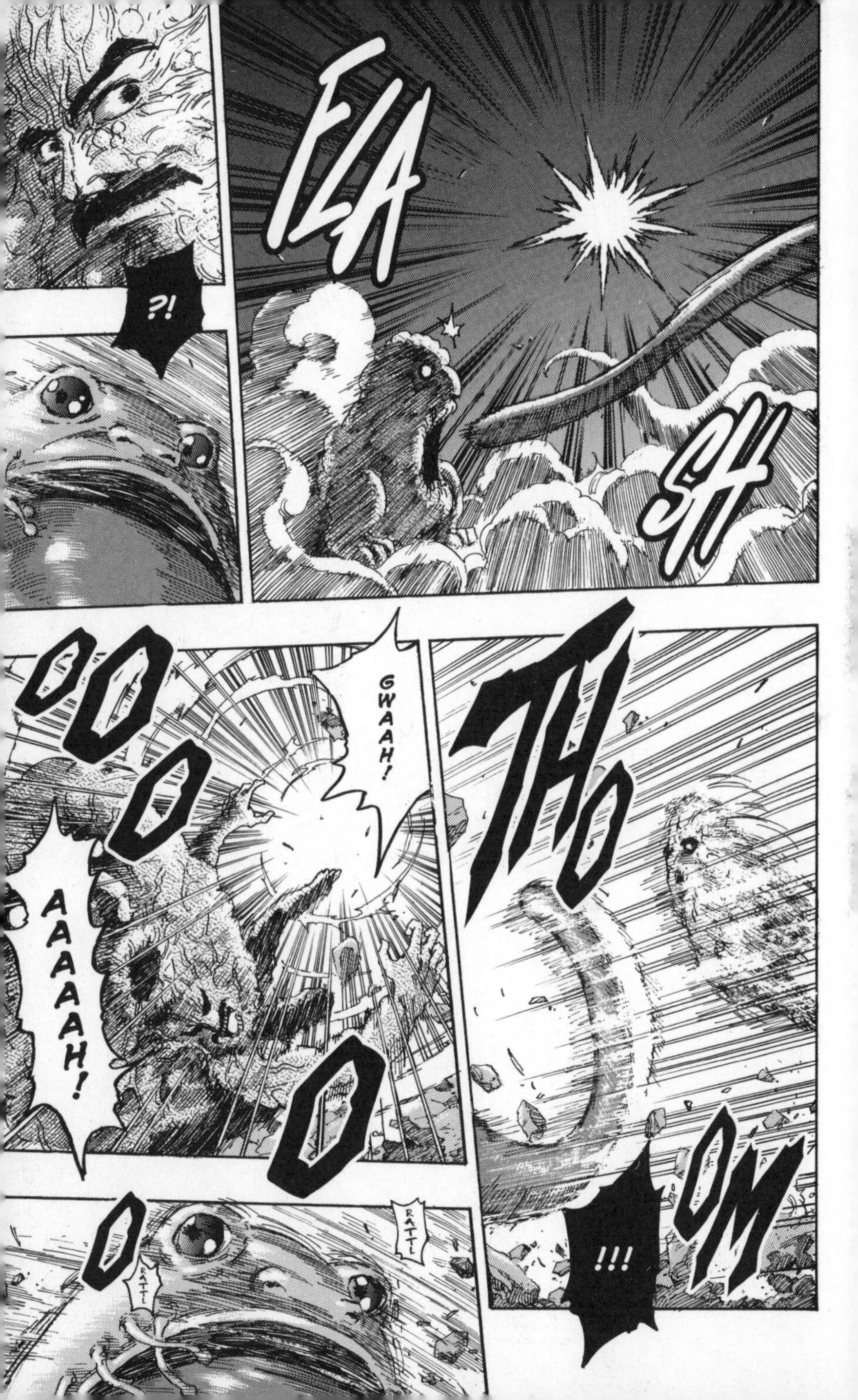
FLA
SH
?!
THO
OM
!!!
DOOOO
GWAAAH!
AAAAAAH!
RATTL
RATTL

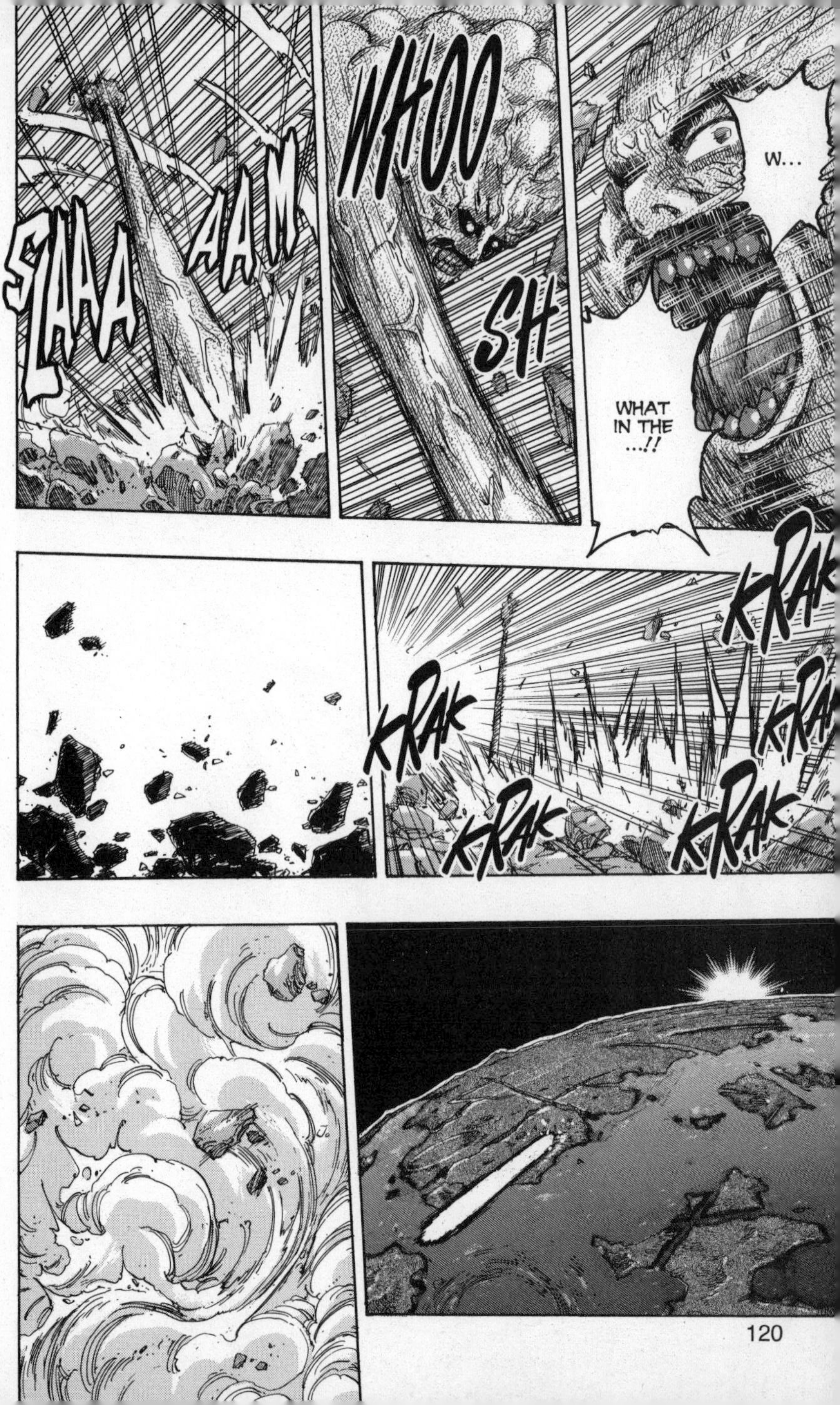
W...
WHAT IN THE ...!!
WHOOSH
SLAAAAM
KRAK KRAK KRAK
KRAK
KRAK
KRAK

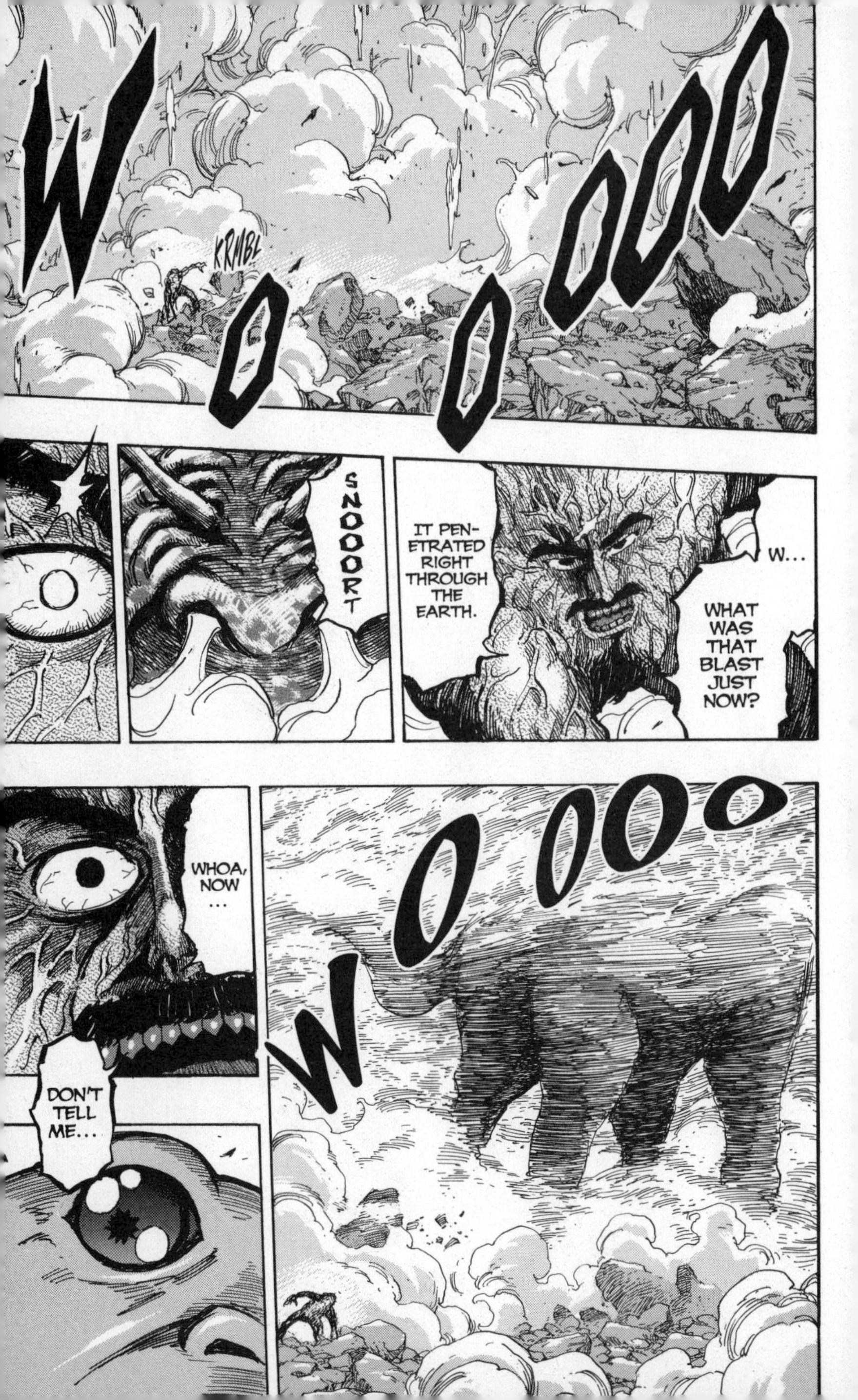

WOOOOOOOO
KRMBL
W...
WHAT WAS THAT BLAST JUST NOW?
IT PEN-ETRATED RIGHT THROUGH THE EARTH.
SNOOORT
WOOOOO
WHOA, NOW...
DON'T TELL ME...

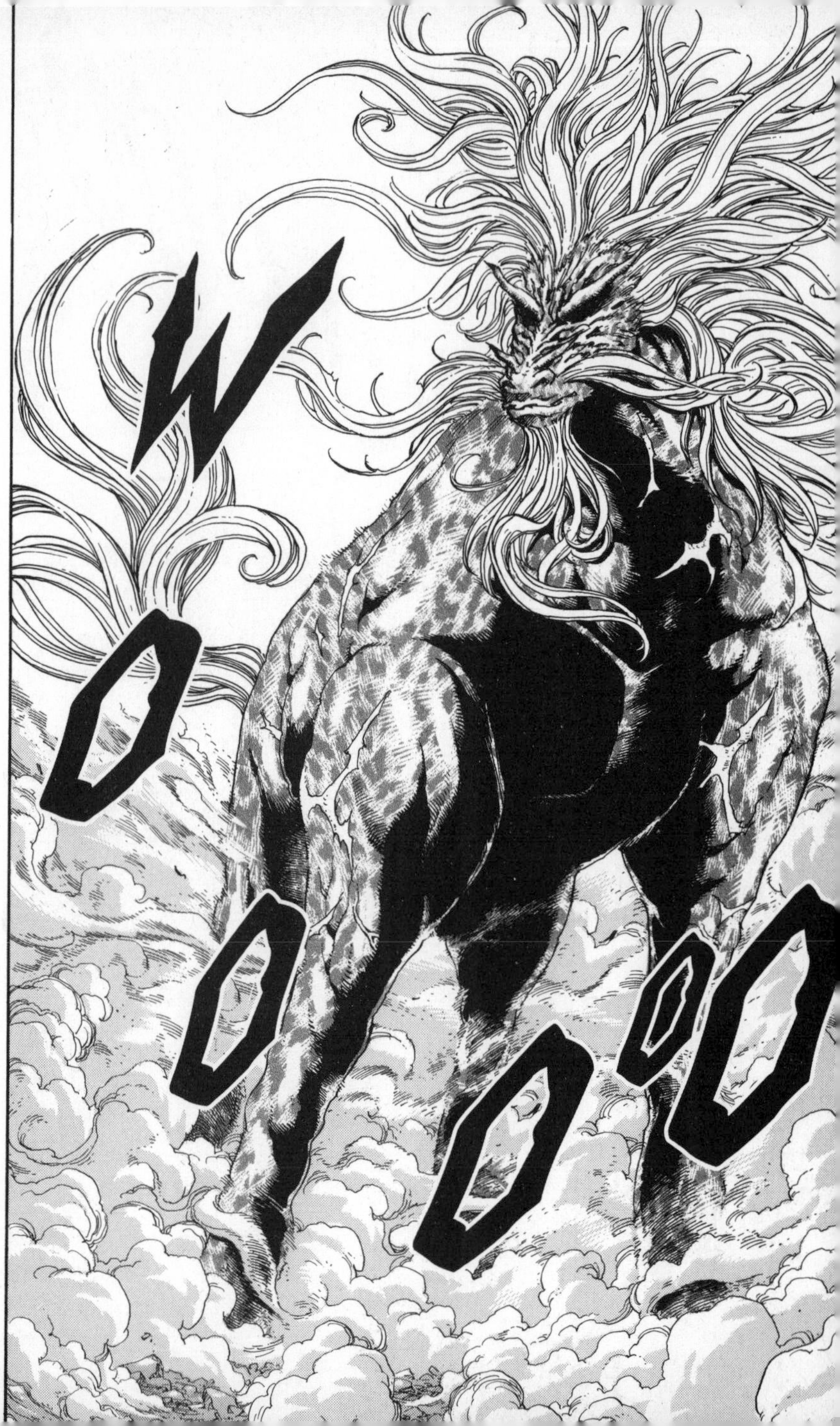
WOOOOO

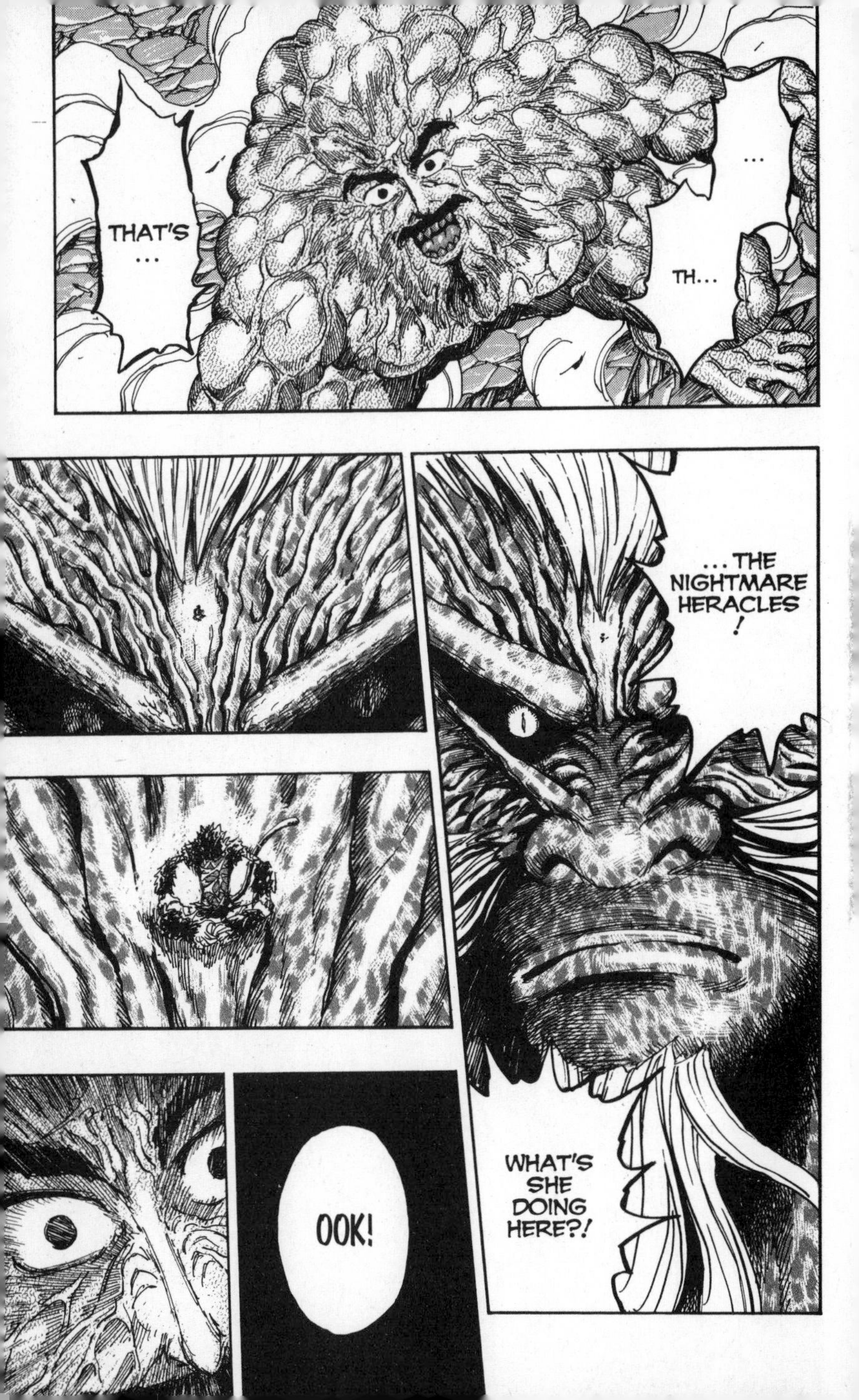
...
TH...
THAT'S ...
...THE NIGHTMARE HERACLES!
WHAT'S SHE DOING HERE?!
OOK!

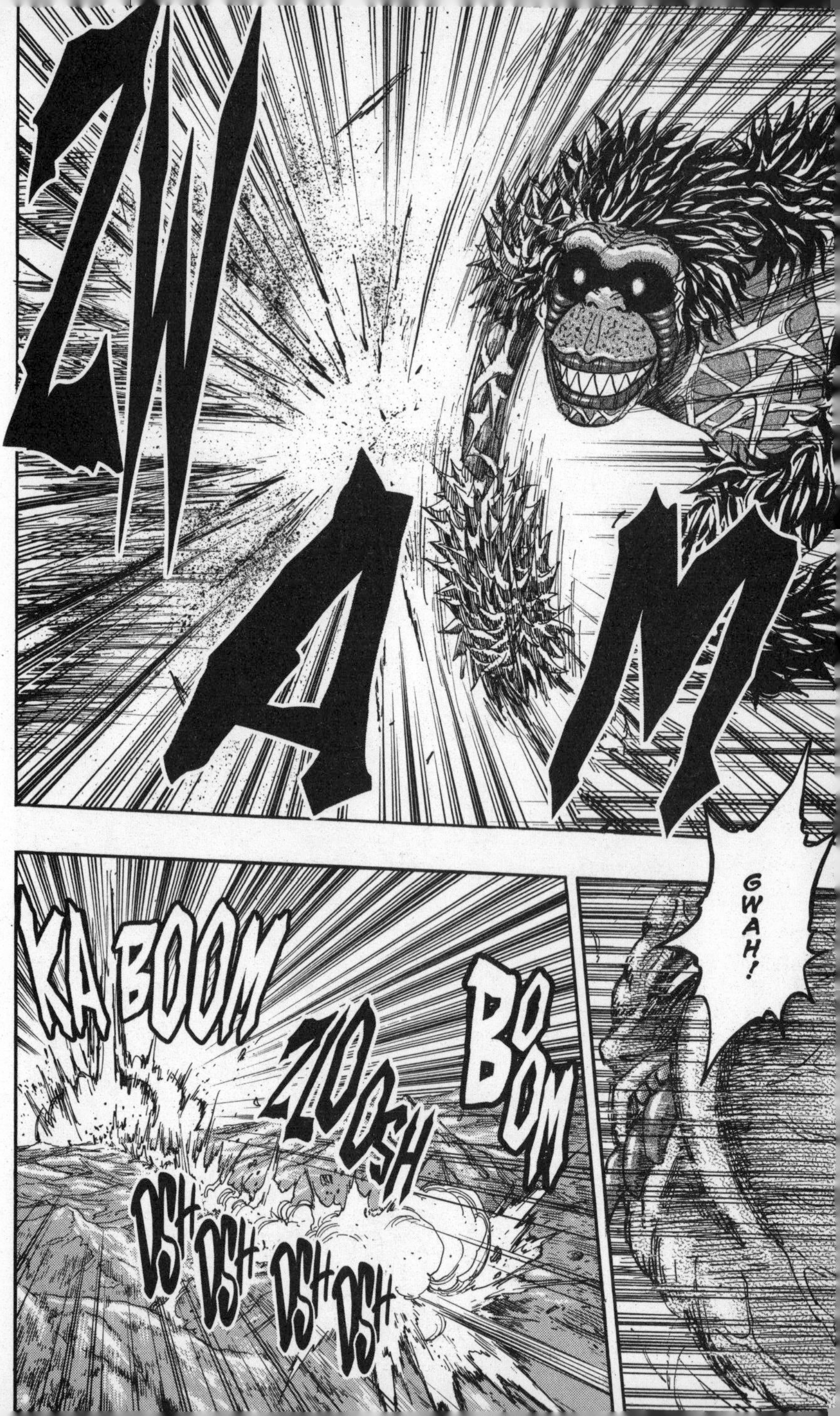
ZWAM
GWAH!
BOOM
ZOOSH
KA BOOM
DSH DSH DSH DSH

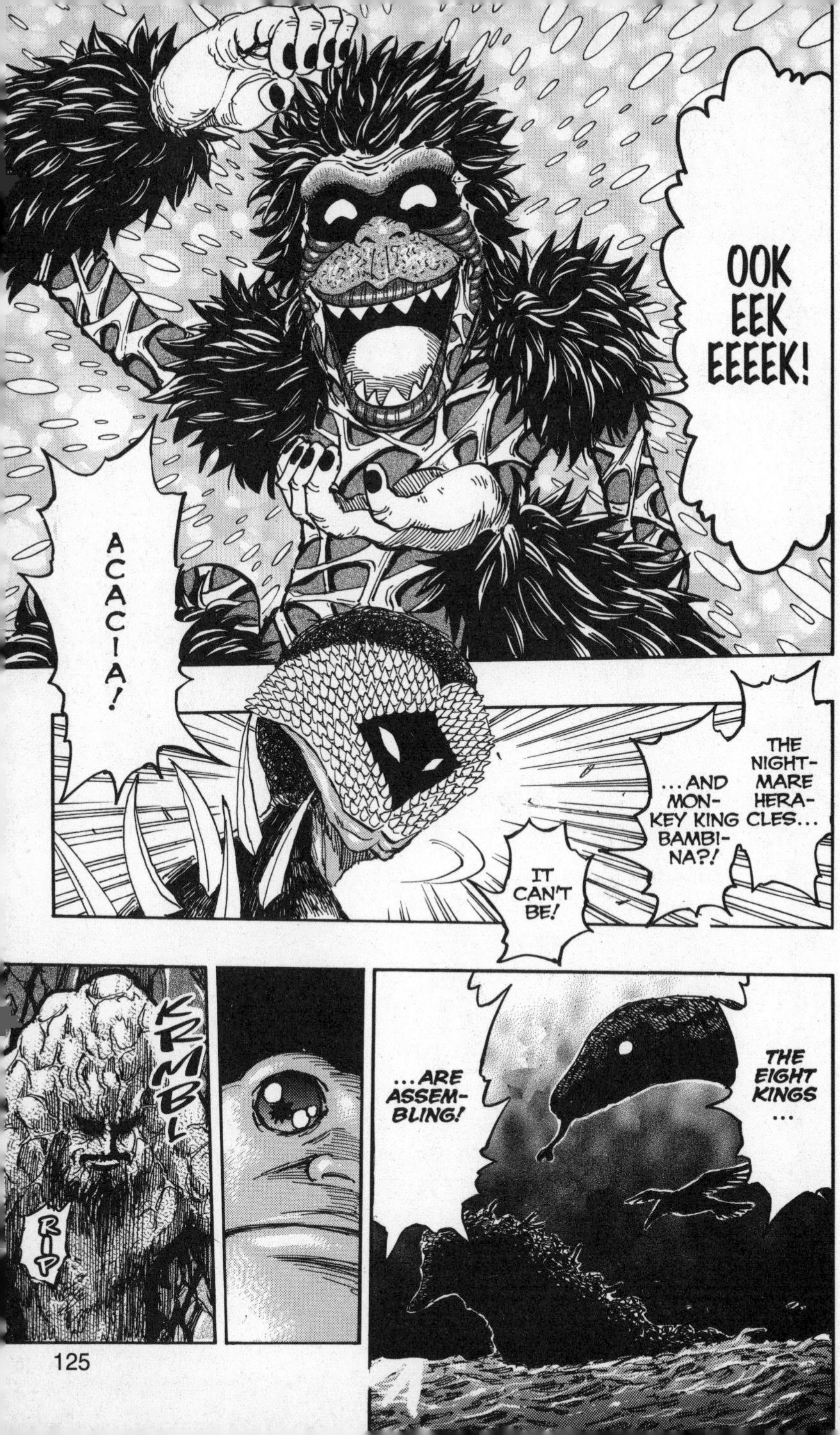
OOK EEK EEEEK!
ACACIA!
THE NIGHTMARE HERACLES...
...AND MONKEY KING BAMBINA?!
IT CAN'T BE!
THE EIGHT KINGS ...
...ARE ASSEMBLING!
KRMBL
RIP

TORIKO

GOURMET CHECKLIST

Vol.407

PLUM STAR
(CLASSIFICATION UNKNOWN)

CAPTURE LEVEL: UNKNOWN
HABITAT: OUTER SPACE
SIZE: UNKNOWN
HEIGHT: UNKNOWN
WEIGHT: UNKNOWN
PRICE: UNKNOWN

HE SAW A *PLUM STAR* THAT FLIES ACROSS THE UNIVERSE.*

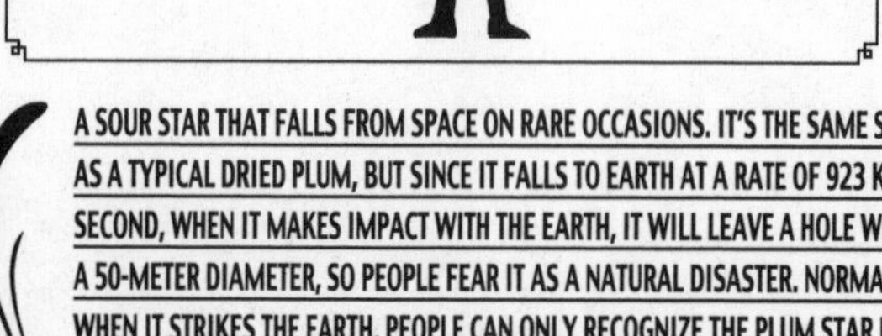

SCALE

A SOUR STAR THAT FALLS FROM SPACE ON RARE OCCASIONS. IT'S THE SAME SIZE AS A TYPICAL DRIED PLUM, BUT SINCE IT FALLS TO EARTH AT A RATE OF 923 KM PER SECOND, WHEN IT MAKES IMPACT WITH THE EARTH, IT WILL LEAVE A HOLE WITH A 50-METER DIAMETER, SO PEOPLE FEAR IT AS A NATURAL DISASTER. NORMALLY, WHEN IT STRIKES THE EARTH, PEOPLE CAN ONLY RECOGNIZE THE PLUM STAR BY ITS SHATTERED REMAINS, BUT THE ONE INSTANCE OF ITS ORIGINAL FORM BEING RECOGNIZABLE IS FROM THE INSIDE OF THE BELLY OF THE SNAKE KING, MOTHER SNAKE, FROM WHEN SHE ATE IT WHILE IT WAS STILL IN OUTER SPACE.

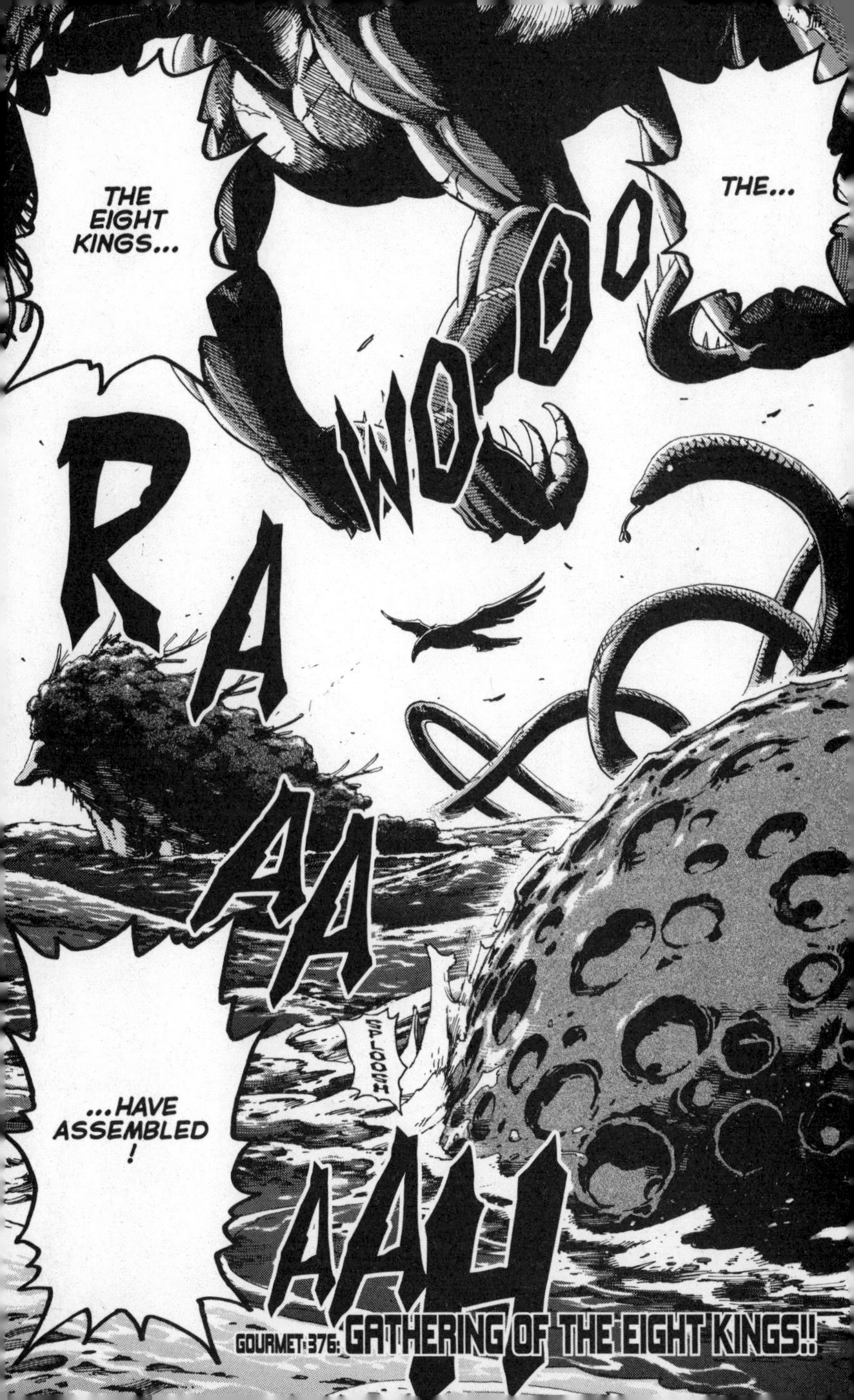
THE...
THE EIGHT KINGS...
RAWOOOAAAAH!
SPLOOSH
...HAVE ASSEMBLED!
GOURMET 376: GATHERING OF THE EIGHT KINGS!!

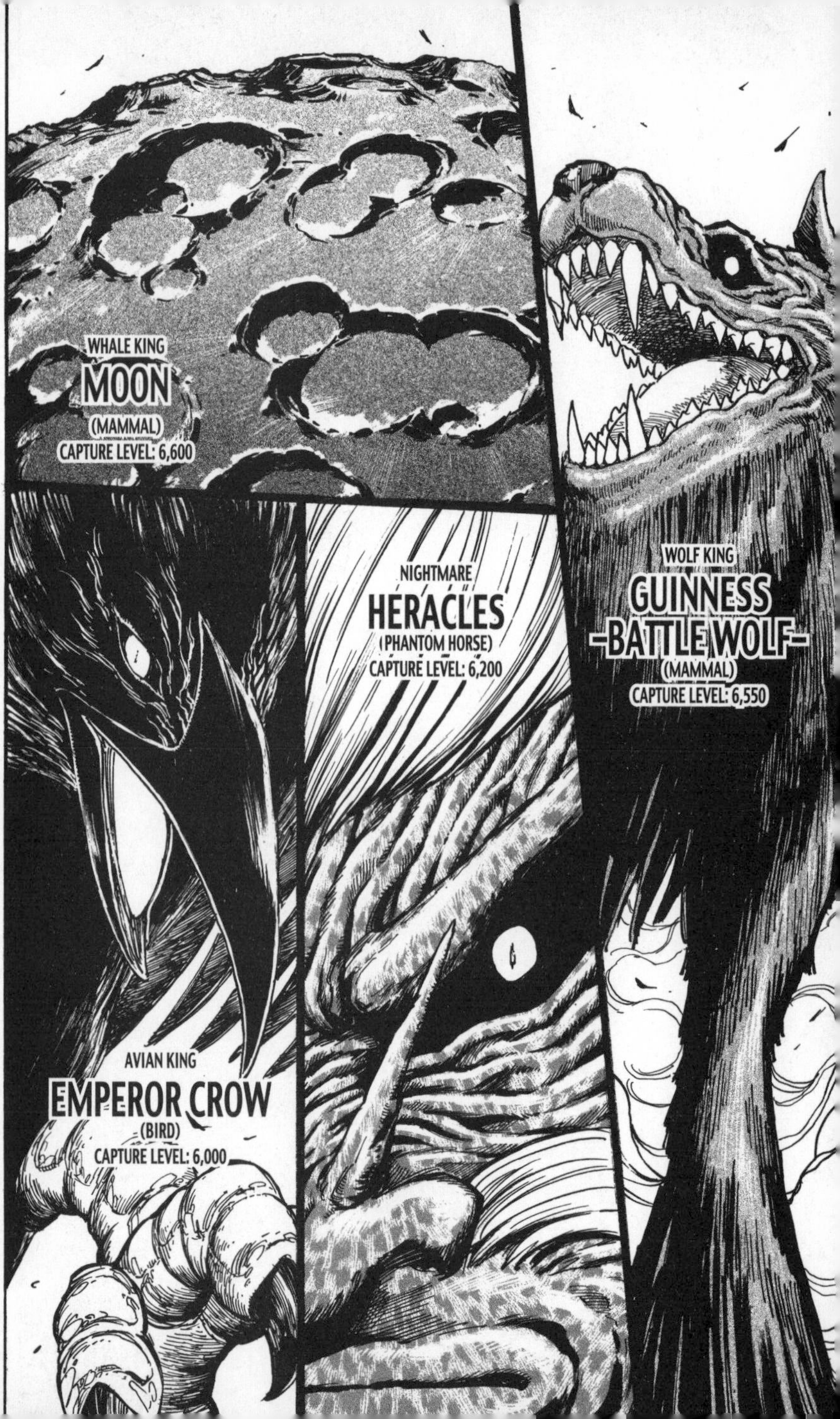
WOLF KING
GUINNESS
-BATTLE WOLF-
(MAMMAL)
CAPTURE LEVEL: 6,550
WHALE KING
MOON
(MAMMAL)
CAPTURE LEVEL: 6,600
NIGHTMARE
HERACLES
(PHANTOM HORSE)
CAPTURE LEVEL: 6,200
AVIAN KING
EMPEROR CROW
(BIRD)
CAPTURE LEVEL: 6,000

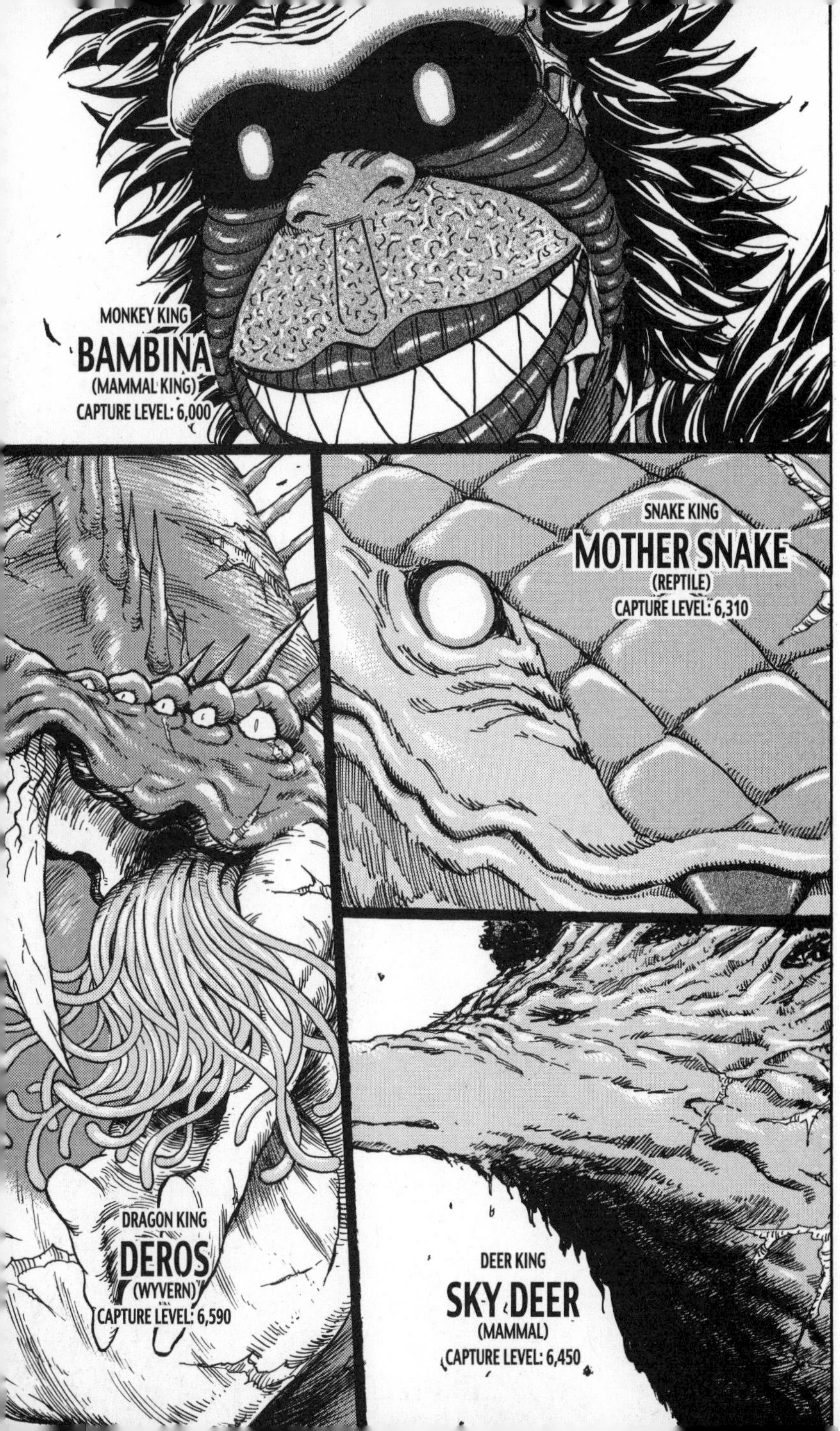
MONKEY KING
BAMBINA
(MAMMAL KING)
CAPTURE LEVEL: 6,000
SNAKE KING
MOTHER SNAKE
(REPTILE)
CAPTURE LEVEL: 6,310
DEER KING
SKY DEER
(MAMMAL)
CAPTURE LEVEL: 6,450
DRAGON KING
DEROS
(WYVERN)
CAPTURE LEVEL: 6,590

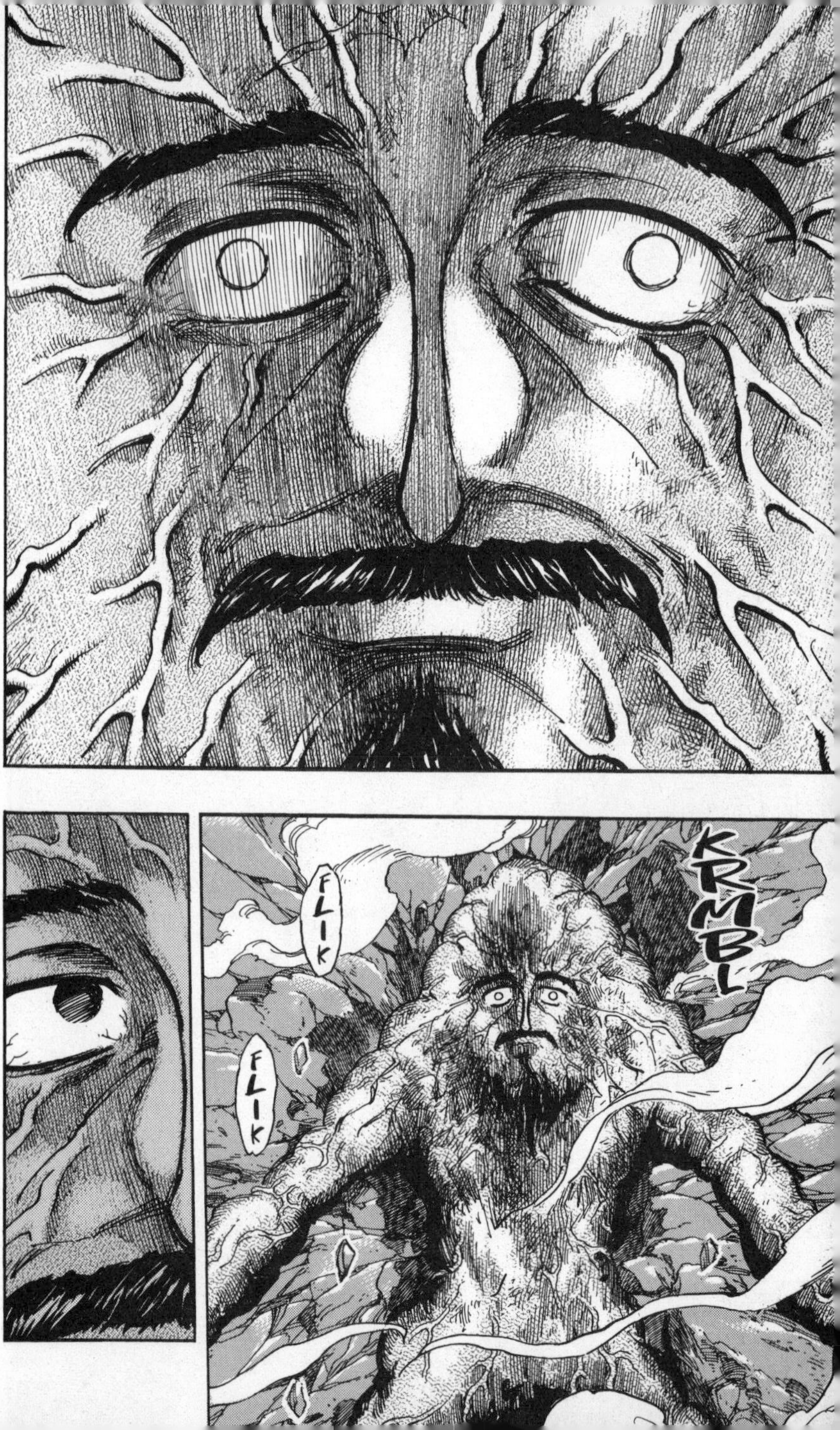
KRMBL
FLIK
FLIK

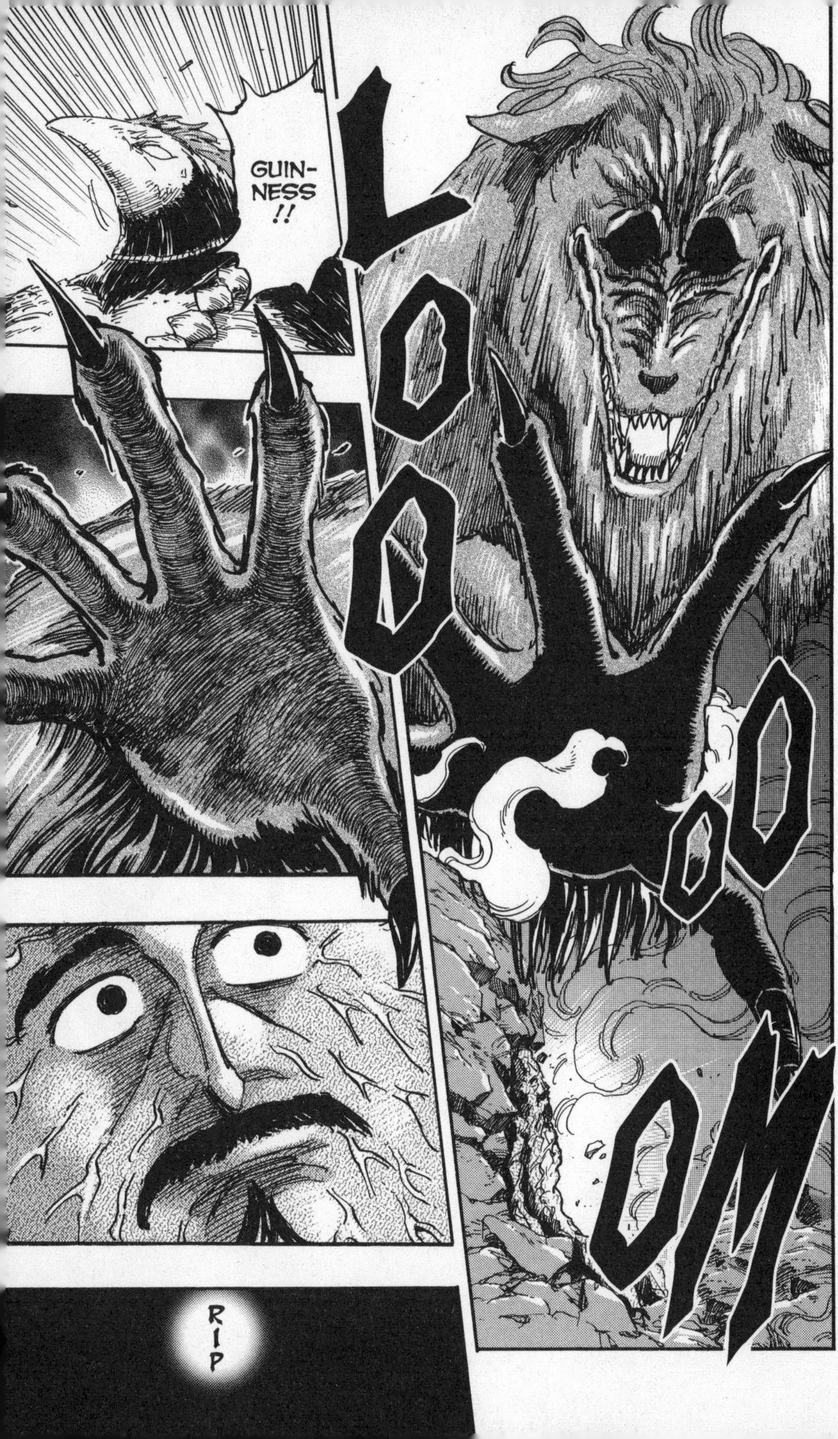

LOOOOOM
GUIN-NESS!!
RIP

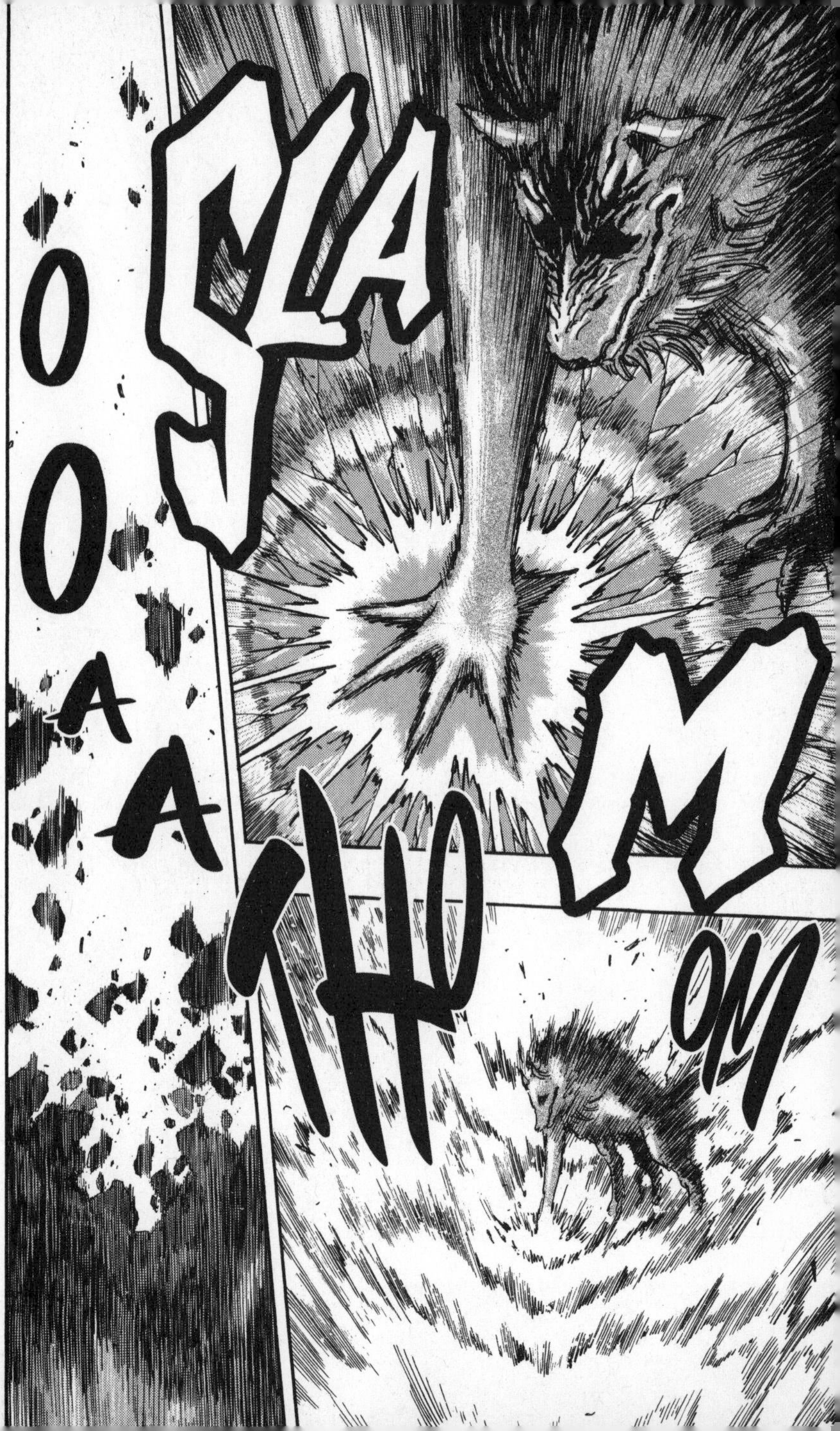
OOAA

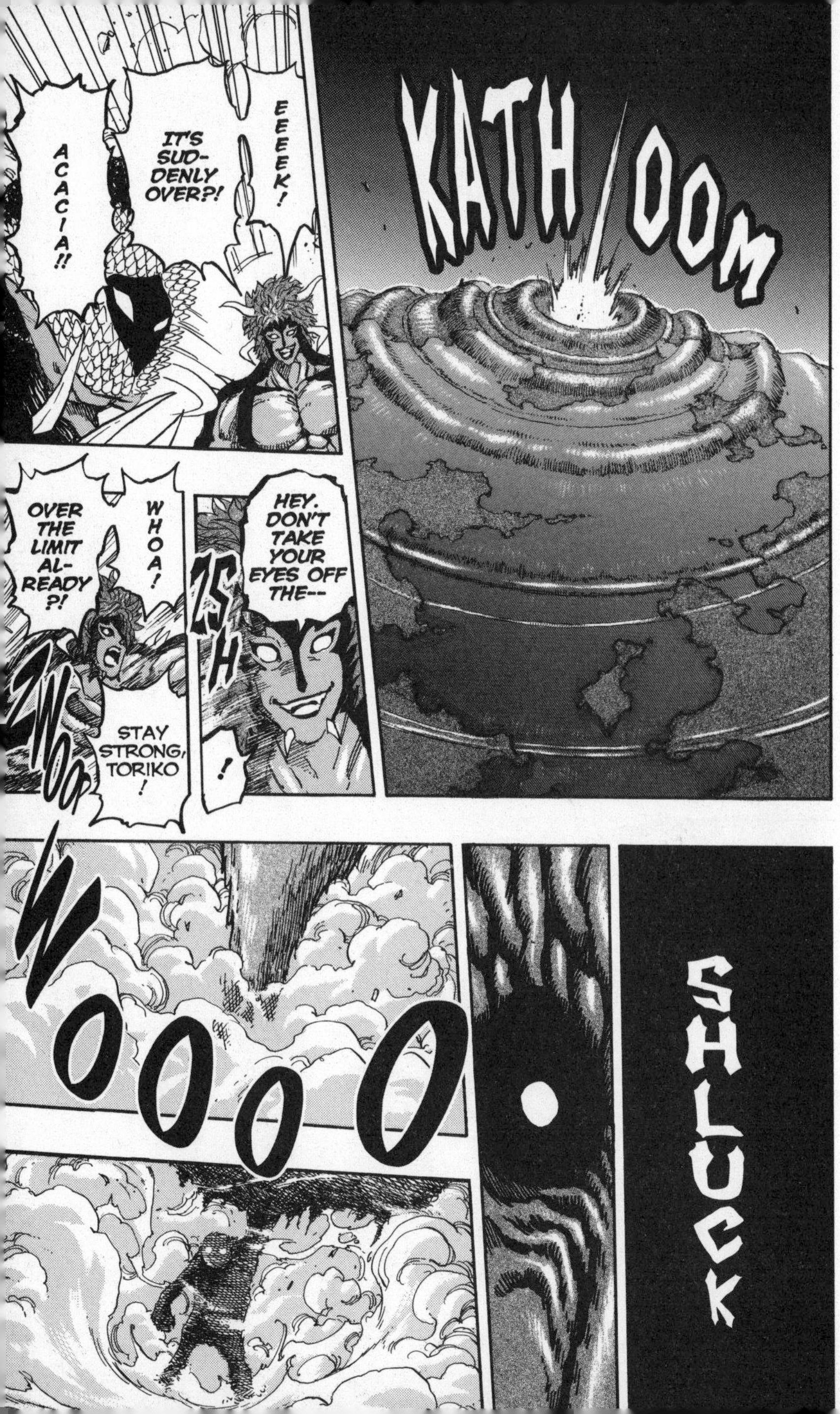
KATHOOM
EEEEEK!
IT'S SUD-DENLY OVER?!
ACACIA!!
HEY. DON'T TAKE YOUR EYES OFF THE--
TSH
!
WHOA!
OVER THE LIMIT AL-READY?!
STAY STRONG, TORIKO!
SHLUCK
WHOOOOO

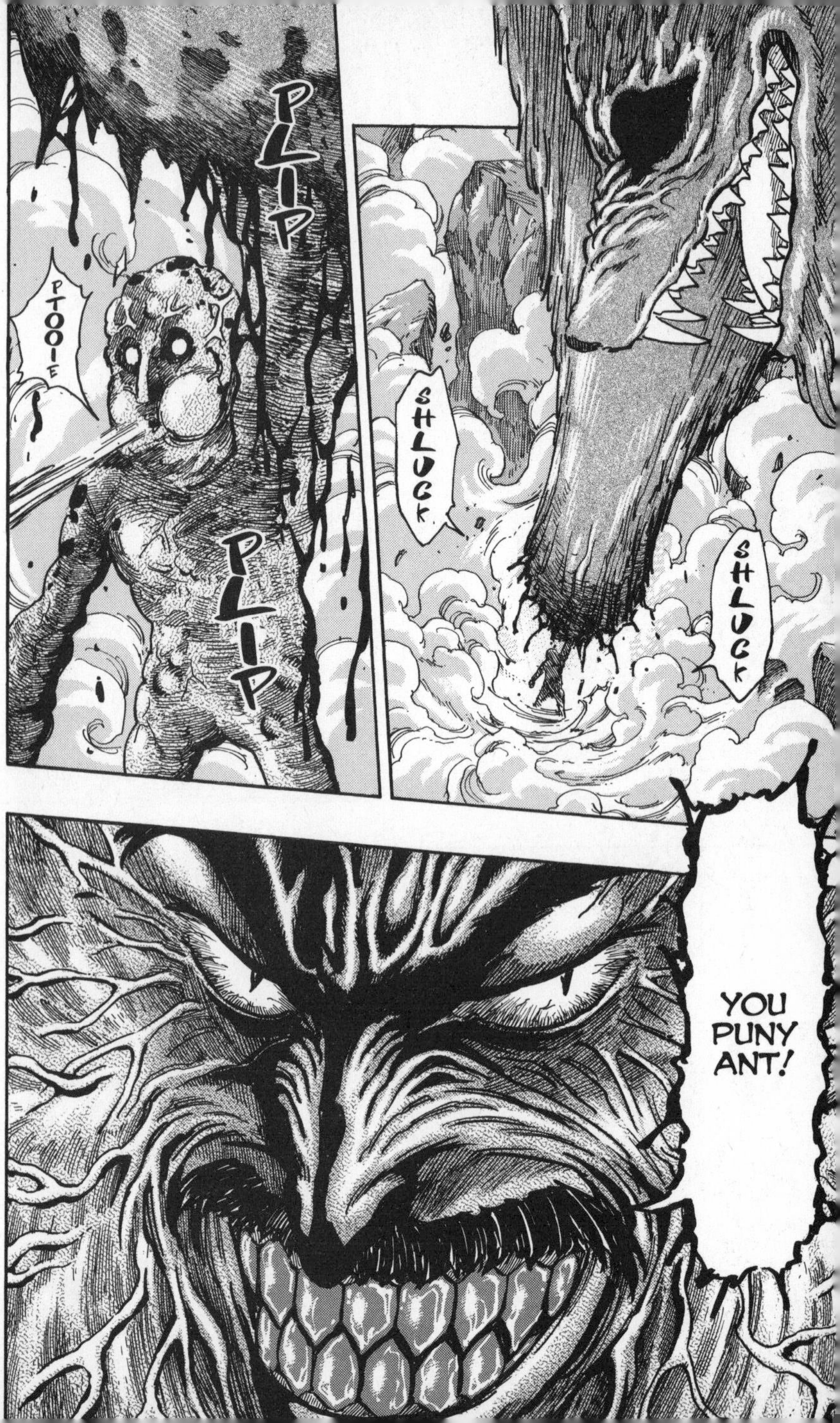
SHLUCK
SHLUCK
PLIP
PTOOIE
PLIP
YOU PUNY ANT!

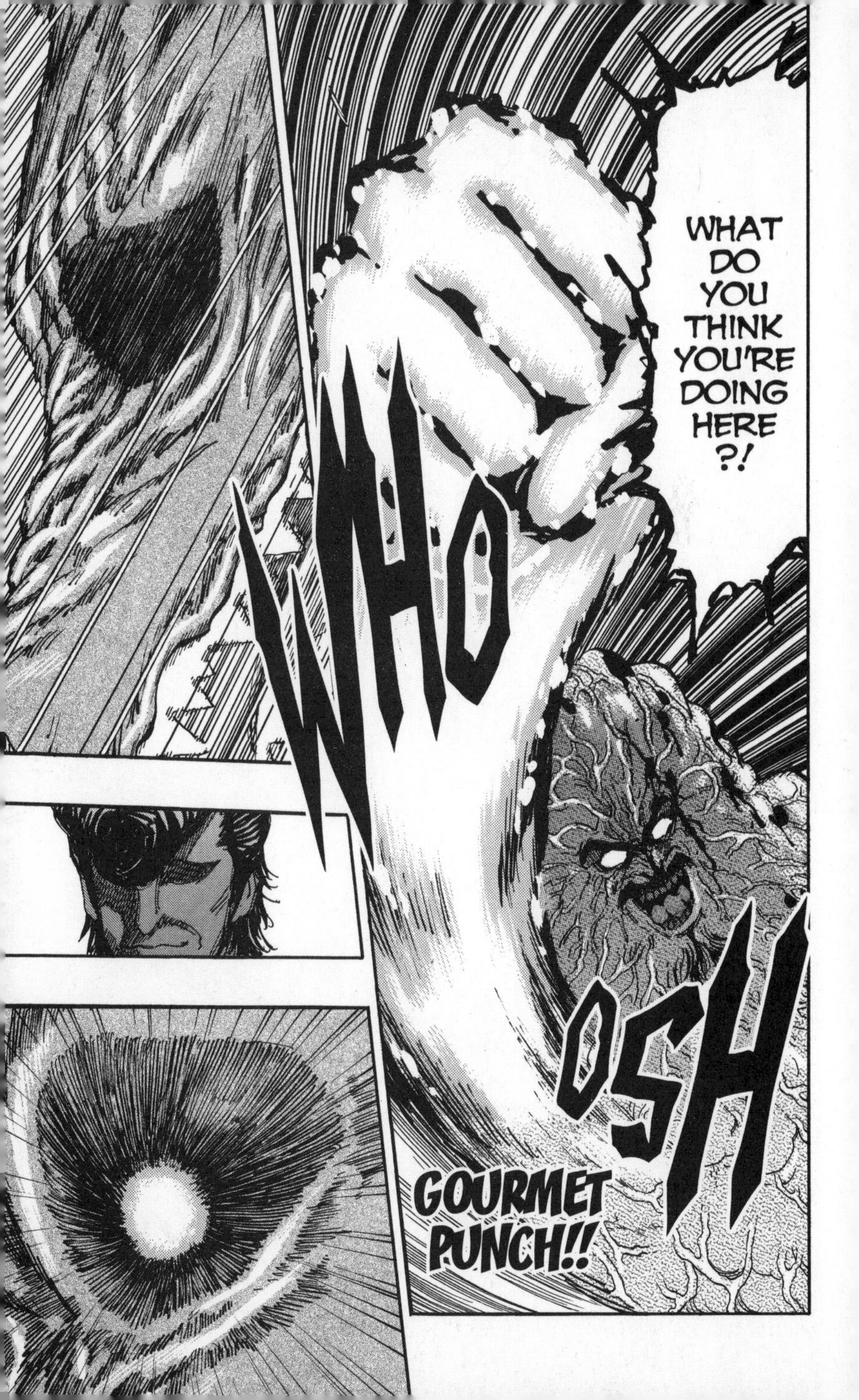
WHAT DO YOU THINK YOU'RE DOING HERE?!
WHOOSH
GOURMET PUNCH!!

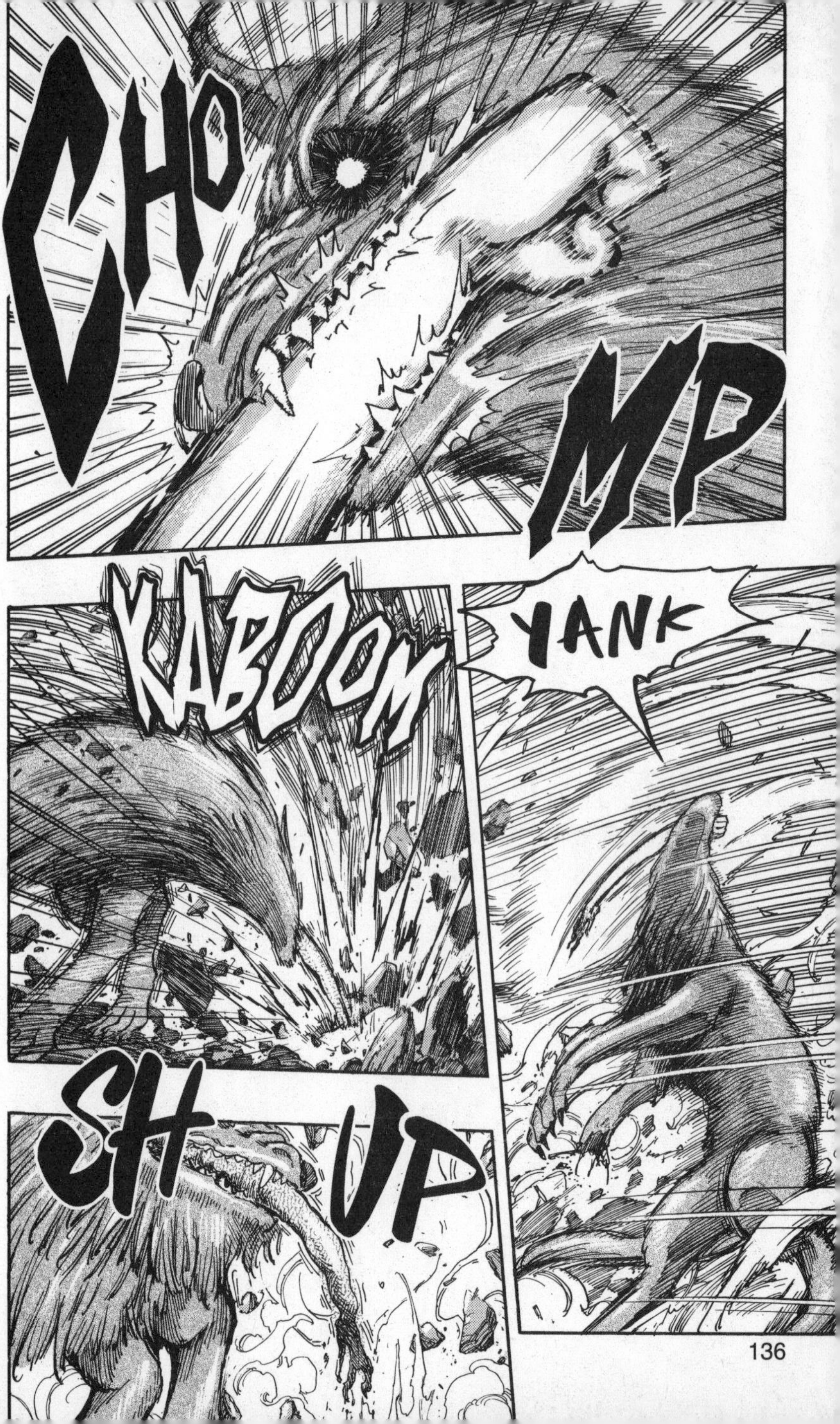
CHOMP
YANK
KABOOM
SHUP

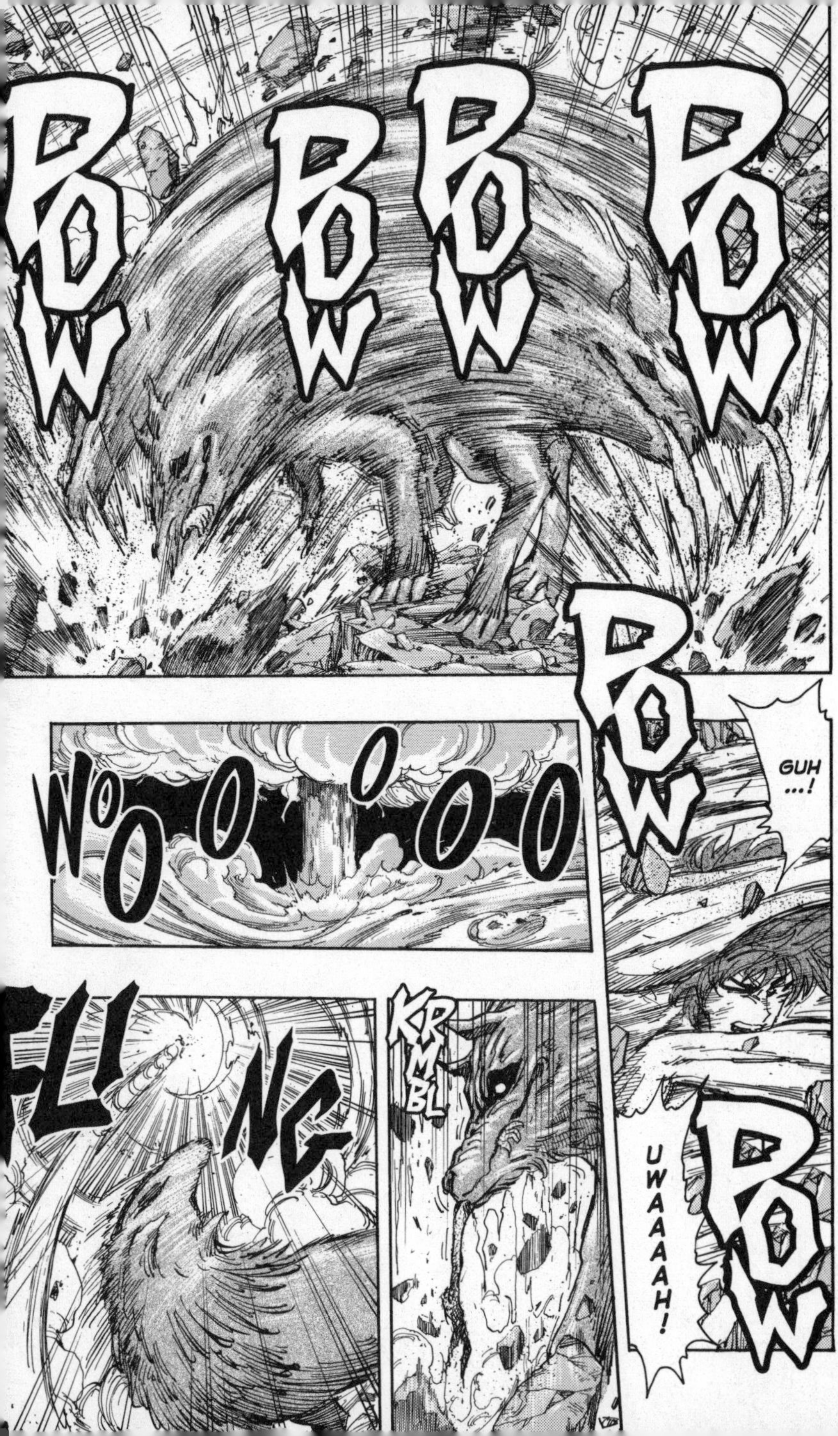
POW
POW
POW
POW
POW
GUH ...!
UWAAAAAH!
POW
WOOOOOOO
KRMMBL
LING

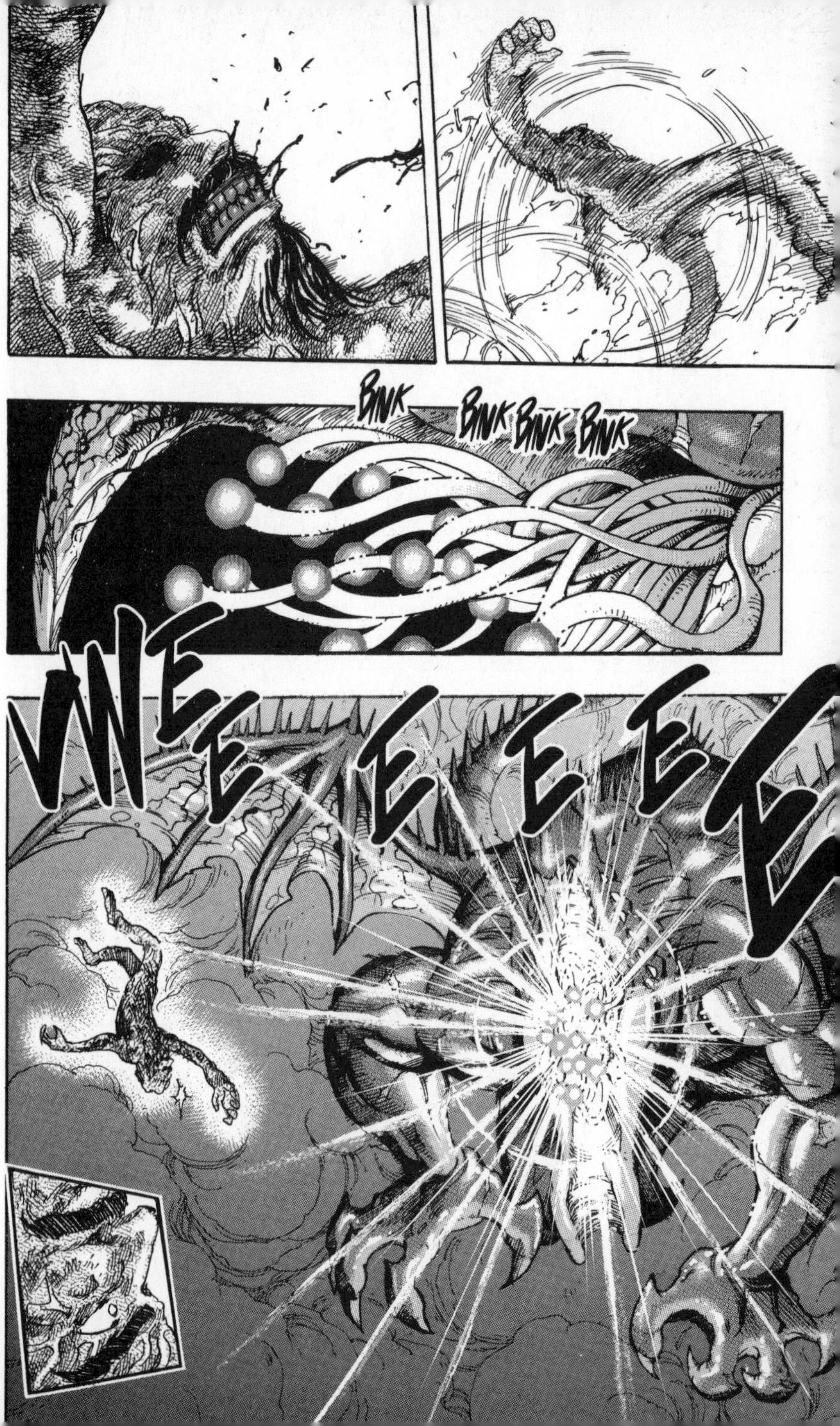
BINK
BINK BINK BINK
VWEEEEEE

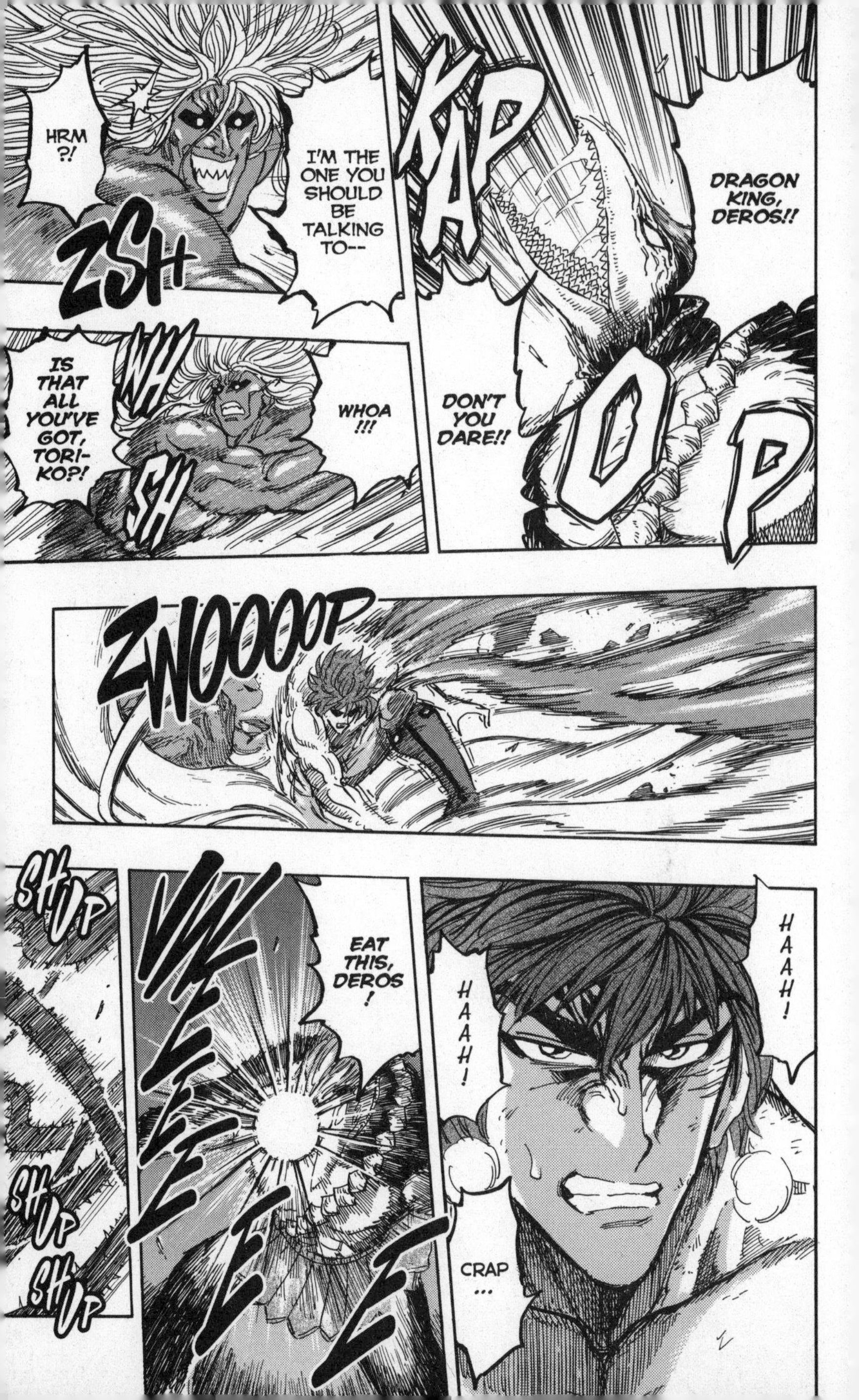
KAP
DRAGON KING, DEROS!!
DON'T YOU DARE!!
OOP
I'M THE ONE YOU SHOULD BE TALKING TO--
HRM ?!
ZSH
WHOA !!!
IS THAT ALL YOU'VE GOT, TORI-KO?!
WHSH
ZWOOOOOP
HAAAH!
HAAAH!
CRAP ...
EAT THIS, DEROS !
SHUP
SHUP
SHUP

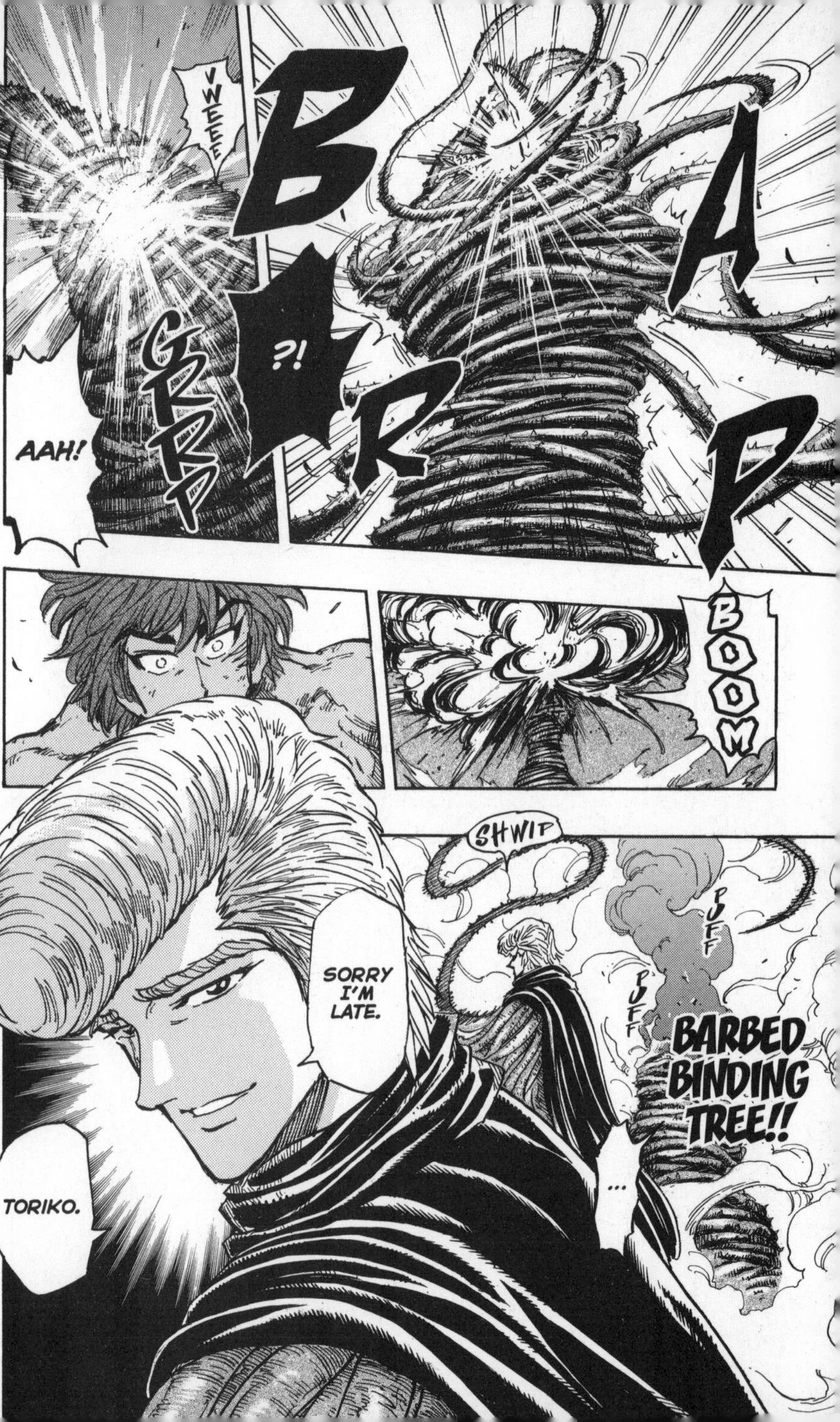
BARP
VWEEE
?!
GRRP
AAH!
BOOM
SHWIP
PUFF
PUFF
BARBED BINDING TREE!!
...
SORRY I'M LATE.
TORIKO.

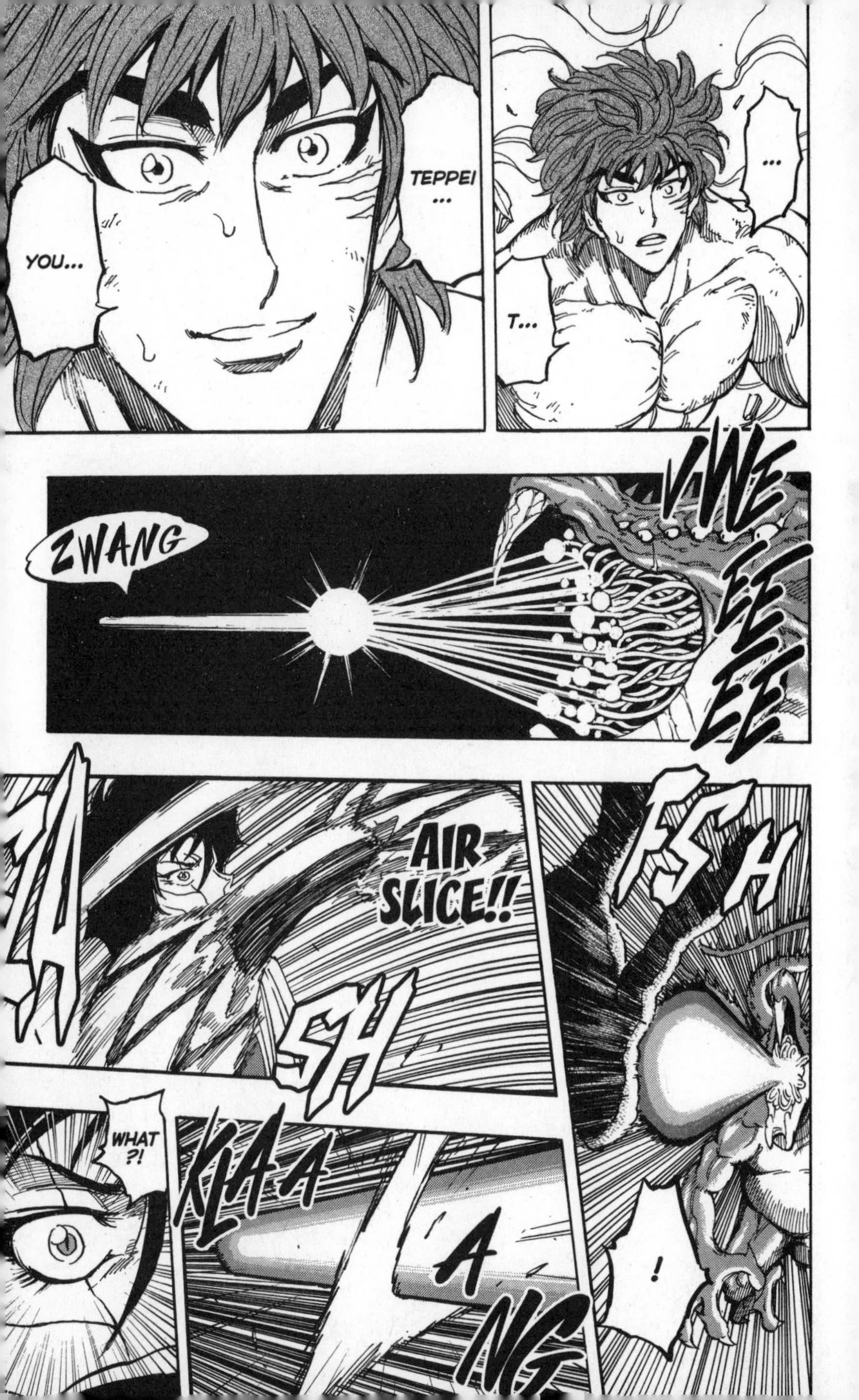
...
T...
TEPPEI ...
YOU...
VWEEEEEEE
ZWANG
FSH
!
AIR SLICE!!
SH
WHAT ?!
KLAAANG

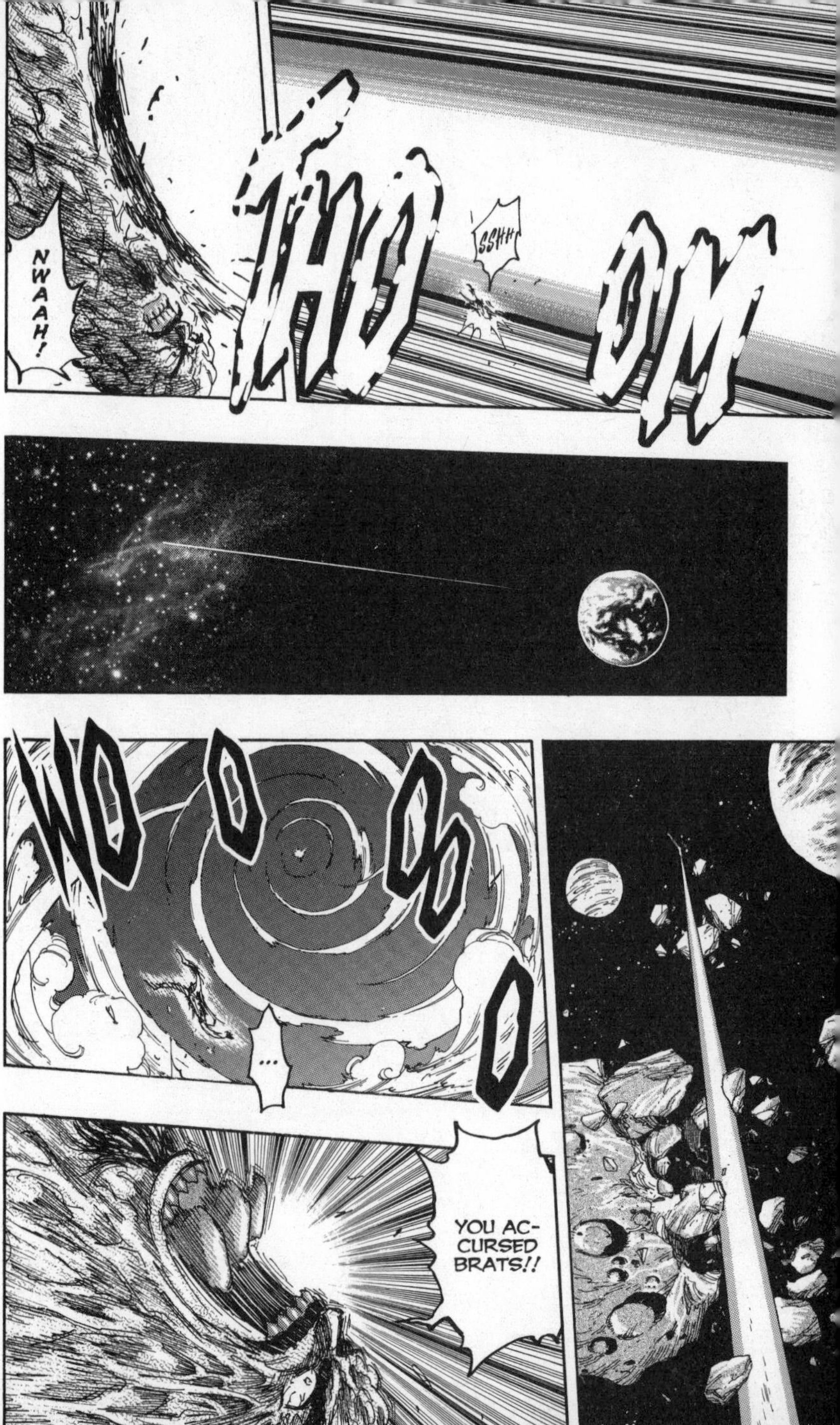
THOOM
SSHH
NWAAAH!
WOOOO
...
YOU ACCURSED BRATS!!

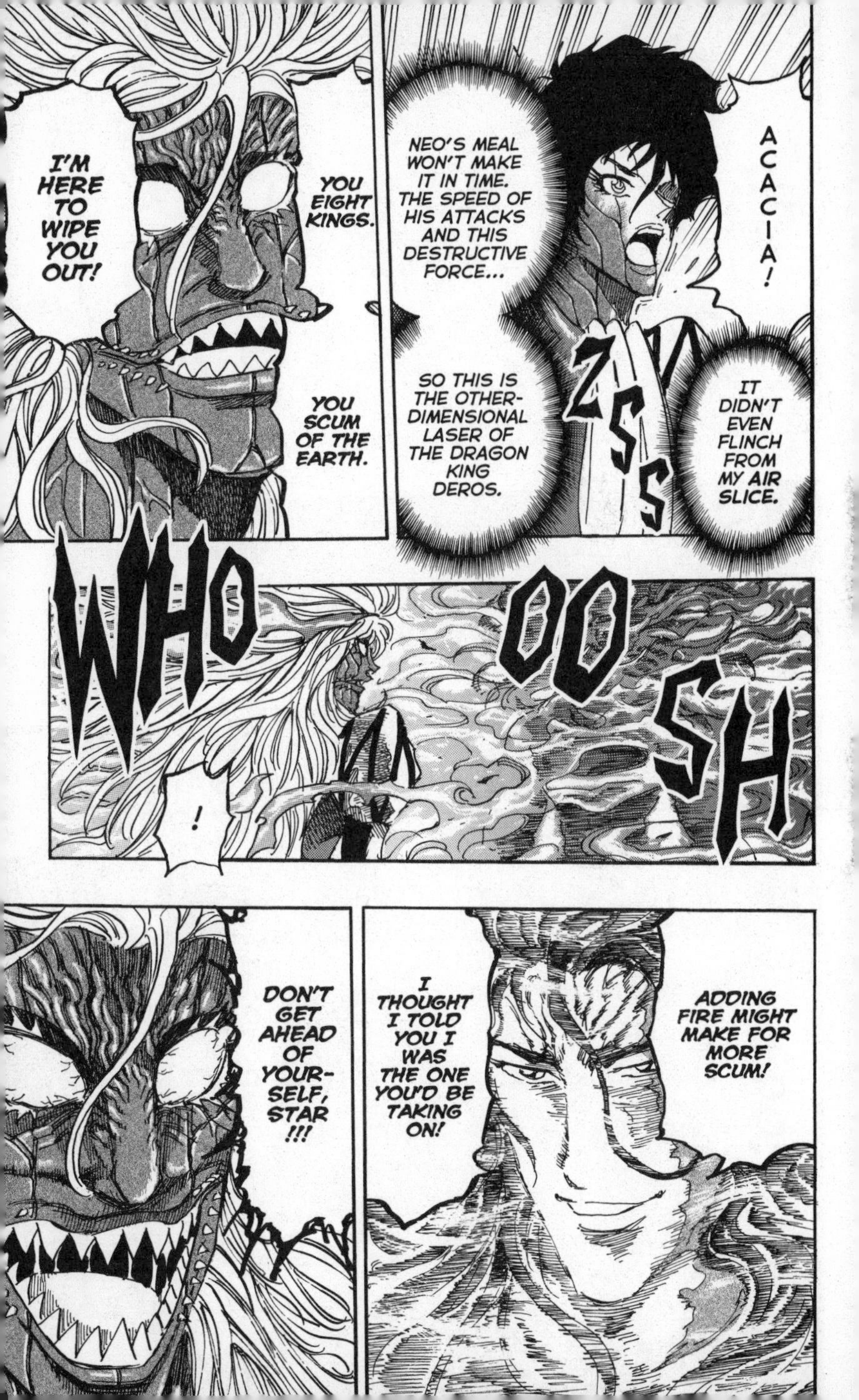
ACACIA!
NEO'S MEAL WON'T MAKE IT IN TIME. THE SPEED OF HIS ATTACKS AND THIS DESTRUCTIVE FORCE...
IT DIDN'T EVEN FLINCH FROM MY AIR SLICE.
ZSSS
SO THIS IS THE OTHER-DIMENSIONAL LASER OF THE DRAGON KING DEROS.
YOU EIGHT KINGS.
YOU SCUM OF THE EARTH.
I'M HERE TO WIPE YOU OUT!
WHOOOSH
!
ADDING FIRE MIGHT MAKE FOR MORE SCUM!
I THOUGHT I TOLD YOU I WAS THE ONE YOU'D BE TAKING ON!
DON'T GET AHEAD OF YOURSELF, STAR!!!

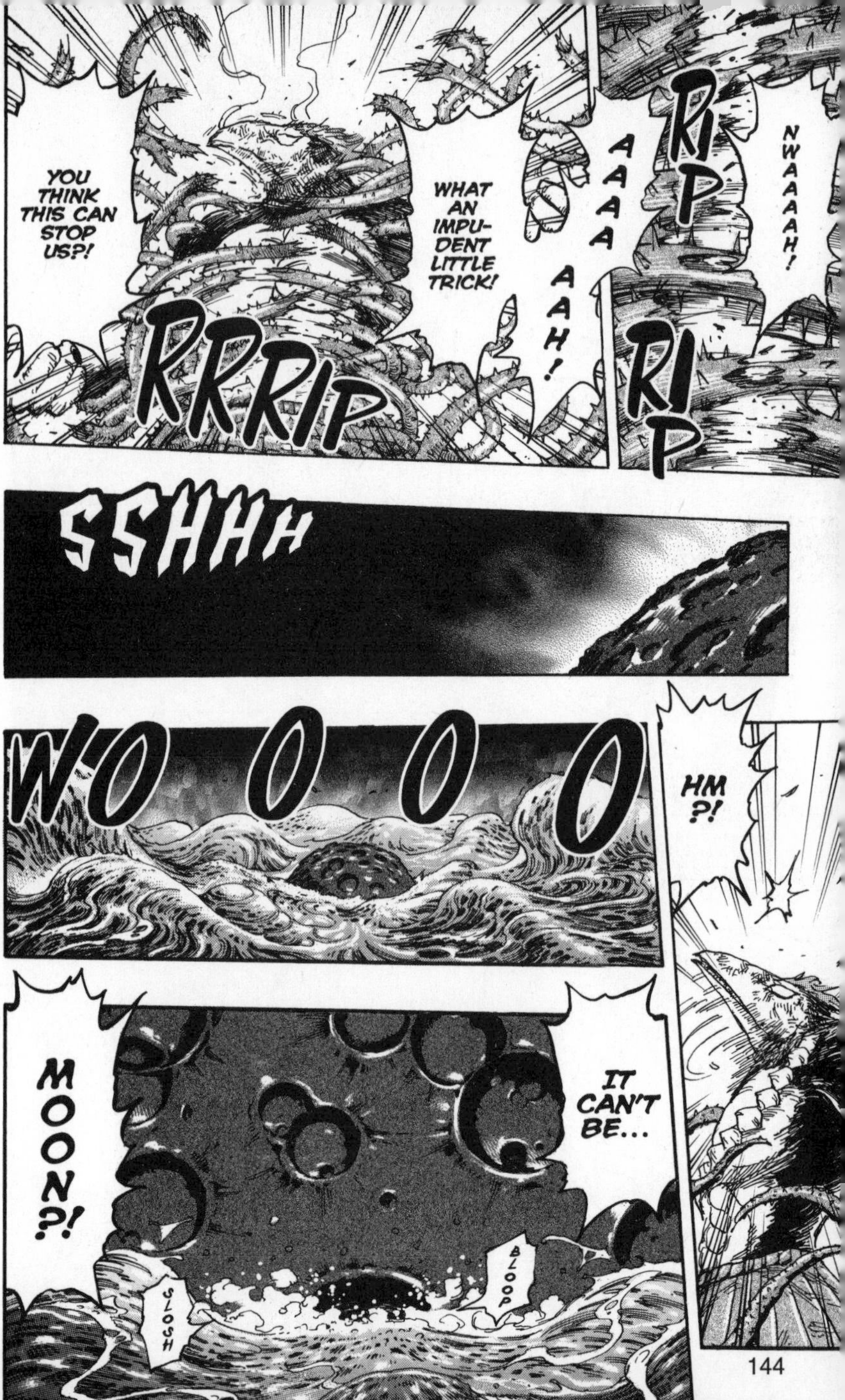

RIP
NWAAAAAH!
RIP
AAAAAAH!
WHAT AN IMPUDENT LITTLE TRICK!
YOU THINK THIS CAN STOP US?!
RRRIP
SSHHH
HM?!
WOOOO
IT CAN'T BE...
MOON?!
BLOOP
SLOSH

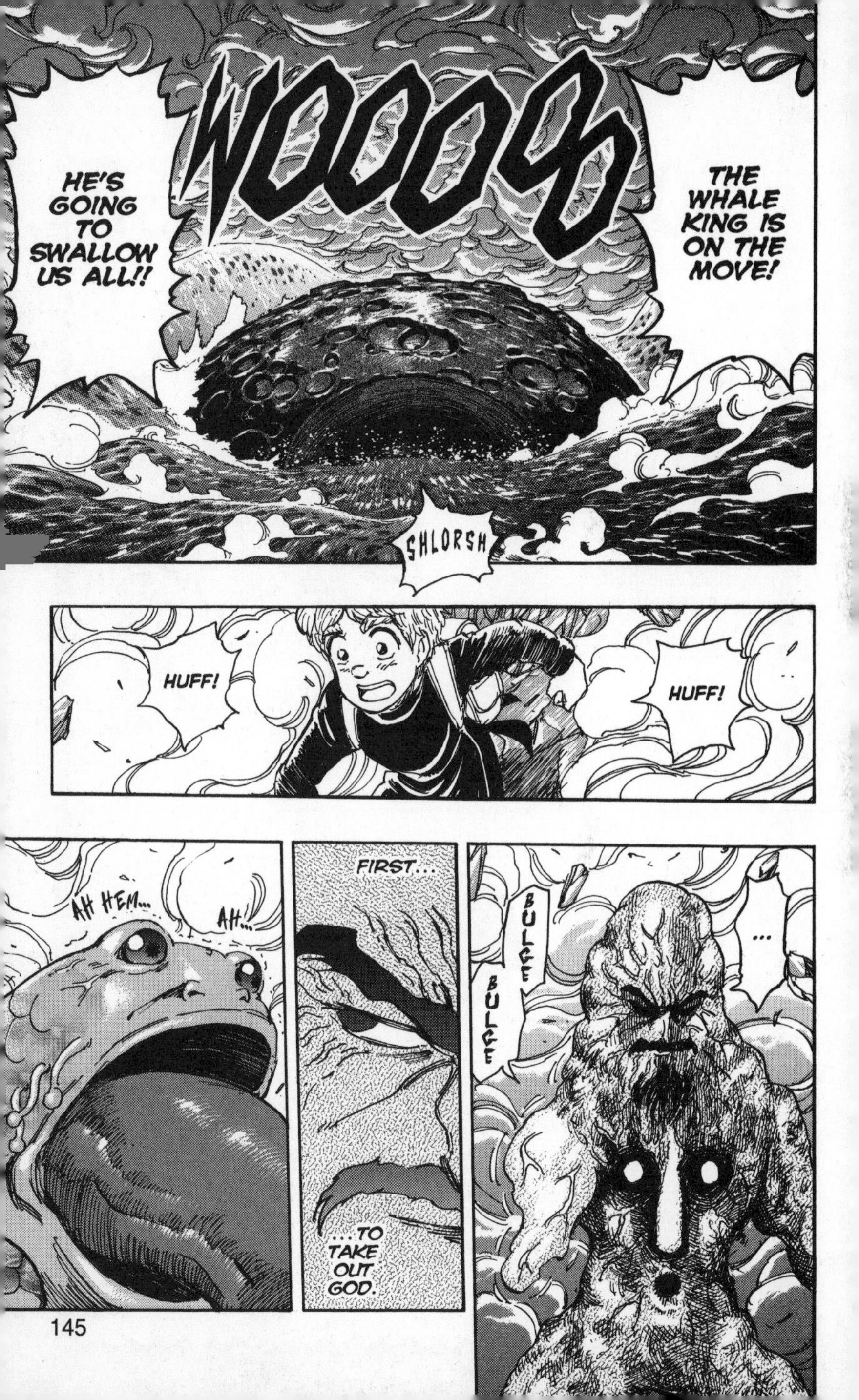
WOOOSH
THE WHALE KING IS ON THE MOVE!
HE'S GOING TO SWALLOW US ALL!!
SHLORSH
HUFF!
HUFF!
...
BULGE
BULGE
FIRST...
...TO TAKE OUT GOD.
AH!...
AH HEM...

TORIKO

GOURMET CHECKLIST

Vol. 408

MOON MUSHROOM
(CLASSIFICATION UNKNOWN)

CAPTURE LEVEL: UNKNOWN
HABITAT: UNKNOWN
SIZE: UNKNOWN
HEIGHT: UNKNOWN
WEIGHT: UNKNOWN
PRICE: UNKNOWN

A MOON MUSHROOM THAT MAGNIFICENTLY SWIMS THE MILKY WAY.**

SCALE

IT SWIMS THROUGHOUT THE MILKY WAY AND WILL ONCE IN A WHILE MAKE AN APPEARANCE IN THE NIGHT SKY OF THE GOURMET WORLD, TAKING THE SHAPE OF A FULL MOON. LEGEND HAS IT THAT IF YOU TOUCH A MOON MUSHROOM, YOUR FOOD LUCK WILL INCREASE, BUT IF YOU EAT IT, YOUR FOOD LUCK WILL PLUMMET. HOWEVER, HAVING NO REGARD FOR SUCH LEGENDS, THE SNAKE KING, MOTHER SNAKE, WILL HAPPILY PREY ON IT IN OUTER SPACE. IT'S ONE OF HER FAVORITE COSMIC INGREDIENTS.

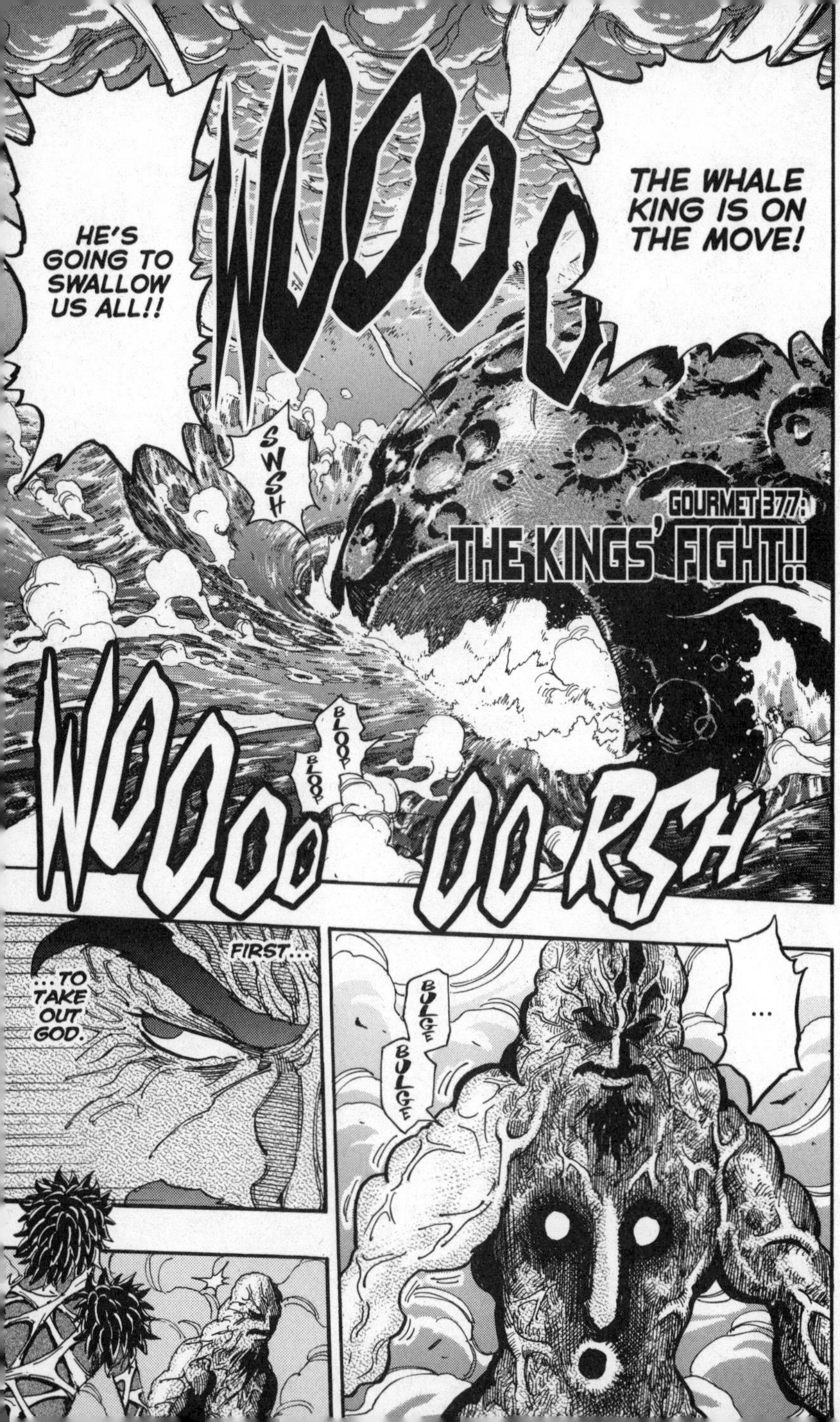
THE WHALE KING IS ON THE MOVE!
HE'S GOING TO SWALLOW US ALL!!
SWSH
GOURMET 377:
THE KINGS' FIGHT!!
BLOOP BLOOP
WOOOO OO RSH
...
BULGE BULGE
FIRST...
...TO TAKE OUT GOD.

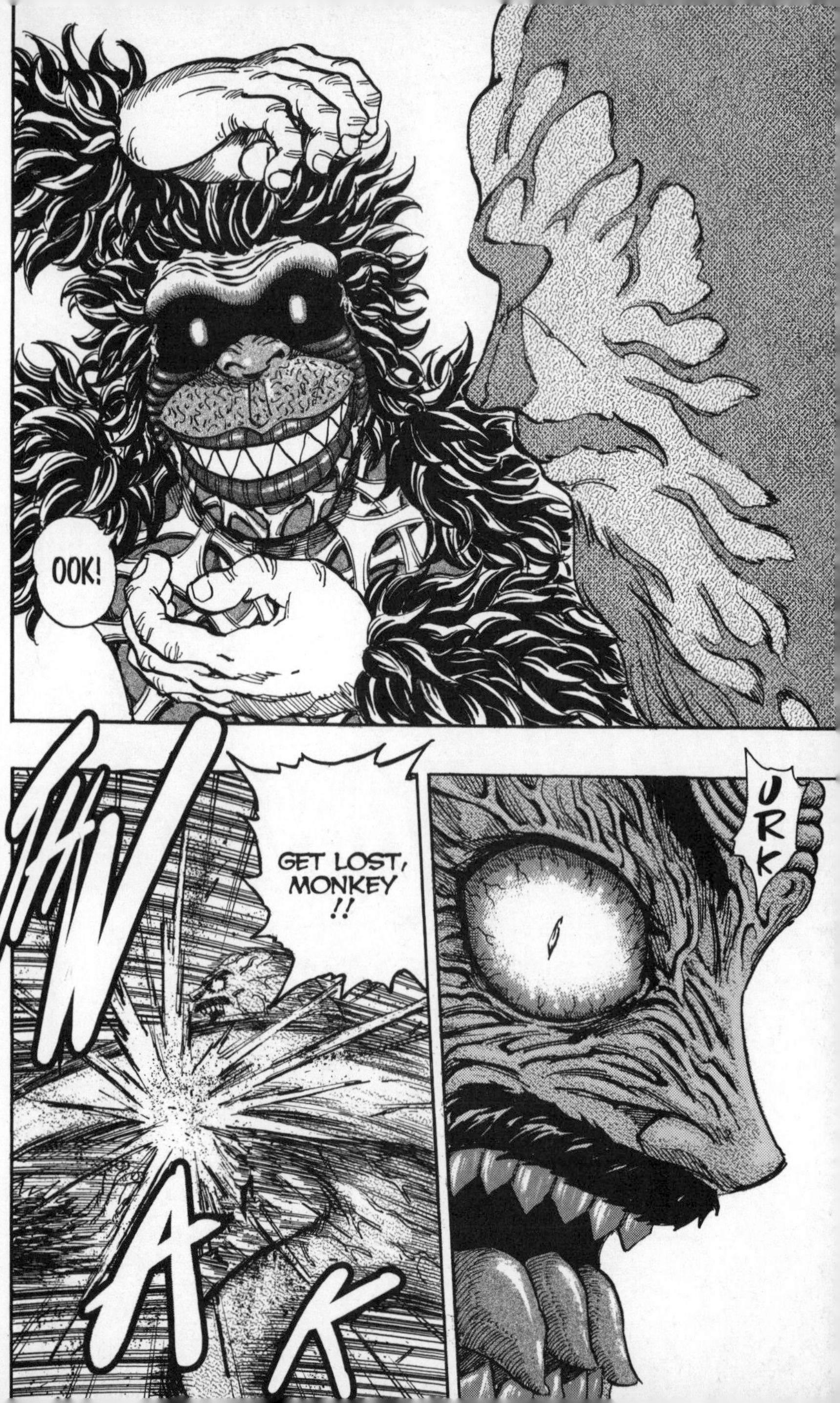
OOK!
URK
GET LOST, MONKEY !!
THWAK

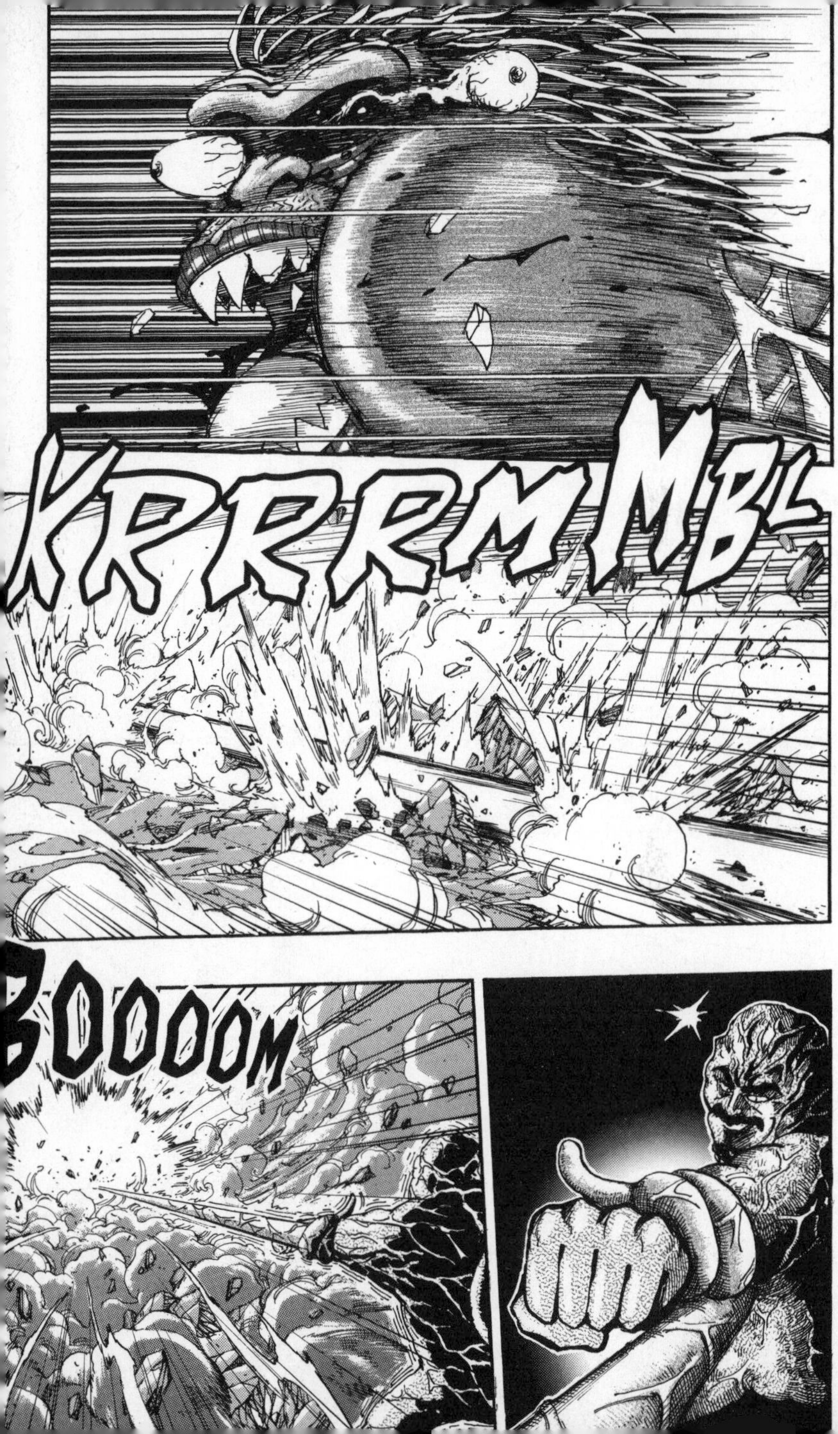
KRRRMMBL
BOOOOM

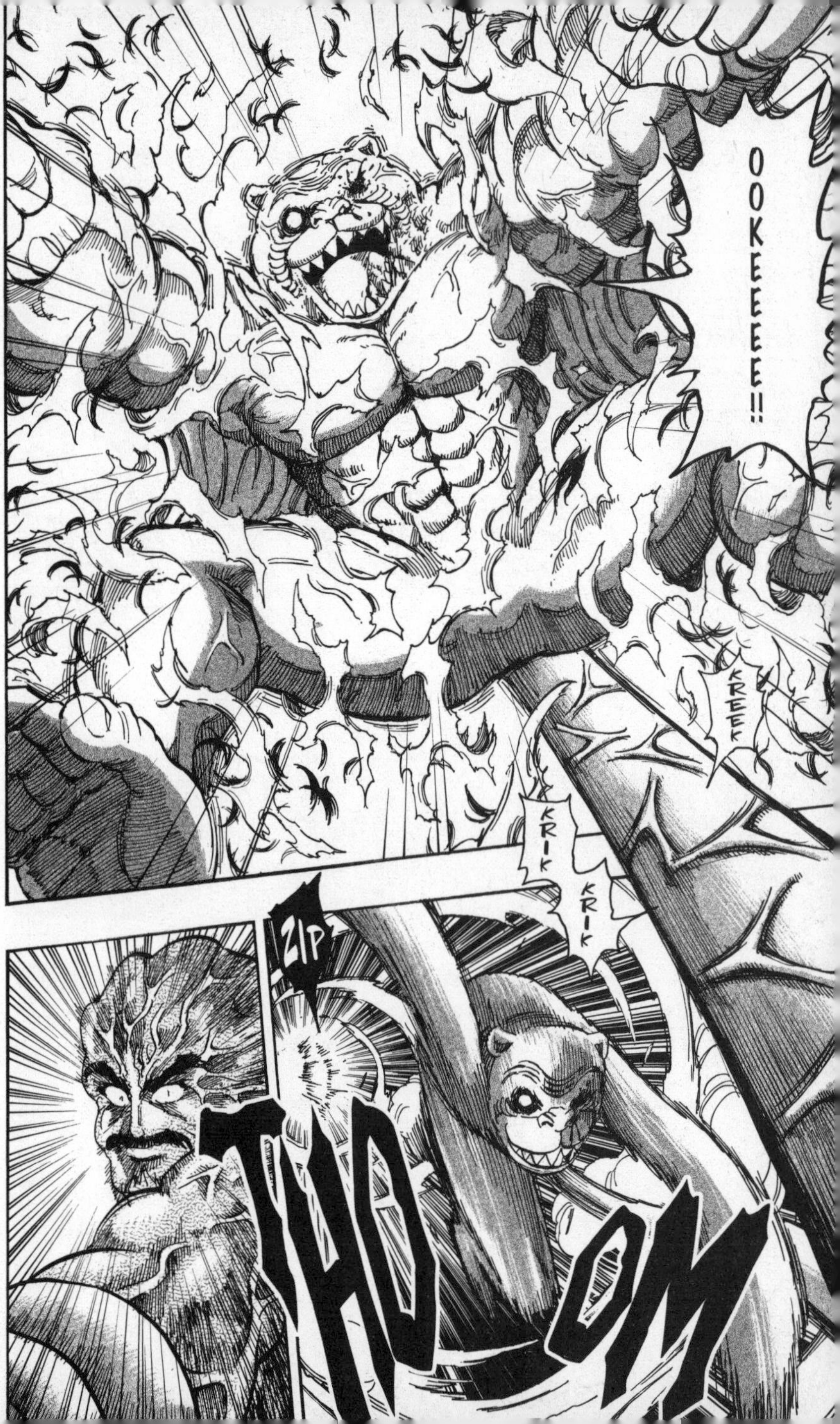
OOKEEEEEE!!
KREEK
KRIK
KRIK
ZIP
THOOM

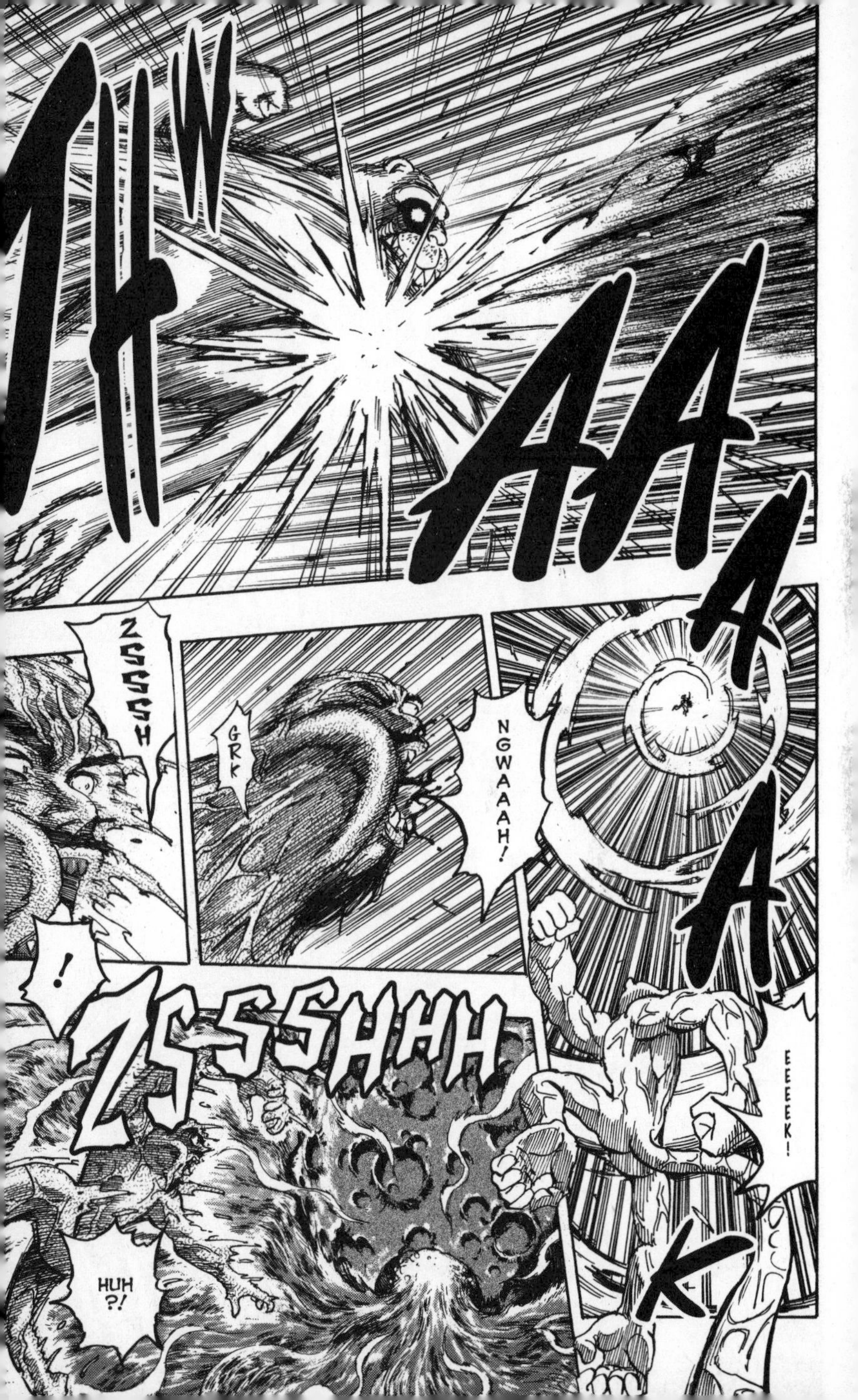
THWAAAAAAK
NGWAAAAH!
GRK
ZSSSH
EEEEK!
ZSSSHHH
!
HUH?!

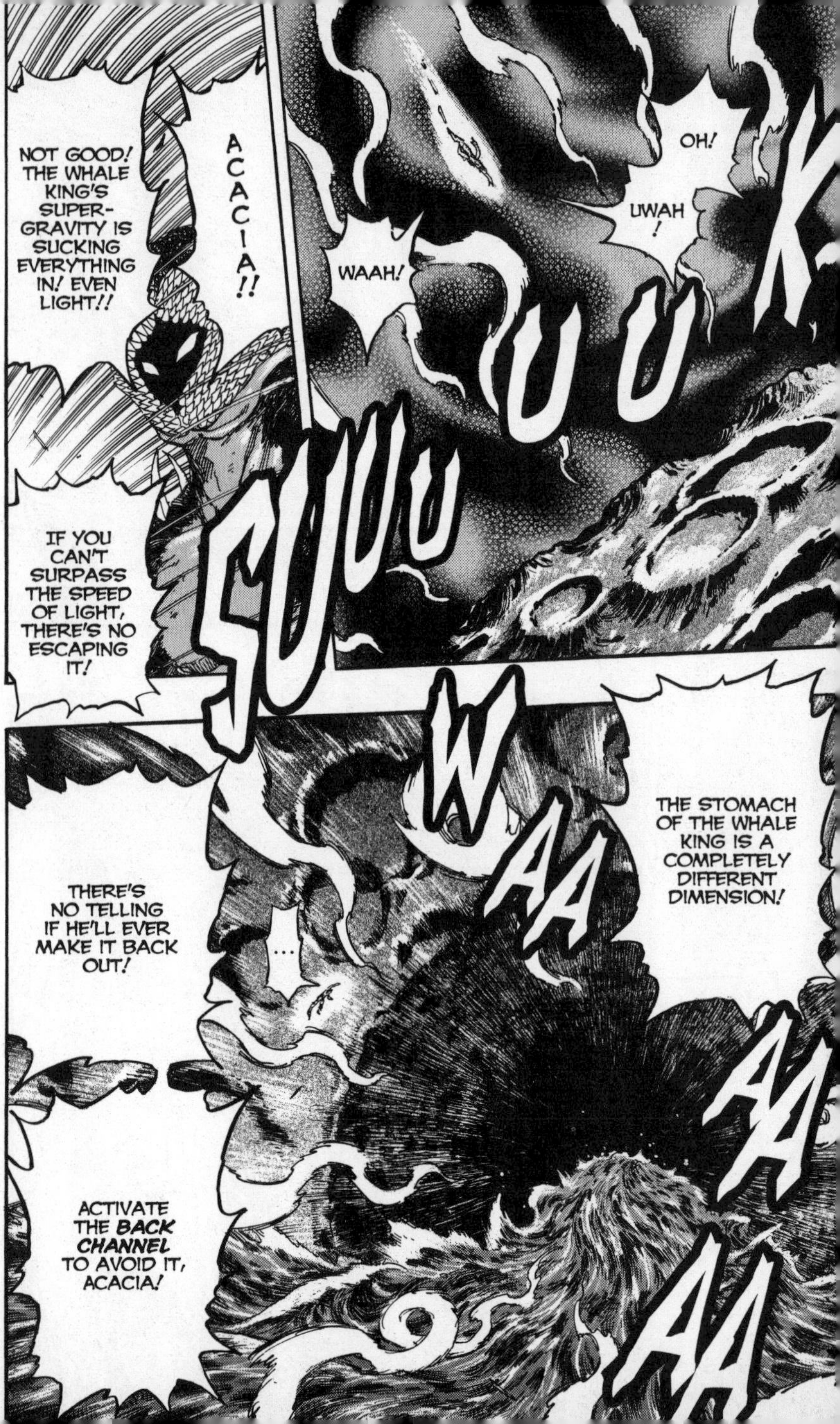
OH!
UWAH!
WAAH!
SUUUUUK
ACACIA!!
NOT GOOD! THE WHALE KING'S SUPER-GRAVITY IS SUCKING EVERYTHING IN! EVEN LIGHT!!
IF YOU CAN'T SURPASS THE SPEED OF LIGHT, THERE'S NO ESCAPING IT!
THE STOMACH OF THE WHALE KING IS A COMPLETELY DIFFERENT DIMENSION!
THERE'S NO TELLING IF HE'LL EVER MAKE IT BACK OUT!
...
ACTIVATE THE ***BACK CHANNEL*** TO AVOID IT, ACACIA!
WAAAAAAA

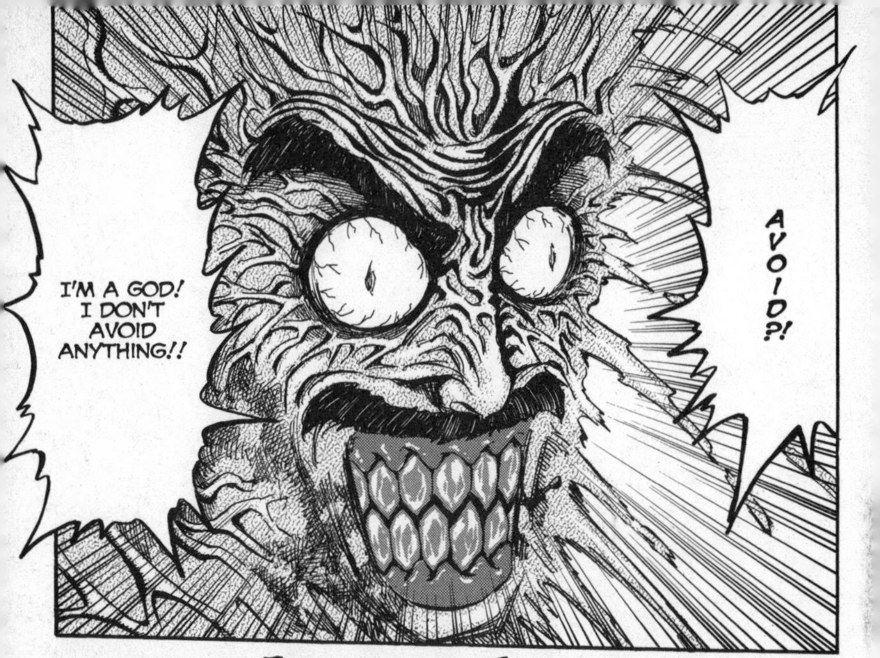
AVOID?!
I'M A GOD! I DON'T AVOID ANYTHING!!

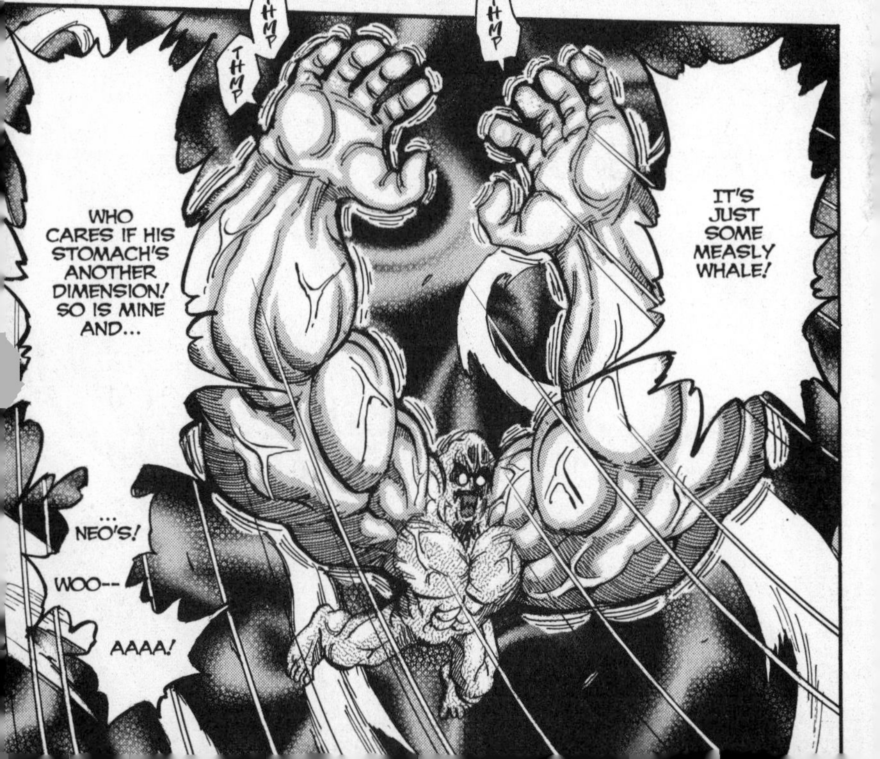
THMP
THMP
THMP
IT'S JUST SOME MEASLY WHALE!
WHO CARES IF HIS STOMACH'S ANOTHER DIMENSION! SO IS MINE AND...
...NEO'S!
WOO--
AAAA!

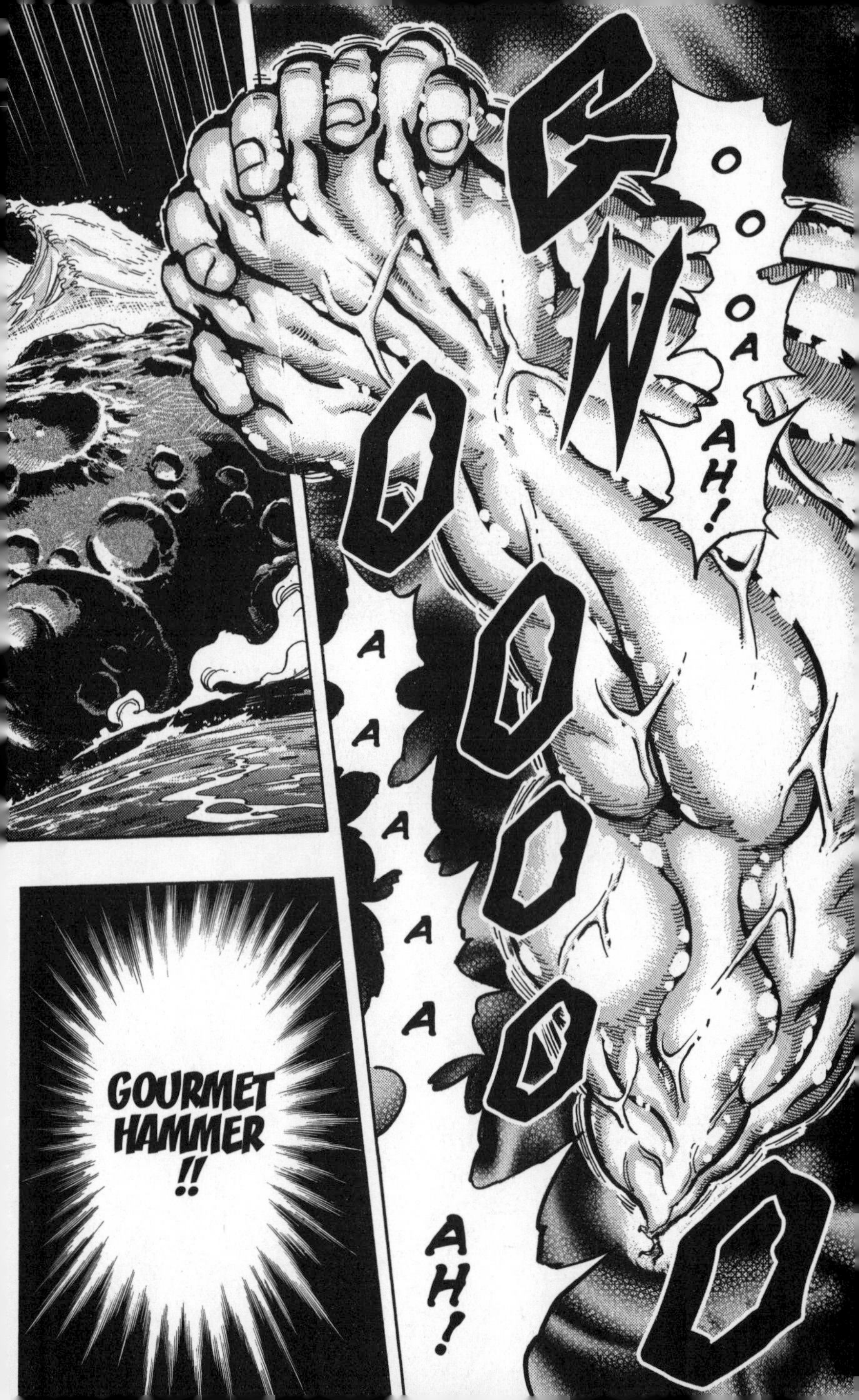
GWOOOOO
OOAAAH!
AAAAAAH!
GOURMET HAMMER!!

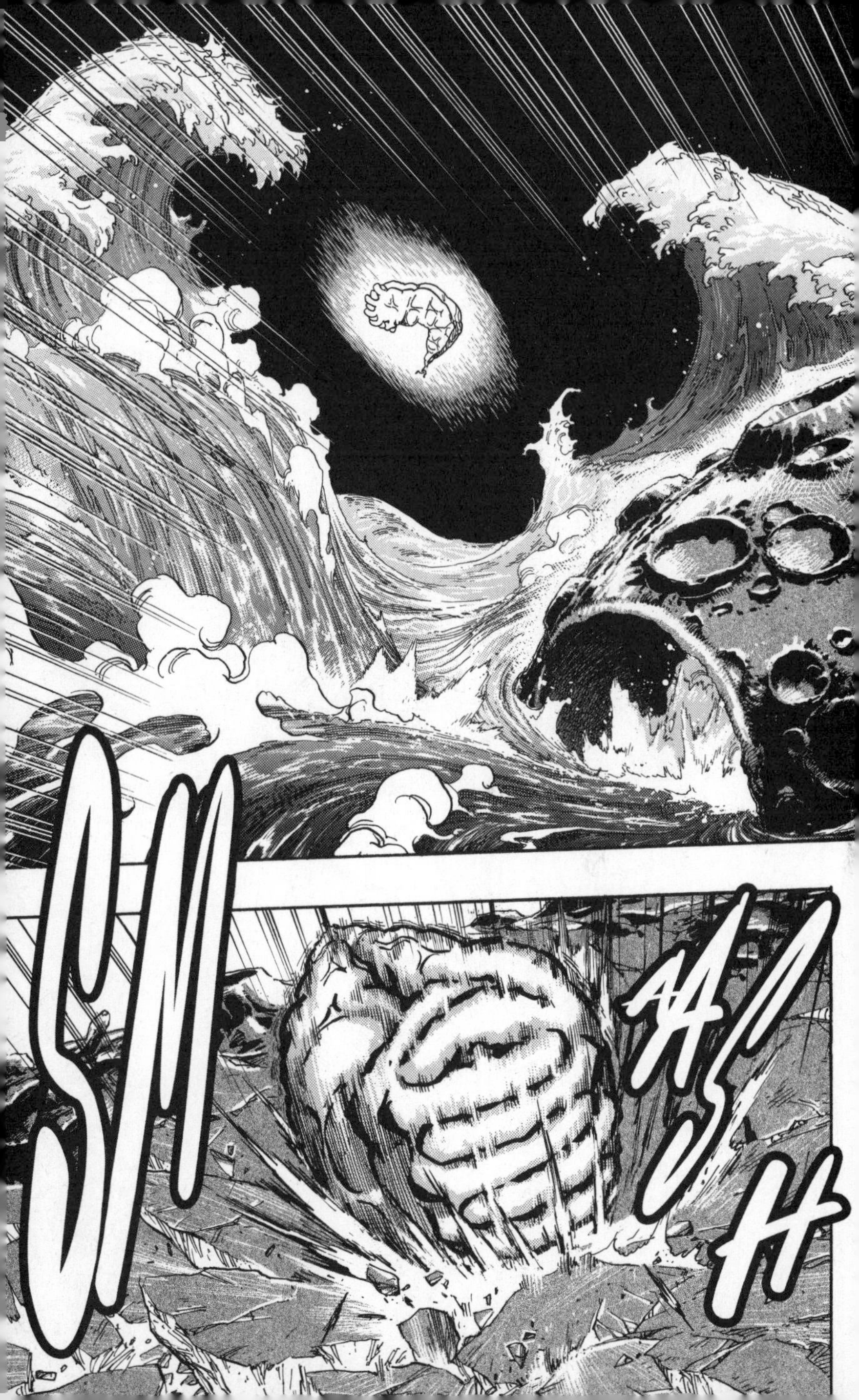
SMASH

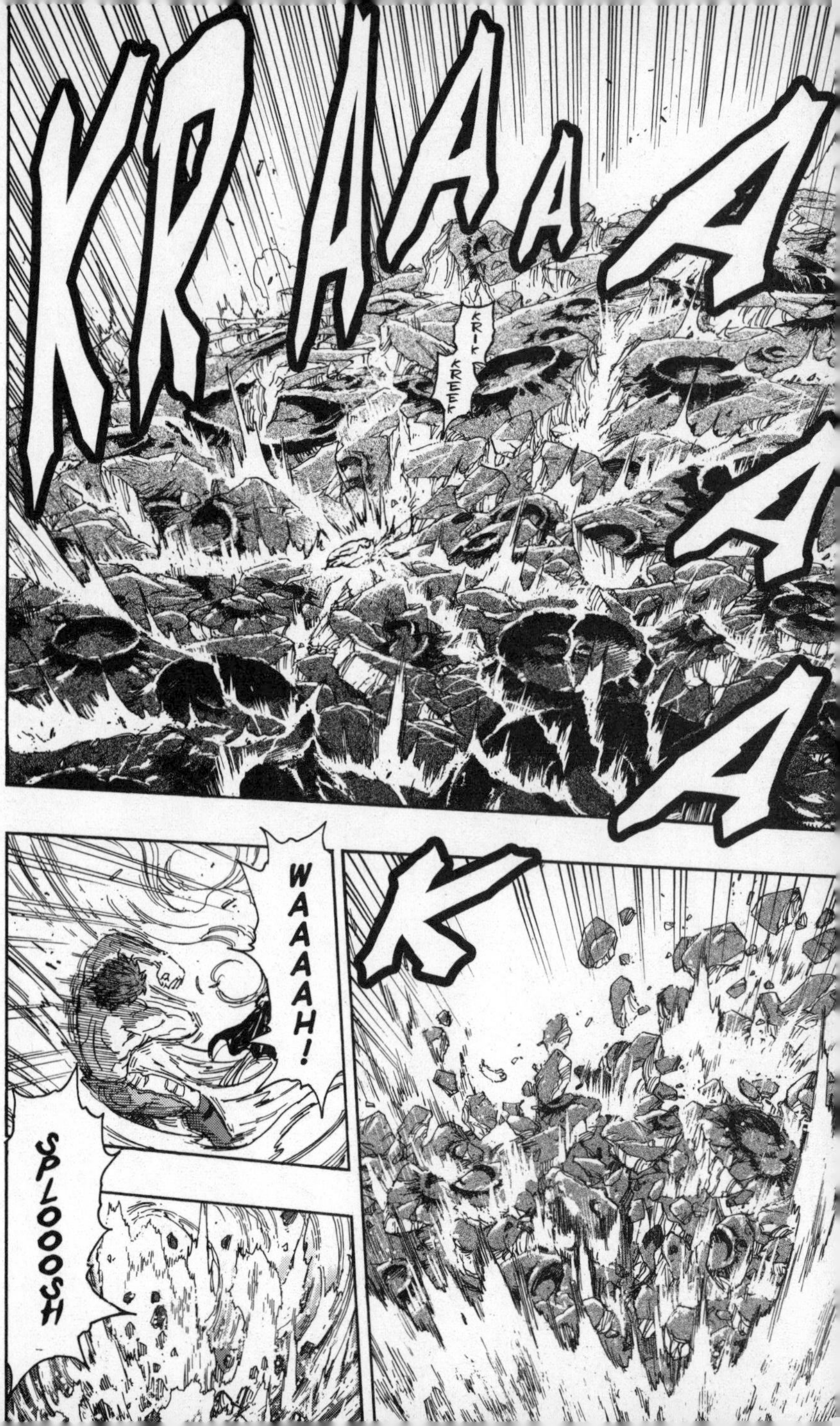
KRAAAAAAAK
KRIK KREEK
WAAAAAH!
SPLOOOOSH

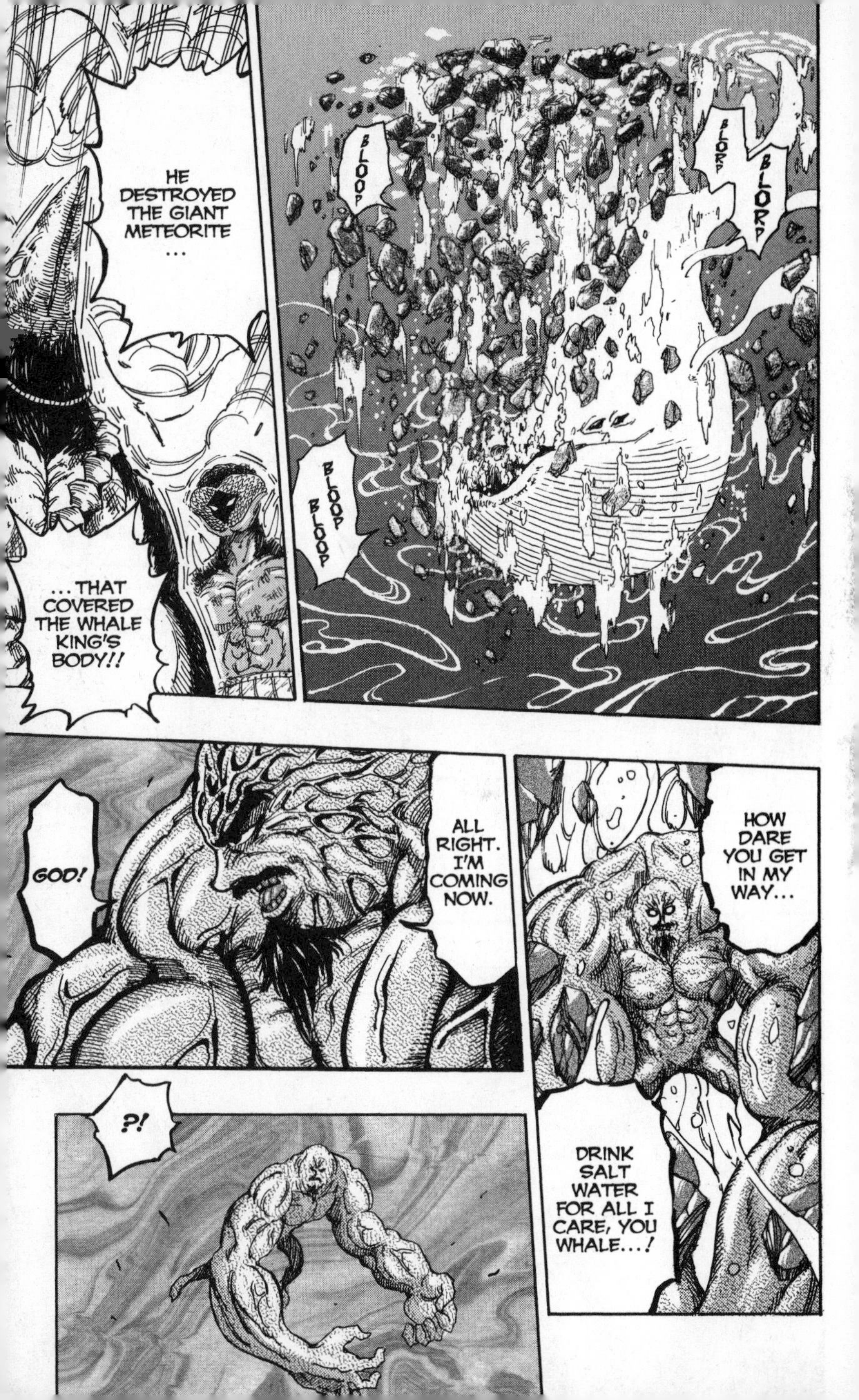
BLORP
BLORP
BLOOP
BLOOP BLOOP
HE DESTROYED THE GIANT METEORITE ...
...THAT COVERED THE WHALE KING'S BODY!!
HOW DARE YOU GET IN MY WAY...
DRINK SALT WATER FOR ALL I CARE, YOU WHALE...!
ALL RIGHT. I'M COMING NOW.
GOD!
?!

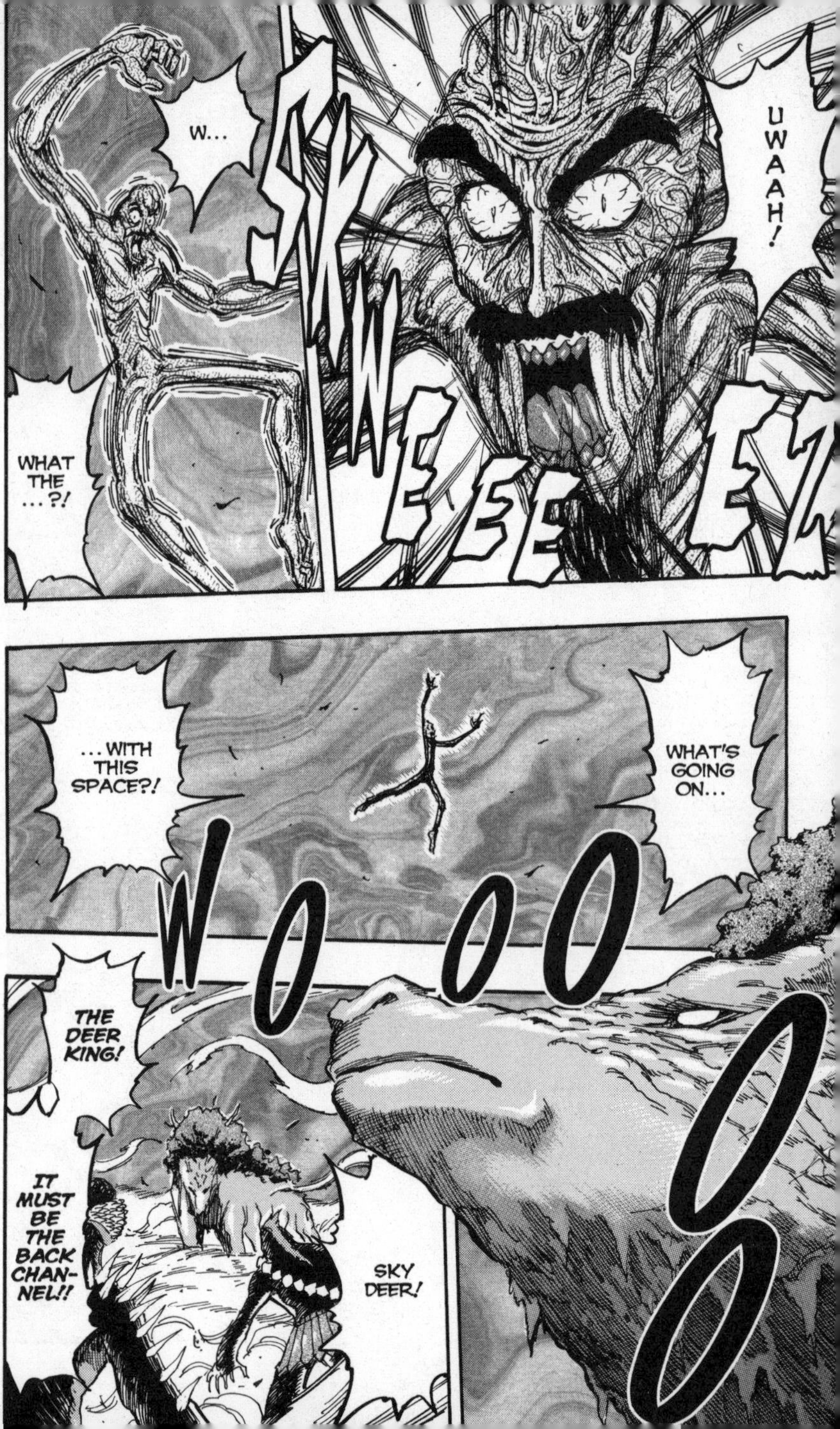
UWAAH!
SKWEEEE
W...
WHAT THE ...?!
WHAT'S GOING ON...
...WITH THIS SPACE?!
WOOOOO
THE DEER KING!
SKY DEER!
IT MUST BE THE BACK CHANNEL!!

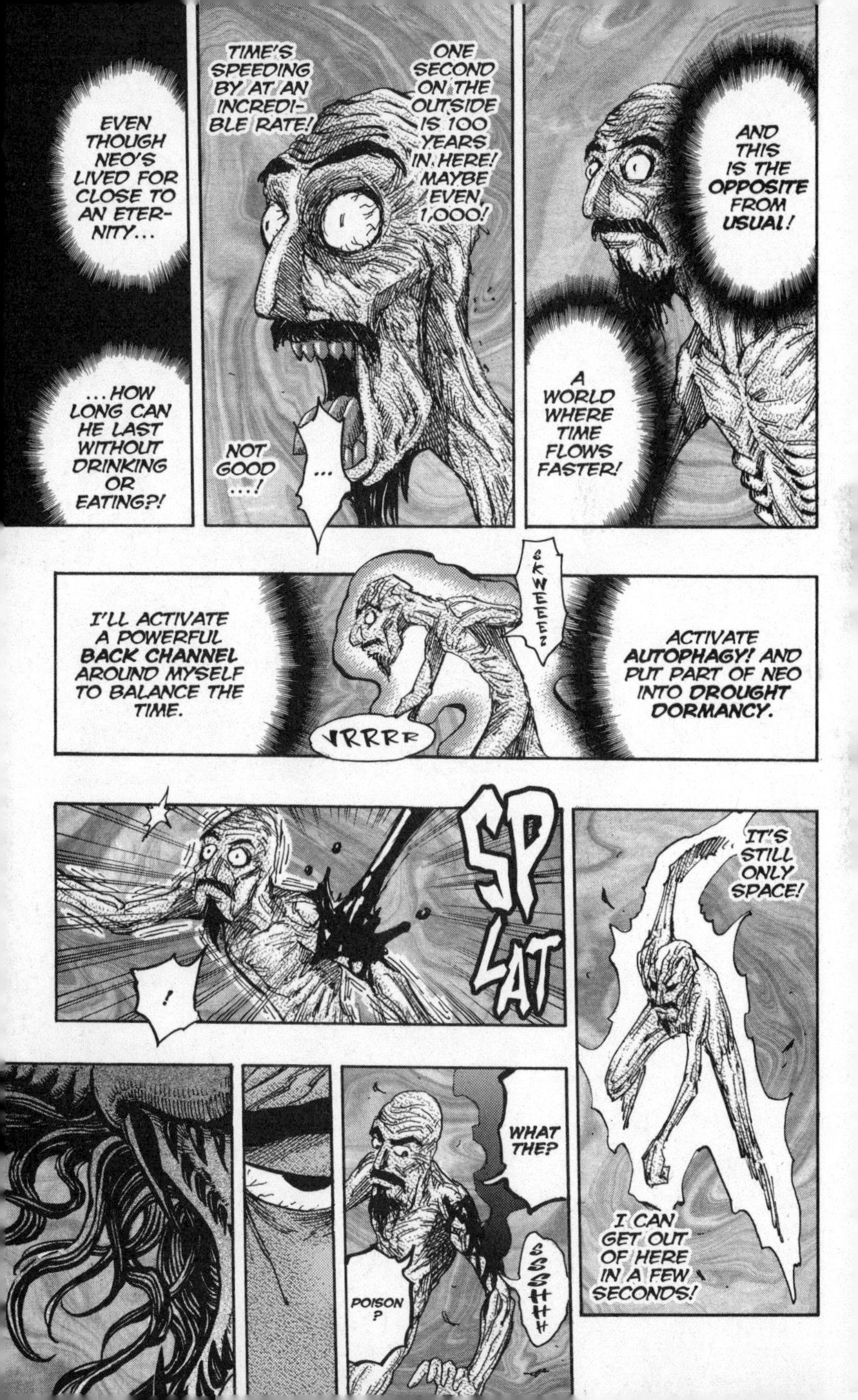
AND THIS IS THE OPPOSITE FROM USUAL!
A WORLD WHERE TIME FLOWS FASTER!
ONE SECOND ON THE OUTSIDE IS 100 YEARS IN HERE! MAYBE EVEN 1,000!
TIME'S SPEEDING BY AT AN INCREDIBLE RATE!
...
NOT GOOD...!
EVEN THOUGH NEO'S LIVED FOR CLOSE TO AN ETERNITY...
...HOW LONG CAN HE LAST WITHOUT DRINKING OR EATING?!
ACTIVATE AUTOPHAGY! AND PUT PART OF NEO INTO DROUGHT DORMANCY.
SKWEEEZ
I'LL ACTIVATE A POWERFUL BACK CHANNEL AROUND MYSELF TO BALANCE THE TIME.
VRRRR
IT'S STILL ONLY SPACE!
I CAN GET OUT OF HERE IN A FEW SECONDS!
SPLAT
!
WHAT THE?
SSSHHH
POISON?

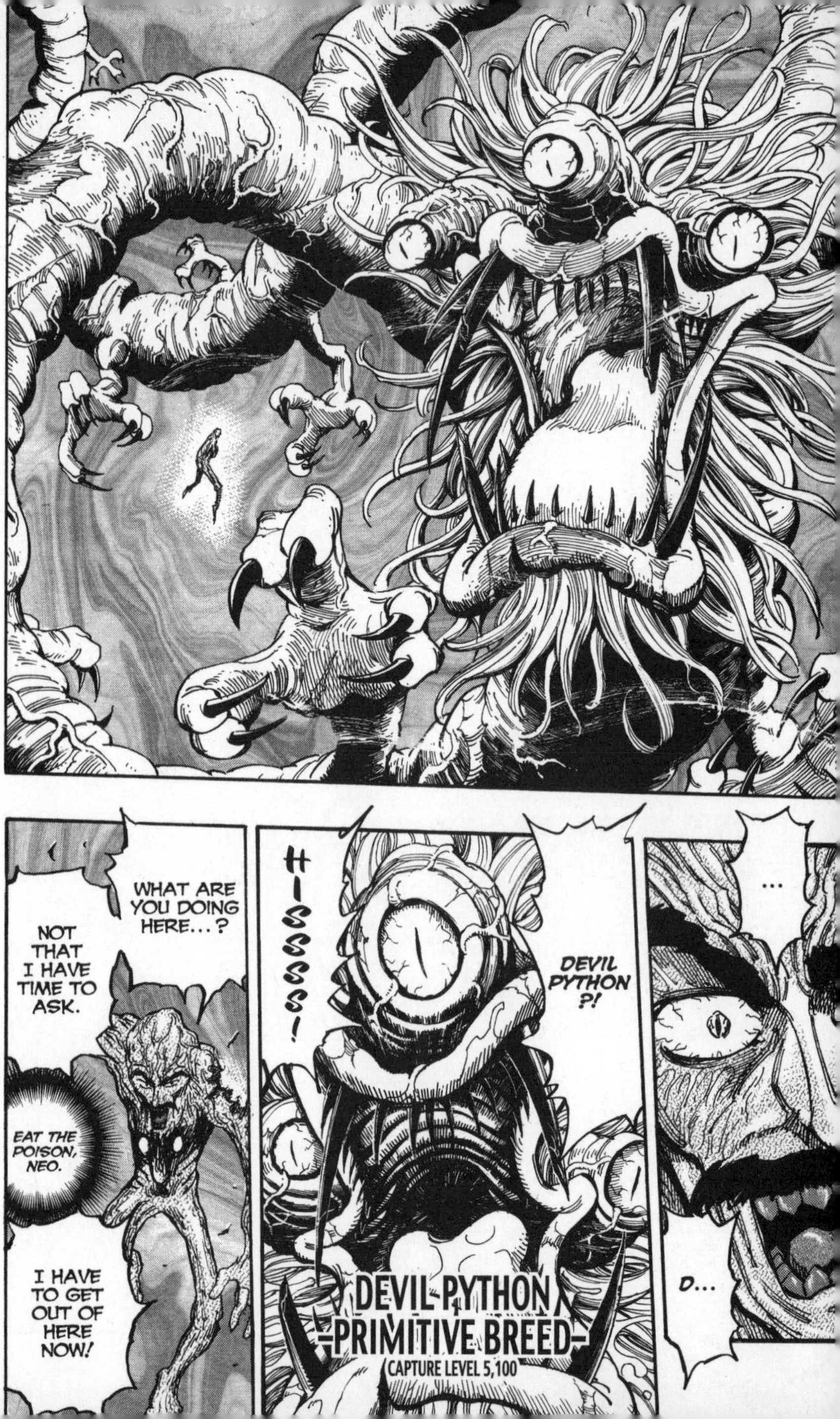
...
D...
DEVIL PYTHON?!
HI-SSSSS!
DEVIL PYTHON
-PRIMITIVE BREED-
CAPTURE LEVEL 5,100
WHAT ARE YOU DOING HERE...?
NOT THAT I HAVE TIME TO ASK.
EAT THE POISON, NEO.
I HAVE TO GET OUT OF HERE NOW!

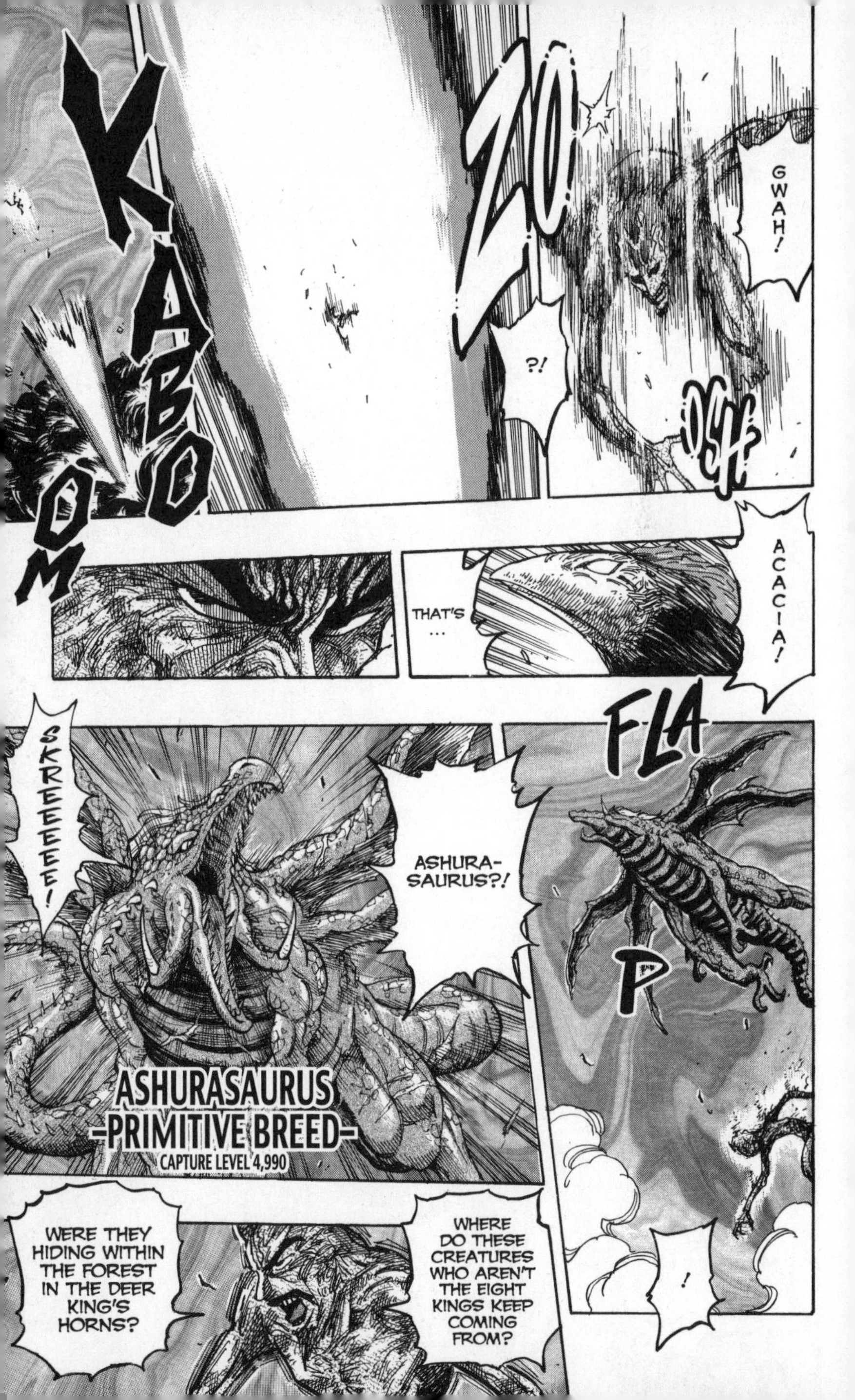
ZO
GWAH!
?!
OSH
KABOOOM
ACACIA!
THAT'S …
FLA
P
!
ASHURA-SAURUS?!
SKREEEEEE!
ASHURASAURUS
-PRIMITIVE BREED-
CAPTURE LEVEL 4,990
WHERE DO THESE CREATURES WHO AREN'T THE EIGHT KINGS KEEP COMING FROM?
WERE THEY HIDING WITHIN THE FOREST IN THE DEER KING'S HORNS?

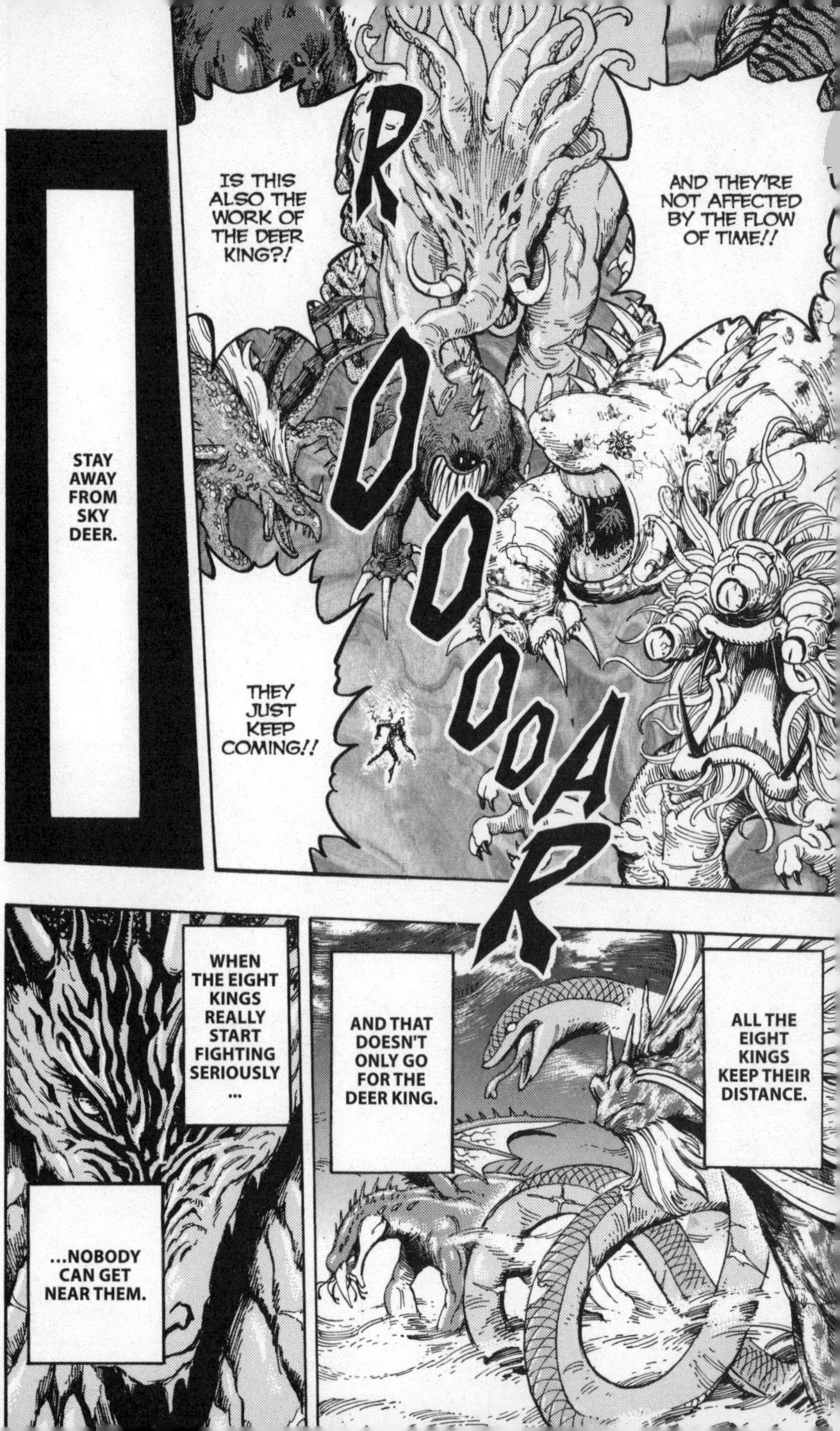
AND THEY'RE NOT AFFECTED BY THE FLOW OF TIME!!
IS THIS ALSO THE WORK OF THE DEER KING?!
ROOOOAR
THEY JUST KEEP COMING!!
STAY AWAY FROM SKY DEER.
ALL THE EIGHT KINGS KEEP THEIR DISTANCE.
AND THAT DOESN'T ONLY GO FOR THE DEER KING.
WHEN THE EIGHT KINGS REALLY START FIGHTING SERIOUSLY ...
...NOBODY CAN GET NEAR THEM.

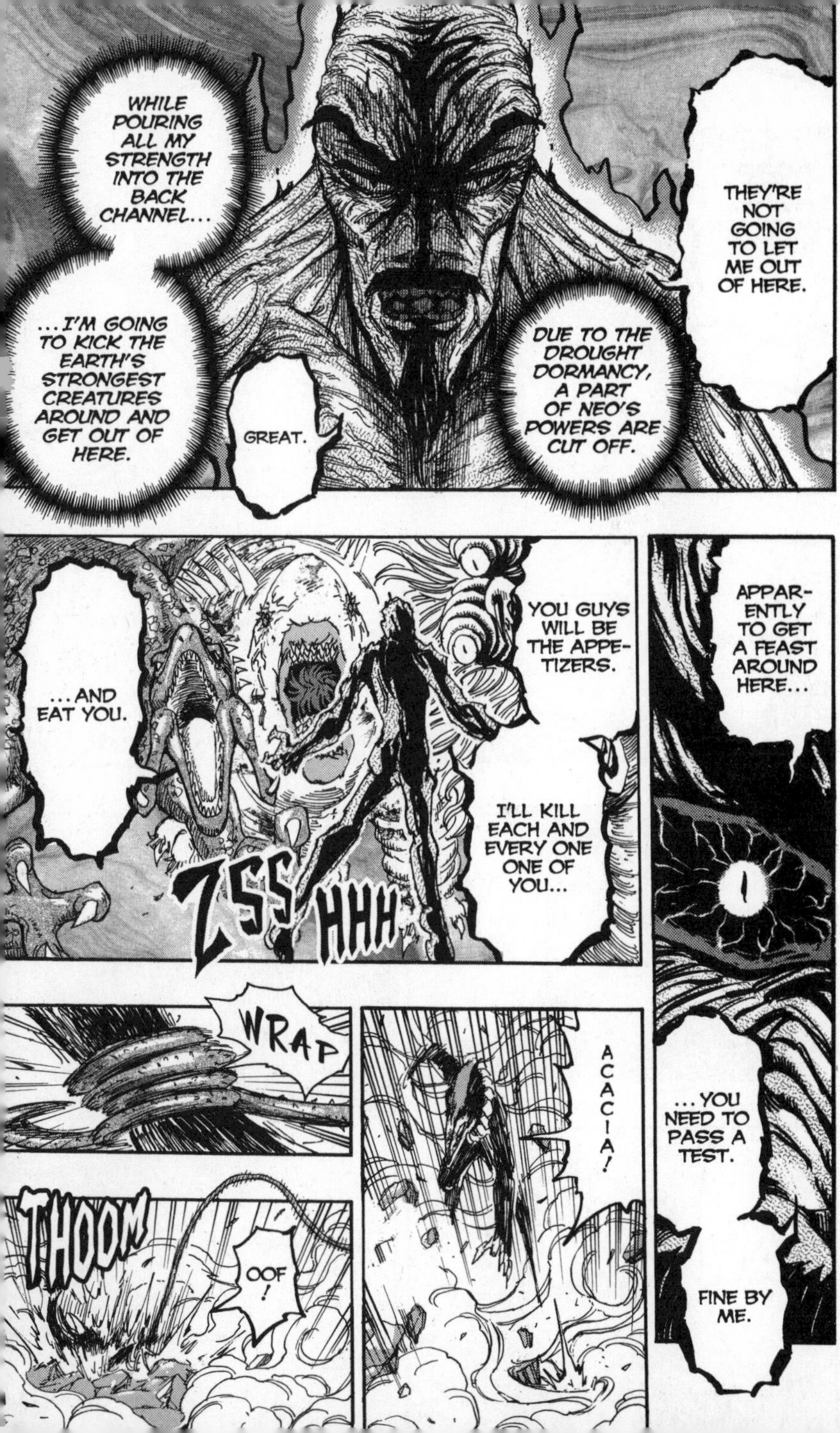
THEY'RE NOT GOING TO LET ME OUT OF HERE.
DUE TO THE DROUGHT DORMANCY, A PART OF NEO'S POWERS ARE CUT OFF.
GREAT.
WHILE POURING ALL MY STRENGTH INTO THE BACK CHANNEL...
...I'M GOING TO KICK THE EARTH'S STRONGEST CREATURES AROUND AND GET OUT OF HERE.
APPAR-ENTLY TO GET A FEAST AROUND HERE...
...YOU NEED TO PASS A TEST.
FINE BY ME.
YOU GUYS WILL BE THE APPE-TIZERS.
I'LL KILL EACH AND EVERY ONE ONE OF YOU...
...AND EAT YOU.
ZSSHHH
ACACIA!
WRAP
THOOM
OOF!

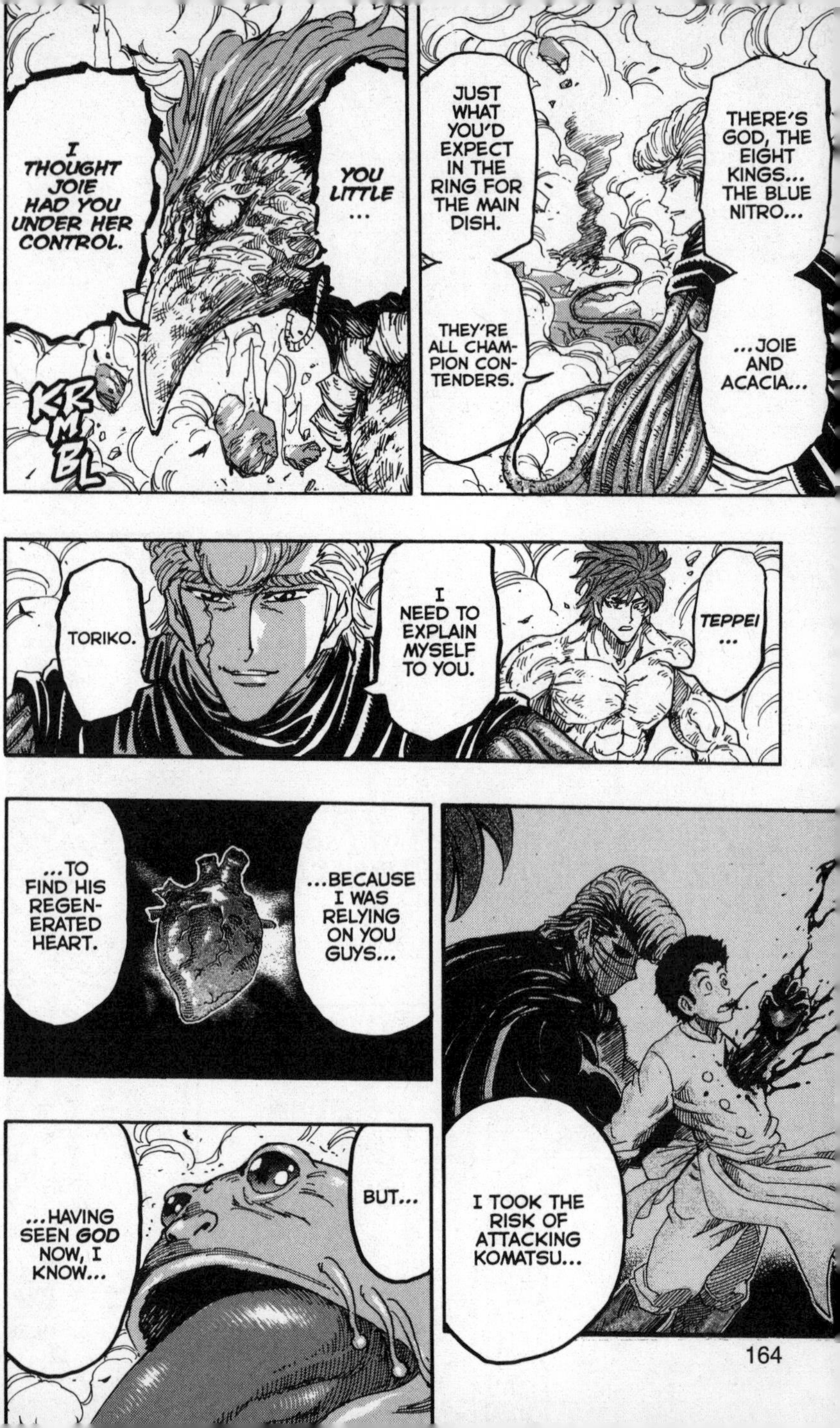
THERE'S GOD, THE EIGHT KINGS... THE BLUE NITRO...
...JOIE AND ACACIA...
THEY'RE ALL CHAMPION CONTENDERS.
JUST WHAT YOU'D EXPECT IN THE RING FOR THE MAIN DISH.
YOU LITTLE...
I THOUGHT JOIE HAD YOU UNDER HER CONTROL.
KRMBL
TEPPEI...
TORIKO.
I NEED TO EXPLAIN MYSELF TO YOU.
I TOOK THE RISK OF ATTACKING KOMATSU...
...BECAUSE I WAS RELYING ON YOU GUYS...
...TO FIND HIS REGENERATED HEART.
BUT...
...HAVING SEEN GOD NOW, I KNOW...

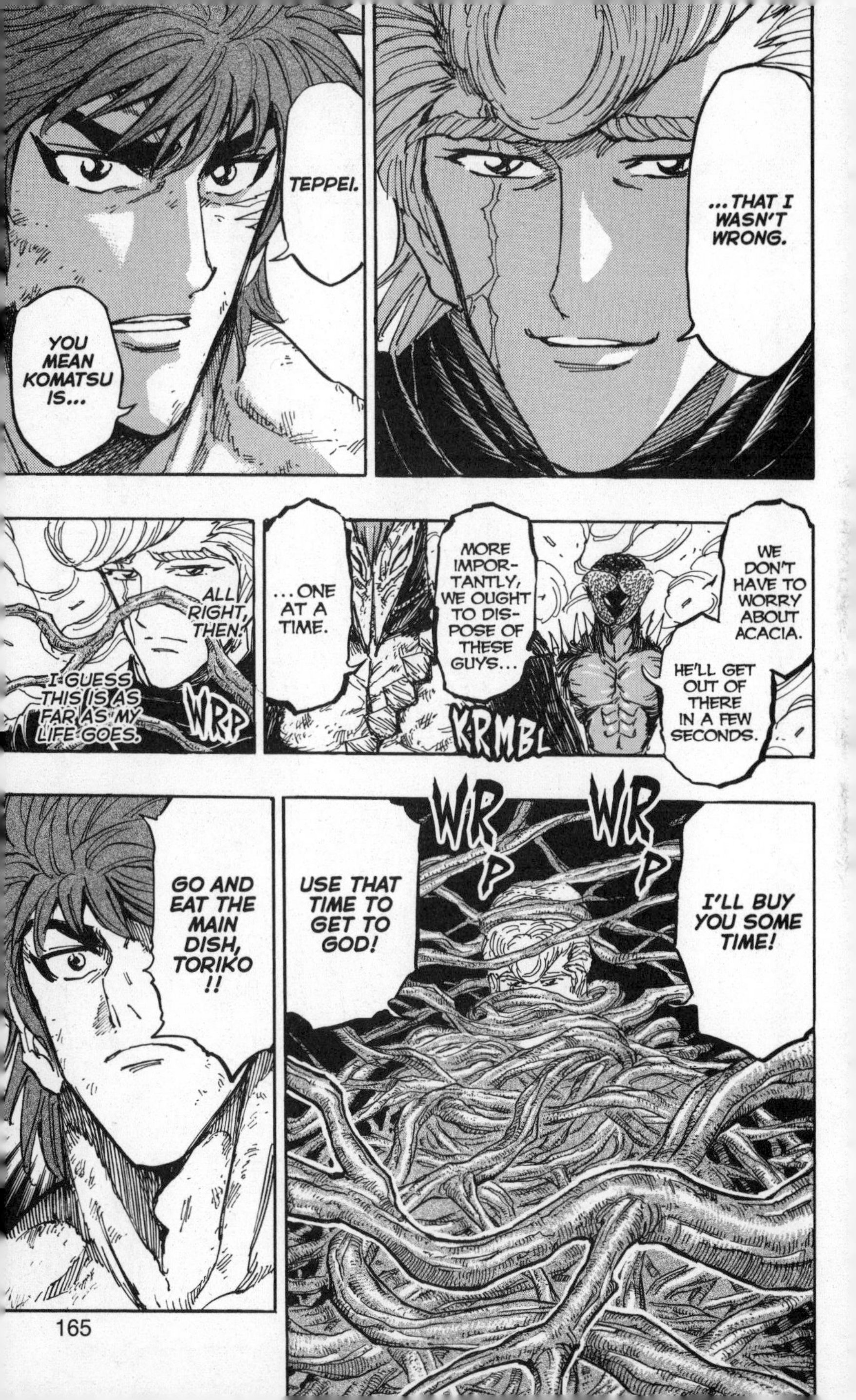
...THAT I WASN'T WRONG.
TEPPEI.
YOU MEAN KOMATSU IS...
WE DON'T HAVE TO WORRY ABOUT ACACIA.
HE'LL GET OUT OF THERE IN A FEW SECONDS.
MORE IMPORTANTLY, WE OUGHT TO DISPOSE OF THESE GUYS...
KRMBL
...ONE AT A TIME.
ALL RIGHT, THEN.
I GUESS THIS IS AS FAR AS MY LIFE GOES.
WRP
WRP
WRP
I'LL BUY YOU SOME TIME!
USE THAT TIME TO GET TO GOD!
GO AND EAT THE MAIN DISH, TORIKO!!

GOURMET CHECKLIST

Vol. 409

RELIC FISH
(CLASSIFICATION UNKNOWN)

CAPTURE LEVEL: UNKNOWN
HABITAT: UNKNOWN
SIZE: UNKNOWN
HEIGHT: UNKNOWN
WEIGHT: UNKNOWN
PRICE: UNKNOWN

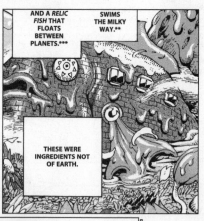

SWIMS THE MILKY WAY.**
AND A *RELIC FISH* THAT FLOATS BETWEEN PLANETS.***
THESE WERE INGREDIENTS NOT OF EARTH.

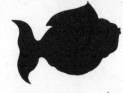

SCALE

A SPACE GOLDFISH THAT FLOATS BETWEEN PLANETS, ABSORBING PLANETS' AND LIFE-FORMS' CULTURES AS NOURISHMENT AS IT MOVES ALONG ITS WAY. THE ORGANS WITHIN ITS BODY ARE WEAPONS CREATED BASED ON ALL THE INFORMATION RECORDED FROM PROSPEROUS CULTURES THROUGHOUT TIME. IT'S VALUED FOR WHAT CAN BE LEARNED FROM IT BY SCHOLARS ALL OVER THE WORLD. BUT FOR THE SNAKE KING, MOTHER SNAKE, IT IS THE EPITOME OF A DIFFICULT CREATURE TO CAPTURE, SO THE DETAILS SURROUNDING ITS ECOLOGY HAVE YET TO BE UNDERSTOOD.

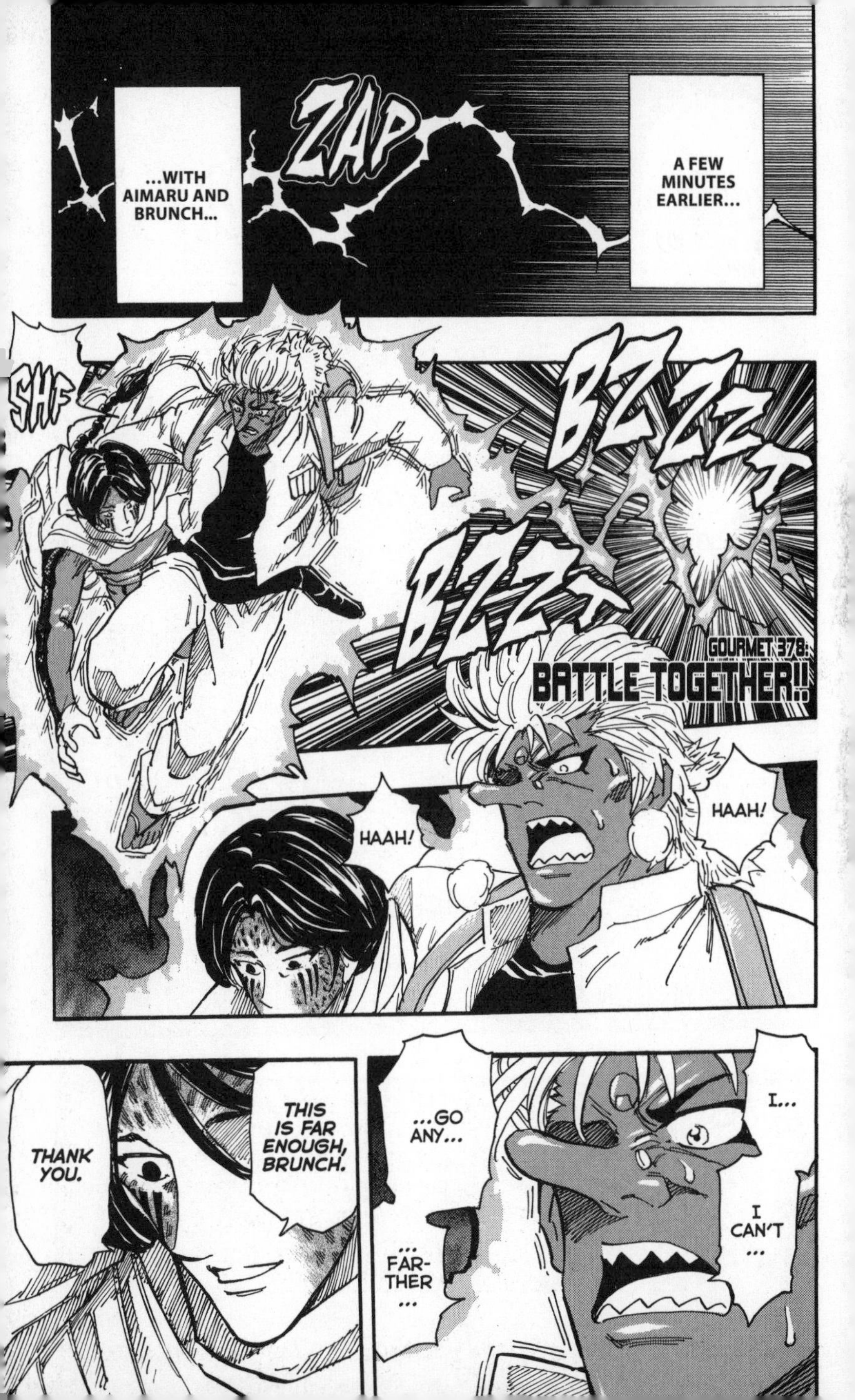
A FEW MINUTES EARLIER...
ZAP
...WITH AIMARU AND BRUNCH...
BZZZT
BZZT
SHF
GOURMET 378:
BATTLE TOGETHER!!
HAAH!
HAAH!
I...
I CAN'T...
...GO ANY...
...FAR-THER...
THIS IS FAR ENOUGH, BRUNCH.
THANK YOU.

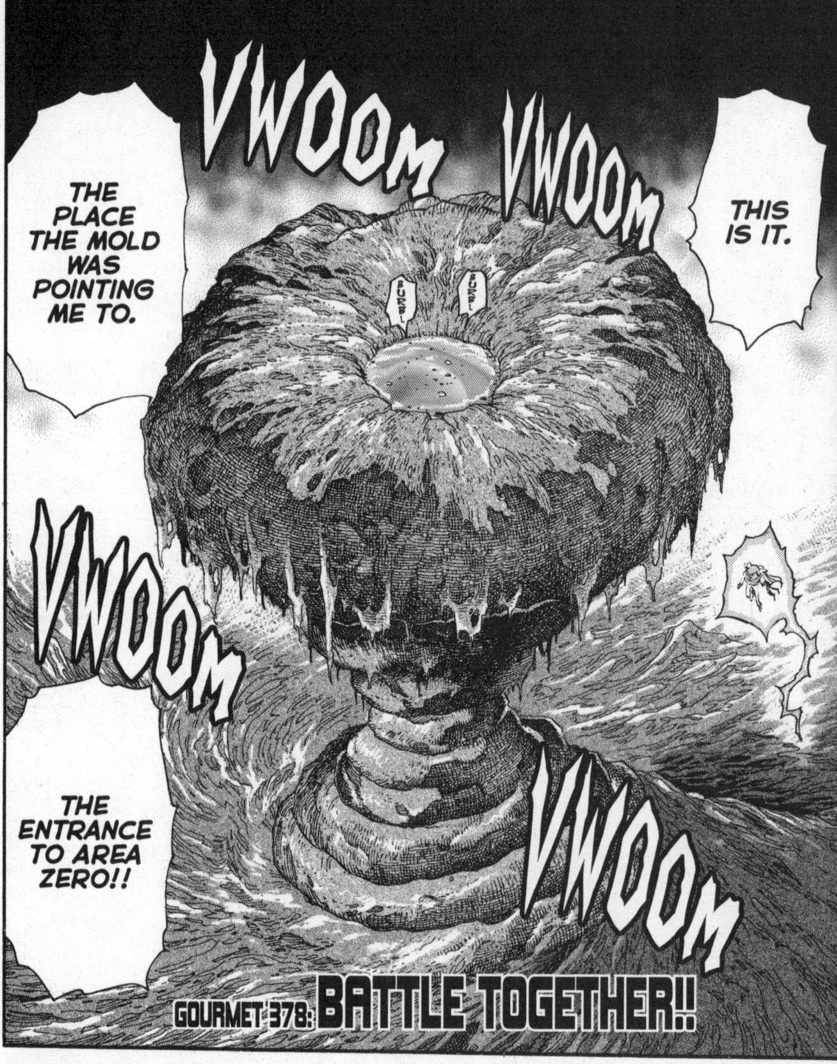
THIS IS IT.
VWOOM
VWOOM
THE PLACE THE MOLD WAS POINTING ME TO.
BURBL
BURBL
VWOOM
VWOOM
THE ENTRANCE TO AREA ZERO!!
GOURMET 378: BATTLE TOGETHER!!

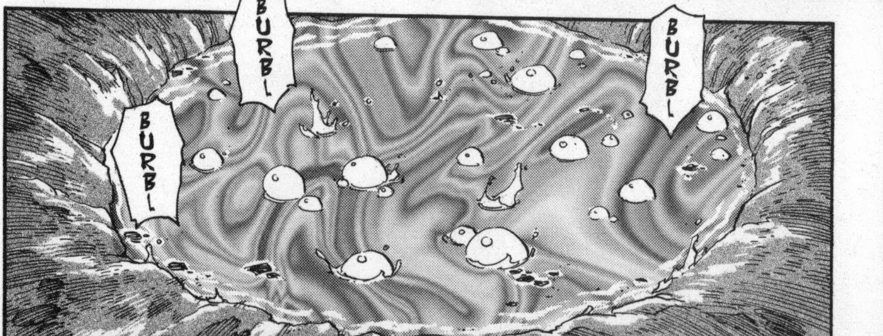
BURBL
BURBL
BURBL

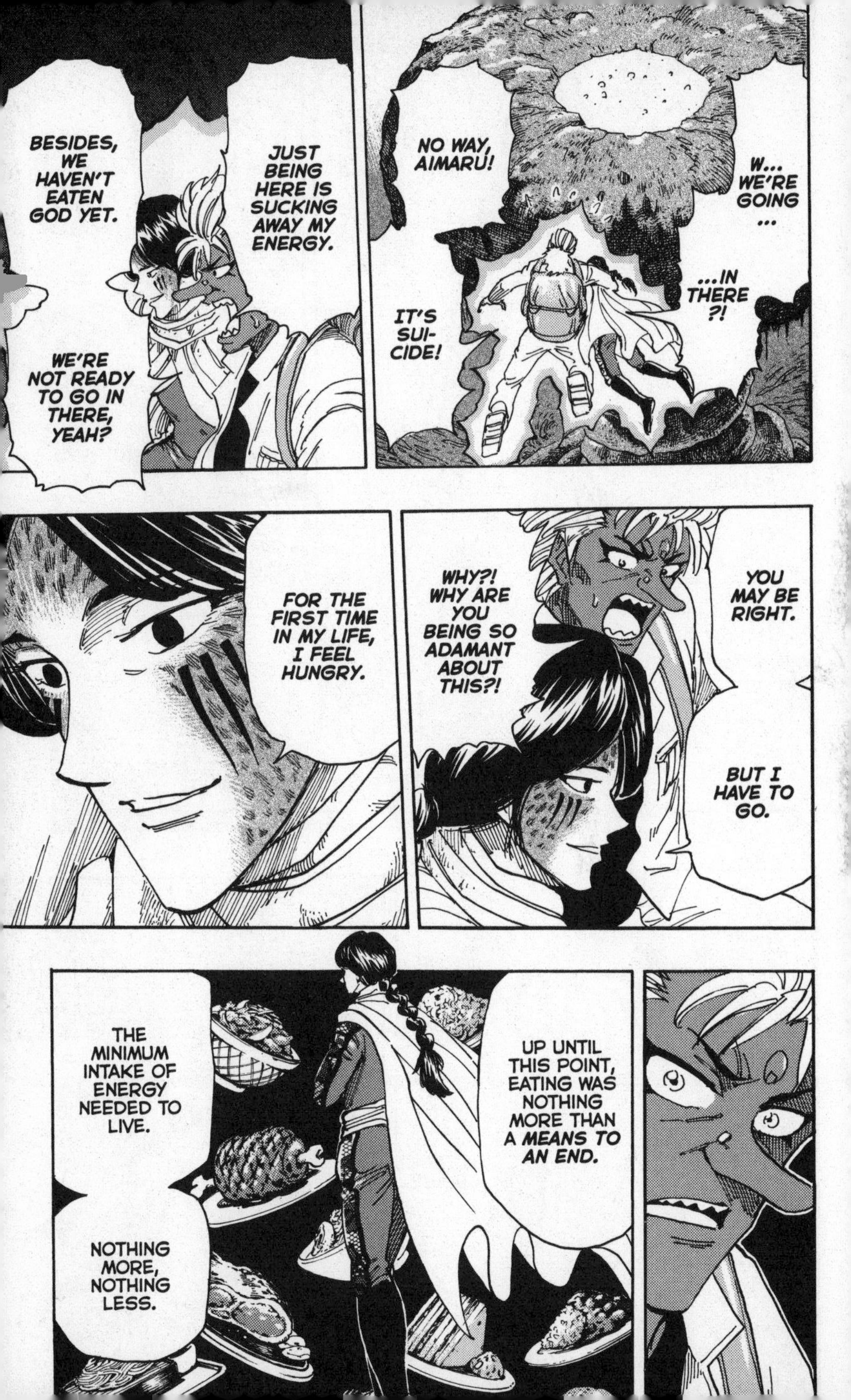
W... WE'RE GOING ...
NO WAY, AIMARU!
...IN THERE?!
IT'S SUI-CIDE!
JUST BEING HERE IS SUCKING AWAY MY ENERGY.
BESIDES, WE HAVEN'T EATEN GOD YET.
WE'RE NOT READY TO GO IN THERE, YEAH?
YOU MAY BE RIGHT.
WHY?! WHY ARE YOU BEING SO ADAMANT ABOUT THIS?!
BUT I HAVE TO GO.
FOR THE FIRST TIME IN MY LIFE, I FEEL HUNGRY.
UP UNTIL THIS POINT, EATING WAS NOTHING MORE THAN A *MEANS TO AN END.*
THE MINIMUM INTAKE OF ENERGY NEEDED TO LIVE.
NOTHING MORE, NOTHING LESS.

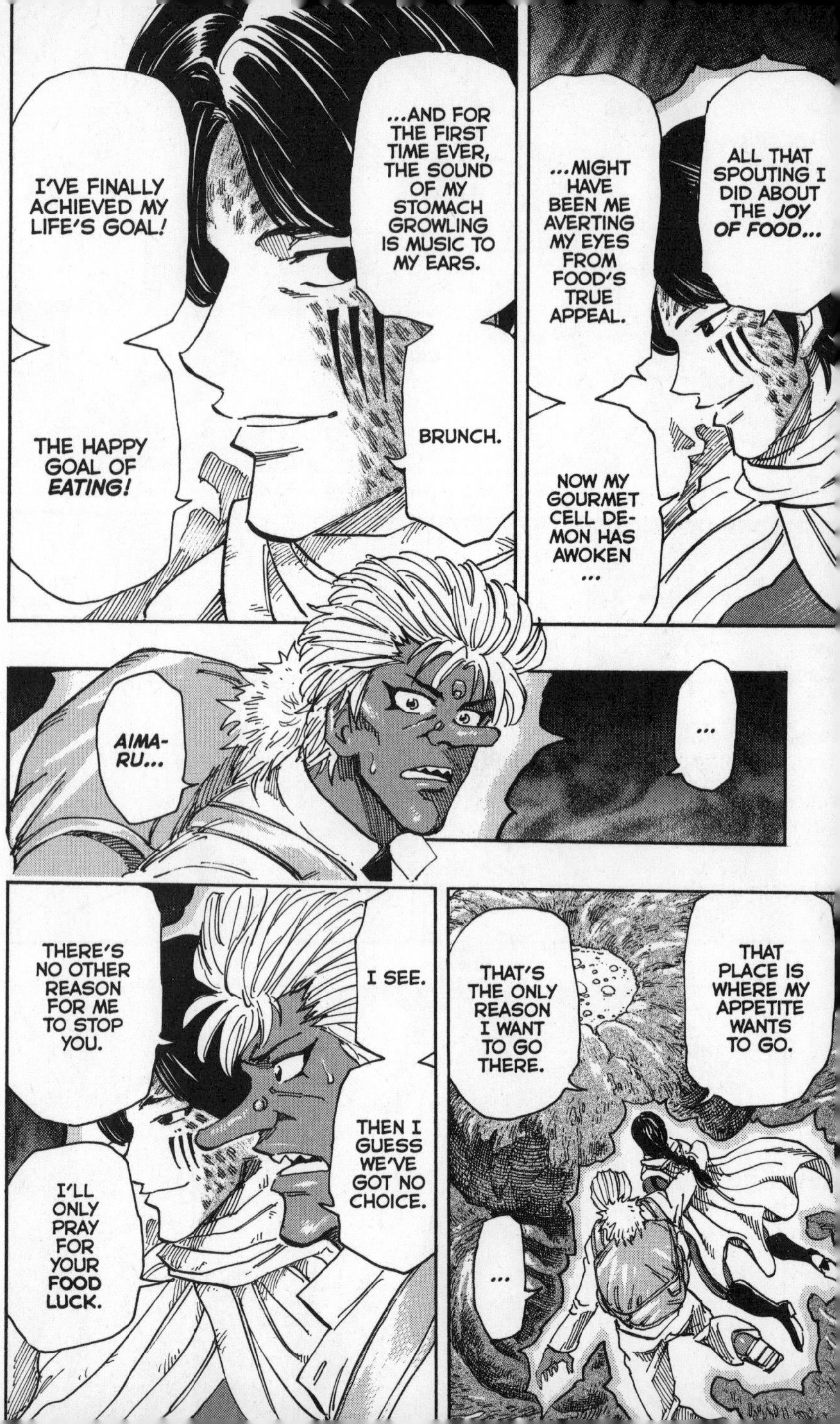
ALL THAT SPOUTING I DID ABOUT THE *JOY OF FOOD*...
...MIGHT HAVE BEEN ME AVERTING MY EYES FROM FOOD'S TRUE APPEAL.
NOW MY GOURMET CELL DEMON HAS AWOKEN...
...AND FOR THE FIRST TIME EVER, THE SOUND OF MY STOMACH GROWLING IS MUSIC TO MY EARS.
BRUNCH.
I'VE FINALLY ACHIEVED MY LIFE'S GOAL!
THE HAPPY GOAL OF *EATING!*
...
AIMARU...
THAT PLACE IS WHERE MY APPETITE WANTS TO GO.
THAT'S THE ONLY REASON I WANT TO GO THERE.
...
I SEE.
THERE'S NO OTHER REASON FOR ME TO STOP YOU.
THEN I GUESS WE'VE GOT NO CHOICE.
I'LL ONLY PRAY FOR YOUR FOOD LUCK.

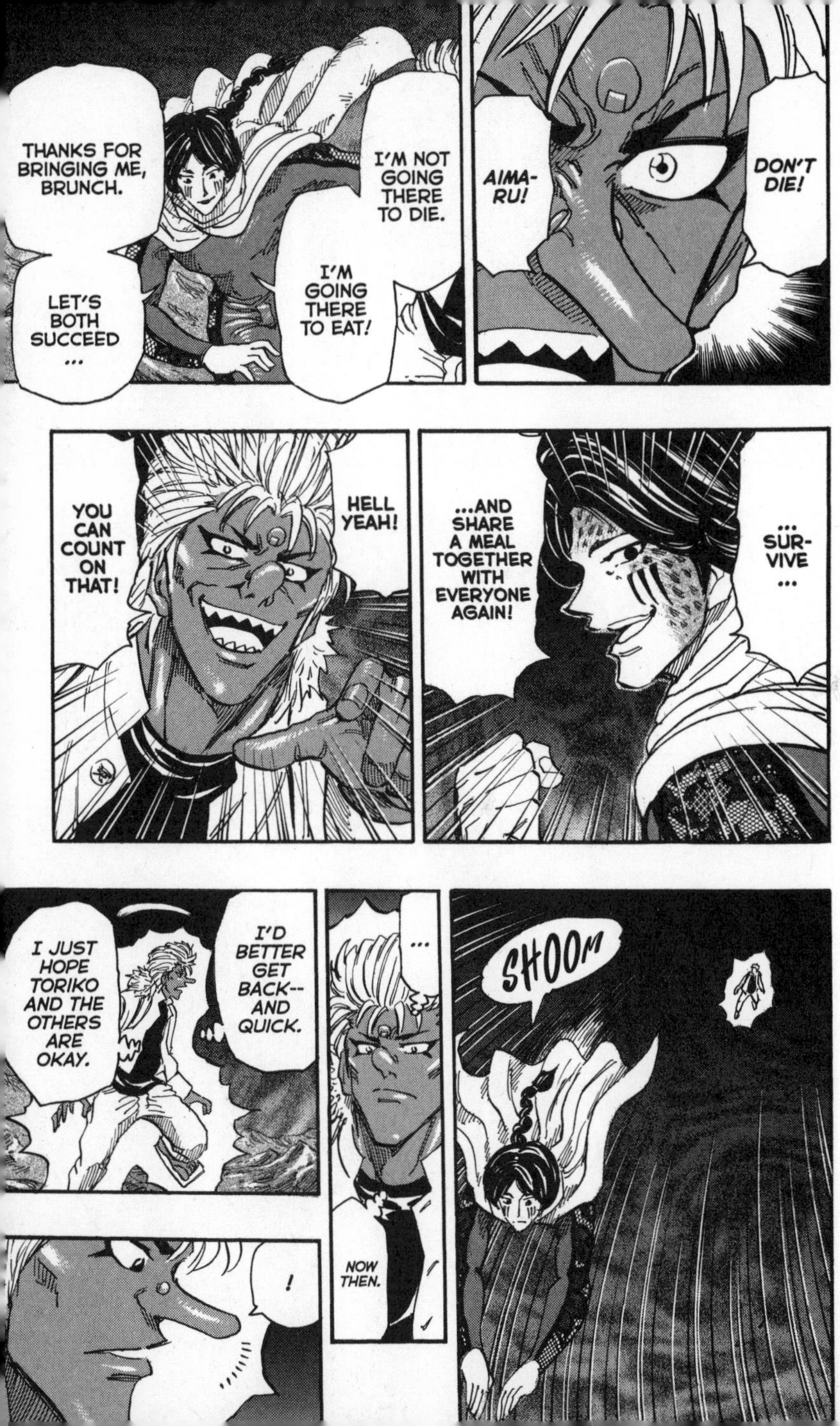
DON'T DIE!
AIMA-RU!
I'M NOT GOING THERE TO DIE.
THANKS FOR BRINGING ME, BRUNCH.
I'M GOING THERE TO EAT!
LET'S BOTH SUCCEED ...
... SUR-VIVE ...
...AND SHARE A MEAL TOGETHER WITH EVERYONE AGAIN!
HELL YEAH!
YOU CAN COUNT ON THAT!
SHOOM
...
NOW THEN.
I'D BETTER GET BACK-- AND QUICK.
I JUST HOPE TORIKO AND THE OTHERS ARE OKAY.
!

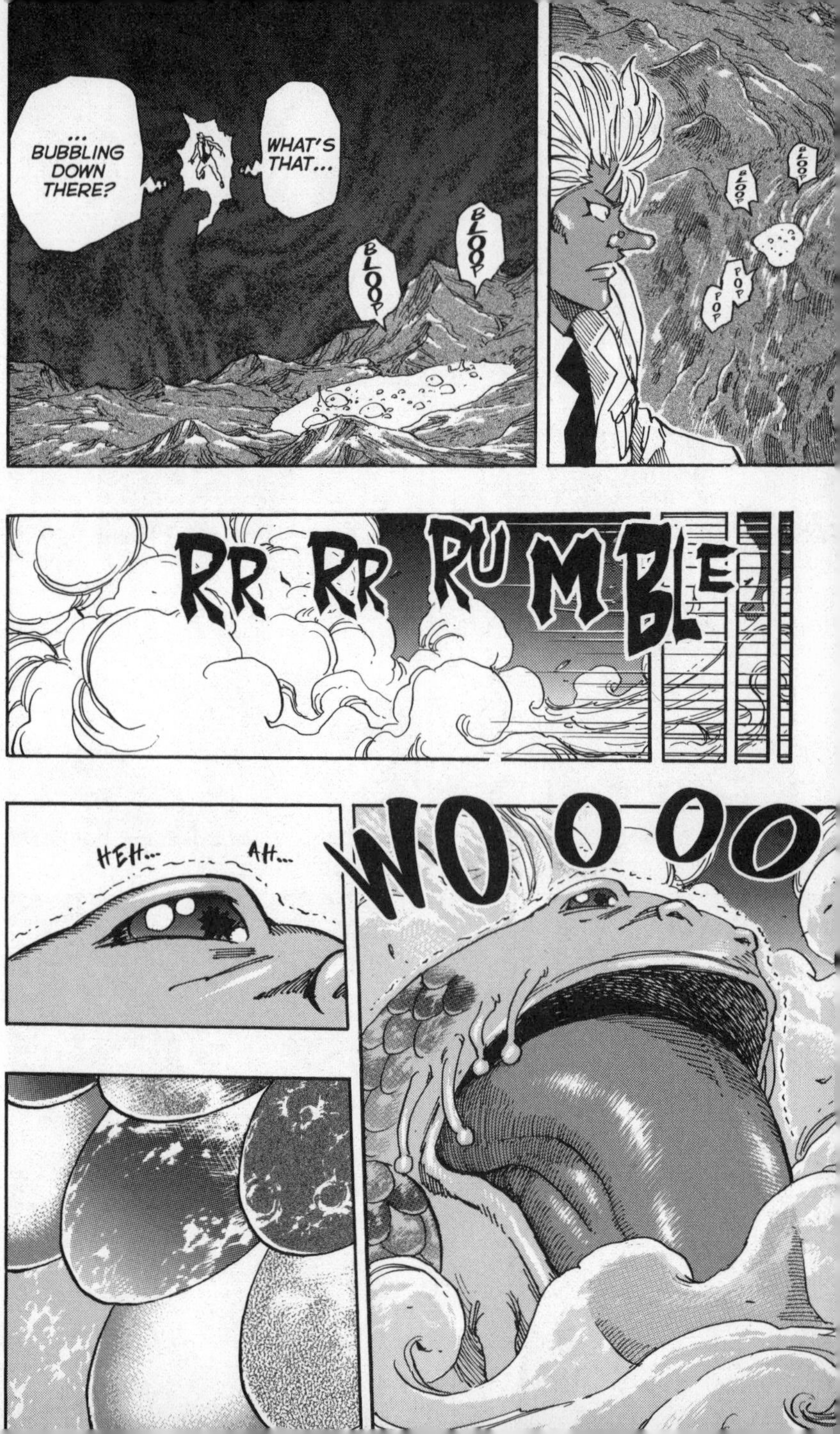
BLOOP
BLOOP
POP
POP
WHAT'S THAT...
...BUBBLING DOWN THERE?
BLOOP
BLOOP
RR RR RUMBLE
WOOOO
HEH...
AH...

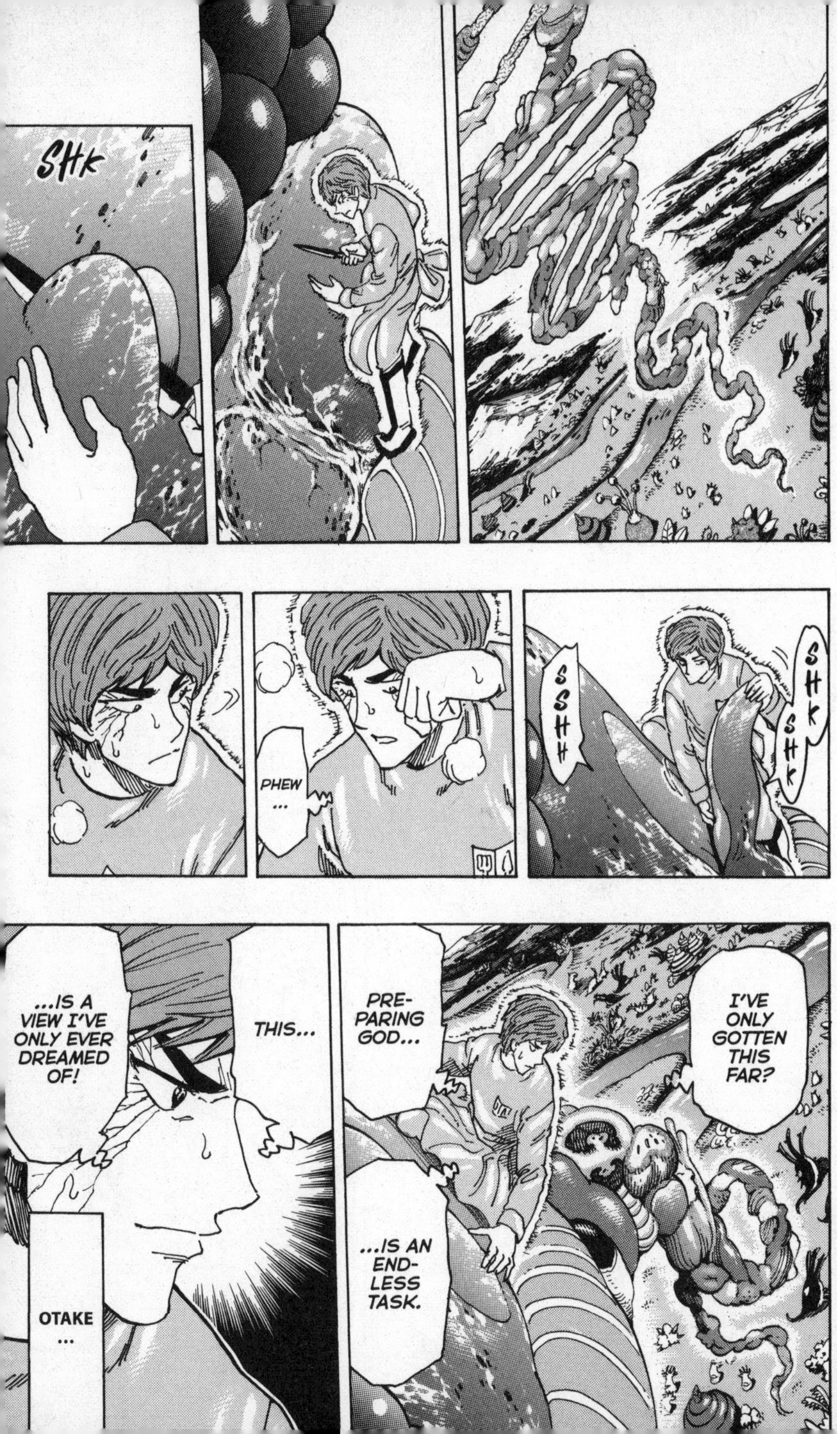
SHK
SHK
SHK
SSHH
PHEW...
I'VE ONLY GOTTEN THIS FAR?
PREPARING GOD...
...IS AN ENDLESS TASK.
THIS...
...IS A VIEW I'VE ONLY EVER DREAMED OF!
OTAKE...

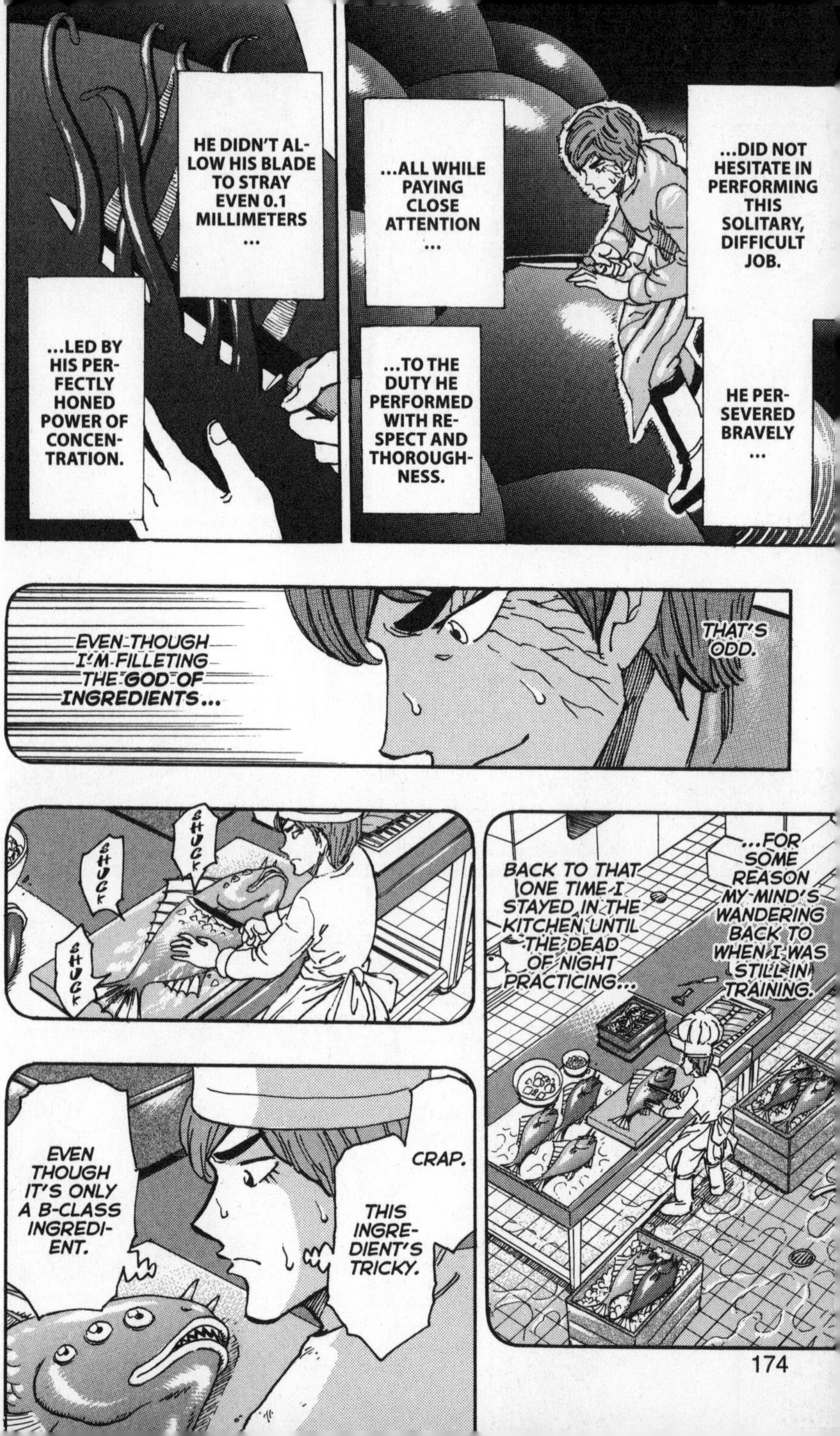
...DID NOT HESITATE IN PERFORMING THIS SOLITARY, DIFFICULT JOB.
HE PERSEVERED BRAVELY ...
...ALL WHILE PAYING CLOSE ATTENTION ...
...TO THE DUTY HE PERFORMED WITH RESPECT AND THOROUGHNESS.
HE DIDN'T ALLOW HIS BLADE TO STRAY EVEN 0.1 MILLIMETERS ...
...LED BY HIS PERFECTLY HONED POWER OF CONCENTRATION.
THAT'S ODD.
EVEN THOUGH I'M FILLETING THE GOD OF INGREDIENTS...
...FOR SOME REASON MY MIND'S WANDERING BACK TO WHEN I WAS STILL IN TRAINING.
BACK TO THAT ONE TIME I STAYED IN THE KITCHEN UNTIL THE DEAD OF NIGHT PRACTICING...
SHUCK
SHUCK
SHUCK
CRAP.
THIS INGREDIENT'S TRICKY.
EVEN THOUGH IT'S ONLY A B-CLASS INGREDIENT.

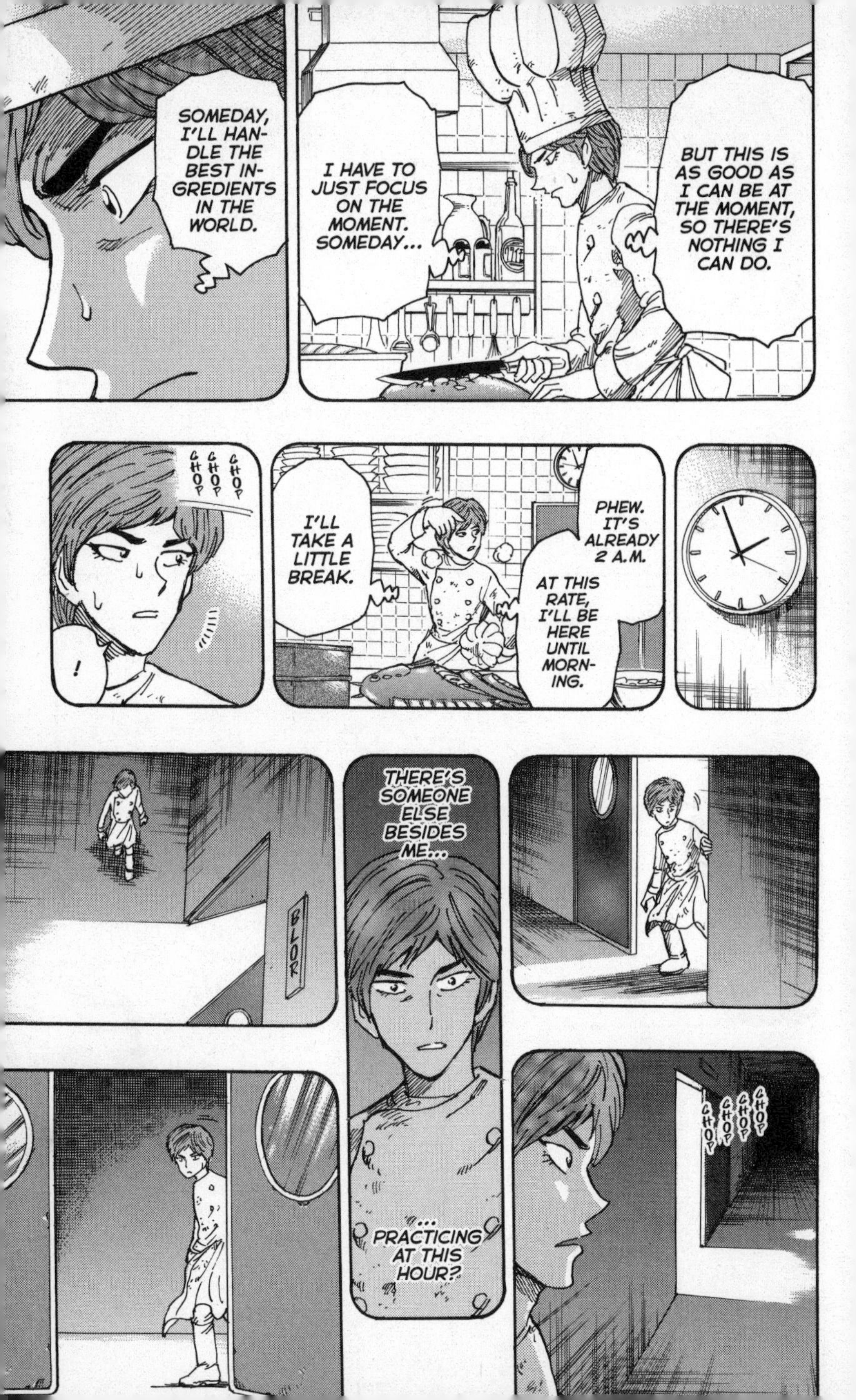
BUT THIS IS AS GOOD AS I CAN BE AT THE MOMENT, SO THERE'S NOTHING I CAN DO.
I HAVE TO JUST FOCUS ON THE MOMENT. SOMEDAY...
SOMEDAY, I'LL HAN-DLE THE BEST IN-GREDIENTS IN THE WORLD.
PHEW. IT'S ALREADY 2 A.M.
AT THIS RATE, I'LL BE HERE UNTIL MORN-ING.
I'LL TAKE A LITTLE BREAK.
CHOP CHOP CHOP
!
CHOP CHOP CHOP CHOP
THERE'S SOMEONE ELSE BESIDES ME...
... PRACTICING AT THIS HOUR?
BLOR

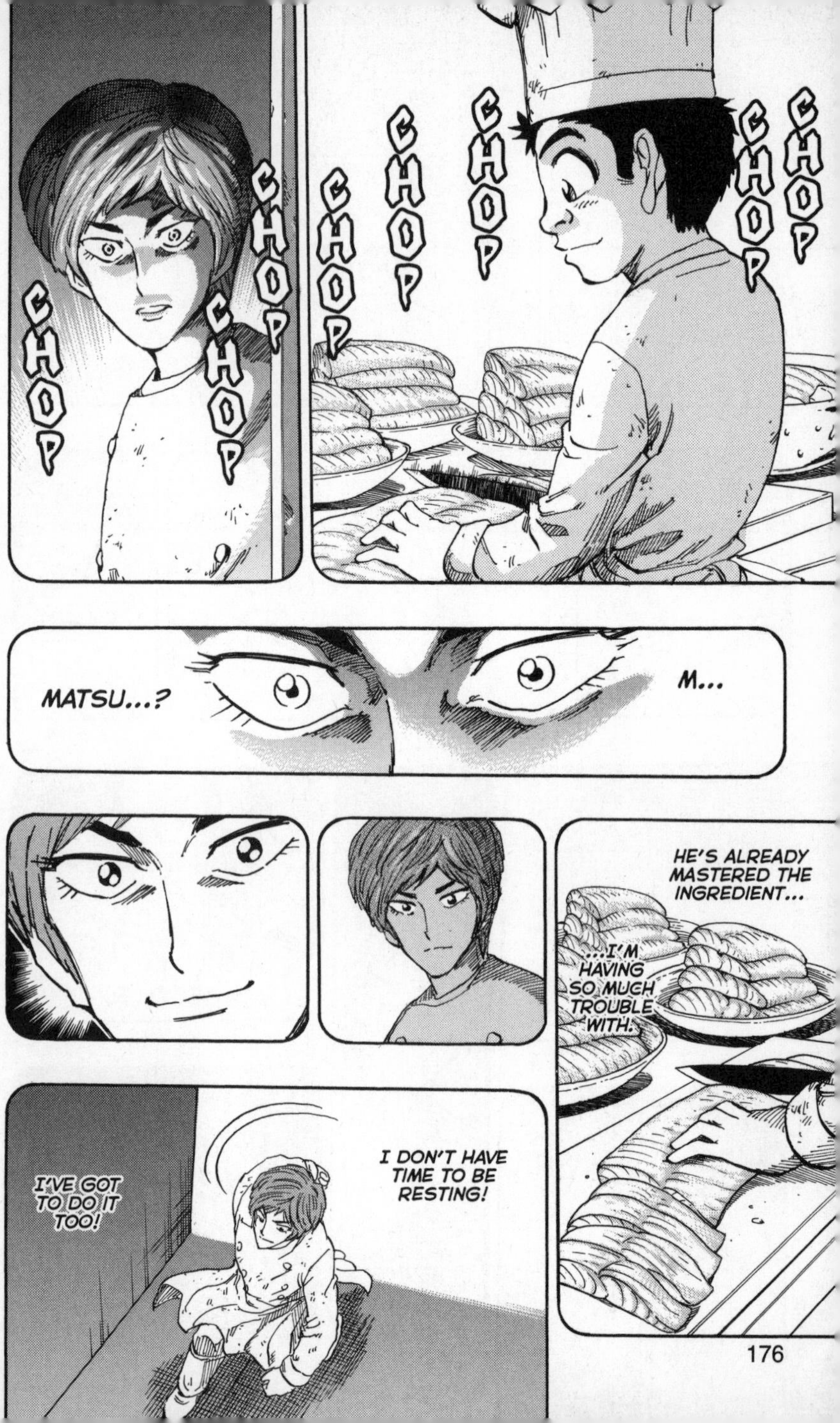
CHOP
CHOP
CHOP
CHOP
CHOP
CHOP
CHOP
CHOP
M...
MATSU...?
HE'S ALREADY MASTERED THE INGREDIENT...
...I'M HAVING SO MUCH TROUBLE WITH.
I DON'T HAVE TIME TO BE RESTING!
I'VE GOT TO DO IT TOO!

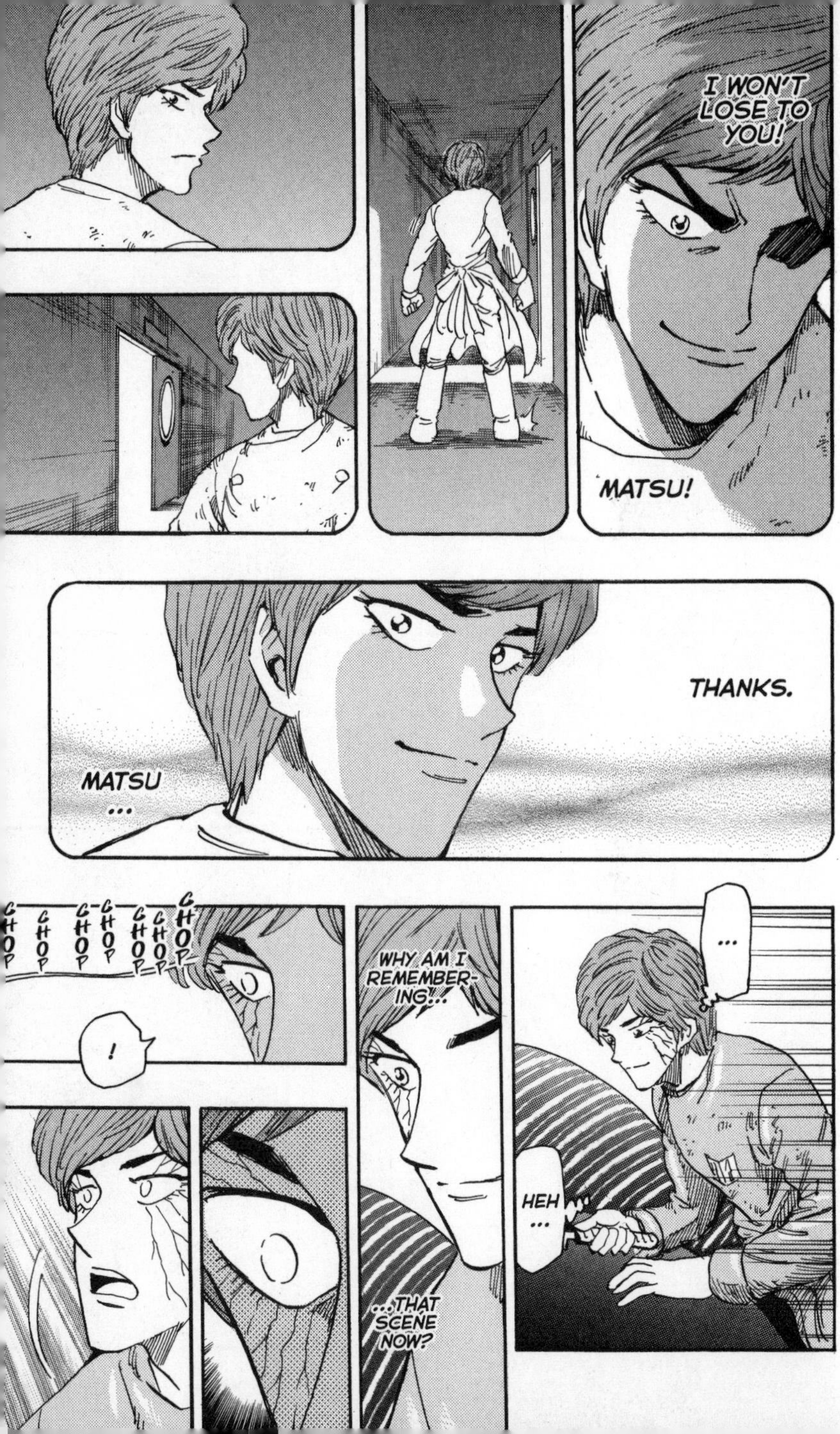
I WON'T LOSE TO YOU!
MATSU!
THANKS.
MATSU ...
...
HEH ...
WHY AM I REMEMBERING...
...THAT SCENE NOW?
CHOP CHOP CHOP CHOP CHOP CHOP CHOP
!

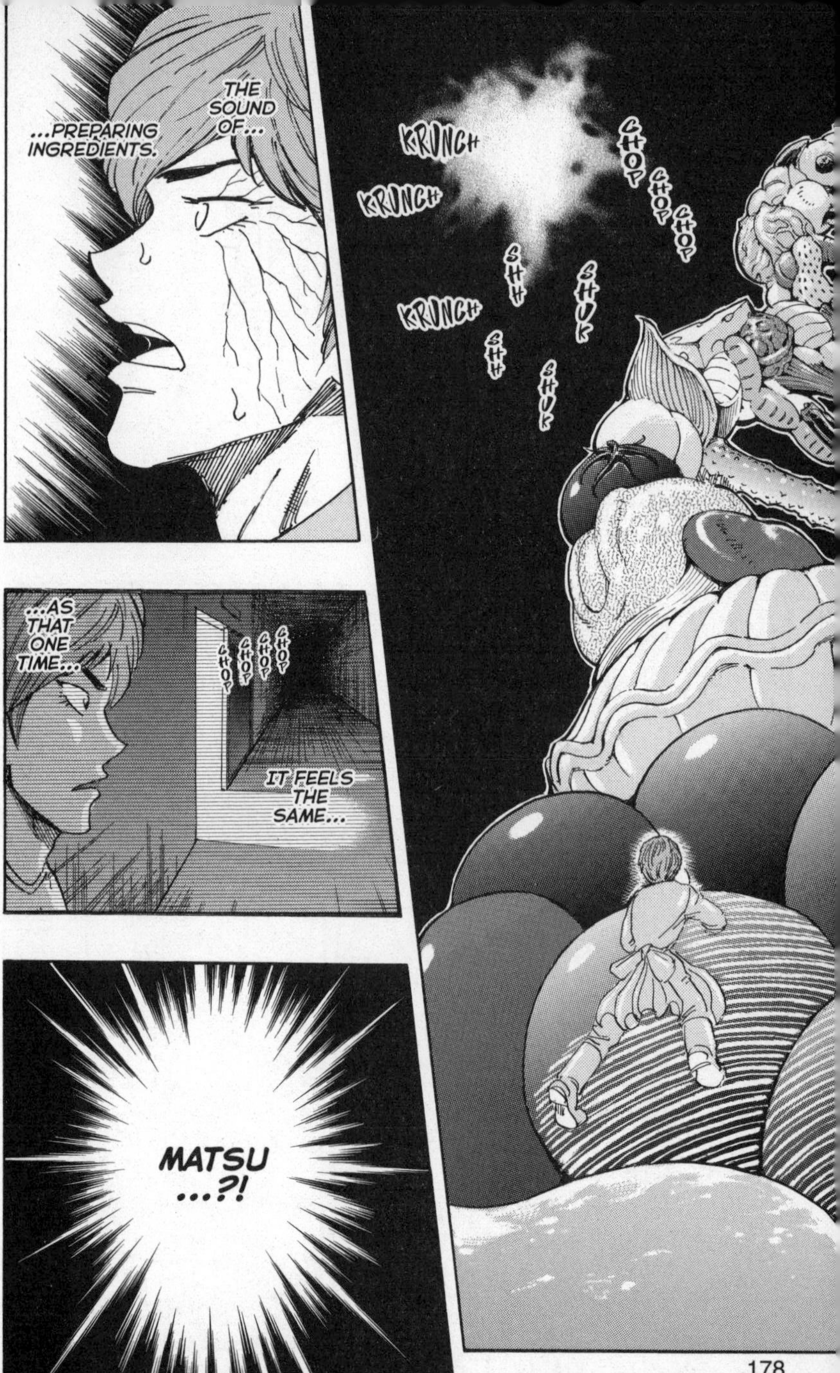
CHOP CHOP CHOP
KRUNCH
KRUNCH
SHUK
SHH
KRUNCH
SHUK
SHH
THE SOUND OF...
...PREPARING INGREDIENTS.
IT FEELS THE SAME...
CHOP CHOP CHOP CHOP
...AS THAT ONE TIME...
MATSU ...?!

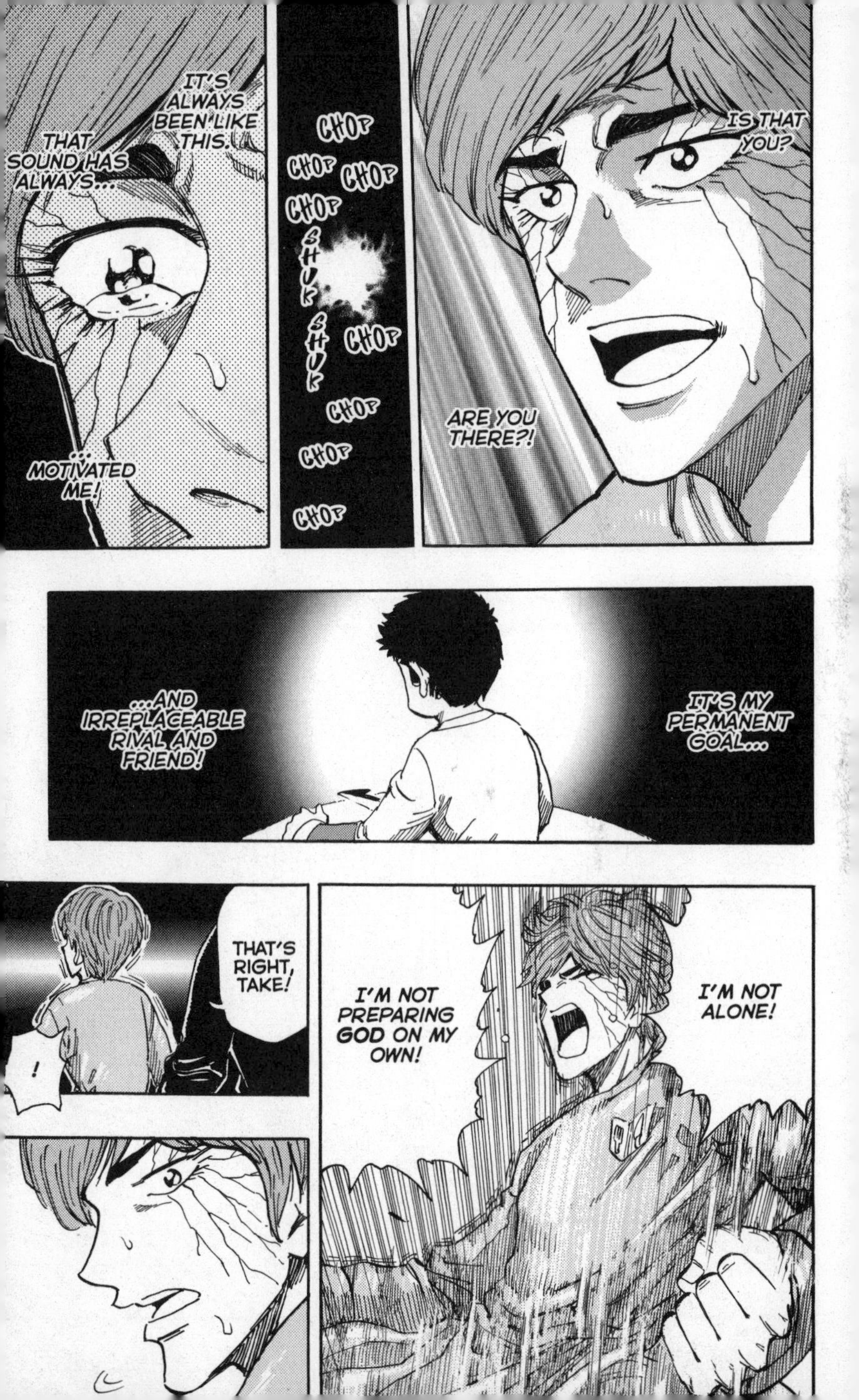
IS THAT YOU?
ARE YOU THERE?!
CHOP
CHOP CHOP
CHOP
SHUK
SHUK
CHOP
CHOP
CHOP
CHOP
IT'S ALWAYS BEEN LIKE THIS.
THAT SOUND HAS ALWAYS...
...MOTIVATED ME!
IT'S MY PERMANENT GOAL...
...AND IRREPLACEABLE RIVAL AND FRIEND!
I'M NOT ALONE!
I'M NOT PREPARING GOD ON MY OWN!
THAT'S RIGHT, TAKE!
!

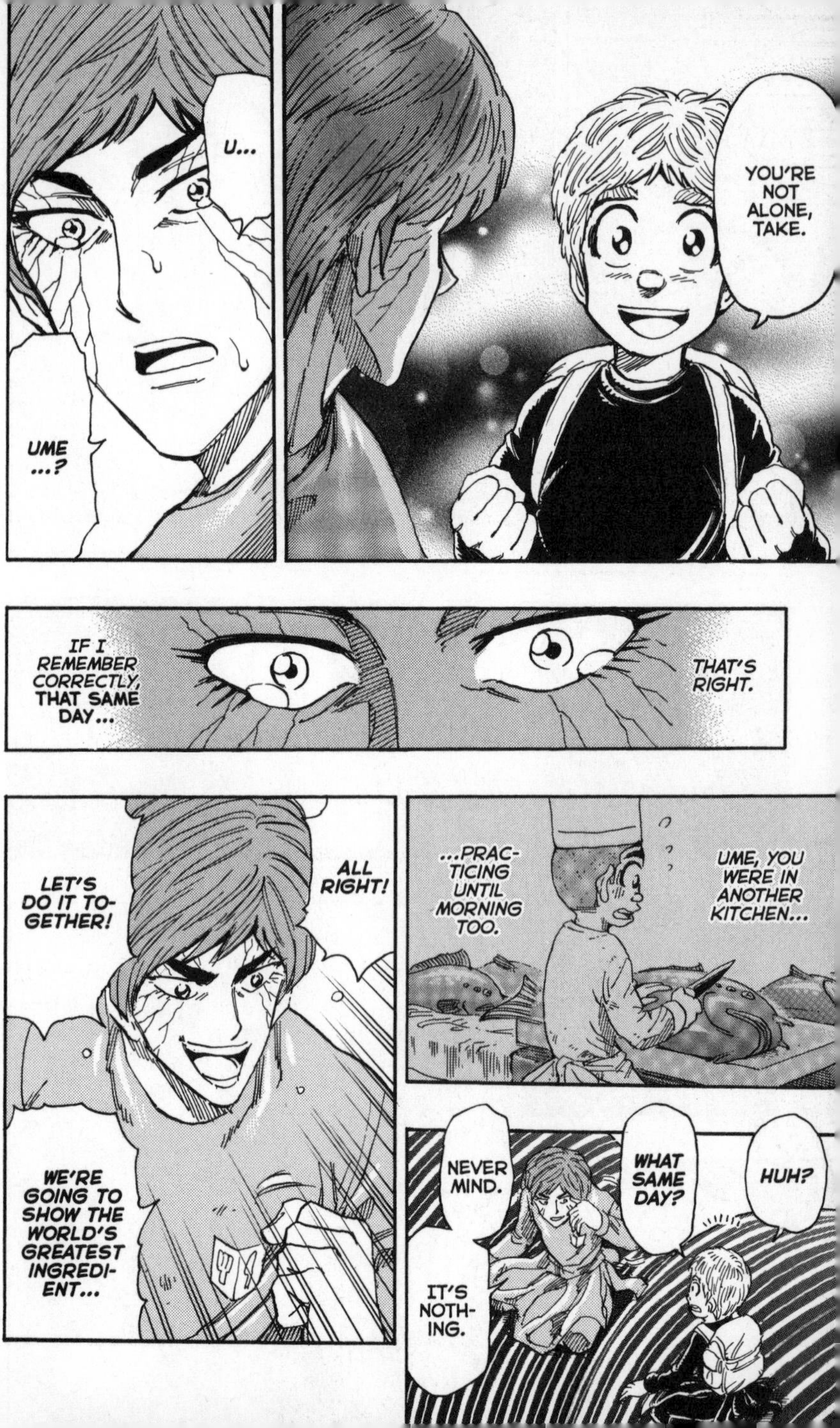
YOU'RE NOT ALONE, TAKE.
U...
UME ...?
THAT'S RIGHT.
IF I REMEMBER CORRECTLY, THAT SAME DAY...
UME, YOU WERE IN ANOTHER KITCHEN...
...PRACTICING UNTIL MORNING TOO.
HUH?
WHAT SAME DAY?
NEVER MIND.
IT'S NOTHING.
ALL RIGHT!
LET'S DO IT TOGETHER!
WE'RE GOING TO SHOW THE WORLD'S GREATEST INGREDIENT...

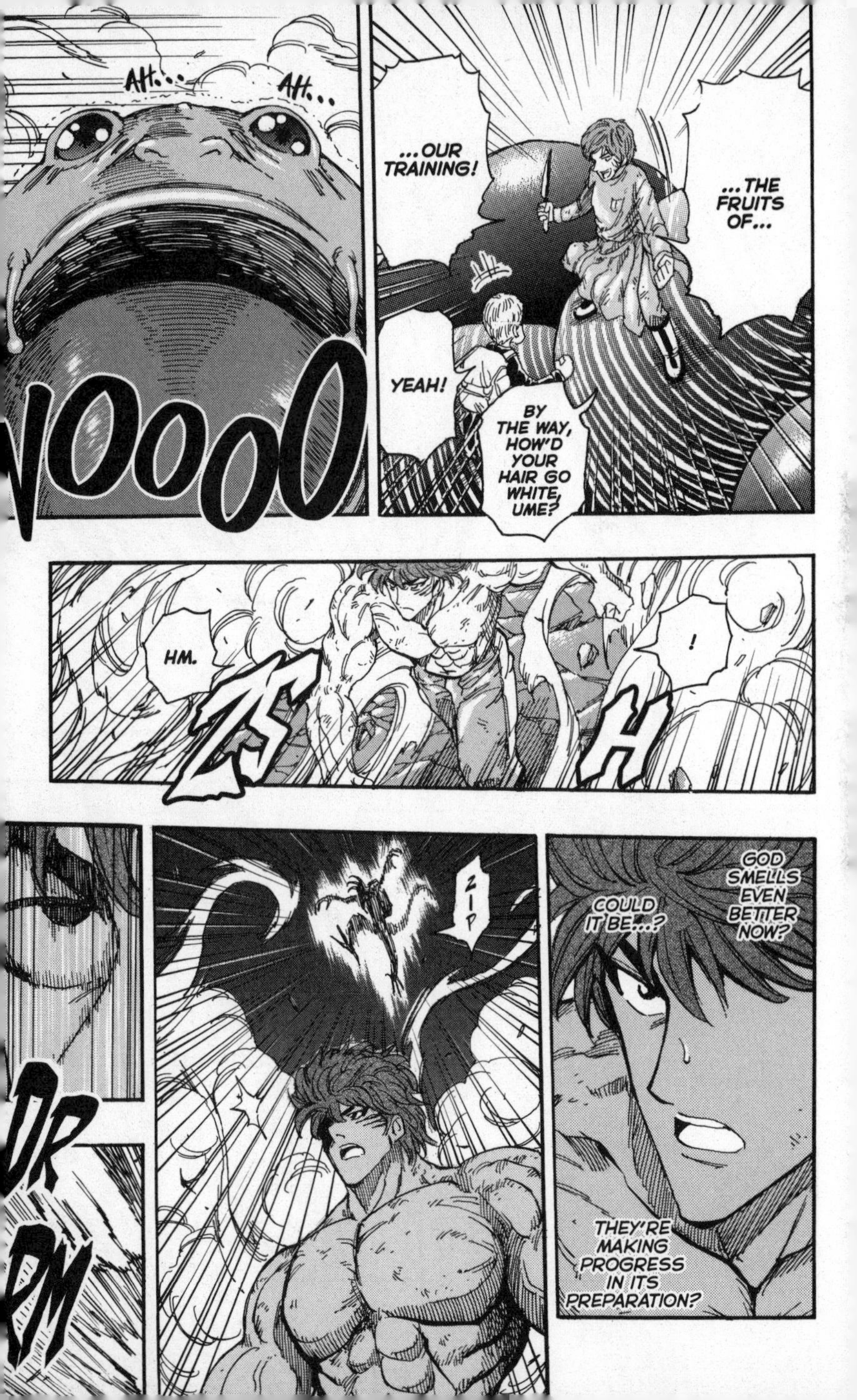
...THE FRUITS OF...
...OUR TRAINING!
BY THE WAY, HOW'D YOUR HAIR GO WHITE, UME?
YEAH!
AH...
AH...
NOOOO
!
H
HM.
ZS
GOD SMELLS EVEN BETTER NOW?
COULD IT BE...?
THEY'RE MAKING PROGRESS IN ITS PREPARATION?
ZIP
DR
DM

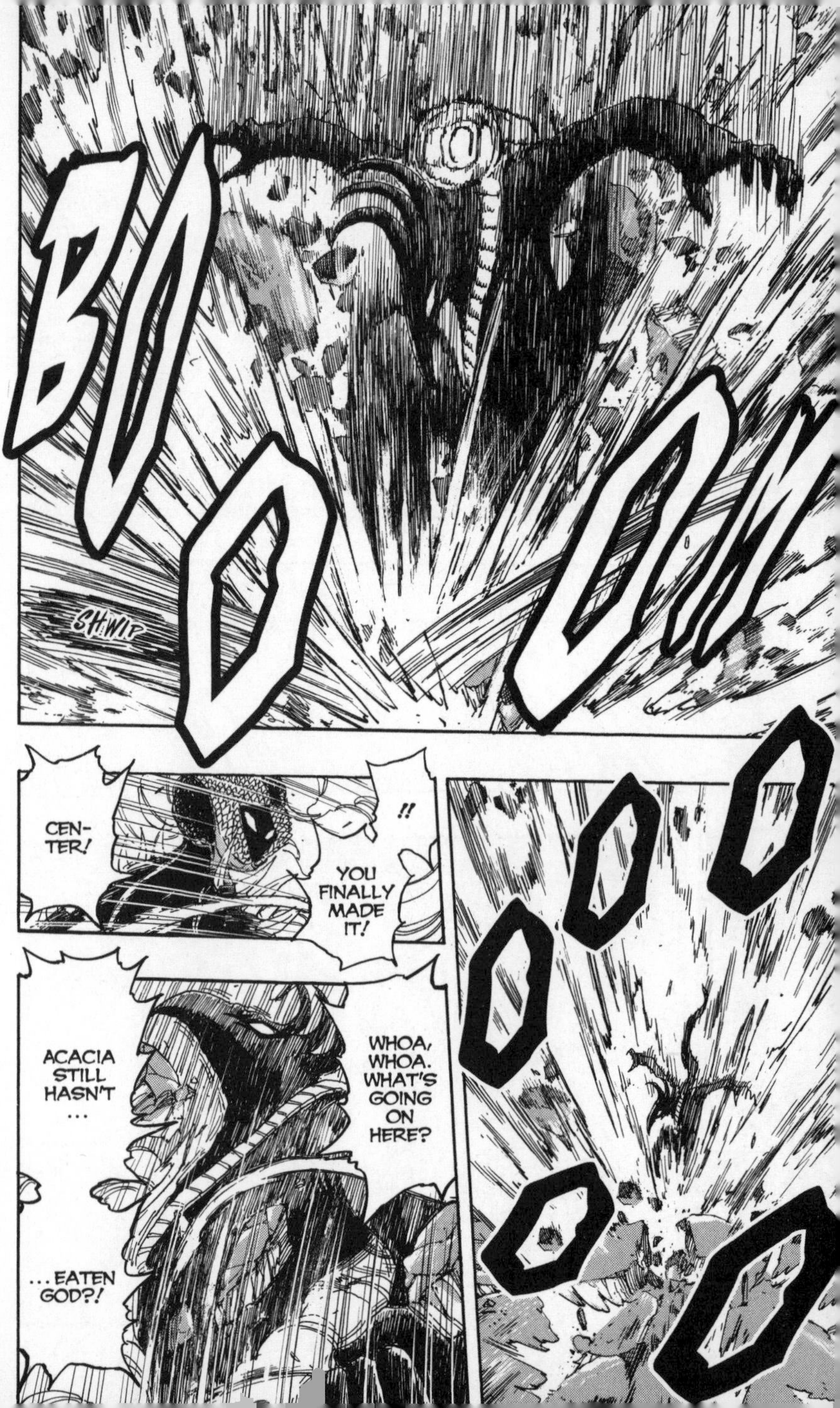
BOOOM
SHWIP
OOOOOOOO
!!
YOU FINALLY MADE IT!
CEN-TER!
WHOA, WHOA. WHAT'S GOING ON HERE?
ACACIA STILL HASN'T ...
...EATEN GOD?!

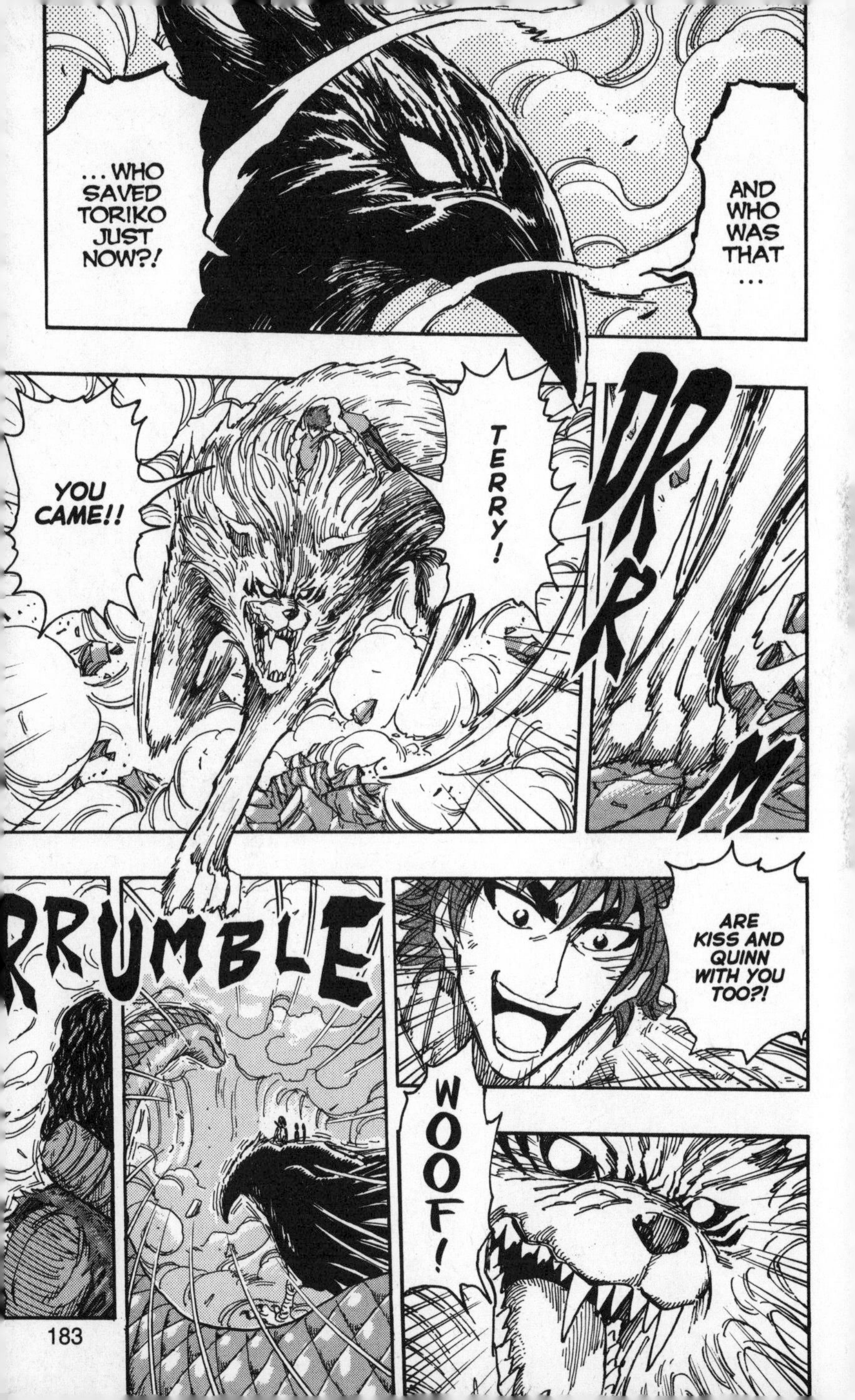
AND WHO WAS THAT...
...WHO SAVED TORIKO JUST NOW?!
DRRRM
TERRY!
YOU CAME!!
ARE KISS AND QUINN WITH YOU TOO?!
WOOF!
RRUMBLE

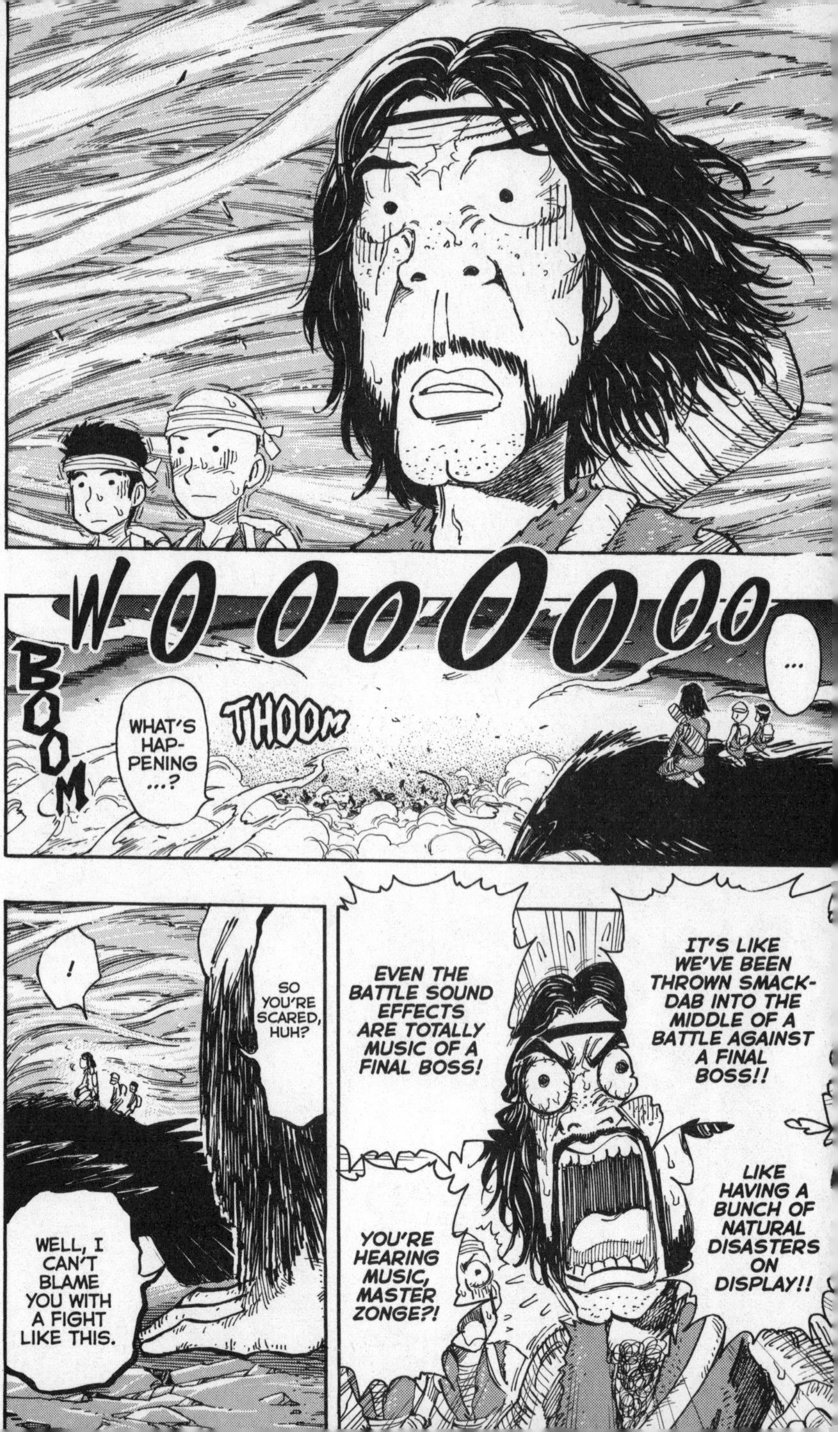
WOOOOOOOOO
...
THOOM
WHAT'S HAP-PENING ...?
BOOM
IT'S LIKE WE'VE BEEN THROWN SMACK-DAB INTO THE MIDDLE OF A BATTLE AGAINST A FINAL BOSS!!
EVEN THE BATTLE SOUND EFFECTS ARE TOTALLY MUSIC OF A FINAL BOSS!
LIKE HAVING A BUNCH OF NATURAL DISASTERS ON DISPLAY!!
YOU'RE HEARING MUSIC, MASTER ZONGE?!
SO YOU'RE SCARED, HUH?
!
WELL, I CAN'T BLAME YOU WITH A FIGHT LIKE THIS.

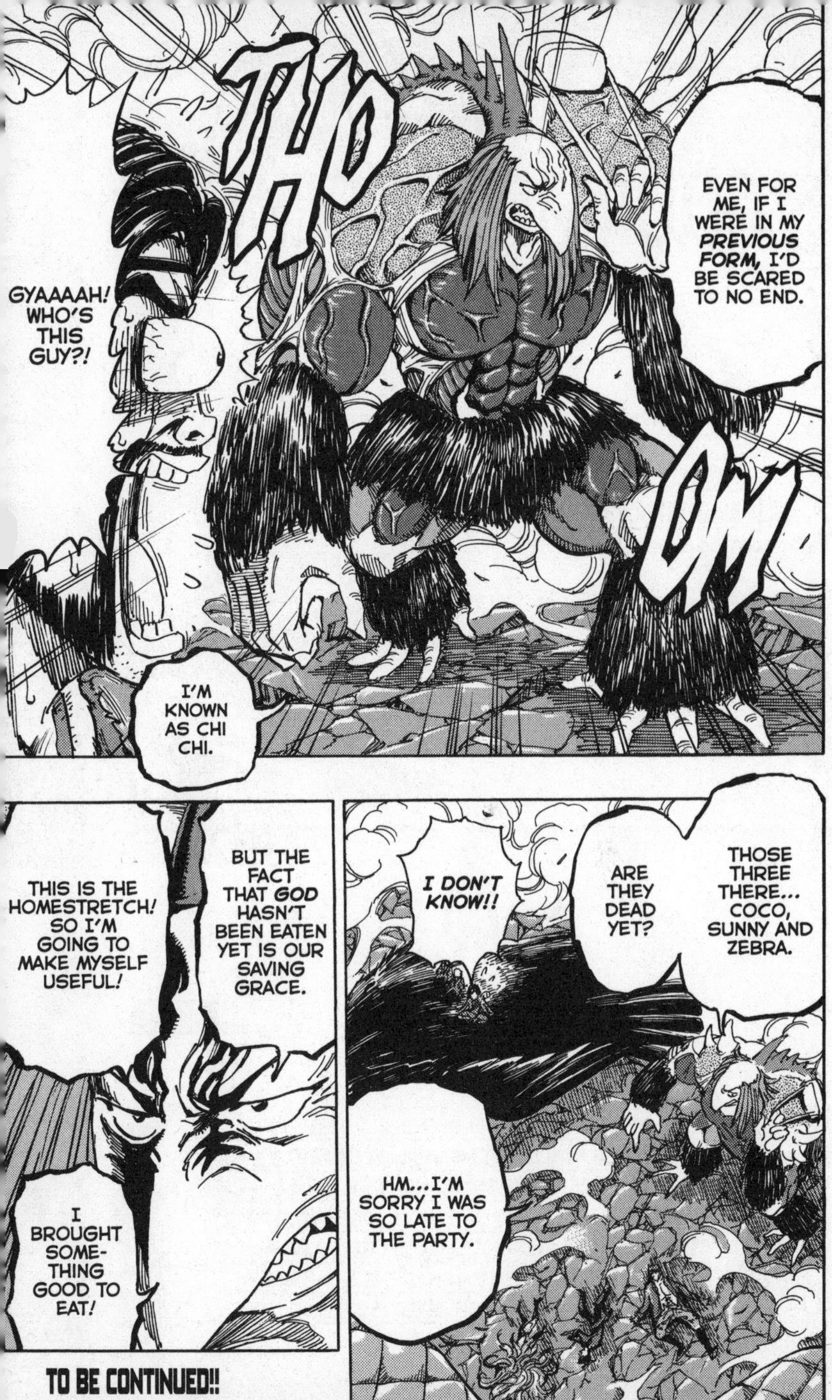
THO
EVEN FOR ME, IF I WERE IN MY *PREVIOUS FORM,* I'D BE SCARED TO NO END.
GYAAAAH! WHO'S THIS GUY?!
OM
I'M KNOWN AS CHI CHI.
THOSE THREE THERE... COCO, SUNNY AND ZEBRA.
ARE THEY DEAD YET?
I DON'T KNOW!!
HM...I'M SORRY I WAS SO LATE TO THE PARTY.
BUT THE FACT THAT *GOD* HASN'T BEEN EATEN YET IS OUR SAVING GRACE.
THIS IS THE HOMESTRETCH! SO I'M GOING TO MAKE MYSELF USEFUL!
I BROUGHT SOME-THING GOOD TO EAT!

TO BE CONTINUED!!

TORIKO

GOURMET CHECKLIST

*Vol.*410

DEMON SHELL
(SHELLFISH)

CAPTURE LEVEL: UNKNOWN
HABITAT: EXTINCT
SIZE: 30 CM
HEIGHT: ---
WEIGHT: ---
PRICE: PRICELESS

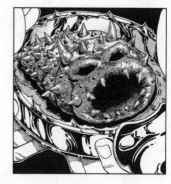

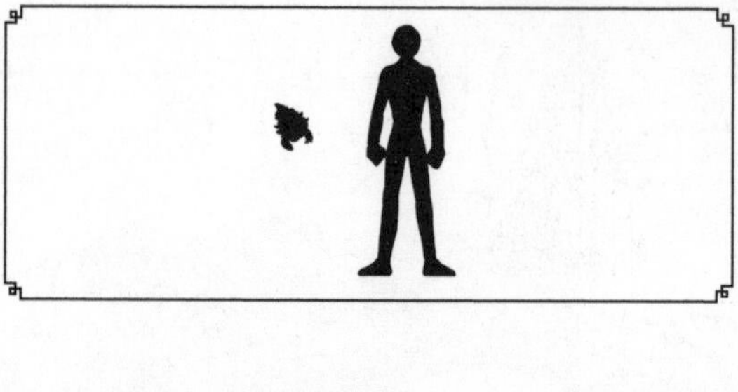

SCALE

A MYSTERIOUS SHELL THAT'S SAID TO HAVE EATEN ALL MANNER OF FISH IN THE PAST. ITS DEMON-LIKE APPETITE AND APPEARANCE EARNED IT THE NAME DEMON SHELL. IT'S ON THE SMALL SIDE, BUT INSIDE IT'S BUILT LIKE AN ENDLESS, EXPANSIVE MAZE AND ITS BODY IS PACKED WITH ALL THE FISH IT'S EVER EATEN. IT'S ALSO CALLED THE "MEMORIES OF THE FARAWAY SEA FLAVORS" AND ALONG WITH BEING A MYSTERIOUS ENTITY THAT CAN BRING BACK THE FLAVORS OF CURRENTLY EXTINCT SPECIES, IT'S A RARE INGREDIENT THAT WAS CHOSEN AS THE FISH DISH IN TORIKO'S FULL-COURSE MEAL.

TORIKO

GOURMET CHECKLIST

Vol. 411

NEWS
(MEAT)

CAPTURE LEVEL: 6,900
HABITAT: GOURMET WORLD AREA 5, FOOD LIMITS FOREST
SIZE: 30 CM
HEIGHT: ---
WEIGHT: 1,200 TONS
PRICE: 50 MILLION YEN PER 100 GRAMS

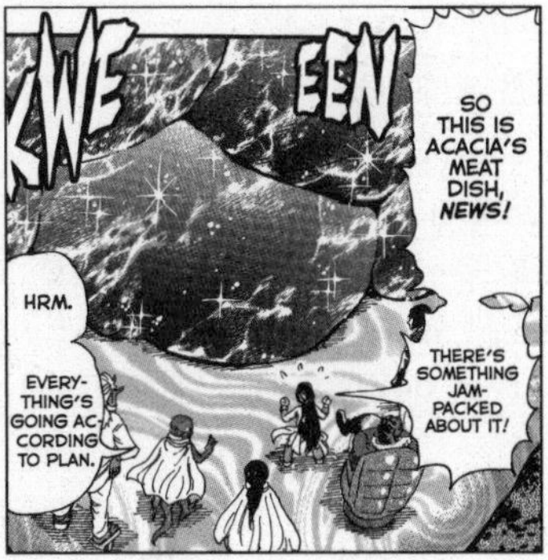
SO THIS IS ACACIA'S MEAT DISH, NEWS!
KWE
EEN
THERE'S SOMETHING JAM-PACKED ABOUT IT!
HRM.
EVERY-THING'S GOING AC-CORDING TO PLAN.

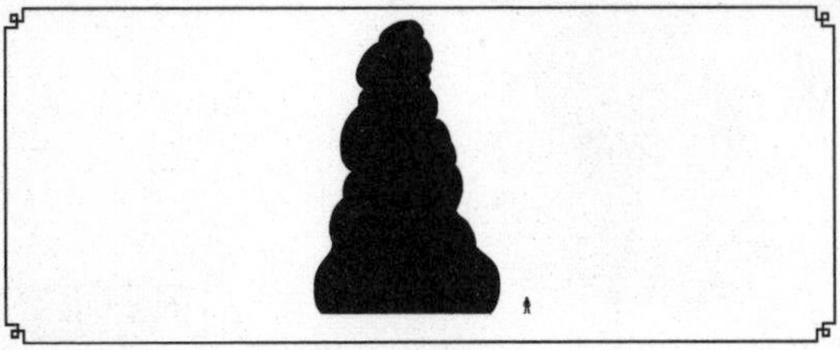

SCALE

THE MEAT DISH IN ACACIA'S FULL-COURSE MEAL THAT COMES FROM THE FOOD LIMITS FOREST. IT'S ONE OF THE MOST TREASURED INGREDIENTS IN THE GOURMET WORLD. MONSTERS ON PAR WITH AREA 6'S SEVEN BEASTS ROAM FREE IN THIS REGION AND THEY ARE SAID TO BE THE STRONGEST IN ALL THE GOURMET WORLD. THE MOST COMBAT-SAVVY DUO IN TORIKO'S PARTY, ZEBRA AND BRUNCH, WERE SENT TO CAPTURE AND PREPARE IT AND SUCCEEDED.

TORIKO

GOURMET CHECKLIST

Vol. 412

EARTH
(DESSERT)

CAPTURE LEVEL: 6,100

HABITAT: GOURMET WORLD AREA 4, GOURMET GARDEN

SIZE: 25 M

HEIGHT: ---

WEIGHT: 500 TONS

PRICE: 40 MILLION YEN PER 100 GRAMS

GLOP
ITS SUGAR CONTENT IS THE GREATEST IN THE WORLD.
THEY SAY THAT NO INGREDIENT SURPASSES EARTH AS AN ENERGY SOURCE.

SCALE

THIS DESSERT IN ACACIA'S FULL-COURSE MEAL COMES FROM THE GOURMET GARDEN, THE BEAUTIFULLY BLOOMING FLOATING GARDEN IN AREA 4. THE ROOTS OF ITS FLOWER FIELDS STRETCH ACROSS THE ENTIRE WORLD, SUCKING UP THE SWEETNESS OF THE EARTH TO GROW THE ULTIMATE DESSERT. THE SUGAR CONTENT OF THIS DESSERT IS THE HIGHEST OF ANY INGREDIENT IN THE WORLD AND THERE'S NO BETTER SOURCE FOR CALORIES ON THE ENTIRE PLANET. BUT JUST GETTING TO THE GOURMET GARDEN REQUIRES PASSING THROUGH THE "CAVE OF OLD AGE" WHICH WILL MAKE YOU AGE AT 200,000 TIMES THE USUAL SPEED. SO UNLESS YOU ACTIVATE A BACK CHANNEL, IT WILL BE IMPOSSIBLE TO CLEAR THE HIGH HURDLES SURROUNDING THIS INGREDIENT. THE DUO THAT STAND OUT THE MOST AMONG TORIKO'S PARTY FOR THEIR POWERS OF PERSUASION, SUNNY AND LIVEBEARER, WERE TOLD ABOUT A SHORTCUT INTO THE GOURMET GARDEN BY THE PEOPLE OF AREA 4 AND SUCCEEDED IN CAPTURING EARTH.

TORIKO

GOURMET CHECKLIST

Vol. 413

ATOM
(DRINK)

JIGGLE
TH...THIS IS *ATOM?*
IT DOESN'T LOOK AS TOXIC AS I WAS EXPECTING.
IT'S GORGEOUS.
ALL THIS LEAVES US NOW IS *GOD* AND THE APPETIZER, *CENTER!*

CAPTURE LEVEL: 7,000
HABITAT: GOURMET WORLD AREA 3
SIZE: ---
HEIGHT: ---
WEIGHT: ---
PRICE: 35 MILLION YEN PER 100 MILLILITERS

SCALE

THE DRINK IN ACACIA'S FULL-COURSE MEAL. IT'S THE MAGMA THAT SPEWS OUT OF CLOUD MOUNTAIN, A GIGANTIC MOUNTAIN OF CLOUDS THAT RISES OVER AREA 3. THE FORCE OF THE ERUPTIONS IS THE STRONGEST IN THE WORLD, AND ONCE THE MAGMA REACHES OUTER SPACE IT ABSORBS THE TOXIC SUBSTANCES AND RETURNS TO EARTH AS A GIANT, POISONOUS WATERFALL. THAT IS WHAT THEY CALL ATOM. THE METHOD FOR EXTRACTING THOSE TOXINS IS SECOND IN DIFFICULTY ONLY TO ANOTHER AND GOD IN ACACIA'S FULL-COURSE MEAL, SO IF IT WEREN'T FOR TORIKO'S POISON MASTER FRIENDS, COCO AND TYLAN, THIS INGREDIENT WOULD PROBABLY BE UTTERLY IMPOSSIBLE TO CAPTURE.

COMING NEXT VOLUME

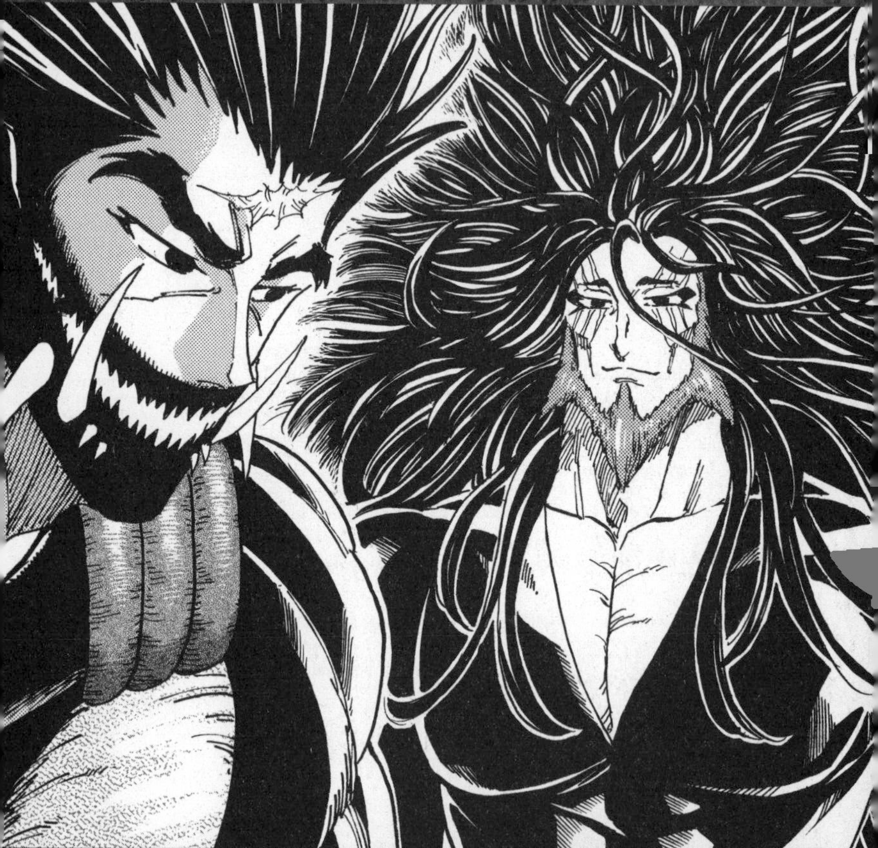

A REUNION WITH APPETITE!!

The battle for the fate of the world rages on as the chefs race to prepare the king of ingredients, God. Meanwhile, Toriko and the other Four Kings, Starjun, Midora and the monstrous Eight Kings take on Neo and Acacia and are felled one by one. Things go from bad to worse when the Blue Nitro assist Acacia with fully reviving Neo! With the Earth itself barely holding up, will Toriko and his friends be able to pull through and save the world from being devoured?

AVAILABLE MAY 2018!

You're Reading in the Wrong Direction!!

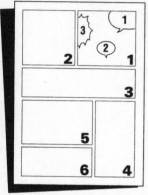

Whoops! Guess what? You're starting at the wrong end of the comic!

...It's true! In keeping with the original Japanese format, **Toriko** is meant to be read from right to left, starting in the upper-right corner.

Unlike English, which is read from left to right, Japanese is read from right to left, meaning that action, sound effects and word-balloon order are completely reversed... something which can make readers unfamiliar with Japanese feel pretty backwards themselves. For this reason, manga or Japanese comics published in the U.S. in English have sometimes been published "flopped" — that is, printed in exact reverse order, as though seen from the other side of a mirror.

By flopping pages, U.S. publishers can avoid confusing readers, but the compromise is not without its downside. For one thing, a character in a flopped manga series who once wore in the original Japanese version a T-shirt emblazoned with "M A Y" (as in "the merry month of") now wears one which reads "Y A M"! Additionally, many manga creators in Japan are themselves unhappy with the process, as some feel the mirror-imaging of their art skews their original intentions.

We are proud to bring you Mitsutoshi Shimabukuro's **Toriko** in the original unflopped format. For now, though, turn to the other side of the book and let the adventure begin...!

—Editor

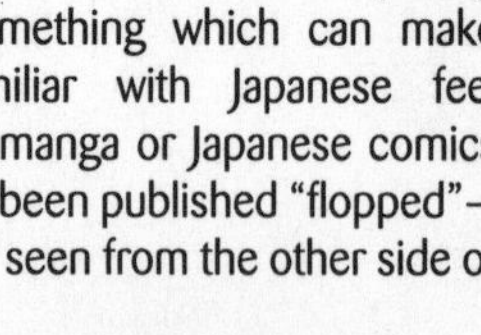